REPRESENTATION AND DERIVATION IN THE THEORY OF GRAMMAR

Studies in Natural Language and Linguistic Theory

VOLUME 22

The titles published in this series are listed at the end of this volume.

REPRESENTATION AND DERIVATION IN THE THEORY OF GRAMMAR

Edited by

HUBERT HAIDER
Institute for German Linguistics, Stuttgart University, Germany

and

KLAUS NETTER
DFKI, Saarbrücken, Germany

KLUWER ACADEMIC PUBLISHERS
DORDRECHT / BOSTON / LONDON

Library of Congress Cataloging-in-Publication Data

Representation and derivation in the theory of grammar / edited by
Hubert Haider, Klaus Netter.
p. cm. -- (Studies in natural language and linguistic theory
; v. 22)
Includes bibliographical references and index.
ISBN 0-7923-1150-7 (HB : acid free paper)
1. Generative grammar. 2. Grammar, Comparative and general.
I. Haider, Hubert. II. Netter, Klaus. III. Series.
P158.R47 1991
415--dc20 91-2122
CIP

ISBN 0-7923-1150-7

Published by Kluwer Academic Publishers,
P.O. Box 17, 3300 AA Dordrecht, The Netherlands.

Kluwer Academic Publishers incorporates
the publishing programmes of
D. Reidel, Martinus Nijhoff, Dr W. Junk and MTP Press.

Sold and distributed in the U.S.A. and Canada
by Kluwer Academic Publishers,
101 Philip Drive, Norwell, MA 02061, U.S.A.

In all other countries, sold and distributed
by Kluwer Academic Publishers Group,
P.O. Box 322, 3300 AH Dordrecht, The Netherlands.

Printed on acid-free paper

Printed in the Netherlands

TABLE OF CONTENTS

HUBERT HAIDER & KLAUS NETTER
Introduction 1

IAN ROBERTS
NP-Movement, Crossover and Chain-Formation 17

KNUT TARALD TARALDSEN
NP-Movement and Expletive Chains 53

WOLFGANG STERNEFELD
Chain Formation, Reanalysis, and the Economy of Levels 71

TILMAN N. HÖHLE
On Reconstruction and Coordination 139

KATALIN É. KISS
An Argument for Movement 199

GISBERT FANSELOW
Barriers and the Theory of Binding 217

HANS-PETER KOLB & CRAIG THIERSCH
Levels and Empty Categories in a Principles and Parameters Approach to Parsing 251

NOTES ON CONTRIBUTORS 303

INDEX OF NAMES 305

INDEX OF SUBJECTS 309

Introduction

Derivation or Representation?

Hubert Haider & Klaus Netter

1 The Issue

Derivation and *Representation* – these keywords refer both to a conceptual as well as to an empirical issue. Transformational grammar was in its outset (Chomsky 1957, 1975) a derivational theory which characterized a well-formed sentence by its derivation, i.e. a set of syntactic representations defined by a set of rules that map one representation into another. The set of mapping-rules, the transformations, eventually became more and more abstract and were trivialized into a single one, namely "move α", a general movement-rule. The constraints on movement were singled out in systems of principles that apply to the resulting representations, i.e. the configurations containing a moved element and its extraction site, the trace. The introduction of trace-theory (cf. Chomsky 1977, ch. 3 §17, ch. 4) in principle opened up the possibility of completely abandoning movement and generating the possible outputs of movement directly, i.e. as structures that contain gaps representing the extraction sites. However, this is only a conceptual shift whereby the concept of movement is replaced by the concept of assigning a set of representations to a given expression. These representations characterize the properties of an expression on various levels together with a set of constraints that specify the possible relations between these levels. Thus, the crucial empirical issue is not the dichotomy of *derivation by movement* vs. *assignment of representations* but rather the question of how many different levels of representation are available.

Of course most approaches would not dispute the need of distinguishing levels of representation in general, like the levels of phonological, syntactic or semantic representation. To avoid misunderstandings we will therefore introduce a terminological distinction for the scope of this introduction. Following a proposal of Ladusaw (1985), we will distinguish *levels* and *strata*: a level is defined by an algebra, i.e. a set of objects and operations defined over it. Different levels will differ in terms of their defining algebras. Representations that employ elements of the same set of objects and the same set of opera-

H. Haider and K. Netter (eds.), Representation and Derivation in the Theory of Grammar, 1–15.

tions will be representations on the same level. If the analysis of a sentence S uses multiple representations on a single level, we will (*pace* Ladusaw) use the term stratum for any sublevel of this level-within-levels-analysis. It should be noted here that the notion of different algebras should not be understood as a pure difference of notation: If identical notations are interpreted differently in distinct representations these representations constitute different levels, if different notations are interpreted identically they should be seen as representing the same level.

The Theory of Government and Binding (GB-Theory, Chomsky 1981), which Chomsky himself prefers to refer to as *The Principles and Parameter Theory*, introduces three strata for the syntactic representation:

- D-Structure
- S-Structure
- Logical Form (LF)

The fact that additional strata have been proposed (cf. NP-structure, suggested by v. Riemsdijk/Williams 1981) indicates that the quest for new strata is taken to be a legitimate theoretical enterprise. It is still a controversial question, however, whether there is an empirically sound basis for the diversification of strata in general, as Chomsky (1981:90f.) admits.

Koster, an advocate of a parsimonius approach, summarizes the issue as follows:

> Traditionally, the idea of distinct levels of representation has played an important role in generative grammar. According to some, it is even the most important idea in generative grammar. (...) Empirically speaking, little is known about these integrated levels. What we find in the current model theoretic approaches to syntax/semantics cannot be the biologically real model we are looking for. The reason is that as yet syntax is often treated in these approaches as something that is already known, whereas only the dimmest outlines have been glimpsed. (...) The idea that distinct levels of representation are the essence of syntax has led to a true proliferation of levels in recent years. Some of these levels are based on elements that have been part of generative grammar since its inception. D-Structure is an example. Others, like LF and NP-structure are relatively new. (Koster 1987:98)

What Koster calls a proliferation of levels is the proliferation of *strata within one level* of syntactic representation. Thus, Koster, in this terminology, argues against introducing additional strata in general and in his recent work (Koster 1987) marshalls evidence for a monostratal organisation of grammar.

In a certain respect, within the family of generative grammars the GB-theory's wealth of syntactic strata is unique, since most other models in the paradigm, such as for example LFG, GPSG and HPSG, are monostratal or at least strictly non-derivational. LFG stands for a theory which involves two levels of representation (constituent structure and functional structure), expressing two different types of information. GPSG illustrates the case of a mono-level and mono-stratal theory of syntax, where all information is expressed by means of phrase structure trees. HPSG can be seen as a mono-level but yet multi-stratal theory of grammar, where different strata relate to different aspects of linguistic information, but are represented by the same algebra, namely feature logics.

With this in mind it appears worthwhile to stress the issue of an empirical motivation for different syntactic strata within the GB framework and focus some research interest on it.

2 Levels and Strata

The stratal or non-stratal design of a model of grammar becomes a crucial issue, if grammar theory is understood as an enterprise that seeks to uncover the organization of an empirical object, namely the design of the particular human capacity to process symbol structures, called natural languages. The basic question is: are there strata?

If there are strata, this means that for a given expression there are multiple representations built up with elements of the same algebra (in Ladusaw's terminology). The technical ways of relating the representations distributed on various strata may turn out to be equivalent, i.e. to be notational variants. In the GB-framework, for instance, the assumption that there is a rule "move α" is not an ontological commitment. There is an equivalent non-transformational account which relates two strata, i.e. deep structure (DS) and surface structure (SS) by means of principles rather than input-output relations.

For example, sentence (1a) can be characterized either transformationally or non-transformationally.

(1) (a) Tabs have been kept on him

(b) Tabs$_i$ have been kept e_i on him

(c) e have been kept tabs on him

In transformational terms, "move α" applies to the D-structure (1c) and moves the object-NP to the empty subject position, hence derives (1b) from (1c). A non-transformational characterization could be framed as follows: Sentence (1a) is assigned two representations, one of which is dependent on the other: (1b) qualifies as a well-formed S-structure assignment to (1a) if there is a well-formed DS-assignment (1c), and (1b) is equivalent to (1c) modulo chain-formation. The constraints on chain-formation have to mirror the constraints on movement-rules.

However, the empirical issue common to both variants remains the same: Do we need the two strata? A natural alternative would be the attempt to exclusively characterize (1a) in terms of (1b), and in general, to assign only a single representation at each level. Of course it is possible to enrich any representation with notational devices such that it can encode any conceivable information. Hence it is a delicate matter to find empirical arguments that provide insight into what the correct form of representation is and whether it is spread across strata or not.

Let us illustrate the points under discussion with the explanation of the strong crossover prohibition under the standard treatment of wh-movement constructions.

(2) (a) *Who$_i$ did he$_i$ say [e_i kissed Antigone]

(b) Who$_i$ e_i said [he$_i$ kissed Antigone$_i$]

According to Chomsky (1981:193f.), the trace of wh-movement is subject to the same binding restrictions as non-pronominal NPs. Hence the trace of *who* in the subject position of the embedded clause in (2a) under the given interpretation violates the binding principle (C), that requires that non-pronominal NPs be unbound. If the traces are replaced by non-pronominal NPs, e.g. a name, the grammaticality pattern is the same:

(3) (a) *He$_i$ said [Oedipus$_i$ kissed Antigone]

(b) Oedipus$_i$ said [he$_i$ kissed Antigone]

However, there are at least two other ways of explaining the difference between (2a) and (2b).

Alternative description 1: Interrogative pronouns, like non-pronominal NPs must not be bound (i.e. coindexed with a c-commanding NP). Binding is checked *before* wh-movement. In (2a) the wh-pronoun occupies the subject position of the embedded clause at the relevant stage of derivation and therefore the sentence is ruled out. This description is available in the approach of v. Riemsdijk/Williams's (1981).

Alternative description 2: There is a wh-chain in (2a), linking the trace with the wh-pronoun. The chain is subject to the binding principles such that the head of the chain (i.e. the wh-element) must fulfill the binding requirements of its foot position. The following solution is proposed by Koster (1987:33):

A dependent element x and an antecedent y satisfy a local relation in a domain z if x and y are in the domain z, or if x or y are respectively related to x′ or y′ in z.

In the standard approach, Chomsky (1981:193f), traces are subject to binding. According to description 2, traces are foots of chains, i.e. extraction sites.

As indicated above, chains mediate between the base position and the 'derived' position of the displaced constituent. However, it is left unspecified what the consequences for the phrases embedded in a complex constituents are. The case illustrated in (4) shows that the accessibility of subconstituents is constrained and that it is not correct to assume that chains mediate any relation whatsoever (cf. v. Riemsdijk/Williams 1981:201).

(4) (a) *He_i likes [the pictures that $John_i$ saw] best

(b) [Which picture that $John_i$ saw] $_j$ did he_i like best e_j

This phenomenon – binding options opened by movement – occurs if the NP in question (in (4) it is the NP *John*) is part of a sentential constituent fronted across the binder.

The constraints involved here have to be further specified, of course. However, even if we do not know what the precise constraints are, it will not come as a surprise that such constraints should exist and that there is a difference between *being in a position* and *being linked to a position* by means of chains. We would expect that the linking mechanism has its own constraints and thereby filters out certain properties. In our case, the domains accessible through chains appear to be those embedded constituents which allow upward percolation of features such as is found with pied-piping. In order to be a candidate for wh-movement, a phrase must be specified positively for a wh-feature. Either the phrase is a wh-element itself or it contains a wh-element in an accessible domain. Accessible domains are, as shown in (5), constituents embedded in APs, PPs and NPs. Clause-internal phrases are not permeable for wh-percolation.

(5) (a) What did you have in mind ?

(b) [How far] is it ?

(c) [With what] shall I fix it ?

(d) [Whose hat] is this ?

(e) *[that you admire whom] did surprise her ?

(5e) is acceptable only as an echo-question, i.e. with heavy stress on the question word, but not as a regular question asked out of the blue, thus illustrating the fact that clauses do not admit pied-piping.

In sum, this set of examples and its account illustrates in a single case what it means to frame GB into a mono-stratal design, with SS as the single syntactic stratum. Whether this approach is superior to the poly-stratal, derivational approach has to remain an open issue until it is worked out in more detail.

Nevertheless, we have to ask ourselves what the criteria of adequacy for a stratal design are and how the present-day version of GB meets these criteria. The basic criterion could be the following Uniqueness Constraint, dictated by Occam's razor:

> For each stratum there must hold at least one constraint that cannot apply to any other stratum.

This criterion is so weak, however, that it is fulfilled even in the trivial case in which each constraint defines a separate stratum. It should be strengthened accordingly and required that there has to be a non-trivial set of constraints for each stratum (cf. Taraldsen, this vol.). Since the choice of the constraints is theory-dependent, the ultimate decision is an empirically based comparison and evaluation of the competing theories or versions of a theory.

2.1 The Strata of GB

In the standard version (Chomsky 1981) there are three syntactic strata, namely DS, SS, and LF. In the overall organization of the grammar four rule-systems (see 6) are distinguished (Chomsky 1981:5), which give rise to four levels (see 7) of representations, three of which meet our criteria for calling them strata, as will become clear below.

(6) a. lexicon

b. syntax
   (i) categorial component
   (ii) transformational component

c. PF-component

d. LF-component

> The lexicon specifies the abstract morpho-phonological structure of each lexical item and its syntactic features, including its categorial features and its contextual features. The rules of the categorial component meet some variety of the $\bar{X}$-theory. Systems (6a.) and (6b.i) constitute the base. Base rules generate D-structures (deep structures) through insertion of lexical material into structures generated by (6b.i), in accordance with their feature structure. These are mapped to S-structure by the rule

> "move α", leaving traces coindexed with their antecedents; this rule constitutes the transformational component (6b.ii), and may also appear in the PF- and LF-component. Thus syntax generates S-structures which are assigned PF- and LF-representations by components (6c) and (6d) of (6), respectively. (Chomsky 1981:5)

(7)

```
      D-structure
           |
      S-Structure
       /       \
     PF         LF
```

(Chomsky 1981:17)

The three strata (D-structure, S-structure, and LF) are subject to a uniformity principle, the projection principle (Chomsky 1981:29). It states that representations at each stratum (LF, D- and S-structure) are projected from the lexicon, in that they observe the subcategorization properties of lexical items.

The definition of the levels in (7) is usually left implicit. Chomsky (1981:39) informally characterizes them as follows:

> D-structure lacks the antecedent-trace relation entirely. At D-structure, then, each argument occupies a θ-Position and each θ-Position is occupied by an argument. In this sense, D-structure is a representation of θ-role assignment – though it has other properties as well, specifically those that follow from $\bar{X}$-theory and from parameters of the base (e.g. ordering of major constitutent) in a particular language.

S-structure is derived from D-structure by applications of "move α". It is a constituent structure enriched with indexing and empty categories, some of which are base-generated (i.e. PRO and pro, the subject of infinitival clauses and the subject of finite clauses in pro-drop languages, respectively), and some are the result of movement (the traces, i.e. the extraction sites and intermediate landing positions of phrases moved by NP-movement or wh-movement).

LF is a stratum that differs minimally from SS. It is derived from SS by so-called LF-movement, the application of "move α" to wh-elements (cf. Chomsky 1973, §16 for an interpretative analysis), quantified elements (cf. May 1977), and focused elements (Chomsky 1981:196), all of which are left unmoved at S-structure. Since S-structure is the input to the phonological representation (PF) LF-movement has no 'visible' effect.

The justification for this stratum rests on the observation that the abovementioned constructions seem to display subject-object asymetries familiar from overt movement constructions, although no movement is visible at surface structure (cf. Chomsky 1981: 235f.)

(8) (a) It is unclear who thinks that we saw who

(b) *It is unclear who thinks that who saw us

On the assumption that every wh-element is moved at LF, there will be a gap at the subject position in the LF of (8b), illustrated by (9). Therefore (8b) will be ill-formed for the same reason that rules out (10a) with the LF (10b).

(9) It is unclear for which person x and which person y, x thinks that y saw us

(10) (a) *It is unclear who_i she thinks that e_i saw us

(b) It is unclear, for which person x, she thinks that x saw us

Subsequently, this approach has been extended to the analysis of scopal relations and focus (cf. May 1985).

LF-movement differs from S-structure-movement in one important respect, however. It does not obey the locality restrictions for movement rules, as Chomsky notes (1981:235f). The following example illustrates the violation of the wh-island constraint:

(11) (a) Who remembers where we bought which book

(b) for which person x and which book y, x remembers for which place z, we bought x at z

(c) for which person x, x remembers for which place z and which book y, we bought y at z

The ambiguity of (11a) is captured on LF. It may be mapped on either of the two LF-representations given in (11b) and (11c). (11b) requires the fronting of the embedded object out of a wh-clause, which is impossible for overt wh-movement. On this evidence Chomsky (1981:236) concludes that LF-movement is unbounded for wh-elements.

This conclusion, however, undermines the programme, since boundedness is considered to be an essential property of movement rules. Huang (1982:383f.) takes this difference to be a primitive universal property, distinguishing LF-movement from SS-movement and proposes a strictly derivational LF-account for describing constructions involving Wh-elements in Chinese, a language without syntactic wh-movement. In the *Barriers*-framework (Chomsky 1986:32), this position is restated.

An explicit discussion of various empirical aspects of this issue, i.e. the discrepancy between LF-operations and SS-operations, can be found in the contributions of G. Fanselow and K. É. Kiss in this volume. Fanselow tries to overcome this theoretical obstacle in terms of a general feature specification principle and level-specific feature distribution. K. É. Kiss's paper offers additional empirical evidence for a systematic differentiation between movement properties and properties of interpretative rules. She analyzes the scopal properties of constructions with left-dislocation and operator movement, respectively, and concludes that a proper analysis calls for a distinction between movement-type representations and base-generated ones.

Recently, there has been a tendency to turn LF into a stratum complementary to SS, the maxim being, that any type of movement found at SS in any language takes place at LF in all those languages that do not move the respective elements at SS.[1]

This move is straightforward only if one assumes that "move α" is the proper level of abstraction for characterizing non-local dependencies. Yet, the fact that we are attuned to assume hidden movements, i.e. movement on a level of representation disconnected from the phonological representation, might just as well be taken as evidence that "move α" is not the appropriate concept, not even on surface structure. It may turn out that the essential properties of UG, that determine the range of facts, have to be captured on a more abstract level which allows a unified treatment on a single, non-stratal representation.

2.2 UG and the Diversification of Strata

The stratification of syntactic properties over three strata is neither an *a priori* quality nor is it learnable, i.e. it cannot be inferred from experience during language acquisition. Hence this property must be a property of Universal Grammar (UG), i.e. the biologically determined system of the human language processing capacity, that constitutes the child's prelinguistic initial state (cf. Chomsky 1981:7).

Viewed from the perspective of our mental design, UG might be characterized as a specific processing unit for data of a specific quality. This processing unit, let us call it the linguistic coprocessor, which evolved as a by-product of the general evolution of our central nervous system, guarantees a highly effective and rapid processing of data structures of a specific kind. It will not come as a surprise that the data structures which we find in natural languages reflect the make-up of UG, if we take into consideration that in the development of

[1] Chomsky (1986a) assumes that anaphors are adjoined to the I position in LF analogously to clitic movement in Romance languages. In Chomsky (1989) he proposes LF-movment of V to I in analogy to overt verb movement in French.

natural languages those data-structures were selected that proved to be efficiently processable. These are the data structures that meet the requirements of UG.

With this in mind, we have to ask ourselves what it could mean that UG requires that syntactic structures be processed on exactly three strata. One possibility, not a very likely one though, is that there is a 'hardwired' triple buffer in which a structure has to be stored in order to be processed by the corresponding set of rules and principles. Each of these buffers then would correspond to one of the strata. Such a picture could possibly suit our conception of simultaneous processing information of different qualities, such as phonological, syntactic and semantic ones. We would not have to presuppose hardwiring, since the difference in processing is a consequence of the intrinsic difference between the data-structures. Strata, however, are by hypothesis designed to characterize data structures of the same kind. It might turn out that the strata of GB are not distinct processing levels but rather virtual constructs that mirror the properties of subunits, i.e. distinct subroutines of UG, and their interfaces. In sum, the stratal organization of the GB-model raises some nontrivial questions for its metatheoretical foundation, which cannot be neglected in an overall assessment of the pros and cons of monostratal vs. polystratal grammar design.

3 The Contributions to this Volume

This volume, then, comprises a selection of papers which try to approach from different aspects the issue of derivation vs. representation in the sense of a non-stratal vs. a stratified theory of syntax.

3.1 Arguments for a Non-stratal Approach

Ian Roberts concludes his investigation of a wide range of crossover-phenomena for NP-movement with the putative result that *movement is really a metaphor for chain-formation and that D-structure is not an independent level of representation but rather a factorization of S-structure and chain-formation.* His analyses are based on Rizzi's (1986) chain formation algorithm, i.e. a restriction on chain formation, which blocks non-local links:

Rizzi's example is given in (12) and illustrates the fact that derived subjects cannot bind a dative reflexive clitic in Italian.

(12) *Giovanni$_i$ si$_i$ è stato affidato t_i' t_i''
Giovanni to-self was entrusted

According to Rizzi, (12) contains an ill-formed chain. It involves two instances of movement, namely NP-movement and clitic-movement, each of which is well-formed by itself. However, the resulting representation becomes ill-formed if the heads of the two chains are coindexed, which is necessitated if a reflexive is involved. In this case the reflexive and the antecedent NP share the same index, hence their traces will share the same index. Thus the reflexive becomes the closer antecedent even to the trace of the NP and thus interrupts the chain of the NP. Roberts carries this approach over to a wide range of phenomena (e.g. reflexive passives, psych-movement and raising constructions, etc.) and tries to explain them in terms of illicit NP-movements ruled out on the basis of Rizzi's locality restriction on chain formation. This approach, if it is correct, presupposes a representational account, since the source of ill-formedness is not found in movement but rather in the resulting configuration. Hence movement in this case is dispensable since the well-formedness restrictions are not captured in terms of restrictions on the mapping of D-structure to S-structure but in terms of S-structure properties itself.

Knut Tarald Taraldsen demonstrates that the same set of restrictions that apply to NP-movement configurations are found with pairs of expletive subject and the NP linked to the expletive. An account in terms of LF-movement, i.e. replacement of the expletive by the linked NP on LF, as suggested by Chomsky (1986a), is shown to be inadequate. Taraldsen concludes *that "move α", and, correspondingly the notion 'derivation' plays no role in syntactic theory, at least as far as the NP-movement subcase is concerned.* The proper level of abstraction is the notion *Argument-chain*, which subsumes expletive/argument-linking as well as the movement relation.

Wolfgang Sternefeld, like Roberts and Taraldsen, casts doubt on the existence of D-structure and S-structure as two distinct levels of representation. He claims that "free chain formation" by means of indexing on S-structure is superior to derivational chain formation. Free chain formation, however, is at odds with the central assumption of Roberts, i.e. the minimality requirement of Rizzi's chain formation algorithm, which he dismisses. Therefore, Sternefeld's and Roberts' proposals are alternative attempts to solve the same problem. Additional empirical evidence will be necessary in order to decide which approach is more fruitful.

The main bulk of the paper is devoted to the analysis of German "verb raising" construction. He defends an analysis in terms of incorporation along the lines of Baker (1988), which works without invoking reanalysis. Reanalysis (cf. Haegeman & Riemsdijk 1986) requires either a derivational or multi-representational approach, both of which are highly controversial. He concludes his paper with a general section on the concept of syntactic level.

Tilman Höhle discusses phenomena of scope and binding in German which fall under the heading of *reconstruction*. In these cases a dislocated phrase *P* behaves in certain respects as if it occupied its base position. In the literature, two approaches to reconstruction can be found:

(i) It is assumed that there is a level of representation – say R-structure – where *P* actually occupies its base position. In this approach of *true reconstruction*, scope and binding relations are computed at R-structure.

(ii) The rules and principles governing the computation of these relations are defined in such a way that they treat *P* at S-structure *as if* it occupied the position of its trace (*psuedo-reconstruction*).

Höhle shows that pseudo-reconstruction – in contrast to true reconstruction – is in conflict with the standard theory of coordination which holds that (a) there is no process of conjunct-initial elision, and (b) that the syntax and semantics of coordinate phrases are evaluated strictly compositionally ("bottom-up").

Coordinate phrases can be treated in accordance with (b) at R-structure but not at S-structure. However, it is not clear whether the assumption (b) is well-founded at all. In fact, several considerations – above all certain parasitic gap phenomena – lead to the conclusion that true reconstruction cannot be adequate – and hence (b) cannot be correct. Höhle suggests that the special properties of parasitic gaps (and parasitic Ā-binding in general), which imply this conclusion, derive from the fact that there are two different aspects of binding, s-binding and f-binding in his terminology, which normally go together, which can be dissociated however under certain conditions.

Hans-Peter Kolb and Craig Thiersch discuss the issue from the point of view of a formalization and axiomatization of GB-Theory by means of a computational reconstruction of the theory. Clearly the construction of a parser which seriously attempts to maintain the essential and distinguishing features of the theory (principles and parameters, modular structure of the well-formedness conditions, projection of all structure from the lexicon), requires a quite different approach from a traditional rule based parser.

In particular, Kolb and Thiersch argue that the attempt to construct a GB-Parser only stands realistic chances of success, if it were to allow incremental parsing with a simultaneous application of all well-formedness conditions as filters on structure building, preventing the generation of faulty structures at the earliest stage possible. Faced with the question of

> whether the relation between the linguistic levels is a truly derivational one, i.e. if there exist specific mappings to derive S- from D-structure and LF and PF from S-structure, with the modules purely functioning as filters on these derivations but too weak to define the levels by themselves; or whether the levels are, in fact, *constituted* by sets of mod-

ules, i.e. if they exist in parallel connected only by the overlap of the conditions that are operative on them

they decide 'in the absence of conclusive linguistic evidence for the necessity of a derivational approach' in favour of the second, more declarative view.

The remaining question of whether the different strata should be constructed in parallel or whether the modules should be compiled to constrain a single annotated S-Structure, encoding the entire information allocated to LF and D-structure in a multi-stratal approach, is rejected as such as a theoretically indistinguishable alternative.

From this point of view the problem to a large degree reduces to a locality problem in terms of the size of the local domain to which the linguistic modules and well-formedness constraints can be applied.

In the second part of their paper Kolb and Thiersch therefore discuss some variants of the G & B theory which crucially involve aspects of locality: the uniform constituent hypothesis, A-chain formation and the status of adjuncts.

3.2 Arguments for Strata

Gisbert Fanselow proposes a relativized minimality condition for government relations, i.e. a locality condition on government. Since government is an essential prerequisite for the well-formedness of empty categories, this condition constrains chain formation as well. Intuitively, the minimality condition states that a governor cannot enter a relation of government for a feature F with a governee G if there is a closer governor for G that governs the same feature F. Although this condition applies to representations, Fanselow claims that a mono-stratal organization is insufficient. Some phenomena could not be captures unless it is assumed that there are different strata which differ in terms of the features specified on them, thus interrupting certain government relations selectively.

Katalin É. Kiss argues for the necessity of distinguishing movement from rules of construal by demonstrating that the rule of "move wh", unlike rules of construal, has the property of creating scope. Evidence is provided by the comparison of two Hungarian constructions: *Operator Movement*, subsuming Focussing, wh-movement and syntactic Q-Raising, and *Left Dislocation*, a base generated construction.

Operator Movement is identified as movement because it observes various manifestations of the Subjacency Condition. These include the Complex NP Constraint, the restrictions that Long Operator Movement can only take place from a governed, complement CP and that it is only possible in the presence of a complementizer, and the fact that the moved element is reassigned case on every cycle by the V currently governing it.

Left Dislocation, on the other hand, is analyzed as a base-generated construction, because, among other reasons, the 'left-dislocated constituent' – 'empty argument' relation does not obey the locality constraints just mentioned.

In the output of Operator Movement, the preposed operator c-commands its scope. In contrast, a left-dislocated operator has narrow scope with respect to the operators preposed by operator movement.

That is, in the case of Operator ... *t* chains, the scope of the operator extends over the c-command domain of the head of the chain, while in the case of base-generated Operator ... *e* chains, the scope of the operator extends over the c-command domain of the root of the chain.

The paper also discusses and refutes two pieces of alleged counter-evidence to the claim that wh-type movement creates scope, namely, example (13) of Haik (1982), containing an apparently narrow-scope wh-moved interrogative phrase, and (14) of Marácz (1987), containing an apparently wide scope wh-phrase in its most deeply embedded clause:

(13) Which men did someone say that we invite for a talk?

(14) What do you think, whom should we invite?

As to the question of Representation versus Derivation, the paper is, in part, agnostic:

> The difference between the outputs of Operator Movement and Left Dislocation can, naturally, also be expressed in a representational framework: Operator Movement results in a chain the links of which locally bind each other, while Left Dislocation results in a chain which is not constrained with respect to locality. The distinction between local and non-local $\bar{A}$-chains, however, amounts to reintroducing the movement rule – rule of construal distinction under a different terminology.

References

Baker, M. (1988) *Incorporation. A theory of Grammatical Function Changing.* University of Chicago Press, Chicago.

Chomsky, N. (1957) *Syntactic structures*, Mouton, The Hague.

Chomsky, N. (1975) *The Logical structure of linguistic theory*, Plenum, New York.

Chomsky, N. (1977) *Essays on Form and Interpretation* North-Holland, Amsterdam.

Chomsky, N. (1981) *Lectures on Government and Binding* (Studies in Generative Grammar 9), Foris, Dordrecht.

Chomsky, N. (1986) *Barriers* (Linguistic Inquiry Monograph 13), The MIT-Press, Cambridge/Mass.

Chomsky, N. (1986a) *Knowledge of Language: Its Nature, Origin, and Use*, Praeger, New York/Westport/London.

Chomsky, N. (1989) "Some Notes on Economy of Derivation and Representation", in: I. Laka & A. Mahajan (eds.) *MIT Working Papers in Linguistics 10 (Functional Heads and Clause Structure)*, 43–74.

Haegeman, L & H.v. Riemsdijk (1986) "Verb Projection Raising, Scope, and the Typology of Rules Affecting Verbs", *Linguistic Inquiry* 17, 417–466.

Haik, I. (1984) "Indirect Binding", *Linguistic Inquiry* 15, 185–223.

Huang, J, (1982) "Move WH in a Language without WH movement", *The Linguistic Review 1*, 369–416

Koster, J. (1987) *Domains and Dynasties: The Radical Autonomy of Syntax*, Foris, Dordrecht.

Ladusaw, W. (1985) "A proposed distinction between *Levels* and *Strata*", *SRC Report*, 85–104

Marácz, L. (1987) "Connectedness and Correspondence Effects in Hungarian", *GLOW Newsletter* 18, 43–45.

May, R. (1985) *Logical Form*, MIT-Press, Cambridge/Mass.

Rizzi, L. (1986) "On Chain Formation", in H. Borer (ed.) *Syntax and Semantics 19: The Syntax of Pronominal Clitics*, Academic Press: New York, 65–96.

Riemsdijk, H.v. & Williams, E. (1981) "NP-Structure", *The Linguistic Review* 1, 171–217

NP-Movement, Crossover and Chain-Formation*

Ian Roberts

1 Introduction

1.1 Strong Crossover and Wh-movement

Example (1) illustrates a standard case of Strong Crossover (SC):

(1) *Who$_i$ does he$_i$ love t$_i$?

Examples of this type were first discussed in Postal (1971). In terms of the binding theory of Chomsky (1981), they are ruled out essentially by Principle C:

(2) A name or variable must be A-free.

An element is A-free iff it is not bound from an A-position. A(rgument)-positions are those which correspond to Grammatical-Function positions in D-Structure: subject, direct object, etc. Binding is defined as follows:

(3) X binds Y iff X c-commands Y and X is coindexed with Y.

We define c-command as in (4):

(4) X c-commands Y iff X does not dominate Y and the first branching node dominating X dominates Y. (cf. Reinhart (1976)).

Consider now the wh-trace in (1). Since it is coindexed with the pronoun in subject position, and since the subject position c-commands the position it occupies, this wh-trace is A-bound from subject position. Moreover, wh-traces are considered to be variables (since wh-words are considered to be quantifiers).

*My thanks to audiences at the following universities for their questions and comments on this material: UC Irvine, RU Utrecht, University of Geneva, University of Stuttgart. Thanks also to the audience at the Workshop on Representational and Derivational Theories, held in Oberkirch, November 1987, and to two anonymous reviewers of this article for this collection.

H. Haider and K. Netter (eds.), Representation and Derivation in the Theory of Grammar, 17–52.

Hence the wh-trace is A-bound by *he* in violation of Principle C of the binding theory, (2).

This account is extended to examples like (5) by assuming a covert level of syntactic representation, known as LF, at which quantifier-variable relations are systematically represented:

(5) *He_i loves $everyone_i$.

In the derivation from S-structure to LF, quantifier phrases like *everyone* are assumed to "raise" to a position adjoined to the clause containing them (cf. May (1977, 1984) for details). This operation, known as Quantifier Raising (QR), yields an LF representation like (6) for (5):

(6) *$Everyone_i$ [he_i loves t_i]

Here too the trace has the status of a variable, bound by *everyone*. Moreover, this trace is A-bound by the pronoun in subject position, exactly like the wh-trace in (1). And, exactly as in (1), the A-bound variable violates Principle C.

The above paragraphs summarize the standard account of strong crossover. Notice that this account is indifferent between a representational and a derivational view of movement. We will argue in this paper, however, that a more complete account of strong crossover implies a representational view of movement.

1.2 Strong Crossover and NP-movement

The above sketch of the standard government-binding account of SC shows one salient property: SC is deduced from Principle C since it is taken to be a property of variables. Variables are the traces of wh-movement and QR. However, although for the purposes of Principle C all variables are traces, not all traces are variables. In particular, the traces of NP-movement are not variables. In fact, NP-traces are considered to be anaphors, and thus fall under Principle A of the binding theory, which requires anaphors to be locally A-bound. It therefore follows that the theory outlined above predicts that there can be no SC with NP-movement.

However, Lasnik (1985) draws attention to a phenomenon which could be considered to be a case of NP-movement SC (NPSC). The examples involve certain "loopholes" in Principle A of the binding theory. Principle A requires anaphors, and therefore NP-traces, to be bound in their minimal binding domain. For our purposes, the minimal binding domain for an anaphor corresponds to the minimal NP or clause containing both the anaphor and a subject. An important consequence of subjecting NP-traces to Principle A in this way is that NP-movement cannot take place across a subject. Thus the ungrammaticality of (7) is explained:

(7) *John$_i$ is believed Fred likes t$_i$.

Here the subject of the lower clause, *Fred*, forms a binding domain for the NP-trace. "Long" movement of *John* gives a representation where this trace is not bound in its binding domain, in violation of Principle A.

However, Lasnik points out that nothing prevents the subject of the lower clause being a pronoun coreferential with the matrix subject, as in (8):

(8) *John$_i$ seems he$_i$ is believed t$_i$ to like Mary.

Here Principle A is satisfied, as the trace is bound by *he*, which is within the relevant binding domain. Nevertheless, (8) is at least as bad as (7). Moreover, Case theory cannot provide an account of this phenomenon; the chain formed by NP-movement in (8) has the standard Case properties of an A-chain in that its head is a Case position, and its foot a non-Case position.

The examples in (7) and (8) instantiate the general schema in (9), which always yields ungrammaticality:

(9) *A$_i$ B$_i$ t$_i$, where A is an argument in a non-θ-position, B is an argument, and A c-commands B and B c-commands t$_i$.

The purpose of this paper is to point out the existence of a wide range of cases of NPSC, i.e. instances of the schema in (9), drawing to a certain extent on observations originally made in Postal's early work on the subject (Postal *op cit*). It should be clear from the above discussion that the current theory offers no natural way of integrating NPSC with the account of "standard" SC (WHSC). Instead, we will adopt the approach of Rizzi (1986) – to be outlined in the next section – and argue that the central notion here is a well-formedness condition on θ-chains. This approach ultimately derives the ungrammaticality of (9) from the general conditions on argument structure, the θ-criterion and the Projection Principle.

1.3 Summary of Paper

The paper is organized as follows: in Section 2 we will present Rizzi's (1986) proposal to account for certain ill-formed occurrences of the Italian reflexive clitic *si* in terms of conditions on chains. We will also show that this account extends to the general absence of reflexive passives, originally noticed by Lees & Klima (1963) and discussed at length by Postal (*op cit*). We will also discuss certain problems raised by Epstein (1986) for Rizzi's approach which arise when Chomsky's (1986a) proposal that reflexives raise at LF is adopted. We will suggest a solution to these problems which has important consequences for the rest of the paper.

In Section 3 we digress to give an account of the different behavior of reflexives and reciprocals in passives. In Section 4, we consider a range of other NP-movement constructions – unaccusatives (in the form of "psych-movement") and raising constructions – where NPSC appears to be relevant. We will also consider one class of cases of *wh*-movement: *easy-to-please* and *too/enough* AP constructions. In some cases, the appearance of NPSC can decide between competing analyses for a given construction. Finally, in Section 5, we suggest that an account of WHSC can be integrated with our account of NPSC, rather than the converse. This leads to a discussion of the role and proper formulation of Principle C.

The major empirical result of this paper, then, is that there is a wider variety of NPSC effects than previously thought, involving all types of NP-movement. While it is not possible to subsume NPSC effects under the standard account for WHSC, by attributing them to Principle C, it is possible to subsume WHSC under NPSC, by taking all SC-effects to be the result of conditions on chain-formation. This move leads to a unified, representational theory of strong crossover.

Since the central formal device which we appeal to throughout is chain-formation, one theoretical result of this paper is a confirmation of the relevance of this notion. Moreover, since the existence of chains calls into question the independent status of the level of D-structure, the necessity of chains in the account of SC demonstrated in this paper casts further doubt on that level's independent status.

2 Rizzi's Chain-Formation Algorithm

2.1 Romance Dative Reflexives

Kayne (1975) originally observed that dative reflexive clitics in Romance could not be bound to a derived subject. Given the crucial fact that only derived subjects yield ungrammaticality, the basic illicit configuration is thus an instantiation of (9) with the derived subject as A and the reflexive clitic as B. This appears, then, to be another case of NPSC.

The analogous Italian data was recently discussed in Rizzi (1986). Rizzi's example is (10):

(10) *Gianni$_i$ si$_i$ è stato affidato t'_i t''_i.
Gianni to-self was entrusted

Rizzi advocates ruling out this example in terms of the interaction of two well-formedness conditions on chains: the θ-criterion and the Chain Formation Algorithm (CFA). The chain (*Gianni*, *si*, t) is ill-formed by the θ-criterion, as it bears two θ-roles, while the CFA guarantees that no other chains may be built, by insisting that intervening binders may not be skipped.

Here we adopt the essentials of Rizzi's analysis, although our definitions differ in detail from Rizzi's:

(11) *Chain*: The sequence (a_1 ... a_n) is a chain only if a_i locally binds a_{i+1}.

(12) a. *Local binding*: X locally binds Y iff X binds Y and there is no Z that binds Y without binding X.

b. *θ-criterion*: Each argument appears in a unique chain containing a unique visible θ-position P, and each θ-position P is visible in a chain containing a unique argument.

(13) a. A θ-chain is a chain which meets (12b).

b. The Projection Principle requires arguments to appear in θ-chains at S-structure.

These definitions allow us to claim that NPSC is to be deduced from well-formedness conditions on chains.

In general, the definitions in (11–13) will rule as ungrammatical any structure of the general form given in (9). This is because, in (9), A requires a θ-role, given the θ-criterion (12b) and the Projection Principle (13b). Since the position it occupies is not a θ-position it must form a θ-chain with some θ-position. For this θ-chain to be well-formed it must contain exactly one argument and one θ-role (13a, 12b), and there must be no "intervening binder", i.e. no coindexed argument which binds the θ-position without binding A, "between" A and the θ-position in question. In (9), the relevant θ-position is occupied by t_i. A cannot form a well-formed θ-chain with this position due to the presence of the intervening binder B. So, if A forms no chain, the θ-criterion and the Projection Principle are violated because A has no θ-role; if A forms a chain with B, the θ-criterion and the Projection Principle are violated because the resulting chain has two θ-roles; if A forms a chain with t_i the θ-criterion and the Projection Principle are violated because the chain (and therefore the θ-chain) is ill-formed, given (12a).

The examples in (8) and (10) instantiate the schema in (9). In (8), the derived subject corresponds to A, an argument in a non-θ-position (recall that it also follows from the Projection Principle that the landing sites for NP-movement must be non-θ-positions) and the complement subject is the intervening binder, an argument preventing the formation of a well-formed chain between the derived subject and its trace. In (10), the derived subject is again A, while the intervening binder is the clitic *si*. We can thus see that the two cases are very similar. Both can be ruled out in terms of conditions on chains.

It seems then that these two cases of NPSC can be accounted for by adopting a version of Rizzi's CFA, a point which was also made by Lasnik. We will now see if this solution extends to other cases.

2.2 Reflexive Passives

Postal (*op cit*, Ch. 1), drawing on observations due to Lees & Klima (1963:21), points out that reflexive passives are at best of questionable grammaticality:

(14) a. ??The man was seen by himself in the mirror.
b. ??She was inadvertently electrocuted by herself.
c. ??You are tortured by yourself/selves.
d. ??We are shaved by ourselves.

In this section we will show how Rizzi's account of (10) carries over to (14). Again, then, the central notion is chain-formation.

Our account of (14) relies on, and indeed argues for, a particular analysis of passives. This analysis is presented and motivated in considerable detail in Baker, Johnson & Roberts (1989), henceforth BJR, and in Roberts (1987). We will not, therefore, linger over it here. The central point of BJR's analysis is the following:

(15) There is a structurally present argument in passives which corresponds to the logical-subject argument of the passivized Verb.

BJR identify this argument with the passive morphology, conventionally *en*. The central properties of passive constructions – absorption of the object's Case and suppression of the subject's θ-role – are deduced from the presence of the passive morphology. The optionally present *by*-phrase, clearly a carrier of the logical-subject θ-role, is related to *en* by means of a "doubling" relationship, giving rise to a kind of "clitic-doubling". Thus BJR assign an S-structure representation like (16) to a typical passive clause:

(16) John_i was see - en_j t_i by Bill_j.

BJR also propose that agentless passives contain a VP-internal empty category, which contracts the same "doubling" relation with *en* as a *by*-phrase does. Thus an agentless passive has the S-structure in (17):

(17) John_i was see - en_j t_i e_j.

Once again, we will not motivate these analyses here. We simply assume them in order to shed further light on NPSC.

The examples in (14) all feature a *by*-phrase containing a reflexive. Alongside these, BJR point out another kind of "covert" NPSC effect. This is seen in examples like (18):

(18) a. They were killed.

b. They were admired.

The relevant fact about examples of this type is that they cannot be construed such that the logical subject and the surface subject refer to the same people. Thus (18a) cannot mean "they committed suicide", and (18b) cannot mean "they admired themselves".

The observation concerning (18) and the Postal-Lees-Klima observation about reflexive passives, illustrated in (14), can be naturally grouped together in terms of BJR's analysis of passives. BJR assign the following representations to (14a) and (18a), respectively:

(19) a. *The man_i was see-en_i t_i by himself_i. (=(14a))

b. *They_i were kill-en_i t_i e_i. (=(18a))

In fact, it is now clear what is wrong with these examples. If the derived subject corresponds to A and the passive morpheme to B, then both representations in (19) instantiate the schema in (9). In that case, reflexive passives are another kind of NPSC which can be accounted for in terms of a version of Rizzi's chain-formation algorithm.

Is the passive affix an intervening binder here in terms of the well-formedness conditions on chains proposed in (11–13)? Assuming c-command (as in (4)) to be relevant for binding relations, the passive affix locally binds t'_i. However, notice that *en* and t'_i symmetrically bind. Suppose now that we adopt the following (from Higginbotham (1983)):

(20) Binding relations are asymmetric.

Given (20), wherever there is a configuration such that A and B bind each other, either A binds B or B binds A. Suppose additionally that chain-formation proceeds in such a way as to form a well-formed chain wherever possible. Thus in cases where a potential intervening binder symmetrically binds a θ-position the potential intervener will not count as an actual intervener. These assumptions rule in the representation (19). Although it may be possible to avoid this problem by appealing to sub-zero bar-levels or by claiming that clitics are adjoined to heads, making V^0 the c-domain of *en*, we prefer to clear the problem up in a different way. We propose that *en* is base-generated in an Infl position which takes the VP headed by the main Verb as its complement (cf. BJR, Section 5, for arguments in favour of this). V incorporates with *en* in the course of the derivation. This gives a structure like the following for (19):

(21) [The man_i was [see-en_i [$_{VP}$ t_v t_i by $himself_i$]]]

In this structure, *en* and t_i are clearly not symmetric binders, so the CFA will be violated.

In this section we have introduced Rizzi's CFA, which amounts to a representational theory of NPSC. We have seen how this mechanism can be extended to account for the ungrammaticality of reflexive passives, including reflexive interpretations of short passives, given certain independently motivated assumptions about passive morphology.[1] We next turn to a class of more serious potential counterexamples to our overall approach.

---

[1]Epstein (1986) points out that Rizzi's account of (10) is incompatible with the proposal in Chomsky (1986a) that anaphors must be governed by their antecedents. This proposal entails that anaphors, in particular reflexives, must move to a position governed by their antecedent in the mapping to LF. Epstein observes that Chomsky's proposal gives rise to a problem with the contrast in grammaticality between the English version of (10), given in (i), and (10) itself:

(i) John was entrusted to himself.

If the reflexive raises to a position governed by the subject at LF, we have an LF representation like (ii) for this sentence (ignoring the Preposition *to* for the moment):

(ii) $John_i$ was [$himself_i$ [entrusted t_i' t_i'']].

This representation is analogous point by point with the S-structure of (10). Epstein rightly puts aside the possibility that the conditions on chains might hold at S-structure only, not at LF (in fact, given our definitions, such a hypothesis would contradict the Projection Principle), and instead suggests modifying the definition of local binding.

Epstein considers two modified definitions of local binding, either of which will give the result that the LF representation of (ii) does not violate the CFA. The definitions are given in (iii):

(iii) a. A locally binds B iff A binds B, and if C binds B, then either C binds A or C = A. (Epstein's (2B), p. 196).

3 Reciprocals

In this section we briefly digress to discuss the behaviour of reciprocals in passive constructions. Reciprocals were not discussed by Postal or by Lees & Klima, as at that time they were considered to have different properties from those of reflexives. In essence, I shall argue in this section that this assumption was right. The crucial property shared by reflexives and reciprocals is that both demand a local antecedent; in other respects, reciprocals differ markedly from

---

b. A locally binds B if A X-binds B and there is no C such that A X-binds B and C X-binds B, where X is uniformly replaced by A or Ā thoughout. (Epstein's (2c), p. 199).

These definitions both mean that *himself* in (ii) does not count as an intervening binder. Let us see how this is achieved.

In (iiia), this is achieved by allowing a mutually binding pair of elements to both count as local binders for some third category they both asymmetrically bind. Assuming *himself* is adjoined to Infl in (ii) then, *pace* Chomsky (1986a), this means that the subject and *himself* symmetrically bind in this structure. Thus *himself* does not count as an intervening binder for the CFA, and (ii) is allowed.

In (iiib), crucial reference is made to the status of the position occupied by the potential intervening binder. An intervening binder does not disrupt local-binding relations if it occupies an A-position and the chain to be formed is an Ā-chain. Conversely, if the intervener occupies an Ā-position and the chain to be formed is an A-chain, local binding relations between the head of the A-chain and some element Ā-bound by the intervener are unaffected. The latter is the situation found in (ii). The reflexive *himself* is in an adjoined position, therefore an Ā-position, and so does not disrupt local A-binding between the subject and its trace. Therefore the operation of the CFA is unaffected.

It makes no difference for our analysis of reflexive passives whether we adopt (iia) or retain the definition in (12a). The analysis of NPSC in reflexive passives stands on either definition. We cannot, however, accept definition (iib). On the reasonable assumption that *himself* and the implicit argument occupy Ā-positions in (19), definition (iib) states that neither of these elements would be able to count as intervening binders. This definition thus predicts that reflexive passives and short passives with a reflexive interpretation of the implicit argument should both be allowed, a false prediction. For this reason, we reject definition (iib).

It seems, then, that the only definition of local binding able to both rule out (19) and rule in (ii) is (iiia). There is, however, another possibility which suggests that we may be able to retain the simpler and more restrictive of the definitions of local binding, that in (12a). Suppose that the reflexive moves to a position adjoined to the PP that dominates it in (i) (this possibility is considered by Epstein (*op cit.*: fn. 14) but rejected by him for reasons to do with the particular definition of government he was assuming: since we assume a different definition, essentially the one in Chomsky (1986b:9), this possibility is open to us). This would give an LF representation like that in (iv):

(iv) John$_i$ was entrusted t'_i [$_{PP}$ himself$_i$ [$_{PP}$ to t''_i]].

If we assume the theory of adjunction structures proposed in May (1985), including the definition of exclusion in Chomsky (*ibid*), the reflexive is able to govern out of PP, because it is only included in a segment of the PP-node. Therefore the reflexive governs t'_i. Thus the reflexive meets the well-formedness condition on anaphors, without violating the conditions on chains.

reflexives.

The basic fact about reciprocals is that they allow binding by a derived subject, while, as we saw earlier, reflexives do not:

(22) a. The men were seen by each other/??themselves in the mirror.

b. They were inadvertently electrocuted by each other/??themselves

c. You are tortured by each other/??yourselves.

In order to account for this contrast and retain our account of the ungrammaticality of reflexive passives, we must say something special about the structure of reciprocals. Drawing partly on suggestions made by Lebeaux (1983), we propose the following structure for reciprocals:

(23)

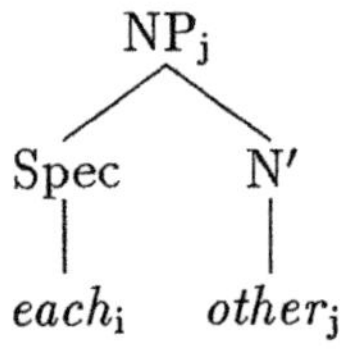

This structure derives from the assumptions of (24):

(24) a. *each* is a quantifier, and QRs in the mapping to LF.

b. *other* is a disjunctive pronoun, and contraindexes with *each.*

There are two arguments that *each* is a quantifier: it shows the effects of scope, and it induces weak crossover.

Concerning scope, Barss (1989) observes that a sentence like (25) has the two readings indicated:

(25) John and Mary said they admired each other.

a. John said: I admire Mary; Mary said: I admire John.

b. John said: I admire Mary and she admires me;

Mary said: I admire John and he admires me.

Reading (a) corresponds to the paraphrase "John and Mary each think ...", while reading (b) corresponds to the paraphrase "John and Mary said they each think ..." The idea that these paraphrases approximate the LFs for the different readings of (25) seems a natural way of accounting for the ambiguity of this sentence. So *each*, like other quantifiers, raises in the mapping to LF.

A second argument comes from weak crossover. Consider the following contrast:

(26) a. They$_i$ gave themselves$_i$ to each$_i$ other.

b. *They$_i$ gave each$_i$ other to themselves$_i$.

(Notice that we are treating *each* as the anaphoric element – see below on this). The assumption that *each* QRs, together with the assumption that reflexives raise at LF (cf. fn. 1), gives the following partial LF-representation for (26b):

(26) c. ... [each$_i$ [gave [t$_i$ other] [themselves$_i$ [to$_i$ [t$_i$]]]]]

(26c) is a weak-crossover configuration: the quantifier *each* locally Ā-binds two variables, t_i and *themselves* (cf. Koopmann & Sportiche (1982)). Notice however that *themselves* c-commands t_i. However, *themselves* is not a quantifier. The local Ā-binding *quantifier* for both variables here is *each*, and this is what leads to a Bijection Principle violation. So, despite the raised reflexive, (26c) is a weak-crossover violation. It is essential to assume that *each* undergoes QR in order to account for this violation.

In (26), we treated the index of *each* as the one shared by the antecedent of the reciprocal. This is consistent with the idea that *each* functions as a bare quantifier at LF (if not before). In general, bare quantifiers have the properties of anaphors, as the following paradigm shows (cf. Belletti (1982)):

(27) a. The kids will each/all go to the movies.

b. The kids tried [PRO to each/all go to the movies].

c. *The kids forced John [PRO to each/all go to the movies].

d. *The kids said that John would each/all go to the movies.

Thus we assume that the anaphoric property of reciprocals derives from the fact that *each* is bare quantifier. Suppose that bare quantifiers in general have to be governed by their antecedents at LF. Then the locality condition on reciprocals will derive from the relevant locality condition on *each*-movement (which amounts to basically the condition that *each* cannot be raised across a c-commanding A-position specifier, a condition presumably deducible from the antecedent-government portion of the ECP).

Another consequence of taking *each* to be a bare quantifier is that it is not an argument. *Each* can thus never count as an intervener for chain-formation. The argumental part of a reciprocal is its head: the disjunctive pronoun *other*. We have proposed that *other* obligatorily carries a distinct index to that carried by *each*. This means that *other* does not share the index of the antecedent of the reciprocal (more precisely, the antecedent of *each*). These considerations lead us to the following representation for passives containing reciprocals:

(28) They_i each_i were see+en_j t_i by $[t_i\ \text{other}_j]_j$

Here there is no CFA violation: *en* does not prevent chain-formation between the subject and the direct-object position, because it has a distinct index from this chain, the one it shares with *other* by the doubling relation; *each* does not block chain-formation because, as a bare quantifier, it is not an argument. Therefore the representation is well-formed.

This is our proposal for the contrasts in (22), then. Briefly, we retain all our assumptions about chain-formation and passives, but consider reciprocals to have a rather different structure from reflexives. The proposals for reciprocals have many wider implications, which we won't go into here. The essential point is that the contrast in (22) can be fairly naturally accounted for. Henceforth, we will use reflexive/reciprocal contrasts of the type in (22) as a diagnostic for instances of NPSC.

4 Further Cases of NPSC

In this section, we will illustrate cases of NPSC involving the two other principal cases of NP-movement besides passive. The constructions in question are psych-movement, which we take to be one kind of unaccusative construction, and raising. In these constructions, unlike in passives and *si*-constructions, clitic-like affixes do not play a crucial role in creating ill-formed chains. Thus we rely throughout on the presence of overt reflexives, together with the assumptions about reflexive-raising adopted in 2.2.

In a final section, we consider some cases of illicit movement which appear similar to the raising cases. These involve various kinds of movement out of AP-complements: *easy-to-please* constructions and *too/enough* complements. We will argue, *pace* Chomsky (1977), that these constructions in fact involve WHSC.

4.1 Psych-Predicates

We divide the discussion of psych-predicates into several subparts, roughly according to the category of the predicate concerned. We adopt the theory of psych-Verbs of Belletti & Rizzi (1988). To some extent, the conclusions we reach provide further evidence for their approach.

4.1.1 Psych-Verbs

The existence of a class of psych-predicates having distinct syntactic and semantic properties from ordinary transitives has long been recognized. Recently, a particular hypothesis about the underlying representation of psych-Verbs has been advanced by Belletti & Rizzi (1988). They distinguish three kinds of psych-Verbs, appearing in the following DS frames:

(29) a. Exp [V Th] – I liked the play.

b. e [[V Th] Exp] – The play amused me.

c. e [V Th [P Exp]] – The play appealed to me.

The first kind of psych-predicate has a D-Structure similar to a standard transitive, except that the θ-roles assigned are different. We will say no more about this type here, except to contrast it with the other types. The second two are both kinds of unaccusative, in the sense of Perlmutter (1978) and Burzio (1986), in that their surface subject corresponds to an underlying object.

For example, a Verb like *amuse* (other members of this class include *amaze, bore, confuse, disgust, excite, frighten, gratify, horrify, irritate, mystify, nauseate, puzzle, rile, surprise, threaten, worry* – cf. Postal (1971:41–42)) in (30a) would have the D-structure in (30b):

(30) a. The play amused me.

b. e [$_{VP}$ [$_{V'}$ amuse the play] me].

Assuming that *amuse* is not a Case-assigner, *the play* moves from the object position to the subject position (cf. the derivation of *John arrived* on standard accounts). A similar derivation takes place with *appeal*, except that here the Experiencer appears in a PP.

As (30b) shows, Belletti & Rizzi (1988) in fact assign a fairly articulated structure to the VP headed by *amuse*. They argue that the Experiencer argument occupies a position higher in the VP than the Theme. This means that the Experiencer argument is outside V′ in (30b), in a relation of asymmetric c-command with the Theme. This analysis predicts that no reflexive can occur as surface Experiencer object of a Verb such as *amuse*, given the theory of chain-formation we have adopted. Consider then the following examples:

(31) a. ??John amuses/disgusts/horrifies/irritates himself.

b. We amuse/disgust/horrify/irritate each other.

(31a) seems to be ungrammatical, as expected.[2] Notice also the minimal pair in (32):

[2]Remember that the agentive (or transitive, as opposed to unaccusative) reading of *amuse* as in *John amuses the kids (with his stories)* is not relevant here. See below for more about the relationship between these two readings. Another factor which could weaken this judgement, as well as (14) above, is the option of stressing the reflexive. When this happens, both (31a) and (14) are fine. For some discussion of why this may be, cf. Belletti & Rizzi (1988: 9–10).

(32) a. John likes himself.

b. ??John pleases himself. (cf. They please each other).[3]

((32b) is not to be taken in the idiomatic sense of "John does whatever he wants to").

A second class of psych-Verbs is the class of perception Verbs with the argument structure (29b), where the Theme argument is an AP small clause. Here the same violation arises as with *amuse* etc., but the judgement is clearer as there is no transitive counterpart to provide a grammatical reading for the sentences:

(33) a. *I_i look old to $myself_i$.

b. $They_i$ look old to each $other_i$.

The VP of (31a) has the following structure:

(34) $John_i$ [[amuses t_i] $himself_i$].

Here, as we said above, the reflexive asymmetrically c-commands the object trace. The reflexive will thus count as the local binder of the object trace. Therefore the reflexive is an intervening binder. Once again, then, the abstract schema in (9) is instantiated here. Notice that this is true independently of the possibility of LF-movement of the reflexive to a VP-adjoined position (although we assume that such movement takes place only if the reflexive does not already govern its antecedent; in fact, in the LF of (34), it governs the object trace, making LF-raising unnecessary. In this respect, reflexives differ from *each*, which, as a quantifier, must raise – cf. fn. 3).

Similarly, (33a) has the LF (35):

(35) I_i [look [t_i old] [$myself_i$ [to t'_i]]].

[3]In fact, the reflexive/reciprocal contrast is less strong with some of the psych-Verbs of (29b) because the reciprocal is somewhat degraded. In addition to ?*They please each other*, consider:

(i) a. ??They worry each other.

b. ?They disturb each other.

Given the proposals made about reciprocals in Section 3, the deviance of these examples cannot be attributed to chain-formation violations induced by the reciprocal. Instead, we propose that the degradation is due to ill-formed *each*-movement at LF, which is turn a consequence of the fact that *each* moves from a position outside V′, thereby crossing one non-L-marked category. Presumably, this is enough to cause a mild violation, even at LF.

Examples of this type, like (31a), are ungrammatical because the reflexive asymmetrically c-commands the trace of the derived subject, which here occupies the subject position of the small clause. So this structure instantiates the schema for chain-formation violations of (9). As we mentioned above, we consider this example to be worse than (31a) because the "psych" reading is the only one available; there is no interference from a competing agentive transitive reading.

Consider finally the third class of psych-Verbs, which we illustrate with *appeal.* These differ from the second type only in that the Experiencer is the indirect object, as the DS of (29c) showed. If the *to*-phrase is outside V′, no reflexive Experiencer should be possible. In fact this is true, as (36) shows:

(36) a. ??John$_i$ appeals t$_i$ to himself$_i$.

b. They$_i$ appeal to each$_i$ other.

(36) seems to have approximately the same status as (31a). We can account for this in the same way as long as we assume that the *to*-phrase is outside V′. Note that this is a minimal difference with the *entrust*-type case discussed in fn. 1 (see example (iv) of that footnote). We will discuss this difference further below, after looking at the behaviour of some types of psych-Adjectives.

In this section we have seen that the two unaccusative classes of psych-Verbs disallow reflexive binding by the derived subject. This can be explained in terms of the chain-formation algorithm of 2.2. So a further case of NPSC admits of a representational account fairly straightforwardly.

4.1.2 Psych-Adjectives

Most Verbs like *amuse* have two Adjectival forms: one in *-ing*, and one in *-ed*. The *-ing* Adjectives contrast directly with the *-ed* Adjectives with respect to the possibility of post-Adjectival reflexives (the data are from Postal (*op cit*: 47)):

(37) a. I am amused with myself.

b. *I am amusing to myself.

(38) a. I am disgusted with myself.

b. *I am disgusting to myself.

(39) a. I am horrified at myself.

b. *I am horrifying to myself.

Two things must be explained in connection with these contrasts: (i) why the *-ing* forms are impossible; (ii) why the apparently passive *-ed* forms are good.

We leave aside point (ii) until the next section. Concerning point (i), we naturally take the contrasts in (37–39) as indicating that the correct DS for an example like (37b) is (40):

(40) e is amusing $John_i$ [to $himself_i$]

The Adjectives assign no θ-role to their subject and no Case to their Theme object (i.e. they obey Burzio's generalization). Because it receives no Case, the object NP moves to subject position. This gives the SS (41):

(41) $John_i$ is amusing t_i [to $himself_i$]

We now obtain the following LF by reflexive raising:

(42) $John_i$ is amusing t_i [$himself_i$ [to t'_i]].

Assuming that the *to*-phrase is $\bar{A}$-external, this structure violates the local-binding condition on chains. The reflexive acts as a binder intervening between the moved NP and its trace, preventing the formation of a well-formed chain between these two positions. So the structure in (42) is another one which instantiates the schema in (9). This is then another case of NPSC, accountable for in the same way as those discussed above.

A further point of interest here is that the existence of an NPSC effect provides evidence that these Adjectives are unaccusatives, in the same sense that psych-Verbs (of Types II and III) are unaccusatives. This conclusion runs counter to the claim (made, e.g. by Levin & Rappaport (1986)) that Adjectives always have an external argument. In this connection, cf. also Cinque (1990), Roberts (1989).

An important question is raised by the ungrammaticality of (36) and the (b)-examples in (37–39) compared to the grammaticality of *entrust*-type cases as in (i) of fn. 1. Superficially, the VPs in the psych-cases and the *entrust*-type case seem to have the same structure, in that both involve a direct object and a *to*-phrase indirect object. However, we are led to claim that the structure of a VP headed by a Verb of the *entrust*-class must be such that the direct and indirect-object arguments are on the same structural level. In that case, the reflexive in an LF-representation like (iv) of fn. 1 will not count as an intervening binder, since it will symmetrically bind the object trace. Thus the sentence will be allowed. We thus assume that Verbs of the *entrust*-class have indirect objects inside V′, while Verbs (and Adjectives) of the psych class have Experiencer arguments which are outside V′. This assumed difference will yield the contrasts we have seen, given our assumptions. The crucial assumption which derives these differences is that binding relations must be asymmetric.

There is some independent evidence in favour of the structural distinction between psych-predicates and ordinary ditransitives of the *entrust*-type. The *entrust*-class allows extraction of a part of the NP inside the PP, while the psych-class does not tolerate this as readily. Cf.:

(43) a. *Which film was Dirk amusing to the director of ?

b. ??Which film did Dean appeal to the director of ?

c. Which film did Sam entrust Marilyn to the director of?

Similar contrasts are observed for Italian by Belletti & Rizzi (1988). We adopt their account for them, which runs as follows: assume that the PP in (43a,b) is outside V′, while that in (43c) inside V′. Assume further that a category outside V′ is not in the canonical L-marking configuration (cf. Chomsky (1986b)). Then the PP in (43a,b) is not L-marked, and so is a barrier for movement (since PP is nevertheless an argument, it cannot be adjoined to). Whether the maximal projection immediately dominating the PP, namely VP, inherits PP's barrierhood is not a question we need to commit ourselves to if we assume that extraction over one barrier can result in a slight subjacency violation. We then account for the contrast in (43) in terms quite consistent with our proposed structural difference between psych-predicates and ordinary ditransitives. So the contrast in (43) is independent motivation for our proposed structural difference.

In this section, we have extended the account of NPSC with psych-Verbs to one class of psych-Adjectives. This is of independent interest, as it suggests that unaccusative Adjectives exist. We also provided independent motivation from extraction contrasts for our proposed structural difference between psych-complements and ditransitive Verbs with a *to*-phrase indirect object. The latter conclusion is consistent with various proposals for a thematic hierarchy (cf. Jackendoff (1972), Belletti & Rizzi (*op cit*), Roberts (1989)); if Experiencers are higher on the hierarchy than Goals, one expects them to occupy higher structural positions, other things being equal. This might explain why Experiencers are outside V′ and Goals inside.

4.1.3 Psych-Passives

In this section we turn now to point (ii) above: the status of the *-ed* Adjectives in (37–39). This question is important because in 2.2, we derived the ban on reflexive passives from very general conditions on θ-role assignment and θ-chain formation. In other words, we are treating the ban on reflexive passives as a very general phenomenon. For this reason we must treat these seemingly passive forms as Adjectival passive participles.

Postal (*op cit*: 43) gives three reasons why these forms should not be considered Verbal passives. First, many of these examples coexist with real passives:

(44) a. I was astonished at his agility.
b. I was astonished by his agility.

The Adjective of (44a) selects the Preposition *at*, while the Verbal passive of (44b) is of course associated with a *by*-phrase.

Compare now the following pair:

(45) a. I was astonished at myself.
b. *I was astonished by myself.

Here we see that the Adjective allows its subject to antecede a reflexive, while the Verbal passive does not, as we saw in 2.2. Second, there are cases of selectional differences, where the real passives pattern with the corresponding actives:

(46) a. *I was mystified at Harry.
b. I was mystified by Harry.
c. Harry mystified me.

Thus many speakers do not allow the Adjective *mystified* to select the Preposition *at* in (46a). Nevertheless the passive participle of (46b) allows a *by*-phrase (*by*-phrases are not selected; cf. BJR).

Third, -*ed* psych-Adjectives take degree modifiers, while true verbal passives of course cannot:

(47) a. I was very astonished at his agility.
b. *I was very astonished by his agility.

The first two of these arguments show that the -*ed* forms are distinct from verbal passives, while the third shows that they are Adjectives. In fact, there is further evidence that these forms must be Adjectival passives.

The crucial fact about the Belletti-Rizzi hypothesis that psych-Verbs are unaccusatives is that it entails that psych-Verbs lack a logical-subject argument. Now, it is a well-known fact that in many (in fact most) languages passivization of Verbs which lack a logical-subject argument is impossible. This is certainly true in English, as the following examples show:

(48) a. *John was seemed to to be smart (by Bill). (raising)

b. *The bridge was existed under (by trolls). (unacc)

c. *John was resembled (by his brother). (copulative)

(These facts fall under the "1-Advancement Exclusiveness Law" of Relational Grammar – cf. Perlmutter & Postal (1984) – which is derived by BJR from the θ-criterion, given that the passive morpheme is an argument). If psych-Verbs lack logical-subject arguments, and Verbs lacking in logical-subject arguments are unable to passivize, the (a)-examples of (37–39) could not be Verbal passives. Therefore they must be Adjectival passives.

What, then, is the structure of these examples? Given the very clear contrast here with the *-ing* Adjectives, we are led to suppose that the Adjectival passives involve no movement. The Experiencer argument is externalized by the operation of a lexical rule (cf. Levin & Rappaport (1986) and below). We thus assign the following structure to the (a)-examples in (37–39):

(49) I_i am [$_{AP}$ amused with/at myself$_i$].

If (49) is the correct representation for the examples in (37–39), then there are no problems with chain-formation, assuming that the Adjectival-passive morphology, unlike Verbal-passive morphology, does not act as an argument. Moreover, Levin & Rappaport (*op cit*) give evidence that Adjectival Passive Formation is a lexical process and so does not involve movement, and so there is no chain formed between the subject position and the object position. For this reason, then, reflexive Adjectival passives do not instantiate the schema in (9), and so they are grammatical.

The conclusion that Adjectival passives allow their subjects to antecede reflexives in following PPs (which may, subject to selection, be *by*-phrases) leads to further consideration. In general, Adjectival Passive Formation (APF) can only convert an argument of the base Verb into the subject of the derived Adjective, as was originally pointed out by Wasow (1977) (although Levin & Rappaport (*op cit*) show that Wasow's original generalization was too strong). This constraint is illustrated in (50):

(50) a. John was (*un)considered a fool.

b. Mary was (*un)baked a cake.

c. Fred was (*un)promised to be left alone.

d. John was (*un)sent a letter.

e. John was (*un)believed to be a genius.

(Here the *un*-prefix forces ungrammaticality because it only attaches to Adjectives, forcing the participle to be construed as Adjectival). We predict that examples like (50) will disallow a reflexive reading or *by*-phrase. This is because they could not be Verbal passives, for the reasons connected with chain-formation described in the previous section. On the other hand, they could not be Adjectival passives, because the thematic constraint is violated. The relevant examples are shown in (51):

(51) a. *John is considered a fool by himself.
b. *Mary was baked a cake by herself.
c. *Fred was promised by himself to be left alone.
d. *John was sent a letter by himself.
e. *John was believed to be a genius by himself.

These examples are in fact considerably worse than examples like (14). This may be because examples like (14) admit a marginal Adjectival passive interpretation, while such an interpretation is ruled out in (51), leading to total ungrammaticality here.

We are thus led to the conclusion that the *-ed* forms in (37–39) are indeed Adjectives. That these are not verbal passives is consistent with our account of reflexive passives in 2.2. There are thus two kinds of Adjective derivable from psych-Verbs like *amuse*; the *-ing* form, which is a true psych-Adjective in that it is unaccusative, and the *-ed* form, which is "transitive" in that it has a thematic Experiencer subject at DS. Again, we are led to these conclusions by our assumptions regarding conditions on chain-formation.

4.1.4 Psych Nominals

Nominalizations of psych-Verbs have some fairly interesting properties. We cannot attempt a full analysis of this area here; instead we will concentrate on the question of "passive in NP", and whether our analysis of illicit NP-movement can tell us anything about the derivation of this construction. If we can find cases of ill-formed reflexivization, we can attribute these to the presence of a derived subject. The existence of derived subjects in nominalizations in turn argues for a syntactic rather than a lexical derivation of passive in NP.

The first fact to note is that only an Experiencer can be the subject of a psych nominal:

(52) a. John's amusement at the stories
b. *The stories' amusement of John
c. ?*The amusement of John at the stories

The natural account of this is that the derived Noun *amusement* lacks the capacity to assign GEN(itive) Case. Note that *amusement* is derived from the unaccusative form of this Verb in (37), suggesting that the derived Noun's Case properties are a function of those of the base Verb – the Verb's original ACC(usative) Case corresponding to the derived Noun's GEN. The following examples show the nominalized transitive *amuse*. Here the derived Noun assigns both GEN Case and a subject θ-role. (53a) is only good if there an implicit Agent of the nominal (or a *by*-phrase). In (53b) the Agent argument is overtly present. So we could conclude from this data that a derived Noun can only assign GEN Case if it also assigns a subject θ-role (cf. Chomsky (1986a)). When contrasted with (52c), these examples suggest that Burzio's generalization is relevant for nominalizations:[4]

(53) a. the amusement of John with the stories

b. Bill's amusement of John with the stories

These considerations suggest that (52c) is ruled out because the unaccusative-derived *amusement* is unable to assign GEN, leading to a violation of the Case Filter by *John.* It is unclear why (52b) is ruled out; this seems to be an instance of the general constraint that only direct arguments of the base Verb may undergo passive in NP. The Experiencer is not a direct argument while the Theme is, leading to the contrast between (52a) and (52b). It is unclear what such a constraint derives from, however.

Our chief concern here is the possibility of a reflexive bound by the subject of a passive nominal like (52a):

(54) a. ?*John's amusement/disgust/astonishment at himself

b. their amusement/disgust/astonishment at each other

(54a) seems highly questionable, and again the contrast with the reciprocal holds. The following analysis of (54a) shows how the reflexive acts as a binder intervening between the derived subject of the NP and its trace:

[4]We cannot maintain this claim in full generality, however, as nominalizations of unaccusative verbs are possible: *the arrival of the guests*, etc. The correct generalization appears to be that Burzio's generalization finds an analogue in ergative but not in unaccusative nominalizations.

(55)

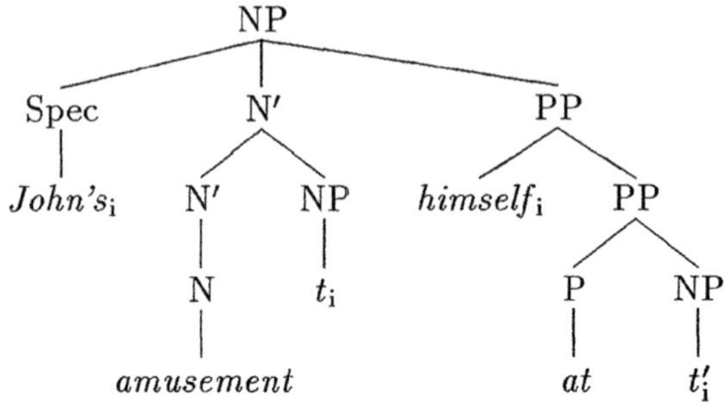

This configuration instantiates the schema in (9) above. The reflexive once again counts as an intervening binder; it governs and asymmetrically c-commands its antecedent t_i. Therefore it asymmetrically binds t_i, and hence counts as an intervening binder. Thus the structure is ruled out.

The result above is only achieved by assuming that passive in NP is an instance of NP-movement.

Finally, notice the ungrammaticality of the following:

(56) *John's amusement with himself

(56) is the passive of the nominalization of the transitive *amuse*. This example can be ruled out in exactly the same way as (54a), which tells us that the *with*-phrase occupies a structural position at least as high as that of the *at*-phrase of (54a), and in any case is outside N′. Notice that this example requires an agent or an agentive implicit argument independently of issues concerning chain-formation. (Furthermore, this implicit argument cannot be coreferent with *John/himself*; unfortunately this fact does not tell us much about how the implicit argument is structurally represented).

In this section we have seen a further case of NPSC, this time involving NP-movement within NP. As in the previous section, the presence of NPSC effects in a given construction can tell us whether that construction involves NP-movement or not. This can then shed light on the overall analysis of a given construction.

4.1.5 Psych-Stems

In this final subsection on psych-predicates we digress slightly from our central topic and attempt to provide a unified analysis of the various kinds of psych-predicates that we have seen in the preceding subsections. An important consideration in this will be the evidence provided by cases of NPSC that certain constructions involve NP-movement while others do not.

We propose the following lexical entry for stems of the *amuse*-class:

(57)

$$\textit{amuse}\left\langle \begin{array}{l} \text{Ag} \ \langle \textit{Exp}, \ (\text{Th})\rangle \\ \langle \textit{Th}, \ \text{Exp}\rangle \end{array}\right.$$

Here we adopt the notation for lexical entries used by Levin & Rappaport (1986): angle brackets surround the internal arguments; the direct argument is underlined – this is the argument which is directly θ-marked in a relation of government and sisterhood with the Verb, without the intervention of any Prepositions, inherent/oblique Cases, etc.; round brackets indicate optionality.

So (57) states that a Verb of the *amuse* class can appear either with an Agent external argument, an Experiencer direct argument and an optional indirect Theme argument, i.e. *John amused the children (with the stories)*, or with no external argument, a direct Theme argument and an Experiencer argument: *The stories amused the children.* In other words, these Verbs show the standard alternation between transitive and unaccusative variants, cf. *break*, *melt* etc. The complicating factor is the presence of the Experiencer argument.

We propose that the transitive variant, with the lexical entry (57a), underlies what we take to be lexical processes of category-conversion: APF and nominalization. Thus, following Levin & Rappaport (1986), the direct argument of the Verb appears as the external argument of the Adjectival passive:

(58) a. I was amused (at the stories).

b. *The stories were amused (to me).

The nominalization of (57a) is that seen in (53). These nominals feature an obligatory Agent, an optional *with*-phrase and optional passive in NP.

Middle-formation is another process which appears to be sensitive to direct arguments, although with some extra restrictions. Middles can be formed from Verbs of the *amuse*-class, but notice again that only the Experiencer and not the Theme can appear as the external argument:

(59) a. Children scare easily.

b. *Stories scare easily.

It is rather hard to get even an internal Theme with (59a); this is an instance of a general and rather mysterious ban on the presence of complements with middles.

No *-ing* Adjective corresponds to the lexical entry in (57a) (cf. **John is very amusing of/to the children with the play*). Arguably, this is because (these) Adjectives neither assign Case nor suppress a θ-role. Thus the Agent is required to be present, blocking movement of the Caseless Experiencer to subject position. On the other hand, a well-formed derivation can ensue on the basis of the lexical entry in (57b), as here the subject position is non-thematic. The Theme externalizes rather than the Experiencer because the lexical entry is different, a point we turn to below.

APF, on the other hand, necessarily involves the suppression of the subject θ-role. Hence APF cannot apply to the representation in (57b), and can apply to the one in (57a). The right theory of implicit arguments could capture this as a kind of "lexical 1-Advancement Exclusiveness Law", a matter we will not go into here (cf. Marantz (1984)). Middle Formation likewise necessarily involves the suppression of the subject θ-role and so cannot apply to the representation in (57b).

Nominalization, on the other hand, is arguably not sensitive in this way to properties of argument structure (cf. Roberts (1987), 4.5). Thus we find nominals corresponding to both variants in (57). The transitive nominal appears in (53); the unaccusative nominal in (52) and (54). Unaccusative nominals have an optional *at*-phrase, no agentive reading of any kind, and no GEN-assignment to the Experiencer. As we mentioned above, the only way to make sense of the latter correlation seems to be to suppose Burzio's generalization to be operative within NPs.

The one question which remains is: why does the order ⟨Exp, Th⟩ switch in psych Cases? We propose a lexical principle:

(60) If a Theme argument is obligatory, then it is the direct argument.

So the Theme argument necessarily precedes the Exp in (54b), as it must be the direct argument. In (54a), on the other hand, the Theme is optional, so the Experiencer can act as the direct argument (this is not necessary, only possible). (60) may follow from a thematic hierarchy for obligatorily present arguments.

Concerning the Case-assignment properties of psych-predicates, the situation is fairly straightforward. In (54) *amuse* obeys Burzio's generalization. It Case-marks its direct (Experiencer) argument in (54a), since it assigns an Agent θ-role. The Theme is marked with *with*, when it appears. In (54b), the Theme receives no Case, and therefore moves, giving rise to the potential CFA violations we have been discussing here. The Experiencer is Case-marked either with *to*, or with an inherent ACC, *pace* Belletti & Rizzi (1988).

It seems, then, that our analysis of NPSC in psych-constructions can lead to a fairly coherent account of the lexical properties of psych-stems. In general, psych-predicates of the *amuse*-class in English show the same transitive/unaccusative alternation as Verbs with a simpler argument structure like *break* etc. The properties of various derived versions of these predicates can be deduced from this assumption along with plausible assumptions about the nature of the morphological processes themselves. While there is clearly much more to be said in this domain, and while it is necessary to test the proposals made for the morphological processes in other lexical domains, the analysis provided here seems promising. Indirectly, this result supports our representational theory of NPSC, since the NPSC effects can be used as a diagnostic for NP-movement and can therefore tell us whether a given construction is lexically or syntactically derived.

4.2 Raising

In this section we turn our attention to another type of NP-movement: raising. We will see that cases of NPSC of the type discussed in previous sections are found with this construction too. Using the same reasoning as the previous section, we will also propose a further case of raising.

With raising predicates, the derived subject cannot bind a reflexive, but can bind a reciprocal:

(61) a. They_i appear to [each_i other]$_j$ t_i to like John.

b. ??They_i appear to themselves_i t_i to like John.

This is the same kind of contrast as the one seen with passives and psych-predicates in previous sections. We account for it in the same way; in particular we assign to (61b) the LF-representation in (62):

(62) They_i [themselves_i [seem [to t'_i [t''_i ...

Here the reflexive has adjoined to VP, a position governed by its antecedent, the subject. In this position, the reflexive counts as an intervening binder, since it clearly asymmetrically c-commands t''_i in the embedded subject position. Thus this example contains another violation of the chain-formation algorithm. The reciprocal in (61a) is well-formed given the assumptions we made about reciprocals in Section 3. Neither *each* nor *other* produces a chain-formation violation.

Another possible case where raising produces a NPSC effect is (63b) (discussed by Rizzi (*op cit*):

(63) a. They_i impress [each_i other]$_j$ as t_i intelligent.

b. ?*They_i impress themselves_i as t_i intelligent.

c. ?*They_i [themselves_i [impress t'_i [as t''_i ...

Here we find the now-usual contrast between the reflexive of (63b) and the reciprocal of (63a). We can account for the ill-formedness of (63b) by assuming that it has an LF representation of the type in (63c). This representation is exactly like (62) in all relevant respects: the reflexive adjoins to VP in order to be governed by its antecedent, the derived subject. In this position, it asymmetrically binds the trace in the subject position of the complement, thereby giving rise to a chain-formation violation. Hence the sentence is ungrammatical. The crucial assumption needed to make this account work is that there is a trace in the subject position of the *as*-clause. *As* must thus be seen as a complementizer associated with a defective IP, defective in the sense that I contains neither Tense nor *to*. Because of the lack of Tense, the subject of the *as*-clause must always raise to a Case-marked position. Presumably *as* does not block antecedent-government of the NP-trace.

It is clear from this brief discussion that raising may give rise to cases of NPSC. We also saw, in the same way as in the previous section, how the presence of NPSC effects can be used as a diagnostic for NP-movement. This led to the suggestion that there is NP-movement in examples like (63).

4.3 APs

In this final section on NP-movement we discuss a number of cases which also seem like instances of NPSC, in that they display similar reflexive/reciprocal contrasts to the ones we have seen up to now. However, the constructions in question must all be analyzed as involving *wh*-movement for independent reasons. We thus propose that they involve a WHSC effect. This conclusion brings us back to the discussion of WHSC, which we take up in the next section.

The main two constructions we are interested in here are *easy-to-please* and *too/enough* complements. In both of these constructions, we find a CP in construction with an Adjective. There is also a *for*-phrase following the Adjective, which may contain a reflexive or reciprocal NP. It is here that we find the contrast that we have seen in the previous sections:

(64) a. ??They are easy for themselves to like.

b. They are easy for each other to like.

c. ??They are too despicable for themselves to like.

d. They are too despicable for each other to like.

We could account for these examples as instances of NPSC by assuming that the subject NP raises from the lower object position. The reflexives would block chain-formation as they would have to adjoin to VP in order to be governed by the derived subject, their antecedent, at LF. We would thus arrive at representations not unlike those we saw for illicit cases of raising in the previous section. Clearly some account would have to be given for why the NP-trace does not violate the Specified Subject Condition: perhaps a restructuring operation between V and A involving the deletion of the PRO subject of the embedded clause (cf. Chomsky (1981)). However, this issue could be avoided by supposing that Adjectives of the *easy*-class are in fact ergative (or psych) Adjectives; in that case, (64a,c) would still be instances of NPSC, only now of the "psych" type rather than of the "raising" type, and the SSC would be irrelevant.

However, there is clear evidence, aside from the issue of NPSC, that these constructions involve WHSC. It is well-known that the rule which relates the lower object position ultimately with the matrix subject is *wh*-movement. The movement appears to be unbounded, and obeys island conditions. Cf. the following examples, which Chomsky (1977:102) uses to establish this analysis for the *easy-to-please* construction:

(65) a. John is easy for us to convince Bill ...
... to do business with t.
... to arrange for Mary to meet t.
... that he should meet t.
... to tell Mary that Tom should meet t.

b. *John is easy for us to describe to Bill a plan to assassinate t.

c. *Who are the presents fun for us to give t to t?

(65a) illustrates the unbounded character of this movement, while (65b) shows that it obeys the Complex NP Constraint and (65c) that it obeys the *wh*-island condition. Similar examples can be constructed for the *too/enough* construction.

So, abstracting away from the issue of the base position of the matrix subject, the examples in (64a,b) have the following LF-representations:

(66) a. *They$_i$ are themselves$_i$ easy for t$_i$ [O$_i$ PRO$_i$ to like t$_i$].

b. They$_i$ are each$_i$ easy for [t$_i$ other$_j$]$_j$ [O$_i$ PRO$_j$ to like t$_i$].

In (66a), reflexive raising has taken place, adjoining the reflexive to VP. The reflexive controls the PRO of the complement clause, as is clear from the sentence's interpretation. So PRO shares the index of the empty operator and its trace, since the empty operator is construed with the matrix subject, and this subject is the antecedent of the reflexive. Therefore transitivity of indexing gives the configuration of the embedded clause shown in (66a). In this configuration, PRO A-binds the *wh*-trace, giving rise to a violation of Principle C. In other words, this is a WHSC violation, exactly like (1). In (64b), on the other hand, our assumptions about reciprocals lead to different indexing configurations, in particular in that *other* controls PRO. Since PRO then has an index distinct from that of the empty operator and its trace, no WHSC violation ensues.

The same analysis holds for (64c,d). These examples, however, permit us to distinguish between an NPSC analysis and a WHSC analysis of the *easy-to-please* examples in (64a,b) independently of the question of the "psych" status of *easy*, as here there are no plausible grounds for assuming that NP-movement is involved in the derivation. A further difference with the *easy-to-please* construction is that the *for*-phrase is in the embedded subject position, and not a matrix benefactive. This is shown by the possibility of an expletive in the *for*-phrase (contrast **Soccer fans are easy for there to be a riot*):

(67) a. Gorbachev is too clever for there to be a war.

b. The police are too vigilant for there to be a riot.

This means that we must assign the following representations to these examples:

(68) a. *They$_i$ are too despicable [$_{CP}$ O$_i$ [$_{C'}$ for [$_{IP}$ themselves$_i$ to like t$_i$]]].

b. They$_i$ are too despicable [$_{CP}$ O$_i$ [$_{C'}$ for [$_{IP}$ [each$_i$ other$_j$]$_j$ to like t$_i$].

Here we have not indicated the movement of the anaphors, *themselves* and *each*. Presumably these elements are able to raise to the matrix AP, but since this hypothesis creates certain difficulties with the statement of the locality conditions on these elements which are extraneous to our present concerns, we abstract away from this raising operation here. In any case, it should be clear that the reflexive (or its trace, after movement) creates a Principle C violation in (68a), in that it A-binds the trace of *wh*-movement. Hence this is another WHSC violation exactly like (66a) and (1). On the other hand, as in (66b), the reciprocal in (68b) does not create such a violation since the NP has the index of *other*, which distinct from the index of *each* and its antecedent.

The examples discussed in this section show that the reflexive/reciprocal contrast is not a diagnostic only for NPSC, but is also relevant for WHSC. However, the treatment of the crossover violation is analogous to the earlier cases, in that a reflexive induces the crucial violation, while a reciprocal, thanks to our assumptions in Section 3, does not. Notice, however, that the two kinds of crossover do not form a natural class: one is attributable to Principle C, the other to conditions on chains. Nevertheless, apart from the difference in the derived position of the moved element, the examples are essentially the same. In particular, they all instantiate the schema in (9). This suggests that a generalization is being missed, and that we should try to assimilate one of the two kinds of SC to the other. It is impossible to assimilate NPSC to WHSC, since NP-movement cannot be thought of as leaving a variable. Therefore, we will try to assimilate WHSC to NPSC. This is the topic of our final section.

5 Principle C

In this section we will attempt to assimilate WHSC and NPSC, drawing on ideas in Hoekstra (1984) and Roberts (1987) (various authors pointed out that WHSC could best be handled representationally: cf. Koopmann & Sportiche (1982), May (1984)). The basic point is that, as we pointed out at the end of the previous section, both types of SC involve the illicit configuration of (9), repeated here:

(69) *A_i B_i t_i, where A is an argument in a non-θ-position, B is an argument, and A c-commands B and B c-commands t_i.

We saw in Section 2.1 how the ill-formedness of constructions of this type can be accounted for in terms of Rizzi's chain-formation algorithm. We will now extend this account to cases of (69) where A_i is an operator (a *wh*-element or a quantifier, cf. (6)).

We are thus interested in standard cases of WHSC of the type in (1), repeated here:

(70) *Who_i does he_i love t_i?

We need to add just one condition on chains to those introduced in 2.1. This is the Bijection Principle of Koopmann & Sportiche (1982):

(71) *Bijection Principle*: Each variable can only be bound by one and only one operator, and each operator can only bind one and only one variable.

We consider (71) to be a further well-formedness condition on chains, applying to exactly those chains formed of operators and variables. Consider then the various possibilities of chain-formation in (70) in terms of the chain-formation algorithm of (11):

(72) a. *wh, he, t*

b. *wh*

c. *wh, he*

d. *wh, t*

Formation of the chain (*wh*, *he*, t), as in (72a), leads to violation of the θ-criterion, as this chain contains the two arguments *he* and the *wh*-trace. The singleton chain (*wh*) in (72b) fails to satisfy the Bijection Principle as it consists of an operator with no variable. The chain (*wh*, *he*) is allowed by the conditions we are using: it satisfies the θ-criterion by containing only one argument, and it satisfies the Bijection Principle as *wh* is an operator and *he* is a variable. Leaving aside the question of licensing resumptive pronouns, then, this is a well-formed chain. However, this leaves the *wh*-trace to form the singleton chain (*t*).[5] This chain contains a variable but no operator, and so violates the Bijection Principle. Finally, the chain (*wh*, t) is ruled out by the local-binding condition on chain-formation. The pronoun *he* counts as an intervening binder and therefore blocks formation of this chain.

So it appears that we can assimilate WHSC to NPSC, and thus unify the theory of crossover in terms of chain formation. So Principle C is no longer necessary to rule out examples like (1). Moreover, Principle C is now redundant with the chain-formation approach in such cases. Is there a way to reformulate Principle C so as to eliminate this redundancy?

Consider once again the formulation of Principle C, repeated from (2):

(73) A name or variable must be A-free.

There are really two parts to this principle: one relevant for variables and one for names. For WHSC it is only the condition on variables which is relevant, and therefore redundant with our chain-based account of this phenomenon. Is this part of Principle C eliminable in favour of conditions on chains? More

[5] We have to say a little more in order to account for the well-formedness of sentences like (i), where the pronoun is interpreted as a bound variable:

(i) Everyone$_i$ loves his$_i$ mother.

Here the quantifier forms the chain (*everyone*, t). The embedded pronoun cannot join this chain, as this would lead to a θ-criterion violation, and does not need to, as it has its own θ-role. Nevertheless it can be interpreted as a variable bound by *everyone*. What we propose, in order to distinguish (i) from (72c), is that pronouns can be interpreted as variables bound by a chain without belonging to that chain, whereas *wh*-traces cannot. In other words, *wh*-traces must belong to a chain containing an operator, while pronouns can belong to such chains. Again unanswered questions arise concerning resumptive pronouns.

generally, can we assume that Principle C only applies to names, with variables being subject only to conditions on chains?

One important case where (73) is relevant is in accounting for the distribution of parasitic gaps. A generalization about parasitic gaps, noted in Engdahl (1983), is that a "real" gap must not c-command a parasitic gap. This is illustrated by the contrast in (74) (where *e* indicates the parasitic gap):

(74) a. Which book did you file t without reading e?

b. *Which book t was filed without reading e?

The ill-formed parasitic gap in (74b) is c-commanded by the real gap in the subject position of the main clause, while the well-formed parasitic gap in (74a) is not c-commanded by the real gap since here the real gap is in the direct-object position of the main clause. Chomsky (1982) derives this from Principle C by assuming that parasitic gaps are variables. As variables these elements are subject to Principle C and therefore cannot be bound from an A-position. Therefore the real gap cannot c-command the parasitic gap. This appears to be a case where Principle C applies to variables in a manner which is not redundant with conditions on chains.

However, Chomsky (1986b) points out that there is evidence that *wh*-movement takes place in the adjunct clause which contains a parasitic gap:

(75) This is the man who I interviewed before ...

a. ??...I knew which job to give to.
b. ??...hearing the rumor that noone likes.
c. ??...meeting the woman who loves. (Chomsky (1986b:55)).

Chomsky therefore proposes that there is movement of an empty operator inside the adjunct. The empty operator is construed with the main-clause *wh*-word by a process of chain-composition (a process which is, by definition, not subject to the θ-criterion). So parasitic gaps have the abstract structure in (76a), rather than that (76b):

(76) a. wh_i t_i [O_i t_i].
b. wh_i t_i [e_i].

The anti-c-command condition now becomes a condition on the operation of chain-composition. We might propose that composition of two chains C_1 and C_2 is possible only where the "foot" (i.e. the θ-position) of C_1 does not c-command the "head" of C_2. This condition is in fact derivable from our conditions on the formation of well-formed chains subject to the θ-criterion: if the foot of C_1

c-commands the head of C_2 C_1 and C_2 will not be analyzed as separate but composed chains, but rather as a single ill-formed chain (this is suggested by Chomsky (*ibid.*)). Although much more needs to be said about conditions on chain-composition, it is clear how an approach along these lines can account for the anti-c-command requirement on parasitic gaps independently of Principle C. We thus tentatively conclude that Principle C is relevant only for names. So this condition remains responsible for violations of disjoint reference like (77):

(77) *$\text{John}_i/\text{he}_i$ saw John_i.

In this section we have assimiliated WHSC to NPSC by making the Bijection Principle (70) a condition on chains headed by operators. This gives us a unified account of SC as a chain-based phenomenon. However, Principle C remains redundant with the conditions on chains for WHSC cases. We thus proposed that Principle C is only relevant for names. We sketched a way that conditions on chains may also account for the anti-c-command constraint on parasitic gaps, another important consequence of taking Principle C to be a condition on variables.

6 Conclusion

In this paper we first discussed a number of cases of "illicit NP-movement", and showed, following Lasnik (1985), how these are all cases of NPSC. The existence of such NPSC effects cannot be attributed to Principle C, but rather must be the result of conditions on chain-formation, *pace* Rizzi. There is a wider variety of such effects than previously thought, involving all types of NP-movement; we illustrated this point with examples from psych-predicates, showing the unaccusative case of NP-movement, and from raising predicates. Finally, we showed that while it is not possible to subsume NPSC under standard accounts of WHSC, it is possible to subsume WHSC under NPSC. This move leads to a unified, representational theory of strong crossover, and the possibility that Principle C can be taken as applying only to names, with variables being subject to conditions on chains.

A number of issues remain unresolved, none of which we can treat here. We will, however, briefly mention them:

a) We have been largely silent on the question of the locality conditions on anaphor movement at LF. This is presumably the ECP, but many conditions remain to be worked out.

b) The possibility of deriving the anti-c-command requirement on parasitic gaps from conditions on chain-formation leaves open certain questions about extending the chain-composition idea. For example, it would be natural to extend this approach to account for the construal between the matrix subject and the empty operator of *easy-to-please* constructions. However, it is clear that here the anti-c-command requirement yields the wrong result, as the matrix subject c-commands the empty operator in the Specifier of the embedded CP. The only way around this seems to be to treat the matrix subject position as non-thematic, requiring chain-composition (= chain-formation in that case) with the empty operator. However, this proposal raises a number of questions which we cannot go into here.

c) Can our approach be extended to weak crossover, particularly if the Bijection Principle, generally assumed to underlie weak crossover, is a condition on chains? The defining characteristic of weak crossover is that the element "crossed over", i.e. the potential intervener, does not c-command the trace of the moved element. This suggests that our approach cannot be extended to weak crossover. However, Lasnik & Stowell (1987) provide evidence that weak crossover is sensitive to aspects of argument structure, and suggest adopting the proposal of Haik (1984) that a category takes the index of a bound variable it contains. This opens up the possibility of accounting for weak crossover using the conditions on chains we have appealed to here.

d) Fourth, there is the question of reconstructing moved anaphors. The most important case of this type involves topicalized anaphors, as in:

   (79) Himself, John likes t.

   This sentences appears to instantiate a strong crossover configuration, and yet it is good. We have nothing to say about this sort of example here, but see Barss (1989) for detailed discussion.

Finally, it is important to stress once again that we have proposed here a representational theory of strong crossover. The central notion in this theory is that of chain. All properties of movement can be deduced from chains, but not all properties of chains can be deduced from movement, in particular the local binding condition. This result, stressed by Rizzi (*op cit*), suggests that movement is really a metaphor for chain-formation and that D-Structure is not an independent level of representation but rather a factorization of S-Structure and chain-formation.

References

Baker, M., K. Johnson & I. Roberts (1989) "Passive Arguments Raised", *Linguistic Inquiry* 20, 219–251.

Barss, A. (1989) "Paths, Connectivity, and Featureless Empty Categories", in A. Cardinaletti, G. Cinque & G. Giusti (eds) *Constituent Structure*, 9–34, Foris, Dordrecht.

Belletti, A. (1982) "On the Anaphoric Status of the Reciprocal Construction in Italian", *The Linguistic Review* 2, 101–37.

Belletti, A. & L. Rizzi (1988) "Psych-Verbs and Theta Theory", *Natural Language and Linguistic Theory* 6, 291–352.

Browning, M. (1987) *Null Operator Constructions*, MIT PhD Dissertation, Cambridge, Mass.

Burzio, L. (1986) *Italian Syntax: A Government-Binding Approach*, Reidel, Dordrecht, The Netherlands.

Chomsky, N. (1977) "On *WH*-Movement", in A. Akmajian, P. Culicover and T. Wasow (eds) *Formal Syntax*, Academic Press, New York, 71–132.

Chomsky, N. (1981) *Lectures on Government and Binding*, Foris Publications, Dordrecht, The Netherlands.

Chomsky, N. (1982) *Some Concepts and Consequences in the Theory of Government and Binding*, MIT Press, Cambridge, Mass.

Chomsky, N. (1986a) *Knowledge of Language: Its Nature, Origins and Use*, Praeger, New York.

Chomsky, N. (1986b) *Barriers*, MIT Press, Cambridge, Mass.

Cinque, G. (1990) "Ergative Adjectives and the Lexicalist Hypothesis", *Natural Language and Linguistic Theory* 8, 1-39.

Engdahl, E. (1983) "Parasitic Gaps", *Linguistics and Philosophy* 6, 5–34.

Epstein, S.D. (1986) "The Local Binding Condition and LF Chains", *Linguistic Inquiry* 17, 187–206.

Faraci, R. (1974) *Aspects of the Grammar of Infinitive and* **for**-phrases, MIT PhD Dissertation, Cambridge, Mass.

Haik, I. (1984) "Indirect Binding", *Linguistic Inquiry* 15, 185–224.

Higginbotham, J. (1983) "Logical Form, Binding and Nominals", in *Linguistic Inquiry* 14, 395–420.

Hoekstra, T. (1984) *Transitivity: Grammatical Relations in Government-Binding Theory*, Foris Publications, Dordrecht, The Netherlands.

Jackendoff, R. (1972) *Semantic Interpretation in Generative Grammar*, MIT Press, Cambridge, Mass.

Jones, C. (1985) *Syntax and Thematics of Infinitival Adjuncts*, PhD Dissertation, University of Massachusetts, Amherst, Mass.

Kayne, R. (1975) *French Syntax*, MIT Press, Cambridge, Mass.

Koopmann, H. & D. Sportiche (1982) "Variables and the Bijection Principle", *The Linguistic Review* 2, 139–160.

Lakoff, G. (1970) *Irregularity in Syntax*, Holt, Reinhart & Winston, New York.

Lasnik, H. (1985) "Illicit NP-Movement: Locality Conditions on Chains?" *Linguistic Inquiry* 16, 481–490.

Lasnik, H. & T. Stowell (1987) "Weakest Crossover", ms. University of Connecticut and University of California, Los Angeles.

Lebeaux, D. (1983) "A Distributional Difference between Reciprocals and Reflexives", *Linguistic Inquiry* 14, 723–730.

Lees, R.B. & E. Klima (1963) "Rules for English Pronominalization", *Language* 39, 17–28.

Levin, B. & M. Rappaport (1986) "The Formation of Adjectival Passives", *Linguistic Inquiry* 17, 623–662.

Marantz, A. (1984) *On the Nature of Grammatical Relations*, MIT Press, Cambridge, Mass.

May, R. (1977) *The Grammar of Quantification*, MIT PhD Dissertation, Cambridge, Mass.

May, R. (1984) *Logical Form: Its Structure and Derivation*, MIT Press, Cambridge, Mass.

Perlmutter, D. (1978) "Impersonal Passives and the Unaccusative Hypothesis", in J. Jaeger *et. al.* (eds) *Proceedings of the Fourth Annual Meeting of the Berkeley Linguistics Society*, University of California, Berkeley.

Perlmutter, D. & P. Postal (1984) "The 1-Advancement Exclusiveness Law", in D. Perlmutter and C. Rosen (eds) *Studies in Relational Grammar 2*, The University of Chicago Press, Chicago.

Postal, P. (1971) *Crossover Phenomena*, Holt, Reinhart & Winston, New York.

Reinhart, T. (1976) *The Syntactic Domain of Anaphora*, MIT PhD Dissertation, Cambridge, Mass.

Rizzi, L. (1986) "On Chain Formation", in H. Borer (ed) *The Syntax of Pronominal Clitics: Syntax and Semantics, Volume 18*, Academic Press, New York.

Roberts, I. (1987) *The Representation of Implicit and Dethematized Subjects*, Foris Publications, Dordrecht, The Netherlands.

Roberts, I. (1989) "Compound Psych-Adjectives and the Ergative Hypothesis", in: Juli Carter & Rose-Marie Dechaine (eds.) *Proceedings of the 19th Meeting of the North Eastern Linguistics Society (NELS 19)*, Graduate Linguistics Students Association, University of Massachusetts, Amherst.

Wasow, T. (1977) "Transformations and the Lexicon", in A. Akmajian, P. Culicover & T. Wasow (eds) *Formal Syntax*, Academic Press, New York.

NP-Movement and Expletive Chains*

Knut Tarald Taraldsen

1 Introduction

We shall consider certain issues relevant to the question of whether the notion "derivation" plays any role in the theory of syntax. If this question is to be answered positively, there must exist some configuration K of properties holding uniquely of the "move α" relation, i.e. of the S-structure pairs (A,B) where B is an empty[1] position classified as an argument position by the (extended) projection principle, and A is an immediate antecedent of B. (We could then say that A fills the position B at D-structure.) Only if such a configuration is found, can one go on to discuss whether the conditions constituting it must be implemented as conditions on derivation rather than conditions on representation.[2]

The most plausible proposal is that the required configuration K corresponds to the following conditions on (A,B):

(1) A is in a non-thematic position.

(2) B is subject to the ECP.

(3) B is subjacent to A.

In the following discussion, we will limit our attention to the subcase of "move α" commonly referred to as NP-movement or A-movement, i.e. to the cases where A is in an A-position. For these cases, one might add the following condition to K:

(4) B is not a Case-marked position.

---

*We owe the inspiration for this work mainly to Franz Fies.

[1]We abstract away from the possibility that certain non-null pronominal element could be analyzed as spelled-out traces under a derivational approach, a possibility that would in particular arise in connection with certain resumptive pronouns that have a distribution similar to wh-traces in some Scandinavian dialects.

[2]The well-known contrasts between wh-traces and parasitic gaps might, for instance, be construed as evidence that the subjacency condition must be stated as a condition on derivations; see Chomsky (1982).

H. Haider and K. Netter (eds.), Representation and Derivation in the Theory of Grammar, 53–69.

Furthermore, the ECP plausibly takes the following form (cf. Chomsky (1986b)):

(5) B is governed by A.

On the other hand, (5) makes (3) redundant for NP-movement, so we shall only consider K = (1), (2)(=(5)) and (4). Only if K so conceived holds uniquely of a subset of the "move α" relation, will NP-movement provide a plausible case for assigning theoretical status to the notion "derivation". Conversely, the demonstration that K does not hold uniquely of the "move α" relation suffices to justify the opposite conclusion.

In order to provide such a demonstration, we now go on to consider some properties of expletive constructions.[3]

2 Expletive chains

We shall begin by showing that the conditions (1) and (4) in the configuration K also hold of the pair (A,B), where A is an expletive subject and B is an NP linked to A (in a sense to be made more precise below). Then, we discuss a proposal by Chomsky to account for this in terms of LF-movement to the expletive position. Three arguments against this hypothesis are given. The most elaborated one is based on past participle agreement in Scandinavian and also provides evidence that condition (2)(=(5)) holds of expletive/argument pairs.

2.1 Two K-properties of expletive/argument pairs

In this subsection, we will show both that the distribution of expletive/argument pairs conforms to conditions (1) and (4), and that this is not an "accidental" consequence of independent properties.

2.1.1 Property (1)

It is in general clear that expletives only occur in non-thematic positions, i.e. only as subjects of passive or "ergative" structures:

(6) *Det skrev en bok.
    it wrote a book

(7) Det ble skrevet en bok.
    it was written a book

[3]Another relevant consideration is found in Rizzi (1986), where it is shown that the "minimality" property of A-chains is not reducible to properties of NP-movement.

(8) Det kom ut en bok.
it came out a book

The parallelism with NP-movement is well-known and in fact constitutes one of the reasons for assigning property (1) to NP-movement:

(9) *En bok skrev t.
a book wrote

(10) En bok ble skrevet t.
a book was written

(11) En bok kom ut t.
a book came out

However, the view that condition (1) holds of expletives, could be challenged on the grounds of Italian sentences like (12):

(12) Canterà Piero.
will-sing Piero

Standardly (e.g. in Chomsky (1981)), such sentences are considered to be derived by "stylistic inversion", i.e. rightward movement of the subject combining with insertion of expletive pro in the vacant thematic subject position:

(13) pro [$_{VP}$[$_{VP}$ canterà] Piero]

Similarly, the expletive subject could be argued to fill a thematic subject position in the Danish example (14), given that the auxiliary is *have*, rather than *be*, as in general required with ergative participles in Danish (see Sprouse & Vikner (1988) for discussion):

(14) Der sover et barn i min seng.
there sleeps a child in my bed

If so, (14) would be essentially an instance of "stylistic inversion" with an overt expletive, and would constitute a counterexample to the claim that condition (1) holds of expletives, analogously to (12).

An alternative way of looking at (12) / (14) leads to the view that these are of the form (15), where the expletive is the subject of IP and the argument NP is the subject of VP:

(15) [$_{IP}$ expl [$_{I}$ V] [$_{VP}$ V′ NP]]

Since it is reasonable to assume that the subject of IP is always non-thematic, this analysis is consistent with the claim that expletives are controlled by condition (1). Given the existence of independent evidence for the structure assigned in (15), we therefore conclude that our claim is not invalidated by (12), (15).

Although we will maintain the preceding analysis, we would also like to point out, perhaps unnecessarily, that the occurrence of expletives in thematic positions would not by itself undermine the argument we are attempting to construct. What potentially defines "move α" (or, more specifically, NP-movement) is the clustering of the properties constituting K. To show that "move α" is really undefined by K, it suffices to show that these properties cluster in the same way with respect to expletive/argument pairs. Hence, we need only show that (1) obtains whenever (2) and (4) do (and vice versa). Thus, if, for instance, the argument (*Piero*) is in a Case-marked position in (12), as frequently claimed (see Chomsky (1981), Jaeggli (1980)), then it is immaterial whether or not the expletive fills a thematic position, since condition (4) does not hold. Conversely, we shall see below that in all cases where condition (2) can be shown to hold, (1) (and (4)) holds as well.

A related remark is this: Suppose that (1) in fact holds true of expletives. Yet, one might hold that this is immaterial to the issue, since obedience to (1) could be considered a consequence of the expletives' being non-arguments rather than a property of the relation between an expletive and an argument. If so, the clustering of property (1) with properties (2) and (4) would in a sense be essentially accidental for expletive/argument pairs.

The opposite view, which we adhere to, claims that condition (1) holds of the relation between an expletive and an argument for the same reason it holds for the relation between a moved NP and its trace. When a pair (A,B) is in this relation, then A must be a non-thematic position. Correspondingly, it is actually only when expletives are paired with arguments in the relevant way, that they must be analyzed as non-arguments. Thus, the expletive (non-referential) subject is an argument in (16), but a non-argument in (17), given the contrast (18) vs (19), which reflects the fact that PRO is always an argument:

(16) Det regner.
it rains

(17) Det regner giftig nedbør.
it rains poisonous rain

(18) Det kan godt være fuktig uten PRO å regne.
it may well be humid without raining

(19) *Det kan godt være fuktig uten PRO å regne giftig nedbør.
it may well be humid without raining poisonous rain

In (16) and (18), the expletive subject forms no link with an argument, but in (17) and (19), it is linked to the argument *giftig nedbør* "poisonous rain".

2.1.2 Property (4)

The distribution of expletive/argument links is in general consistent with property (4):

(4) B is not a Case-marked position.

Thus, B (the argument) is in general the object of a passive or an unaccusative verb. Such verbs are standardly considered not to assign Case (obligatorily).

When an expletive subject is paired with an argument governed by a Case-assigning verb form, the result is ill-formed:

(20) *Det skrev en bok.
it wrote a book

Obviously, the ill-formedness could be attributed to the fact that the subject position is thematic in (20), so that condition (1) is violated. On the other hand, this leads to the question why the subject of (20) must be thematic. It seems that most accounts more or less explicitly assume some version of Burzio's generalization (21):

(21) A verb assigns a θ-role to its subject if and only if it Case-marks its object (if there is one).

Yet, (21) is not likely to be an axiom of syntactic theory. Rather, it should derive from other principles. In fact, the *if*-part of (21) can be derived from property (4) and the θ-criterion. By the θ-criterion, each A-chain (containing an argument) must be assigned a thematic role. The subject either constitutes an A-chain all by itself, or else it heads an A-chain containing also some other NP. Suppose now that property (4) holds of A-chain links (A,B). Then, the fact that the verb Case-marks its object, means that the subject cannot form a chain together with the object. Therefore, it must head a chain with no other members. But this chain is assigned a thematic role, only if the verb assigns a thematic role to its subject.[4]

Apart from conceptual reasons, there is some empirical motivation for deriving obligatory θ-role assignment to subjects from the θ-criterion and condition (4) rather than from (21). Consider the following example:

[4]The *only-if* part of (21) is a consequence of the requirement that every A-chain must have a Case-marked member.

(22) John$_i$ was given t$_i$ the award.

Here, the verb fails to assign a θ-role to its subject, although it presumably Case-marks its object (*the award*). This is at odds with (21), but is perfectly consistent with the θ-criterion and condition (4), since Case is not assigned to the trace, the second member of the A-chain link (*John,t*).

Clearly, if the if-part of (21) is in general induced by condition (4), we will want to say that the obligatory θ-role assignment to the subject of (20) is also induced by this condition, although the subject is here a non-argument. The optimal way of expressing this is to say that the θ-criterion holds for all A-chains, also those that only contain non-arguments. (It follows from this that all well-formed A-chains also must contain at least one argument.) Then, the fact that condition (4) is a property of expletive/argument pairs, simply reflects the fact that such pairs now must be links of A-chains and that condition (4) is a property of A-chain links.[5]

If the relation between an expletive and an argument is an instance of the more general A-chain relation, then a natural consequence of our preceding observations is to hypothesize that conditions (1) and (4) both are properties of A-chain links. Below, we shall argue that this is true of the ECP (condition (2)) as well.

But if the A-chain relation subsumes the expletive/argument pairing, then it cannot be equal to the "move α" relation, as characterized above, since clearly B in an expletive/argument pair (A,B) is not a position filled by A at D-structure, i.e. the two positions are not related by a mapping between D-structure and S-structure. Hence, if the configuration K in fact holds of the A-chain relation in this more general sense, K fails to isolate the "move α" relation. This is the conclusion we want to establish.

2.2 Expletive replacement at LF

There is an alternative to this conclusion, which seems compatible with all observations made up to this point: Assume that B in an S-structure expletive/argument pair (A,B) must be moved to A, replacing the expletive, between S-structure and LF. This leads to the formation of a standard A-chain link antecedent/trace at LF. Even if all conditions constituting the configuration K only hold of such links (at LF and/or at S-structure), they would still in general have to be satisfied by any expletive/argument pair at S-structure, since they could otherwise not be met by the A-chain link resulting from expletive

[5]The requirement that every A-chain must contain a Case-marked member (see footnote 4) provides an extra reason why an argument B forms an A-chain headed by an (Case-marked) expletive A, when B is not Case-marked.

replacement at LF (assuming a suitably restricted mapping from S-structure to LF).

If this program can be successfully implemented, it again becomes possible to see A-chain formation as a reflex of "move α" (NP-movement), since the A-chain properties (the configuration K) now hold of S-structure expletive/argument pairs only derivatively.

The alternative analysis described here corresponds essentially to a proposal by Chomsky (1986a:179). In the remainder of this subsection, we present two arguments directed against the idea that expletives must be replaced by arguments at LF. In the next section, we give the argument from Scandinavian past participle agreement to show that even if one assumes expletive replacement at LF, there are certain classes of expletive/argument pairs whose S-structure sensitivity to K (in particular, the ECP) fails to be correctly induced (even assuming well-motivated restrictions on the mapping from S-structure to LF; see paragraph 2.3.3).

2.2.1 Ne-extraction

The arguments in this and the following section are both based on Italian data. First, consider the well-known subject/object asymmetry displayed in (23)–(24):

(23) Ne arrivarono solo tre.
of-them arrived only three

(24) *Solo tre ne arrivarono.
only three of-them arrived

According to Belletti & Rizzi (1981), the clitic *ne* represents the head of the NP it is linked to in sentences like (23)–(24). Thus, the structures look like (25)–(26):[6]

(25) pro $[_{VP}$ ne$_i$ + arrivarono $[_{NP}$ solo tre t$_i]]$

(26) $[_{NP}$ solo tre t$_i]$ $[_{VP}$ ne$_i$ + arrivarono t$_i]$

(25) is well-formed by most versions of GB-theory. In (26), however, the clitic fails to c-command the trace inside the subject NP. To this we could attribute its ill-formedness, for instance, by adopting Chomsky's (1986b) view that traces

[6]To simplify exposition, we omit a representation of Infl.

of heads must be antecedent-governed. Alternatively, we could deduce an ECP-violation by assuming that subjects are not L-marked, in Chomsky's (1986b) sense, and therefore are barriers to government, making c-command irrelevant.[7]

Either way, the possibility of drawing the required distinction between (23) and (24) seems to rest on the non-existence of expletive replacement at LF. For if expletives are replaced by arguments at LF, (23) and (24) will both have the representation (26) at LF. Hence, both should violate the ECP, contrary to fact.

Notice that one cannot avoid this problem by stipulating that the ECP does not hold at LF, if expletive replacement is to induce the full range of A-chain properties that expletive/argument links have at S-structure. This is so, because the ECP is one of those properties, as we will show in the next subsection.

2.2.2 Wh-subjects

Consider the implications of the fact that the that-trace effect is absent under wh-movement in Italian:

(27) Chi credi che comprerà questi quadri?
who you-think that will-buy these paintings

If (27) had to be analyzed as shown in (28), we would have an ECP-violation at the embedded subject position:

(28) chi$_i$ pro credi [$_{CP}$ (t$_i$) che [$_{IP}$ t$_i$ [$_{VP}$ comprerà questi quadri]]]

However, Rizzi (1982) shows that the correct analysis is the one in (29), where the rightmost *pro* is an expletive subject licensed by the null-subject property of Italian:

(29) chi$_i$ pro credi [$_{CP}$ (t$_i$) che [$_{IP}$ pro [$_{VP}$ [$_{VP}$ comprerà questi libri] t$_i$]]]

In (29), the trace position can be taken to be governed by the verb and satisfies the ECP in the same way as wh-extracted objects.[8]

But if expletives must be replaced by arguments at LF, the LF representation corresponding to (29) must be essentially similar to (28):

[7]Actually, this option is perhaps at odds with the simplest formulation of Chomsky's (1986b:24 ff) idea that if X L-marks some phrase P, it also L-marks its specifier, given specifier/head agreement. If specifier/head agreement applies between the embedded subject and the infinitive in **Piero lascia solo tre cantarne* "Peter lets only three sing-of them", we would then, incorrectly, expect this sentence to be grammatical, in contrast with (24).

[8]In order to consider (28) as an ECP-violation, we may either assume that a C′ with a lexical head (*che/that*) is a minimality-barrier (cf. Chomsky (1986b:47)), or else take IP to be

(30) chi$_i$ pro credi [$_{CP}$ (t$_i$) che [$_{IP}$ t$_i$ [$_{VP}$ [$_{VP}$ comprerà questi quadri] t$_i$]]]

In particular, there should again be an ECP-violation at the embedded subject position.

We cannot evade this conclusion by making it possible for a subject to somehow escape the ECP at LF. Rizzi also shows that the ECP must rule out the LF-representation (32) of (31) to exclude the unavailable reading "I want that no one sing":[9]

(31) *Non voglio che nessuno canti.
not I-want that no one sing
"I do not want that no one sing."

(32) nessuno$_i$ [$_{IP}$ pro non voglio [$_{CP}$ (t$_i$) che [$_{IP}$ t$_i$ [$_{VP}$ canti]]]]

We conclude from this and the preceding argument that obligatory expletive replacement at LF is not easily reconcilable with other, perhaps more well-motivated, hypotheses.[10]

---

an inherent barrier, if not L-marked, contrary to Chomsky (1986b). The latter option permits a trace at the subject position just in case its antecedent can be successfully adjoined to IP, which would be incompatible with non-null complementizers, if these select IP, although not sufficiently lexical for L-marking, and adjunction to a selected complement is forbidden, as an extension of Chomsky's (1986b:16) suggestion. The fact that even "short" wh-movement of the subject seems illicit in Italian (cf. Rizzi (1982)), may favor the second approach, which would allow one to claim that even empty C selects IP in Italian.

[9] Compare: *Non voglio che tu canti niente* "I want that you sing nothing".

[10] We only see the following way of avoiding our conclusion: Taking the ECP-effect in (28) to be caused by the minimality condition as described in footnote 8, we let in (30) by allowing *che* to delete at LF. To exclude (32), it then suffices to disallow iteration of LF-movement, eliminating the trace in the specifier position of the embedded CP.

However, we have hinted at reasons for not thinking of (28) in terms of minimality. Moreover, banning iterated movement at LF would be at odds with an LF account of the facts discussed in the next subsection.

2.3 Expletives and past participle agreement

We now turn to another type of argument. There are two ingredients: An analysis of past participle agreement (pp-agr) developed in Kayne (1985, 1986, 1989), and certain facts about pp-agr in Scandinavian.[11]

2.3.1 An analysis of pp-agr

Consider the following Italian sentence:

(33) Maria è partita/*-o.
Maria is left-f.sg/*-Ø

Kayne (1985, 1986, 1989) argues that a verbal form can only agree with a local subject. Hence, (33) must allow the analysis in (34):

(34) Maria$_i$ è [$_{VP}$ t$_i$ [$_{V'}$ partita t$_i$]]

Moreover, the analysis in (35) must not be available, since we would otherwise fail to make pp-agr obligatory in (33):

(35) Maria$_i$ è [$_{VP}$ [$_{V'}$ partita t$_i$]]

Kayne shows that the required ill-formedness of (35) can be traced back to the ECP, if the ECP requires A to govern B in A-chain links (A,B), as stipulated in condition (5) above. Adapting Kayne's analysis, let us say that the embedded V′ is a barrier by the minimality condition (cf. Chomsky (1986b:42ff)):

(36) A does not govern B if A is outside the least phrasal projection P containing B, where B is not the head of P.

According to (36), the object trace is not governed by its immediate antecedent (*Maria*) in (35), or in (34) (by the subject trace). But the subject trace in (34) permits agreement, which, conceived of as co-indexing between the subject and the verb, turns the participle into an antecedent-governor of the object trace (cf. Chomsky (1986b:74-75)). Hence, there is a well-formed ("extended") A- chain (*Maria, è, t, arrivata, t*), as required by the θ-criterion.

On this view, obligatory pp-agr always reflects the property that the object of the participle is part of a link (A,B) subject to the ECP (thought of as condition (5)).

[11]The discussion is based on the analysis presented in more detail in Christensen & Taraldsen (1989).

2.3.2 Pp-agr in Swedish

Traditional Swedish grammar makes a distinction between the participle and the "supine". The participle occurs with the passive auxiliary *bliva* "become" and the supine only occurs with the auxiliary *hava* "have":

(37) Boken blev skriven förra året.
the book was written last year

(38) Jens har skrivit en bok.
Jens has written a book

Clearly, we can unify the two categories "participle" and "supine" by taking advantage of the fact that a participle always agrees with the subject, while a supine never shows agreement:[12]

(39) Boken blev skriven/*-et/*-a.
the book (c) was written-c/*-n/*pl

(40) Brevet blev skrivet/*-en/*-a.
the letter was written-n/*-c/*-pl

(41) Böckerna blev skrivna/*-en/*-et.
the books were written-pl/*-c/*-n

(42) Jens/lejonet/barnen har kommit/*-en/*-et/*-a.
Jens the lion (n) the children have come-Ø/*-c/*-n/*-pl

In other words, the supine can simply be seen as the non-agreeing form of the participle. Then, its distribution follows from the more general fact that pp-agr never happens under auxiliary *have* in any language (except when induced by clitic placement; cf. Kayne (1985)).[13]

In Swedish, then, the morphological shape of the participle will show whether it agrees with a neuter singular (V-*et*) or does not agree at all (V-*it*). With this in mind, consider example (43):

(43) Det blev skjutet/*-it en älg.
it was shot-n/*-Ø a moose (c)

[12]In Swedish, but not in Norwegian (or Danish), only the have auxiliary is used with unaccusative verbs, like *komma* "come".

The notation used in the glosses is as follows: c = common gender singular, n = neuter singular, pl = plural (where gender oppositions are neutralized in the participle inflection).

[13]Christensen & Taraldsen (1989) reproduces Kayne's (1986) account why, in general, pp-agr with the subject of the auxiliary, mediated by a subject trace in the participial VP, is possible only with the *be* auxiliary, but see Kayne (1989: footnote 27).

We see that pp-agr in passives is obligatory even when the subject is an expletive (*det* "it"). In terms of Kayne's theory of pp-agr, this means that the expletive and the object of the participle must be part of a relation subject to the ECP (=condition (5)), so that the only permissible structure is (44), where A governs B for every link (A,B) in the relation (=(*det, blev, t, skjutet, t, en älg*)):

(44) det_i blev $[_{VP}$ t_i $[_{V'}$skjutet en $\text{älg}_i]]$

This establishes two things. First, there is clear evidence that the links relating an expletive to an argument, are also subject to the ECP, formulated as condition (5) above, so that the entire configuration K holds of the expletive/argument relation. Second, it is impossible to use expletive replacement at LF to induce all the effects of K for S-structure expletive/argument pairs. Agreement is reflected in morphological form and must therefore take place at S-structure. Hence, the trace in the subject position of the embedded VP must be present at S-structure.[14]

But there is no reason why this trace must occur in an S-structure representation like (44), unless the ECP holds directly of the expletive/argument relation at S-structure. If the ECP held only of the output of expletive replacement, the crucial subject trace could be created after S-structure by iterated NP-movement at LF leading to expletive replacement at its second application.[15]

2.3.3 Pp-agr in Norwegian

An argument similar to the immediately preceding one can be constructed on the basis of data from certain Norwegian dialects, although it is harder to discover because of the lack of a morphological distinction between non-agreeing participles and participles agreeing with a neuter singular NP:

(45) Brevet vart skrive.
the letter (n) was written-n

[14]One might attempt to evade this conclusion by allowing random agreement at S-structure, requiring the result to satisfy the configurational conditions on pp-agr only at LF, where expletive replacement could create the subject licensing agreement. (I owe this observation to an anonymous reviewer.) But in that case, one would incorrectly predict the participle in (43) to agree with the argument, *en älg*, rather than with the expletive:

*Det blev skjuten en âlg.
it was shot-c a moose(c)

[15]This argument rests on the assumption that the landing site for the first application of LF NP-movement would not be forced to be represented as an empty NP, linked to the matrix subject, at S-structure by considerations relating to structure preservation. We discuss this possibility in 2.3.4.

(46) Jens har skrive ei bok.
Jens has written-Ø a book

The relevant dialects show pp-agr in passives and in participles occurring with the auxiliary *vera* "be". We will consider the interaction between pp-agr and the fronting of a quantified NP illustrated in (47)–(48):[16]

(47) Vi har ikkje skrive nokon bok.
we have not written any book

(48) Vi har ingen bok skrive.
we have no book written

From its basic postverbal position, a quantified NP may be moved leftward. We assume that it is adjoined to VP rather than moved into the subject position of VP, since this fronting does not induce pp-agr:[17] [18]

(49) Vi har ingen bok skrive/*-en.
we have no book (c) written-Ø/*-c

More precisely, we assume that a quantified NP is adjoined to some locally maximal V-projection. In (48), this is V′.[19]

Yet, we find obligatory pp-agr with the fronted NP in sentences like (50):

(50) Det vart ingen bok skriven/*-e.
it was no book written-c/*-n

[16]On the alternation between *nokon* and *ingen*, see Christensen (1986).

[17]The notation used in the glosses is identical to the one adopted for the Swedish examples. Although the relevant Norwegian dialects in fact have three distinct genders in the nominal system, the participle inflection neutralizes the opposition between masculine and feminine gender, both being glossed as common gender (c).

[18]If Kayne (1989) is right, auxiliary *have* is not a Case-assigner. Then, the A-chain in

...[$_{VP}$ ingen bok$_i$ [$_{VP}$ t$_i$ [$_{V'}$ lesen t$_i$]]]

is Case-marked, only if the participle assigns Case to its foot. This would violate condition (4), as it stands. But to allow for Romance type pp-agr with a clitic pronoun (with auxiliary *have*), we would also have to adopt Kayne's formulation of condition (4), which suspends its effects for A-chains headed by an adjoined (Ā) position, the head being the clitic in

Pierre les$_i$ + a [$_{VP}$ t$_i$ [$_{V'}$ mises t$_i$ à la porte]].

To exclude the incorrect pp-agr in (49), we would then say that the adjoined NP is an operator and therefore cannot head the A-chain, correlating this with its being quantified.

[19]We assume that a projection need not reach its potentially maximal $\bar{X}$ level, when, as in this case, there is no specifier to force it. The reason we do not have the NP adjoin to VP dominating V′ exhaustively in (49), is that we consider the trace of the adjoined NP to require antecedent-government; see Christensen & Taraldsen (1989). But the adjoined NP governs the object position, only if it is adjoined to V′ rather than VP, given our formulation of the minimality condition.

Given that a quantified NP can adjoin to the locally maximal V-projection, there is no explanation of this instance of obligatory pp-agr, unless we assume that an expletive/argument link (A,B) must satisfy the requirement that A governs B, just like standard A-chain links. Then, the analysis in (51) is ruled out in favor of the one in (52):[20]

(51) det_i vart $[_{V'}$ ingen bok_j $[_{V'}$ skrive $t_{i,j}$]]

(52) det_i vart $[_{VP}$ ingen bok_j $[_{VP}$ $t_{i,j}$ $[_{V'}$ skrive t_i]]]

Pp-agr is now determined by the features assigned to the trace in the subject position of the participial VP. Since an Ā-bound trace has the same grammatical features as its Ā antecedent (see Christensen & Taraldsen (1989)), it follows that the participle takes on the common gender singular form.

Thus, the obligatory pp-agr found in Norwegian sentences like (50) provides further evidence that expletive/argument links obey the ECP just like standard A-chain links.[21] Given the morphological reflexes of pp-agr, this piece of evidence cannot be reinterpreted in terms of LF expletive replacement for the reasons already discussed in connection with the Swedish example considered earlier.

The Norwegian example also illustrates another A-chain like property of expletive/argument links. Attributing the ill-formedness of (51) to the ECP (= condition (5)), we tacitly assumed that the relation between the expletive and the argument, the object trace, could not be mediated by a link formed by the VP-adjoined NP and the trace, giving (*det, ingen bok, t*) composed entirely of links (A,B) where A governs B. In other words, we must assume that the relation between an expletive and an argument cannot be mediated by Ā positions. But this is exactly what is generally assumed for the relation between the head and the foot of a standard A-chain.

The entire discussion of course presupposes that the ECP (or at least the part of it corresponding to condition (5)) is really not an "empty category

[20]The subscripts indicate chain membership. Thus, we take it that a trace can simultaneuously be the foot of an Ā chain and a (non-head) member of an A-chain. This is rather obviously true for wh-movement structures in Scandinavian; cf. Christensen & Taraldsen (1989). The crucial fact seems to be that the foot of an Ā chain must be analyzed as an argument, so that such an element can only be included in an A-chain that does not contain other arguments, as is the case when the A-chain is headed by an expletive. As for the potential violation of the Binding Theory's principle C, we may assume that principle C does not apply to A,B members of the same A-chain.

[21]In fact, this version of the argument is somewhat stronger than the one based on Swedish. In the Swedish case, one might consider the possibility that the agreement is caused by co-indexing between the expletive and a (subjectless) participial VP, reflecting an expletive/argument pairing where this VP is the argument; cf. Pollock (1985). This alternative is not available in the Norwegian case, since the agreement is not with the expletive (although induced by it).

principle", but rather a property of the links relating two positions in some specific way. On the one hand, it would not otherwise make sense to consider expletive/argument links (A,B) as subject to the ECP, since B need not in general be empty. On the other hand, we have seen that it is not sufficient for an empty category B, like the trace in (51), to be antecedent-governed by some A, like the adjoined NP in (51), if (A,B) cannot be a link for all ECP-sensitive relations that B enters into. Hence, we are led to view the (relevant part of the) ECP more as a "bounding condition" conceptually akin to the subjacency condition than as a condition relating to the identification of empty categories.

2.3.4 A remark on structure preservation

To conclude this subsection, we will consider a potential counterargument to the claim that the pp-agr facts are beyond the reach of a theory incorporating expletive replacement at LF. At the end of 2.3.1, we pointed out that expletive replacement, an instance of NP-movement, could create the pp-agr inducing trace in (44) and (52) (repeated below) at LF, too late for it to be reflected in the morphological shape of the participle:

(44) det_i blev $[_{VP}\ t_i\ [_{V'}$ skjutet en $\text{älg}_i]]$

(52) det_i vart $[_{VP}$ ingen $\text{bok}_j\ [_{VP}\ t_{i,j}\ [_{V'}$ skrive $t_i\ ]]]$

The counterargument would run as follows: Since NP-movement is structure preserving, the NP holding the critical trace created by expletive replacement, must be present as an empty element at S-structure. If we assume that this empty element must be antecedent-governed, it must be co-indexed with the expletive or with the adjoined NP (in (52)), and pp-agr will occur.

We think that this line of reasoning starts out from an unwarranted assumption, viz. that structure preservation holds in the required sense. The essence of structure preservation is the idea that (structure preserving) transformations can only create configurations conforming to the basic phrase structure skeletons. From this point of view, the notion that a structure preserving rule must move to pre-generated positions is in fact a relic of earlier versions of generative grammar in which the range of permissible phrase structures was defined once, by the phrase structure rules located in the grammar's base component. If instead the building of phrase structures is controlled by a set of general principles holding at every level, as would seem to be in the spirit of the projection principle, this conception of structure preservation loses its motivation. We would have an equally restrictive theory of derived phrase structure by thinking of movement as structure building subject to the general principles of phrase structure. In particular, there would be no reason at all for disallowing expletive replacement to create the crucial traces in (44) and (52) *ex nihilo* under iterated NP-movement.[22]

3 Conclusion

We started out from the premise that the "move α" relation would be a significant element of syntactic theory just in case the conditions constituting the configuration K could be considered properties uniquely assignable to this relation. Our examination of the expletive/argument relation has led us to think that the configuration K holds (directly) of this relation as well. Therefore, we conclude that "move α", and, correspondingly, the notion "derivation" plays no role in syntactic theory, at least as far as the NP-movement subcase is concerned. Putting it in slightly different terms, we hold that the only truely significant theoretical entity in this domain is the notion of "A-chain" suitably extended to subsume expletive/argument linking as well as the NP-movement relation, with the latter losing its status as an autonomous component of the grammar. The configuration K should then be seen as a property of A-chain links.

References

Belletti, A. & L. Rizzi (1981) "The Syntax of *ne*: Some Theoretical Implications", *The Linguistic Review* 1, 117–154

Benincà, P. (ed) (1989) *Dialect Variation and the Theory of Grammar*, Foris, Dordrecht

Chomsky, N. (1986a) *Knowledge of Language*, Praeger, New York

Chomsky, N. (1986b) *Barriers*, MIT Press, Cambridge

Chomsky, N. (1981) *Lectures on Government and Binding*, Foris, Dordrecht

Christensen, K. K. (1986) "Norwegian *ingen*: a case of postsyntactic lexicalization", in: Dahl & Holmberg (1986)

Christensen, K. K. & K. T. Taraldsen (1989) "Expletive Chain Formation and Past Participle Agreement in Scandinavian Dialects", in: Benincà (1989)

[22]We also note that if expletive replacement must pass through a previously generated subject position inducing pp-agr at S-structure, as presupposed in the putative counterargument, we might expect feature conflict between the agreement morpheme and the new subject at LF.

Dahl, Ø. & A. Holmberg (eds) (1986) *Scandinavian Syntax*, University of Stockholm

Jaeggli, O. (1980) *On Some Phonologically Null Elements in Syntax*, unpublished ph.d. diss., MIT

Kayne, R. S. (1985) "L'Accord du Participe Passé en Français et en Italien", *Modèles Linguistiques* 7, 73–89

Kayne, R. S. (1986) "Thematic and Case-assigning Properties of Past Participles", paper presented at the Princeton Workshop of Comparative Grammar

Kayne, R. S. (1989) "Facets of Romance Past Participle Agreement", in: P. Benincà (1989)

Pollock, J.-Y. (1985) "Il", unpublished ms, Université de Paris 12

Rizzi, L. (1982) *Issues in Italian Syntax*, Foris, Dordrecht

Rizzi, L. (1986) "On Chain Formation", in H. Borer (ed) *The Syntax of Pronominal Clitics: Syntax and Semantics, Volume 18*, Academic Press, New York.

Sprouse, R. & S. Vikner (1988) "Have/be selection as an A-chain membership requirement", *Working Papers in Scandinavian Syntax* 38

Chain Formation, Reanalysis, and the Economy of Levels*

Wolfgang Sternefeld

0 Overview

The purpose of this paper is to (re-)examine a number of arguments that have been used to corroborate the hypothesis that S-structure and D-structure are distinct, independently justified levels of representation. The discussion aims to show that on the basis of existing grammatical description no convincing motivation for the level of D-structure has been given. Moreover, I argue that a restricted system of UG should not allow for a level of representation that does not qualify as a branching point in a derivation.

In section 1, I investigate the role of chain formation in derivational and representational theories of "move α". I argue that "free chain formation" is superior to the more restricted mechanism of chain formation proposed in Chomsky (1981). The review of a number of constructions in this section will give empirical and conceptual support to a more liberal linking device that builds up chains in accordance with grammatical restrictions such as subjacency and the ECP. The arguments will also show that the necessity of an independent level of D-structure has not yet been established.

In section 2 the discussion of several analyses of the "verbal complex" in Germanic languages compares a structure changing account with theories that derive the verbal complex by movement or "incorporation" (in the sense of Baker (1988)). It will be shown that an incorporation-like theory successfully accounts for a considerable range of data; as opposed to an account in terms of reanalysis (and contrary to Baker's intention), the proposed theory will also be shown to be essentially mono-representational.

Section 3 contains some general and hypothetical remarks concerning the legitimacy of stipulating levels of representation. An attempt is made to define levels on the basis of universal rules and constraints. It turns out, however, that the intuitive concept of a level cannot be characterized by arbitrary systems of principles of UG alone. To obtain intuitively correct results, these systems

---

*For critical comments and discussions I wish to thank Mark Baker, Kathrin Cooper, Regine Eckhard, Fritz Hamm, Gereon Müller, Klaus Netter and Arnim v. Stechow.

H. Haider and K. Netter (eds.), Representation and Derivation in the Theory of Grammar, 71–137.

must be "rich enough" so as to pick out levels with highly specific properties. The considerations in this section also suggest that only "very few" levels can exist; in particular, I propose that levels can only arise from branchings in a derivation.

1 Free Chain Formation

Within the theory of "principles and parameters", the concept of chain formation is crucial in any part of the theory that deals with empty categories; in particular, the θ-criterion as formulated in Chomsky (1981) relies on a specific mechanism of chain formation that requires local binding as a link between the elements of a chain. The local binding property of links in a chain is defined by clauses (1) to (3), where X and Y may be replaced by A or $\bar{\text{A}}$:

(1) α is X-bound by β iff α is bound by β and β is in an X-position.

(2) α is locally bound by β iff α is X-bound by β, and if γ Y-binds α, then either γ Y-binds β or $\gamma = \beta$.

(3) α is locally X-bound by β iff α is locally bound and X-bound by β.

For illustration consider a structure such as (4) and assume that α and β are in A-positions, while α' occupies an $\bar{\text{A}}$-position. Furthermore, it is required that α, α', and β be coindexed:

(4) ... [α' [α [... β ...]]]

In this configuration, α' binds and locally binds α; α in turn binds and locally binds β; but α' does not locally bind β; therefore, α' locally $\bar{\text{A}}$-binds α, α locally A-binds β, but α' does not locally $\bar{\text{A}}$-bind β.

In "*Government and Binding*", Chomsky uses local A-binding as the only relevant property that ties together elements in an A-chain. According to this definition of A-chains, the pair (α, β) in (4) will necessarily constitute an A-chain as soon as β is a coindexed non-pronominal empty category. The θ-criterion is formulated in such a way that maximal A-chains must link exactly one argument to exactly one θ-position.

As another illustration of (1)–(3), consider (4) again, but assume now that α' is an A-position whereas α is an $\bar{\text{A}}$-position. In this case α' does not locally A-bind β, therefore (α', β) does not constitute an A-chain. Rather, the elements (α') and (β) constitute A-chains of their own.

In Chomsky (1986) the concept of chain formation is extended to $\bar{\text{A}}$-chains. No formal definition of this generalized type of chain formation is given there, but the discussion does not presuppose that chain formation always involves local binding, where binding is either A-binding or $\bar{A}$-binding. $\bar{A}$-chains are headed by $\bar{A}$-positions, whereas A-chains are headed by A-positions. We may add two further requirements which are taken from the definition of A-chains in Chomsky (1981) and can be carried over to the definition of $\bar{A}$-chains:

(5) Every chain is maximal, i.e. cannot be embedded into a chain that meets all the requirements of chain formation.

(6) If (α, β) is a link in a chain and α is an A-position, then β is an A-position.

The first requirement will be discussed at length in the following subsections; the second requirement expresses a certain well-formedness condition on A-chains, namely, that $\bar{A}$-positions may not intervene between A-positions in a chain: $\bar{A}$-positions are said to "break" A-chains. I will return to this condition in subsection 1.6.

The development of GB-theory has shown that local binding is not the only locality constraint that could reasonably be attributed to links in a chain. It was proposed in Chomsky (1986a) that other well-formedness conditions on chains are antecedent-government and subjacency. Depending on the kind of entity involved in a chain, each link (α, β) in a chain has to satisfy one of the following conditions: Either β is subjacently bound to α, or α antecedent-governs β. From the definition of chain formation informally given above, it would now follow that A-chains are restricted by local binding *and* by government. Likewise, $\bar{A}$-chains of arguments are restricted both by local binding *and* by subjacency, whereas $\bar{A}$-chains of non-arguments are restricted by local binding *and* by government.

I aim to eliminate this redundancy below. Following Chomsky (1986: 181f.), I argue that the local binding requirement on chain formation should be dropped. According to this proposal, chains can be formed by arbitrary co-indexation; they will be said to result from "free chain formation" (FCF). Chains resulting from the local binding mechanism introduced in Chomsky (1981) will be called "GB-chains". It will be taken for granted that the locality constraints introduced in Chomsky (1986a) are sufficient to ensure correct binding. The bulk of the arguments in the following subsections will serve to verify that GB-chain-formation is too restrictive.

In the context of the discussion of locality constraints, I also point out some consequences of FCF for the concept of derivational chain formation. Since FCF arises from free indexing, this concept is at odds with a mechanism that derives chains from the derivational history of "move α". Within this conception, derivational chains encode the derivational history of movement. Not only is a theory which is committed to derivational chain formation cumbersome to formalize, it also has to build in some mechanism that blocks FCF. I argue that derivational chains and additional machinery of this sort are unnecessary, because FCF is sufficient to obtain the correct results. Moreover, I try to show that in cases of head movement representational chain formation is superior to derivational chain formation. I will conclude by showing that as a consequence of the representational view of chain formation the level of D-structure can be dispensed with in the organization of UG.

1.1 Raising

To begin our review of locality constraints on chain formation, consider the following construction from German[1]:

(1)	weil	Johann$_i$	ihr	$[_\alpha$ t_i	dumm]	vorkommt
	because	John	her		foolish	appears

'because John strikes her as foolish'

Let us assume that α is a small clause projected by the adjective *dumm* such that α is the upper segment of an AP. The small clause analysis is motivated by the fact that the adjective *dumm* θ-marks the chain of the subject-NP *Johann*. For illustration compare (2) with (3):

(2)	weil	(es)	ihr	[t_i	unstatthaft]	vorkommt	[da"s	sie	Geld	bekam]$_i$
	because	(it)	her		illegal	appears	that	she	money	got

(3)	*weil	Johann$_i$	ihr	unstatthaft	vorkommt
	because	John	her	illegal	appears

In (3) the adjective has θ-marked *Johann*, whereas in (2) it has θ-marked an extraposed clause, with extraposition leaving behind an optional expletive element *es*. The difference in grammaticality is explained by the fact that *unstatthaft* ("illegal") selects only propositional complements. This requirement is satisfied in (2), but it is violated in (3).

Further motivation for this analysis comes from the observation that *vorkommen* is an ergative verb meeting all the criteria for ergativity: its participle is formed with *sein* ("to be"); it does not allow passivization; it resists nominalization even when combined with an adjective (cf. **ein ihr-dumm-Vorkommer*); it induces "Dative precedes Nominative" as an unmarked word

[1] For ease of exposition, German examples will always be presented as subordinate clauses, which display the basic position of the verb.

order etc. Summing up, we may safely conclude that *vorkommen* does not θ-mark the subject position.

Given that a small clause analysis along these lines is correct, a surprising property of this kind of construction is given in (4):

(4) weil Johann$_i$ sich [$_\alpha$ t_i dumm] vorkommt
because John himself foolish appears

'because John strikes himself as foolish'

As has been pointed out in Sternefeld (1984), coreference of the anaphoric argument-NP *sich* with the derived subject is completely grammatical. From the present perspective, the problem with (4) is chain formation: According to the GB-definition of a chain, *sich* and the trace of *Johann* should form a chain, since *sich* locally binds the trace. Moreover, (*sich*, t_i) is the only chain that is well-formed according to GB-theory. However, this chain violates the θ-criterion because it contains two θ-positions.

Let us first see how a derivational theory of chain formation could handle the problem. The solution seems to be very simple. Within such a theory, the proper representation of (4) is something like (4#):[2]

(4#) weil #Johann$_i$# sich$_i$ [#t_i# dumm] vorkommt

A derivational theory of "move α" has been advocated in Chomsky (1981) and (1986). In GB, the notion "t-antecedent" is introduced, and the notion "trace-of" is distinguished from the notion "trace". According to derivational terminology, the trace in (4#) is not the trace of *sich* since *Johann* is the t-antecedent of t_i. Intuitively, *sich* and t_i cannot constitute a link in a chain, because the anaphor is not the t-antecedent of the trace. The formal mechanism of GB chain formation, however, has not been defined in terms of t-antecedents but in terms of local binding.

Turning now to a representational theory, "move α" is a relation that must be read off a representation. We define chains in the usual way except for the difference that binding in a chain need not be local. As a further step towards a relaxation of requirements on chain formation, we also drop Chomsky's condition that chains must be maximal:

(5) *Free Chain Formation*:

C = (α_1, ... α_n) is a chain iff
(a) α_i binds α_{i+1}, and
(b) α_{i+1} is a trace.

[2]For mnemonic purposes, I use the diacritic "#" to represent movement in a derivational theory. More precisely, the elements marked with # are the last ones affected by "move α" in the course of a derivation.

As a consequence of treating $\bar{A}$-chains and A-chains alike, the formulation of the θ-criterion of GB has to be slightly revised. One way to achieve consistency with GB is to ignore $\bar{A}$-positions in a chain. In the following definition, I use the term "argument position" as an abbreviation for "A-position that contains an argument". The θ-criterion can now be stated (informally) as follows:

(6) *θ-Criterion*: Given a structure Σ, there is a one-to-one mapping μ from θ-positions in Σ onto argument positions in Σ such that for each $\langle\theta, \mu(\theta)\rangle \in \mu$ there is a chain in Σ with θ as its only θ-position and $\mu(\theta)$ as its only argument position.

Strictly speaking "θ-position" should be understood as "Grammatical Function that bears a θ-role" (GF-θ) and "argument position" as "Grammatical Function that qualifies as an A-position and contains an argument". The relevance of these qualifications will become clear in sections 1.4 and 1.5. For the present purpose it is sufficient to note that the above definition and FCF solve our problem, because *sich* and the trace of *Johann* do not necessarily enter into a chain. Note also that the θ-criterion in GB and our informal specification in (6) do not require *each* chain to be subject to the θ-criterion. Again in (4) there are three chains that include the trace: (t), (*sich*, t), and (*Johann*, t). Clearly, only the last chain satisfies the θ-criterion and the first two chains can simply be ignored.

In GB all chains in a well-formed structure satisfy the θ-criterion, i.e. they contain exactly one argument whenever they contain a θ-position and vice versa. This is not the case with FCF, because chains may be too short to satisfy the θ-criterion. In both theories, however, the θ-criterion only requires the existence of one chain that links θ-positions to arguments; it does not require that *all* chains establish such a link. Therefore, FCF is consistent with the θ-criterion of GB. The only difference, namely that less restrictive chain formation allows for more chains, is immaterial for the purpose of θ-theory.

1.2 Scrambling and Topicalization

Let us explore some further consequences of FCF now. Turning from NP-movement to subcases of *wh*-movement, we find analogous crossover configurations in "topicalizations" and in "cliticizations":

(1) Himself$_i$, he$_i$ cannot stand t_i

(2) da"s sich$_i$ der Hund$_i$ t_i in den Schwanz bei"st
that himself the dog in the tail bites

Although nothing important hinges on it, I will assume that movement in (1) and (2) is adjunction to IP (cf. Baltin (1982)). Cliticization in (2) can be described as a subcase of Scrambling. In both structures we can assume that the landing site of movement is an Ā-position. The obvious problem is again chain formation. Strictly local linking and maximality of chains would predict that only (*he*$_i$, t_i) and (*der Hund*$_i$, t_i) are well-formed chains, although they obviously violate the θ-criterion.

Within a derivational theory of movement the Ā-chains involved can be represented as in (3):

(3) (a) #Himself$_i$# he$_i$ cannot stand #t_i#

(b) da"s #sich$_i$# der Hund$_i$ #t_i# in den Schwanz bei"st

Although the #-chains conform to our intuition about the generation of these structures, the question arises how the θ-criterion should be formulated, i.e. whether or not the θ-criterion should refer to Ā-chains and arguments in Ā-positions or whether it should focus upon A-positions within A- and Ā-chains. Above, we pursued an approach in the spirit of GB-theory and restricted the θ-criterion to A-positions in chains. I will refer to this formulation of the θ-criterion as to its "GB-version". Alternatively, we could interpret the θ-criterion such that we take arguments in Ā-positions into consideration. This means that we drop the restrictions to A-positions in the notion "argument position" defined above. The resulting variant of the θ-criterion will be called the "Ā-version" of the θ-criterion.

Regardless of which version is adopted some changes in the definition of argumenthood of empty categories are required. Consider the status of the traces with respect to argumenthood. In both (1) and (2) the traces are locally A-bound and according to the standard (contextual) definition of empty categories they should be anaphors. Of course we want to maintain this result, because the anaphoric status of the trace is responsible for the fact that the moved NP must be a reflexive pronoun. But for the purpose of θ-theory of GB we have to restrict our attention to the A-position in the chain of the anaphor. In GB the A-chain headed by the trace is subject to the θ-criterion, therefore the trace should be an argument. On the other hand, empty anaphors can't be arguments in GB. We thus have to conclude that contrary to what is predicted in GB some anaphors must be arguments. Alternatively, we could presuppose the Ā-version of the θ-criterion. In this case the assumption that all variables are arguments causes problems, which is illustrated in (4):

(4) Who$_i$ t_i saw what?

Clearly, *who* and *what* are both arguments. But if the variable in (4) is an argument, the $\bar{A}$-chain of *who* contains two arguments. This contradiction requires a modification of the definition of argumenthood.

Let us first consider the $\bar{A}$-version of the θ-criterion. As a consequence of the above considerations we have to drop the requirement that variables are arguments. Intuitively this makes sense, because – apart from cases like (4) – variables (as defined in GB) do not always correspond to arguments. In GB, the concept of a variable intuitively presupposes binding by an operator. But as soon as binding by some other element is considered, the notion "variable" turns out to be a misnomer. For example, we do not want to claim that the trace left behind by movement of a non-argument is an argument because it has Case, nor do we want to conclude that it must be an argument qua being locally $\bar{A}$-bound. A case in point is movement of an expletive element to SpecC in verb-second constructions, as in the derivations of V/2 clauses in (6) from the V/1-structures in (5):

(5) (a) Wird es dunkel werden?
Will it dark become

(b) Stimmt es^i, [da"s sie kommt $]^i$?
Is-correct it that she comes

(6) (a) Es_i wird t_i dunkel werden.

(b) Es_i stimmt t_i, da"s sie kommt.

The standard definition would imply that an $\bar{A}$-bound trace (or a trace in a Case position) is a variable and therefore should be an argument. But it is obvious that the trace of a non-argument must be a non-argument.

Given this revised understanding of argumenthood, the $\bar{A}$-version of the θ-criterion seems to work fine and there seems to be no reason to return to the more complicated GB-version. We will see in the next subsection, however, that this reformulation of the θ-criterion still could lead to problems.

1.3 Parasitic Gaps

We now turn to a more complicated case of FCF. Parasitic gap constructions are particularly interesting for derivational theories of movement, because they seem to exhibit a difference between gaps produced by movement and gaps produced by co-indexing:

(1) (a) #Which book# did you review #*t*# [$_{PP}$ without reading *e*]?
(b) a person #who# [$_{NP}$ close friends of *e*] admire #*t*#

Within a derivational theory, it is argued that the "real" trace t is generated by movement, whereas the trace e (an argument and a variable) is parasitic on "real movement" and results from free (co-)indexing. The difference in the status of the traces is reflected by the fact that the real trace must be subjacently bound to its antecedent, whereas the relation between the parasitic gap and its Ā-binder typically violates subjacency (cf. Chomsky (1982)).

If subjacency is a property of chains, the parasitic gap must be a chain of its own. The same conclusion follows from the θ-criterion: If the parasitic gap were a non-argument that has to be bound to an operator in a chain, there is no one-to-one correspondence between arguments and θ-positions. Therefore, a revision of basic principles of θ-theory seems to be necessary.

Chomsky (1986a) argues that parasitic gaps are subjacently bound to empty operators in a chain. This move would solve all our problems, because empty operators are arguments and thereby help to preserve the one-to-one correspondence between arguments and θ-positions. On the other hand, examples like (1b) suggest that this solution cannot always work in case of parasitic gaps within subject NPs, because there seems to be no landing site for an empty operator that could bind the parasitic gap.

If we are to take examples like (1b) seriously, the notion of argumenthood has to be revised again. Once again, we have to decide which of the versions of the θ-criterion should be the basis for a definition of argumenthood. The Ā-version correctly predicts that an argument in an Ā-position has to be bound to a θ-position in a chain that satisfies grammatical restrictions on movement (subjacency, antecedent-government). This does not follow from the GB-version of the θ-criterion but must be stipulated. I will therefore adopt the Ā-version as the basic principle to which the following discussion will refer.

Examples like (2) suggest that well-formedness principles on chains, like subjacency, cannot always decide which trace has to be taken as parasitic:

(2) Who did you give a picture of t to t'

Both traces are subjacently and locally bound by an operator. Therefore, we cannot *a priori* decide which of the two variables must be an argument, i.e. we cannot make our definition of argumenthood depend on a decision on which of the empty elements is an argument and which one is not. (For some motivation to take t as the parasitic gap, see the "Clause Non-Final Incomplete Constituent Constraint" in Kuno (1973)). In the following, I will first define the notion of a potential argument. "Real" arguments will be potential arguments that head a chain. In (2) both empty categories will be potential arguments, but only the empty category that is not be bound to the operator in a chain will be a ("real") argument.

(3) A trace α in an A-position is a potential argument iff α is $\bar{A}$-bound by an argument β, and if β binds a trace γ, γ does not bind α, nor does α bind γ.

(3) embodies the anti-c-command requirement for parasitic gaps (cf. Chomsky (1982)). In particular, constructions like (4) will be excluded by the θ-criterion:

(4) (a) *Who *t* gives a picture of John to *e*

(b) *Who *e* gives a picture of John to *t*

In (4a) we would like to exclude *e* as a potential argument. Although *e* is $\bar{A}$-bound by the argument *who*, *who* also binds the trace *t* which violates the c-command requirement expressed in (3). In (4b), the same holds with respect to the reversed assumptions about binding of *who* in a chain.

Clearly, the non-maximality of chains is still consistent with the usual analysis of (1a) and the claim that subjacency is a property of chains. Non-maximality is also illustrated in the following parasitic gap construction in Dutch, which is discussed in Bennis (1986) and Bennis & Hoekstra (1984):

(5) dat Jan$_i$ [$_{VP}$ zich$_i$ [$_{VP}$ [$_{CP}$ zonder PRO$_i$ e_i te bedenken] t_i
that Jan himself without to reflect
in het water stortte]]
into the water hurls

Following Felix (1983), Bennis and Hoekstra argue that a scrambling rule has adjoined *zich* to the VP. Definition (3) implies that the parasitic gap is a potential argument. Since e_i cannot be in a chain with *zich*$_i$, it must be the head of a chain and according to (3) it is an argument that satisfies the θ-criterion. Observe also that the parasitic gap is not a variable, because it is not locally $\bar{A}$-bound. As a consequence it must be an anaphor. Furthermore, it is very likely that this property must be realized on the element that induces argumenthood on the anaphor, i.e. the argument that induces argumenthood on the anaphor must itself be an anaphor. Similarly, the real trace must be an anaphor, because it is A-bound by *Jan*. However, since the empty anaphor t_i in (5) is not locally A-bound, the example shows that the definition of empty anaphors must be revised. Suppose we adopt the following definition:

(6) A governed empty category in an A-position is an anaphor iff it is either locally A-bound or if it is A-bound in its minimal governing category.

The first part might be redundant, but could be useful in excluding cases of super-raising. The nature of the second alternative is much like the constraint on chain formation in terms of grammatical restrictions. Since the locality constraints on movement (subjacency, antecedent-government) are sufficiently local to guarantee correct chain formation, I suggest that the locality constraint on anaphors is also sufficient to define anaphoricity.

The grammaticality of (5) now follows without further stipulation, whereas strict locality in the definition of chains, anaphoricity, and argumenthood would lead to unsurmountable difficulties.

1.4 Serial Verb Constructions

So far, derivational chain formation and FCF exhibit roughly the same empirical effects, this being a consequence of the fact that each *t*-chain unambiguously corresponds to a chain formed by FCF on some level of representation. In this section, I will go on to show that the opposite does not hold. I will exemplify a case of chain formation that makes sense in a non-derivational theory but becomes entirely meaningless when interpretated in a derivational manner.

The envisaged counter-example to derivational chain formation has been brought to my attention by Mark Baker (p.c.). In his analysis of serial verb constructions Baker (1989) suggested that the structure in (1) should serve as base generated source for an analysis of object sharing constructions to be illustrated below:

(1)

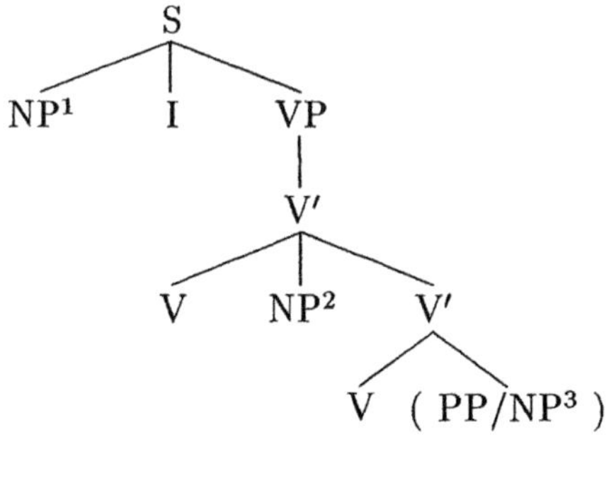

The VP is analysed as having two verbal heads both of which θ-mark the shared object NP². Instances of (1) are shown in (2).[3]

(2) (a) Yoruba
$[_S$ Bàbá mi $[_{VP}$ $[_{V'}$ ra ẹ̀wù $[_{V'}$ bùn mi]]]]
father my buy garment present me
'My father bought me a garment'

[3] All linguistic material in this subsection is drawn from Baker (1989).

(b) Sranan

$[_S$ Kownu $[_{VP}$ $[_{V'}$ seni $[_{NP}$ wan boskopu] gi Tigri]]]
King send a message give Tiger
'King sent a message to Tiger'

Baker's Projection Principle implies that θ-marking of the NP^2 between the two verbs is obligatory for both of them: NP^2 must be θ-marked by two object θ-roles, one being assigned by the first, the other being assigned by the second verb of the VP. The subject may also receive two θ-roles. Note that assignment of two roles to a θ-position is not incompatible with the θ-criterion as stated in Chomsky (1986). Hence, the above analysis predicts that a transitive first verb always induces transitivity or ergativity (in the sense of Burzio (1981)) on the second verb, otherwise no second θ-role could be assigned to NP^2.

If the first verb is intransitive, however, NP^2 will not be generated and must be omitted from the representation in (1). In this case no restriction is imposed on the second verb. We thus find constructions with the second verb being intransitive, transitive (with its object θ-role realized on NP^3), or ergative; cf. Baker (1989:533f). It is interesting to note that Baker observes an asymmetry when an ergative verb is combined with an intransitive verb; the ergative verb must always be chosen as the second predicate of a serial verb construction. He first shows that the combination of two intransitive verbs or two ergative verbs is unproblematic. These cases are illustrated in (3) with the arrows indicating θ-assignment:

(3) Yoruba

(a) Adé $[_{VP}$ rìn jó]
Ade walk dance

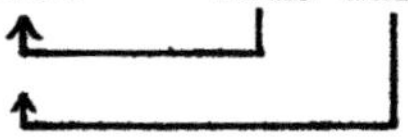

(b) ó$_i$ $[_{VP}$ $[_{V'}$ pọ́n t_i $[_{V'}$ rà]]]
it ripen rot

'It has ripened to the point of rotting'

Combining an ergative verb with an intransitive verb will yield the two possible structures in (4):

(4) Sranan

(a) *Kofi$_i$ [$_{VP}$ kon t_i [$_{V'}$ waka]]
Kofi come walk

(b) Kofi$_i$ [$_{VP}$ waka [$_{V'}$ kon t_i]]
Kofi walk come

'Kofi walks hither'

The ungrammaticality of (a) is explained by the Projection Principle. Above we already showed that the intermediate object must receive two θ-roles, but here the object of *kon* = *come* cannot be θ-marked by *waka* = *walk* which only assigns a VP-external θ-role. The grammaticality of (b), however, poses a problem. The requirement of maximality in chain formation would yield the chain (*Kofi*$_i$, t_i) which is inconsistent with the θ-criterion. Although FCF would allow both NPs to form single-element chains, there seems to be no way to derive that t_i is an argument. Moreover and most importantly, the example also shows that the concept of a t-chain does not help to solve the problem. This concept does not even make sense when applied to the relation between *Kofi* and the trace.

A solution to the paradox of θ-theory emerges if we take into account a formal detail of chain formation in GB, where chains are made up from grammatical functions (GFs) rather than positions in a tree. A GF will count as argumental if and only if its position is filled by an argument expression. θ-assignment is to GFs rather than to positions in a tree. We can therefore require that each GF bears no more than one θ-role. The θ-criterion then expresses a one-to-one correspondence between argumental GFs and θ-marked GFs.

Given that chains are made up from GFs the paradox disappears if one shifts from the grammatical functions (GFs) of GB to the definitions of GFs given by Williams, Emonds, Pesetsky, and others. These authors replace the notion "subject of S" by the more traditional notion "subject of a predicate" or "subject of VP." Following di Sciullo & Williams (1987) we will relativize this notion to the respective head of VP. Accordingly, the GF "subject" may have different values (NP, VP_{head}) and (NP, $VP_{head'}$) that refer to the same position in a tree.

In serial verb constructions we are usually forced to assume two values of the GF "subject", which is a consequence of our requirement that the two subject θ-roles of the verbs are assigned to different values of GFs. This symmetry cannot be perfect however, because verbs need not assign a θ-role to their subject GF. Baker mentions a number of asymmetries to the effect that the first verb has some (morphological) prominence over the second. We may add here that the prominence of the first verb in a serial verb construction is also reflected by the fact that the subject position obligatorily enters into the GF "subject" only with the first verb. Although the second verb will in general also be linked to the subject position in the GF "subject", it only serves as a secondory head of VP: Constructions like (5) show that the assignment of a second GF (related to the second V) is not obligatory:

(5) Yoruba
Olú [$_{VP}$ ti [$_{NP}$ ọmọ náà] subú]
Olu push child the fall

'Olu pushed the child down'

Here, the subject position is θ-marked only by the first verb and does not enter into any θ-relation or chain with the argument of the ergative verb *subú*. On the basis of the concept of GF proposed above it would lead to a violation of θ-theory if we were to assume a GF "subject of *subú*": This GF would be assigned to a position that contains an argument, therefore it must receive a θ-role in a chain, which seems to be implausible in (5).

It might be argued, however, that one could have linked the object GF in (5) to the GF "subject of *ti*" in a chain which displays something like NP-raising without movement. Although this step would reconcile the existence of a secondary GF with the θ-criterion, such a chain would be exceptional, however, because it lacks a well-defined hierarchical relation between the two values of the GF subject: Which value is to be considered as the head of the chain? Referring to the aforementioned asymmetry between heads we could conclude that the subject of *ti* must be the head of this chain. In that case, however, we would have to face a violation of the groundedness condition on chains, because we would have produced the analogue of "movement into a θ-position" (see section 1.9 for a discussion of groundedness). To summarize, we assume that assignment of a value of the GF subject is obligatory only for the first verb in a serial verb construction.

Returning now to the problematic example (4b) it is easy to see that the one-to-one correspondence between arguments and θ-roles can be maintained only by referring to argumental GFs and θ-marked GFs. θ_1, i.e. the θ-role of *waka* = *walk*, must be assigned to the subject of *walk*, the position of this subject being occupied by an argument that satisfies the θ-criterion. θ_2, the

θ-role of the ergative verb *kon* = *come*, must be assigned to an object position. But according to standard assumptions this position is an anaphor and a non-argument, therefore it has to be linked to a position occupied by an argument. Hence, we have to construct the following chains:

(6) $C_1 = (\langle NP_{Kofi}, VP_{waka}\rangle)$ for θ_1, and
$C_2 = (\langle NP_{Kofi}, VP_{kon}\rangle, \langle NP_t, V_{kon}\rangle)$ for θ_2.

The categories that enter into chain formation are indexed with the lexical expressions of their heads. This is essential for categories with more than one head, because we just hypothesized that the relation "subject of a VP" must be relativized to the head(s) of VP. Therefore $\langle NP, VP_x\rangle$ and $\langle NP, VP_y\rangle$ can be two different elements of the GF "subject", even if both NPs and both VPs occupy the same position in a tree. The indices on the NPs indicate different positions in the tree, they have been added only for mnemonic purposes. Since both chains satisfy the θ-criterion (when relativized to chains of GFs), the construction is accounted for in a systematic way that leaves the basic principles of θ-theory unaffected.

Once again we have seen that FCF helps to solve a problem that obviously cannot be handled by GB chain formation. The gist of the argument, however, consists in having given an example that cannot be handled by *t*-chain formation either. The problem here arises from the GB concept of D-structure which evolved from the requirement that D-structure trivially satisfies the θ-criterion, implying that at D-structure each argument is in a θ-position and each θ-position is filled by an argument (cf. section 1.9 below for a discussion of this principle). Applying the principle to (4b) we are now faced with the problem that an argument has to be raised into a position already being an argument position in D-structure. With (7) as the only conceivable D-structure sources of (4b) we cannot avoid the conclusion that all NP-positions must be θ-positions.

(7) (a) $[_S\ [_{NP}$??? $]\ [_{VP}$ waka $[_{V'}$ con kofi $]]]$
(b) $[_S\ [_{NP}$ kofi $]\ [_{VP}$ waka $[_{V'}$ con ??? $]]]$

The positions filled with question marks cannot be featureless, because they must contain arguments in D-structure. Apart from that, however, it appears that nothing meaningful can be said about the identity of "???" nor about the derivation of the S-structure (4b), casting doubt on concepts like D-structure, "transformational" derivation, and *t*-chain formation.

Note in passing that roughly the same argument would carry over to asymmetric coordinations like "*John robbed the bank and was arrested by the police*". We do not claim, however, that the present theory solves any of the problems posed by coordinate structures (cf. Chomsky (1982a) or Pesetsky (1982) for some discussion). Notwithstanding these problems it seems worth noting at this point that the above discussion is completely independent from the issue of coordinate structures and ATB-movement. Therefore the argument against *t*-chain formation is much stronger than the one that could be deduced from coordinations.

Similarly, our arguments in favor of FCF are much stronger than the arguments for FCF in Chomsky (1986), who also introduces some limited kind of "CHAIN" formation by free coindexation, to the effect that "CHAINs" of this type can arise from coindexing an argument expression with an expletive element like *it* or *there*. Again, our arguments in favor of FCF do not rely on particular structures involving expletives but go right into the heart of trace theory.

Crucially, however, our theory rests on a rather different concept of GFs, and it will be one of my aims in the next subsection to give some independent motivation for the relational use of GFs introduced above. As it turns out the following discussion will also illustrate another case of chain formation without movement.

1.5 GF-Projections

In the following we turn to an analysis of so-called coherent constructions in German and Dutch that has been proposed by Haegeman & Riemsdijk (1986), henceforth H&R. A more comprehensive analysis of these constructions will be the topic of section 2. At this point, I merely want to point out a problem for this analysis that seems to have escaped the attention of H&R; the problem can be solved by employing the relational notion of GFs introduced above.

H&R's analysis of coherent constructions proceeds in three steps. Starting with a D-structure like (1a), H&R first form the verbal complex in (1b) by erasing the projections of the embedded verb and all but the topmost projection of the matrix verb:

(1) (a) weil [$_{IP}$ Johann [$_{VP}$ [$_{CP}$ PRO [$_{VP}$ die Frau küssen]]] will]
because John the woman to-kiss wants

(b) weil [$_{IP}$ Johann [$_{VP}$ PRO die Frau [$_{V^0}$ küssen will]]]

In the resulting structure the nodes of PRO and *die Frau* are dangling. The latter one will be reconnected to the rest of the tree in the next step which rebuilds the structure according to the principles of $\bar{X}$-theory. The result is given in (2):

(2) weil [$_{IP}$ Johann [$_{VP}$ die Frau [$_{V^0}$ küssen will]]]

The final step in their analysis concerns some language specific reordering within V^0 (I will return to this in section 2). Now observe that, as a consequence of the requirement that PRO cannot be governed, PRO must be deleted from the reanalysed structure (2). We therefore have to admit a violation of the Extended Projection Principle. Besides, some limited violation of the Projection Principle has to be accepted as an effect of the very nature of reanalysis. As it is clear from the above exposition the CP-object of the matrix verb cannot be projected onto the reanalysed structure.

Consider next an example not found in H&R (1986):

(3) weil Johann [$_{VP}$ [$_{CP}$ [$_{IP}$ e [$_{VP}$ PRO gekü"st werden]]]] will
because John kissed to-be wants

(3) shows a D-structure with the embedded predicate in passive voice before the raising of PRO has occurred. After raising we get the following structure:

(4) weil Johann$_i$ [$_{VP}$ [$_{CP}$ [$_{IP}$ PRO$_i$ [$_{VP}$ t_i gekü"st werden]]]] will

(4) can be taken as a legitimate S-structure except that obligatory reanalysis still has to apply. After the reanalysis and deletion of PRO, we end up with something like (5):

(5) weil Johann$_i$ [$_{VP}$ t_i [$_{V^0}$ gekü"st werden will]]

GB chain formation will connect *Johann* and t_i in a chain that violates the θ-criterion. We therefore must conclude that not only PRO has to be deleted but also its trace. On the other hand, we now face a further violation of the Projection Principle, one that is more severe and does not directly follow from the very nature of reanalysis. The question arises whether such a violation can be tolerated. In any case, it seems that some kind of restriction is required in order to rule out the abuse of deletion of empty categories.

As a partial solution to this problem, it was proposed in v. Stechow & Sternefeld (1988) that the mechanism of recoverability of deletion should be made more explicit in the following way. In some sense, PRO is not really "deleted", but the value of its GF is "projected" on the matrix subject. This seems to be a natural way of looking at reanalysed infinitives: Defining the notion subject in relation to a verb would, in any case, imply that the closest VP-external NP that c-commands a verb (or any of the verbs of the cluster) is its subject. Therefore, GF projection follows automatically from reanalysis and the relational approach to GFs.

The mechanism of "GF-projection" now provides a solution for the problem of chain formation in (5). As in the preceding subsection, the subject-position receives "two GFs" (or more precisely, it is an element in two values of the GF subject) that can connect this position to two different chains. In conjunction with the θ-criterion, FCF will connect only the intuitively correct GFs into chains. The value (*Johann, will*) of the GF "subject" has received a θ-role and cannot be connected to another GF-θ. The value (*t, gekü"st*) of the GF "object" has received a θ-role but does not contain an argument. The only available argument position is the subject position; the only available choice for a GF-value in a chain is of course (*Johann, gekü"st*), because this GF-value contains an argument but has not already been assigned a θ-role.

We see that GF-projection and FCF provide the key for a proper working of reanalysis; one that is capable of maintaining a structure like (5) while sticking to the Projection Principle in its most restrictive version. Since the GF of PRO has "survived" in the relational representation of GFs, we can claim that not only the Projection Principle itself but even the Extended Projection Principle is satisfied with respect to the revised concept of GFs. Moreover, we have found another application of chain formation that does not involve "real movement".

1.6 Si-Constructions

Having investigated a number of reasons for adopting FCF, we now turn to an argument that runs counter to the proposals made above. Rizzi (1986) analyses the ungrammaticality of constructions like (1b) and (2b) as a violation of strictly local chain formation:

(1) (a) Gianni$_i$ è stato affidato t_i a se stesso$_i$
Gianni was entrusted to himself

(b) *Gianni$_i$ si$_i$ è stato affidato t_i t'_i

(2) (a) I due nemici$_i$ spesso vengono t_i in mente l'uno all'altro
The two enemies often come to mind to each other

(b) *I due nemici$_i$ spesso si$_i$ vengono t_i in mente t'_i

His explanation contrasts with our previous analysis where we assumed FCF to be available for scrambling, topicalization, and NP-movement. If our analysis is correct, there is no reason to assume that the observed interaction between clitic movement and NP-movement should obey local binding properties.

Of course, we could refer to the intuition originally derived from super-raising, namely that coindexed elements between NP-chains "break" chains:

(3) John$_i$ seems [$_{CP}$ t_i that [$_{IP}$ Mary [$_{VP}$ t_i [hates t_i]]]]

We then have to assume that the clitic position is an $\bar{A}$-position and thereby breaks chains. This explanation would appeal to the kind of locality condition already envisaged as condition (6) of section 1.1. In the context of the present discussion, however, one would prefer a theory that can avoid additional requirements on chain formation.

Explaining the "odd behaviour" of clitic placement in accordance with FCF could take advantage of the (perhaps unexpected) fact that nearly all of Rizzi's ungrammatical examples are of the type illustrated above and crucially involve two gaps. Following a proposal by Chomsky (1986:217, fn. 115) and adopting Pesetsky's (1982) theory of paths,[4] one can easily derive a violation of the Path Containment Condition (PCC). Assume that cliticization in Italian can be described as movement to the specifier position of "agreement object", as in Chomsky (1989). The structure of (1b), then, is something like (1c):

(1) (c) *Gianni$_i$ si$_i$ è [$_{V'}$ stato affidato t_i] t'_i

Assume furthermore that the two landing sites involved, namely the respective specifier positions of AGR-subject and AGR-object, interact with respect to Pesetsky's Path Containment Condition if and only if both agreement positions are coindexed. To see this, observe that the ergative verb in (1c) is subcategorized for a direct object NP and an indirect object PP. We can assume that the clitic *si* is an NP that will be generated as a complement of an empty preposition. Alternatively, we could take *si* as an N^0-category such that the path of N^0-movement will begin at the $\bar{N}$ node, resembling the COMP-INFL path that starts with $\bar{I}$. In each case, we derive a violation of the PCC. The clitic's path to SpecAGR-object (or to AGR-object in case of N^0-movement) will overlap with the object's path to SpecAGR-subject, but neither one is properly contained in the other. This immediately explains the ungrammaticality of (1b).

Apart from Pesetsky's PCC, another solution that does not require additional restrictions on chain formation could involve the empirical generalization that *si* must be bound to a subject; cf. Rizzi's example

(4)	* Si$_i$	inimicherà	Gianni$_i$ t_i
	(I) against-himself	will push	Gianni

To explain the ungrammaticality of (4), we cannot appeal to principles of binding theory (i.e. we cannot claim that *si* is free and violates principle (A), nor that *Gianni* is bound and violates principle (C)) because we have seen in section 1.2 that analogous crossovers are grammatical in German, as long as

[4]which received some corroboration from May (1985) and from numerous others working in that framework; cf. Kim & Larson (1989) for a recent example.

the clitic *sich* corefers with a subject. But clearly we can rule out (4) directly by referring to *si*'s property of being subject oriented: As is the case with many anaphors in the majority of the languages of the world, *si* must be bound to a subject.

Before we return to (1) and (2), note that it is necessary to distinguish between the impersonal *si* and the reflexive *si*. We observe that the impersonal *si*, which is base generated in a θ-position (cf. Chomsky 1981)), must be bound to a non-θ-subject position, whereas the reflexive *si* must be bound to a θ-subject. This property of the distribution of *si* allows us to argue as follows: In (1) and (2) *si* is bound to a non-θ-subject, therefore it will be understood as an impersonal *si*. But clearly, *si* cannot be understood as having "absorbed" the subject's θ-role in (1)–(2), because there is no such θ-role. Therefore, the construction violates the θ-criterion. Being bound to a non-θ-position *si* must be impersonal, but as such it did not get an appropriate θ-role in (1) and (2).

Another rather trivial solution to Rizzi's problem would be to say that there is an accidental gap in the distribution of clitics. There simply are no reflexive dative clitics in Italian; therefore the constructions considered by Rizzi are ungrammatical. Perhaps Rizzi could claim that one should to be able to show that this gap cannot be accidental. The above considerations establish the more general claim that clitics can never be bound to derived subjects. I suspect, however, that such a claim might be too strong.

Let us finally turn to another type of example that was designed to corroborate GB-chains but which could receive an explanation entirely independent of chain formation:

(5) *Gianni$_i$ si$_i$ sembra [$_{IP}$ t_i non fare il suo dovere]
Gianni to-himself seems not do his duty

The clitic must have been moved out of an (optional) dative complement of *sembra*. Following Emonds (1985), one could assume that this complement is headed by an empty preposition. Again we can derive a violation of the PCC, either on the assumption that the path begins with PP or on the assumption that N^0's path starts with N′. An analysis along these lines cannot be on the right track, however, because we have to take into account that the construction is ungrammatical even if there is no cliticization of the PP. But if there is no movement of the anaphor, we must find an explanation which is also independent of the PCC.

For the present purpose, it suffices to make it plausible that non-local chain formation will not be the only reason for the observed ungrammaticality. Consider the contrast between (6a) and (6b):

(6) (a) *John seems to himself to have neglected his duty.

(b) ?They seemed to each other to have neglected their duties.

The constructions seem parallel as far as the relevant aspects of syntax are concerned. The only difference results from meaning: In (a) the experiencer attributes a property to himself, whereas in (b) the experiencers do not self-attribute the property of neglecting one's duty. That some non-syntactic aspects might be involved is also confirmed by Rizzi's own example (7), which is taken to be grammatical because the anaphor is stressed:

(7) Perfino a se stesso$_i$ Gianni$_i$ sembra [t_i non fare il suo dovere]
Even to himself Gianni seems not do his duty

Since the ungrammaticality of (5) seems to depend on the ungrammaticality of (the Italian analogue of) (6a), we either have to say that the ungrammaticality of (6a) *and* (5) cannot be explained by a mechanism like chain formation, or we could explain (6a) by chain formation but have to ignore the preposition. In this case, however, Rizzi would be committed to the rather implausible assumption that the stressed anaphor in (7) has not been moved. Otherwise the construction should be as unacceptable as (5), because an intervening binder blocks GB-chain formation between *Gianni* and t_i:

(7′) [(a) se stesso]$_{i'}$ Gianni$_i$ sembra t'_i [t_i non fare il suo dovere]

These examples strongly suggest that the ungrammaticality of (5) is independent of FCF. As the empirical evidence presented is rather poor, there is considerable room for manœuvering and reinterpreting of the data (cf. also Lasnik (1985), Epstein (1986) or our discussion of a Larsonian VP-structure in Corver & Riemsdijk (forthcoming proceedings of the Tilburg conference on Scrambling)).

1.7 Head Movement

So far we have not considered more complex chains such as (α, β, γ). Chains with more than two elements normally arise when the position β is used *en route* as an escape hatch for movement from γ to α. I will now examine chains that cannot be interpreted literally in such a way. Chain formation of the kind introduced below will encode aspects of the derivational history but cannot strictly be interpreted as "derivational" in the usual sense of the term. Relevant examples of this kind will be gained from an investigation of properties of head movement.

Baker (1988) showed that head movement can remove barrierhood from a maximal projection. His definition of barrierhood by minimality is given in (1):

(1) Let D be the smallest maximal projection containing A. Then C is a *barrier* between A and B iff C is a maximal projection that contains B and excludes A, and the head of C is distinct from the head of D and selects some WP equal to or containing B.

Before discussing (1) in relation to FCF I will show that this definition is both too strong and too weak.

Consider cyclical head movement as in verb-second movement in German. The verb first adjoins to I and then the inflected verb adjoins to C. This movement is schematically given in (2) (the order of constituents being neglected):

(2)

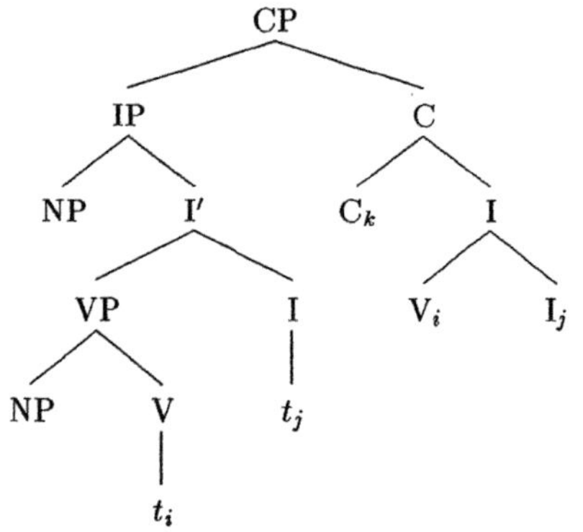

I will assume that head movement in German is less "incorporative" than Baker's theory would predict, in particular, the trace of head movement retains its ability to assign Case unless otherwise indicated. Given the definition of distinctness in (3) below, the reader may verify that the chains (V_i, t_i) and (I_j, t_j) are well-formed with respect to the ECP. No barrier intervenes between the antecedent and its trace.

(3) X is *distinct* from Y only if no part of Y is a member of a chain containing X.

Consider now the deplorable fate of the lower NP in (2) when V is an ergative verb. The situation is illustrated by V-second movement in V/2-clauses in Swedish, a language that does not exhibit small pro and therefore enforces raising of the argument of an ergative verb into the subject position. Somewhat surprisingly, the VP turns out to be a barrier for movement of the object NP to the subject position. This is the case because the position of t_i is distinct from the position of t_j; therefore V erects a barrier for movement of the object-NP to the subject position. (Note that VP would not be a barrier for moving the object directly to the SpecC position.) As the object of an ergative verb cannot receive Case *in situ*, we have to conclude that Baker's mechanism is too strong.

To solve this problem I turn to a completely different but, as we will see, related difficulty. Baker (1988) observed that (1) does not exclude "acyclic movement", which would arise from first moving I to C and then adjoining V to C:

(4)

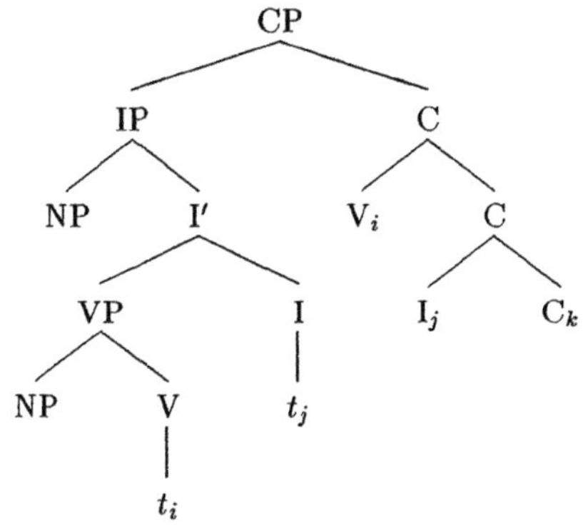

As Baker has shown on the basis of relevant data, this type of movement must be excluded. His own attempt to do so is unsatisfactory, however, because he explicitly builds the head-movement constraint into the definition of antecedenthood in an X^0-chain. The problem is much more interesting since some authors assume a kind of co-indexation (between heads) that does not involve movement (cf. V and I coindexing in Chomsky (1986a) or C and I coindexation in Müller (1989)). As a fatal consequence of this base generated identification of heads, V can move directly to C and it becomes impossible to derive the head movement constraint from minimality alone.

In order to regain the explanatory power to derive the Head Movement Constraint from the ECP, I start with the assumption that head movement can remove barrierhood for phrases but not for heads. The reason for this would be that adjoined heads can be analysed as non-distinct from the perspective of maximal projections, but will still appear as distinct on the X^0-level itself. It is easy to make this precise by substituting the clause "the head of C is distinct from the head of D" in (1) by "B considers the head of C distinct from the head of D". Distinctness will then take into account the additional requirement that a zero-bar category will always consider α distinct from β unless α is the trace of β:

(3′) *Distinctness*:

For Z, X is *distinct from* Y iff

(a) Z is phrasal and no part of Y is a member of a chain containing X, or
(b) Z is not phrasal and X is the trace of Y.

Distinctness will be a three place relation, just like the notion of barrierhood defined in (1). As a first result of this move cyclical movement as in (2) will be blocked because t_j is not the trace of C. Therefore IP is a barrier between t_i and its antecedent V_i. To remedy this damage, we adopt a variant of Baker's proposal which states that indices of adjuncts should percolate up to their hosts. Given the convention that the host still retains its own index as a designated index, we arrive at the following representation of (2):[5]

(5)

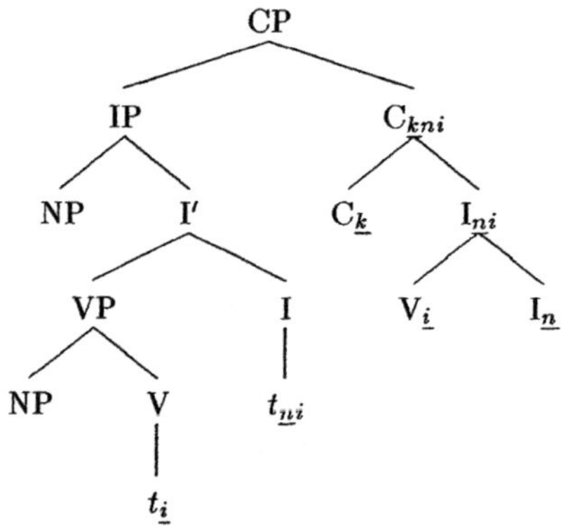

However, this does not yet solve the problem because $t_{\underline{n}i}$ is still not the trace of the head of CP. Accordingly, there is still a barrier between t_i and V_i. On the other hand, V_i is an adjunct and therefore has to be connected to a head position with V's index as a designated index in such a way that no barrier is crossed. To resolve the conflict, I propose the natural convention that chain formation and antecedent government extends to links in a chain that share a common index:

(6) $C = (\alpha_1, ... \alpha_n)$ is a *chain* iff

(a) α_i m-commands α_{i+1},
(b) α_{i+1} is a trace, and
(c) α_i and α_{i+1} share a common index.

[5]In this representation, the designated index has been underlined. If only one index is attached to a category, underlining will be omitted.

(7) α_i *antecedent governs* α_{i+1} iff

(a) α_i governs α_{i+1}, and
(b) (α_i, α_{i+1}) is a link in a chain.

Having extended chain formation to elements that share an index, it is easy to show that the relevant chains in (5) do not cross barriers. The first chain is $(V_i, t_{\underline{n}i}, t_i)$ which connects V_i to a trace with its (designated) index. The second chain is $(I_n, t_{\underline{n}i})$ which connects I with its trace. As a result, the derivation of the head movement constraint has become rather trivial. Consider (4) again which violates the head movement constraint because acyclic movement has generated the following representation of (4):

(8)

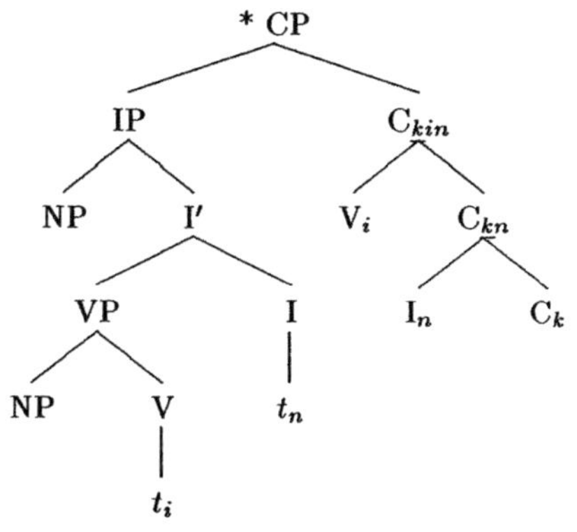

Since there is no way to bring t_i and t_n into a chain, this representation is ruled out by the ECP: t_n and $C_{\underline{k}in}$ are still distinct for t_i because t_n is not the trace of $C_{\underline{k}in}$. Therefore, IP is a barrier for the movement of V.

As it is clear from the exposition of our problem, chain formation as conceived above cannot exactly result from moving V through the position of the intermediate trace, because the trace is not the trace of V but rather the trace of V+I. Nevertheless, this less restricted kind of chain formation does a useful job in a representational theory: it ensures the locality of chain formation that has been obscured in a representation like (2).

Turning next to the problem of ergative verbs and NP movement, we will restate the condition that triggered the VP barrier between subject and object position. Applied to a representation like (5), the crucial condition that could block movement is that t_{ni} would not contain an element that is a member of a chain containing t_i. But since t_{ni} itself is an element in t_i's chain, t_i cannot be distinct from I for NP-movement. Therefore, the unwarranted barrier between the two NP positions has disappeared.

1.8 Base Generated Incorporation

A possible objection to the formalism proposed above could be that there is no need for multiple indices, if proper government is a derivational property of movement. In other words, the assignment of γ-features could apply immediately after movement of an item at any stage of a derivation. To see the advantage of a derivational approach to γ-assignment, note that we are able to find a derivation of NP-movement in the ergative-V-raising construction above that is consistent with Baker's definitions. We proceed in three steps and check proper government at three points of the derivation. First, we move the ergative V to I; next, we move the NP to the subject position, leaving behind the feature $[+\gamma]$; and finally we move I to C.

Indeed, such a solution would be simpler than the conventions governing multiple indices. But as has been shown by Lasnik & Saito (1984), this approach is not tenable, because γ-features must be assigned at a particular level. The intuitive reason is that we encounter an ordering problem for LF-movement of adjuncts. Since deletion of traces is an operation that links S-structure and LF, we might move adjuncts "too far", assign the feature $[-\gamma]$ to the trace, and finally delete the trace on the way to LF. Therefore, deletion of traces must precede γ-assignment. To avoid an ordering problem, the checking of proper government has to be on a level, not during a derivation.

Although Baker is in accord with Lasnik & Saito (1984), he claims that his theory provides strong evidence for an independent level like D-structure. Somewhat ironically, however, Baker does not give any real argument in favor of his view. The only thing he shows is that incorporation involves "move α" and therefore cannot be "base generated" in the sense of lexical theories that do not allow more abstract representations.

In fact, the only more explicit reasoning Baker offers is the following: "... it has been proposed within the GB framework that D-structure be dispensed with, and that the thematic information traditionally there be recovered by Chain Formation algorithms defined on S-structure (cf. Chomsky (1981, chapter 6), Rizzi (1983) [=Rizzi (1986)], Sportiche (1983)). But consider what implications this move would have for the analysis of complex examples of polysynthesis such as (1) from Southern Tiwa:

(1) Ti-seuan-p'akhu-kumwia-'am-ban wisi te-khaba-'i.
    1sS:A-man-bread-sell-CAUS-PAST two 1s:C-bake-SUBORD
    'I made the man sell the two breads that I baked.'

Grant that an algorithm could recognize all the morphemes and deduce from them the basic structure of the sentence by making use of the Projection Principle. This would get one as far as (2):

(2)

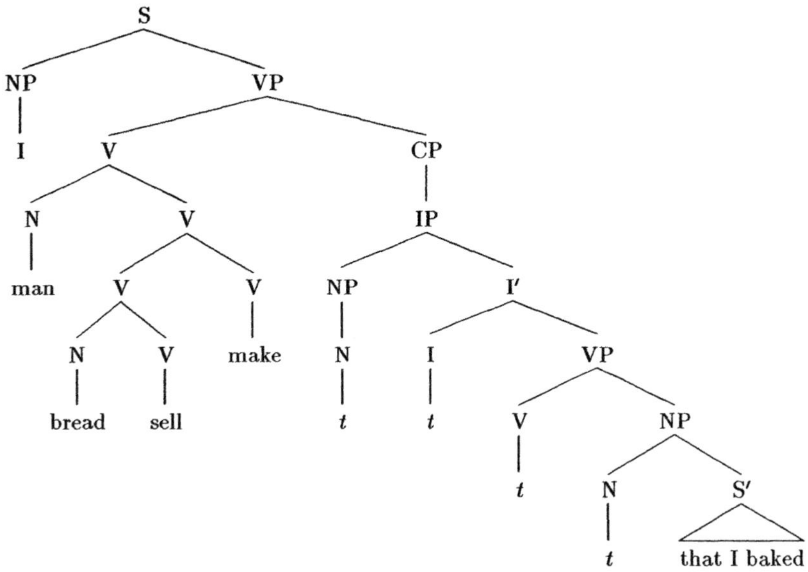

However, the algorithm still must correctly index the traces with the morphemes on the verb in such a way that 'man' is matched with the higher NP and 'bread' with the lower. Moreover, the algorithm must fail if the morphological structure of the complex verb in (2) is changed, thereby accounting for the ungrammaticality of the resulting sentence. No doubt an algorithm with these properties can be constructed, but it seems clear that it will not be a simple one, it will be arbitrary to a degree, and it will have the content of the Mirror Principle built into it rather explicitly." (p. 426f)

Contrary to what is conjectured by Baker, it is easy to see that no such problem will arise in the modification of his theory proposed above. Given the structure (2), we first label the lexical items by arbitrarily chosen indices. Next we project indices onto higher constituents, as has been proposed in Chapter 7 of Baker (1988). Analysing the example along the lines discussed on p. 378, Baker has to assume that the I-projection must be ignored. In the present framework no such ad-hoc stipulation is necessary. Indexing of heads and the percolation mechanism will analyse (2) as follows:

(3)

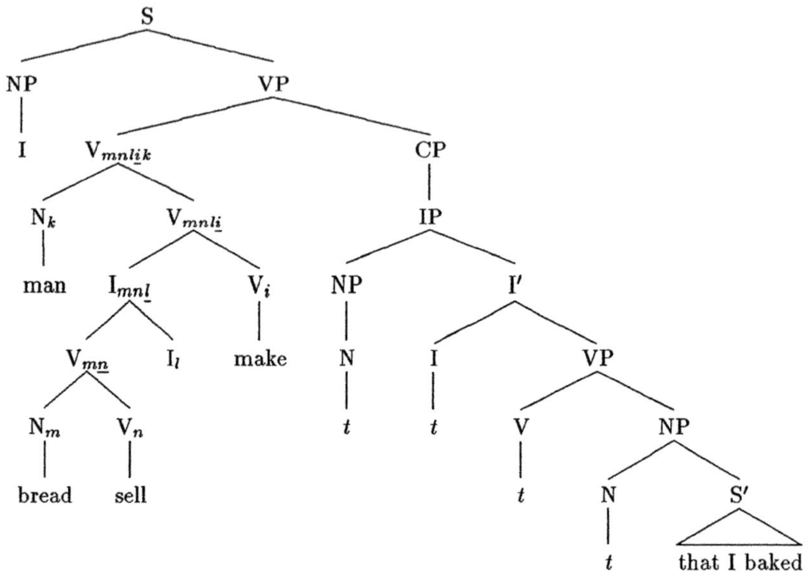

The last step is to correctly identify the traces. But this step is completely determined by the given structure: Arbitrary indexing and FCF will give exactly the correct results, which is achieved as a consequence of the ECP and the requirement that each trace must match an antecedent with identical indices. The only additional principle we must make explicit is (4):

(4) An adjoined head α must be linked to a trace β in a chain, such that the index of α is the designated index of β.

In order to make it plausible that assignment of indices is unique, let us see what happens if we assign the wrong indices to the N-traces:

(5)

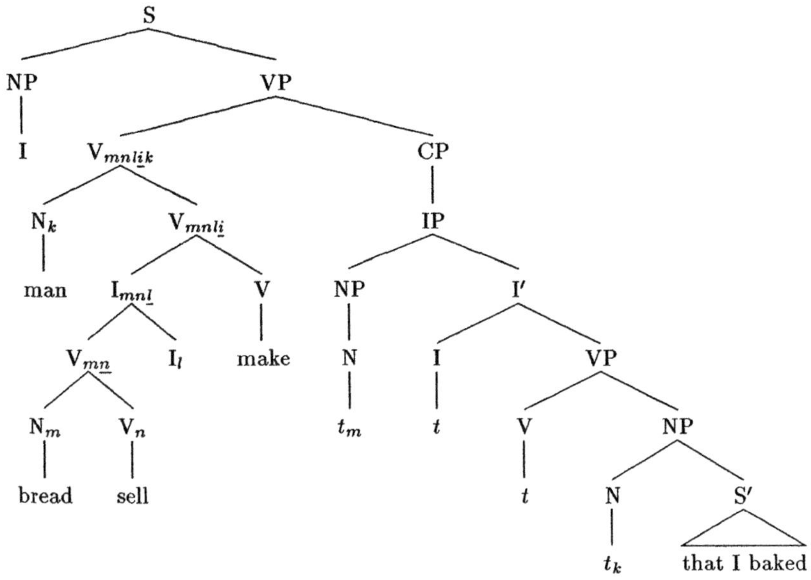

The problem now is to fill in additional indices in such a way that all traces are bound and have an "antecedent" that properly governs the trace. For the latter requirement, we have to find an antecedent for t_k, therefore the trace of *sell* must have the index k. If this were the only index of the trace, $sell_n$ could not be bound to a V-position with n as its designated index. We therefore have to assume that the trace of V is $t_{\underline{n}k}$. But this trace cannot have an antecedent in the tree. The only element that contains these indices is the matrix verb itself. But this element has i as its designated index. Therefore the assumption that the lower N has k as its index yields a contradiction. In fact, the only distribution of indices that would be allowed by the mechanism proposed is the intuitively correct one. The same conclusion could be drawn if we tried another "incorrect" distribution of indices. We can therefore safely conclude that the only correct indexing is the one that would also result from "real movement".

These considerations may suffice to show that Baker's claim cannot be substantiated by reference to computational difficulties. Another claim concerns the purported advantage of D-structure in that it is the one level that conforms to the principle of $\bar{X}$-theory. Proposals of this sort can often be found in the literature, nevertheless they seem to miss the point. In most modern theorizing, the Projection Principle guarantees that S-structure does not differ from D-structure except for adjunctions created by "move α". But since some amount of base generated adjunction has to be admitted in any theory of phrase structure, it seems that one has to clarify why certain adjunctions could *not* be base generated. The additional task of excluding these base generated adjunctions (while admitting base generated adjunctions of APs, relative clauses, modifiers, adverbs, APs, and other "recursive" categories) seems to be completely independent of $\bar{X}$-theory and might turn out as complicated as (or even equivalent to) the task of taking into account base generated adjunctions directly.

Likewise, no argument in favor of D-structure can be drawn from the assumption that this level is a "pure representation of θ-assignment". Since all θ-positions must be projected onto S-structure, there seems to be no point in "abstracting away" from S-structure by some mechanism that recovers D-structures again. At least, this will be unnecessary for the purpose of θ-assignment.

The arguments in this section have shown that structures that involve incorporation can be generated directly in the base. In section 2.4 I present some further evidence against a derivational treatment of incorporation.

1.9 D-Structure in GB

In the preceding sections I analysed a number of phenomena that could have an impact on the question of whether or not D-structure is a legitimate level of representation. Some arguments in favor of FCF can be reinterpreted in favor of a derivational concept of chain formation. This is clearly the case with the analyses proposed in the first two subsections. The latter sections provided evidence against a purely derivational concept of chain formation. Up to now we have not recognised any real argument that turns directly against the unification of D- and S-structure: FCF preserves all the advantages of derivation chain formation but does not presuppose it; in fact, I attempted to show in the last section that some extension of chain formation could have advantages over a purely derivational conception of chains.

I now turn to considerations that address the issue more directly, discussing in this final subsection the only presently still relevant arguments in favor of D-structure that can be found in Chomsky (1981).[6]

[6]I leave aside an argument concerning D-structure agreement (p. 259f) that presupposes the GB-account of pro-drop. Except for Chomsky (1982b), more recent developments unanimously reject this theory. (Cf. Adams (1987), Jaeggli (1984), Platzack (1986) Rizzi (1982a), Rizzi (1986a); see also Müller & Rohrbacher (1989) for a useful overview and Durie (1988) for another rejection of D-structure agreement.) Likewise, Chomsky's arguments on p. 203 of GB are inconsistent with the existence of parasitic gaps and can therefore be ignored. I also ignore his discussion of idioms, because it becomes inconclusive as soon as it is recognized that some amount of reconstruction is necessary in LF. There are two remaining arguments which will be discussed at length in the next two subsections.

1.9.1 The Non-Existence of 'SEEM'

Let me begin with Chomsky's proof that there cannot exist an intransitive verb "SEEM" which is like *seem* in that it induces $\bar{S}$-deletion, but which is unlike *seem* in that it assigns a θ-role to its subject position.

As it stands, this claim is too strong. A counterexample is provided by the causative verb *lassen* (to let) in German which can be analysed as having a θ-subject, inducing $\bar{S}$-deletion, but not being transitive, i.e. not being subcategorized for an NP. I therefore change Chomsky's formulation slightly by replacing "transitivity" with "Case assignment". We thus arrive at the following descriptive generalization:

(1) There is no verb V that triggers $\bar{S}$-deletion (i.e. selects IP), θ-marks its subject, but does not assign Case to the embedded subject governed by V.

To illustrate this claim, we construct a syntactic frame that permits insertion of a hypothetical verb exhibiting the properties described in (1). In order to obtain an argument in favor of the explanatory value of D-structure, we then have to show that the construction can be barred by independently motivated principles of a derivational theory which would imply (1) as a theorem.

Following GB, p. 112f, assume that English used *Jove* instead of *it* in expressions similar to *"it is raining"*, where *to rain* does not θ-mark the subject and *Jove* is an R-expression. Consider the D-structure (2) and the S-structure (3):

(2) $[_{NP}$ e] SEEMs $[_{CP}$ Jove to rain]

(3) $[_{NP}$ Jove$_i$] SEEMs $[_{IP}$ t_i to rain]

Since SEEM does not assign Case, (2) violates the Case Filter, therefore *Jove* has to move to the matrix subject position. The argument in favor of a derivational theory is drawn from the assumption that (2) cannot be a well-formed D-structure for (3). Since the θ-criterion applies at all levels of representation, (2) violates the θ-criterion on D-structure twice: The argument *Jove* is in a non-θ-position, whereas the non-argument e is in a θ-position.

On the other hand, it is easy to see that the chain in (3) does not violate the θ-criterion. This structure is well-formed with respect to the principles of grammar considered so far. Since only the D-structure is defective, it seems that we have a strong argument in support of D-structure and a derivational theory.

Let us examine the argument more closely. Clearly, it is legitimate to assume that (in one variant of GB) both the S-structure (3) and the D-structure (4) are well-formed representations:

(4) $[_{NP}$ Jove] SEEMs $[_{CP}$ e to rain]

In (4) the θ-criterion is satisfied, so neither (3) nor (4) could be barred by any principle that governs the well-formedness of representations. For Chomsky's argument to be valid, we have to establish that something has gone wrong with the mapping from (4) to (3): (4) cannot be the D-structure of (3); i.e. the derivation from (4) to (3) should not be allowed by the rule system of GB. In the context of his discussion of *SEEM* Chomsky did not explicitly show why (3) could not be derived *from (4)*. In another context (p. 203), he remarks: "Notice that it is the *derivation* ... just considered rather than the structure itself that must be barred. The structure itself does not violate any of the subsystems of principles ... of the GB-theory, but it is not derivable by the rule system of this theory."

An implicit answer to the problem at hand can be found in chapter 6 of GB, where Chomsky discusses two different versions of the notion "trace". Let us therefore speculate upon the appropriate pairings of D- and S-structure along the lines indicated there.

Suppose we proceed in the usual way, i.e. we build up the D-structure (4) and check it with respect to the relevant conditions. Next, we apply rules that convert (4) into (3). Two things could be done. First, we may coindex *Jove* and e. Next, we (contextually) classify empty categories. As it turns out, e is a trace, because e became bound as a result of free indexing. Next, we check S-structure conditions on binding, θ-marking, chain formation, etc. Up to now, everything is fine. But finally, we have to look at the pair ⟨D, S⟩. In order to establish that something went wrong "during the derivation", we have to observe that the trace is not the trace of *Jove*. To see this we move *Jove* back to the position of the trace and compare the resulting structure D′ (=2) with D (=3). If the reconstructed representation were in fact the D-structure source of the derivation, the derivation is well-formed (and t is "the trace of *John*").

To make this idea precise, we can exploit the idea of a *history-chain*. A history-chain is a chain which has resulted from real movement in a derivation.[7] We now represent the derivation of (3) from its D-structure source (2) as follows:

(3#) $[_{NP}$ #Jove#] SEEMs $[_{IP}$ #t# to rain]

By the conventions introduced above, the former representation (3) itself (as opposed to the representation (3#)) cannot result from movement, because it lacks a history chain. The chain in (3) must be the result of coindexing without movement. Let us assume now that each A-chain must be a history-chain.

[7] In accordance with the convention introduced in section 1.1, we will use the double-cross notation as a mnemonic device to represent "real" movement.

This requirement rules out (3) in a more or less informal way; in a more technical treatment one has to restrict free indexing in some way or another. Alternatively, we could modify the notion "trace", distinguishing the representational notion "trace", and the derivational notion "trace of". Formally, this would imply that an empty category could be a trace in a chain only if it has been given the #-mark at some previous stage of the derivation. It is not entirely clear how such proposals could be spelled out technically; but, for the sake of the argument, let us assume that in some way or another we can rule out "co-indexing chains" that fail to be history chains.

Having established that (3#) cannot be properly generated (because the derivation is ruled out by the θ-criterion on D-structure), we seem to have established that there is no proper way to derive the surface string *Jove SEEMs to rain.*

This does not completely solve the problem, however, because it still remains to be shown why the empty element [e] could not constitute a chain of its own. Informally speaking, this empty category must then be an expletive "small pro". Although English does not exhibit small pro's, it is clear that other languages do. We now have to show that there is no language which could have an element like *SEEM* that could license pro. But this is clearly contrary to the facts; German causative constructions exemplify embedded pro's in passive constructions like (5):

(5) Er lä"st $[_{IP}$ *pro* $[_{VP}$ ihr_{DAT} von niemandem]] helfen
He lets her by nobody help

'He doesn't allow anybody to help her'

The only way to derive theorem (1) from independently motivated principles is to require that pro needs Case, which in turn could be derived from the following principles of GB:[8]

(6) Each NP is an "element" of a chain.

(7) Each chain is "headed" by a Case marked position or by PRO.

Since the empty element governed by SEEM cannot be PRO, it needs Case. But *ex hypothesis* the matrix verb cannot assign Case. This contradiction rules out (3)/(4) as possible S-structures.

A proponent of a mono-representational theory will recall Chomsky's general condition on "CHAINs" in *Knowledge of Language* (1986). Since there is no

[8]The quotes indicate sloppyness of expression: strictly speaking, the positions are not elements of a chain, rather they are values of GFs that enter into chains.

D-structure in a non-derivational theory, a CHAIN is always generated by binding. By definition a well-formed chain must be headed by a Case-marked position (or PRO). Chomsky adds the requirement that a chain be *grounded* in a θ-position, a condition which was first formulated by Koster (1982/83) as a representational equivalent to the θ-criterion on D-structure, this requirement now being part of the θ-criterion:

(8) "If C = $(\alpha_1, ..., \alpha_n)$ is a maximal CHAIN, then α_n occupies its unique θ-position and α_1 its unique Case-marked position."
(Chomsky 1986: 137)

In a non-derivational theory, we have to argue as follows. Assume that *Jove* and [e] are not coindexed. As before, the second part of (8) rules out the Case-less element [e]. Next, consider the chain (*Jove*, *t*). This chain clearly violates the groundedness condition, i.e. the first part of (8), because the chain is headed by a θ-position α_1 and $\alpha_n = t$ is not θ-marked.

The discussion has shown that the relevant part of (8), namely groundedness, has to be stated as an independent principle of a representational theory T_r but can be derived in the derivational grammar T_d. This fact alone seems to suggest that – other things being equal – T_d is explanatorily superior and therefore should be preferred on methodological grounds. The argument is flawed, however, by the fact that T_d has to use additional machinery which is superfluous in T_r. It is not *a priori* clear, for instance, how #-chains should formally be defined, i.e. how these chains (as the formal S-structure object to which the θ-criterion has to apply) should be exactly represented on one level as an encoding of previous levels. In any case, we would have to add some otherwise unmotivated restrictions to T_d to the effect of ensuring that an alternative like T_r is not an available option of UG.

In addition, constraints such as the structure-preserving constraint or various versions of the Projection Principle are traditionally postulated in T_d-theories, whereas none of these devices makes sense in T_r. If one were to decide between both theories, it would be difficult to tell which one is really more explanatory. If elegance and simplicity is the only guide we have at present, it seems clear to me that one would prefer T_r – even at the risk of sacrificing explanatory power when it comes to explain the non-existence of SEEM.

1.9.2 Tough Movement

Chomsky's second example that crucially relies on the existence of D-structure is his derivational account of *tough* movement. The analysis involves the only non-trivial use of reanalyis in GB-theory. Consider the following derivation:

(1) (a) e is easy [$_{S'}$ PRO to please PRO] (D-structure)
(b) e is easy [$_{S'}$ #PRO$_i$# [$_S$ PRO to please #t_i#]] (movement)
(c) e is [$_{AP}$ [$_A$ easy to please] t_i] (reanalysis)
(d) John$_i$ is [[easy to please] t_i] (lexical insertion, S-structure)

Reanalysis generates a complex adjective *easy to please* and thereby eliminates the S-boundaries, the empty operator in COMP, and the PRO-subject. The resulting structure (c) is not well-formed, however, because the trace needs an argument as an antecedent. Therefore lexical insertion of a binder of the trace has to be permitted on the way to the final S-structure (d).

I do not want to go into the motivation for this analysis. The interesting feature of (1) consists in the fact that it violates otherwise well-motivated principles of GB and also our earlier assumptions about chain formation. First note that the structure (d) contains a chain which cannot be the result of movement. The existence of such a chain is inconsistent with the derivational theory reported in the last section. Ignoring this contradiction, Chomsky's analysis of *tough* movement, if correct, could supply further evidence against derivational chain formation.

On the other hand, we are about to show that D-structure can be dismissed with. Apart from this predominant objective, I would also prefer an alternative analysis that avoids a violation of the Extended Projection Principle. Moreover, Chomsky's analysis crucially relies on the possibility of lexical insertion in S-structure. Therefore we might suspect that one could do better with a theory where all lexical insertion occurs at S-structure.

A straightforward way to proceed is to assume that structures arising from operator movement into the embedded specifier position permit for a compositional θ-marking of the subject position. This is to say that the predicates *easy* and the CP "Op$_i$ PRO *to please* t_i" compositionally specify the θ-role of the subject John. No further change of the phrasal make-up of tough movement constructions would be required. We simply end up with a structure like (2):

(2) [John$_i$ is easy [Op_i [PRO to please t_i]]]

This analysis, however, does not express the intuition captured in (1c), namely, that the expression *easy to please* is a complex adjective that exhibits the distributional properties of simple adjectives:

(3) John is an easy to please guy

Note also that the type of analysis proposed in (2) permits unbounded dependencies created by long operator movement:

(4) John is easy to imagine to please

On the other hand, it has been observed by Nanni (1978) that this type of construction does not have the same distribution as the attributive adjectival construction, cf. (5):

(5) * John is an easy to try/imagine to please guy

In order to account for this difference is seems that we have to admit two different analyses; one that allows long operator movement as in (2) and one that more closely resembles Chomsky's original proposal but at the same time excludes unbounded dependencies. The difficulty is to account for this second derivation in a structure preserving way. To this end I want to propose an analysis along the lines of Baker (1988). First the embedded VP (or tense phrase) moves into the specifier position of the embedded clause, as shown in (6).

(6) e is easy $[_{CP}$ $[_{VP}$ to please John $]_i$ $[_{IP}$ PRO t_i]]

The representation (6) is somewhat imprecise, however, because according to traditional assumptions the [−tense] element *to* is generated outside VP. Assuming that *to* is generated as the head of a tense phrase inside and different from the IP (cf. Chomsky (1989)) it is actually this tense phrase that moves into SpecC. The notation "VP" then is misleading but has been adopted for convenience. Inside this phrase the verb can move to tense = *to*; again this type of movement has been omitted from the representation (6).

The next step is to incorporate a transitive verb into the adjective, this process being lexically governed by the matrix predicate. In particular, only those verbs can undergo incorporation into the *tough* movement class of adjectives that can be understood as specifying the agent's intention (cf. Nanni (1978)):

(7) e is $[_{AP}$ $[_{A}$ easy to please$_j$]$[_{CP}$ t_j John $[_{IP}$ PRO t_i]]] (incorporation)

According to Baker (1988), one effect of incorporation is that the verb loses its ability to assign Case. I have already indicated above that Case absorption is not necessarily a consequence of incorporation. Nevertheless, in the case at hand I assume that the adjective is "strong enough" to remove the trace's ability to assign Case. Therefore, the NP has to move into the subject position to get Case:

(8) John$_n$ is $[_{AP}[_{A}$ easy to please$_j$ $][_{CP}\ t_j\ t_n\ [_{IP}$ PRO t_i $]]]$ (NP-movement)

Note that this analysis is consistent with the theory of barriers in Chomsky (1986a). In GB the motivation for assuming an operator in (1b) has been derived from the observation that only non-idiomatic material can be bound by an empty operator. Therefore, only non-idiomatic material can undergo *tough* movement. An analogous restriction holds in (8), if one assumes that only non-idiomatic material can be separated from the verb by incorporation.

Although the details of this proposal will require some elaboration and the discussion of this type of construction is far from exhaustive, it is easy to see that the analysis does not violate the Extended Projection Principle. As we have pointed out in section 1.8, (8) can be directly generated by FCF; this result being obtained by re-analysing reanalysis as "structure preserving" incorporation. The details of the above analysis could be considered immaterial, however, because the main purpose of this subsection has been to prepare the reader for an analysis of data from a more exotic language (namely, German), which will exploit exactly the same mechanism that has been introduced in this section.

In the next sections I turn to another area of theorizing that crucially involves reanalysis and the distinction between levels. I reformulate a derivational approach to reanalysis in terms of a representational theory of incorporation. The analysis will avoid some pitfalls of the theory of reanalysis and will resemble the analysis of *tough* movement.[9]

2 Reanalysis and Incorporation

2.1 The Problem: A Construction from Züritüütsch

Züritüütsch, a dialect of Swiss German spoken in Zürich, provides us with another example of a phenomenon which has received different treatments in derivational and representational theories. We will see that the so-called Verb Raising Construction in Züritüütsch actually involves a kind of VP-raising quite similar to VP movement in *easy-to-please* constructions. Whereas this kind of raising is string-vacuous, VP raising will go further up into the matrix clause and has visible effects by reordering the matrix predicate and the embedded VP, as will be shown below.[10]

[9]The analysis could be presented as a part of this section. The complexity of the data and of existing grammatical descriptions, however, justify a new chapter that is completely devoted to this topic.

[10]For more extensive discussions of the data, cf. Lötscher (1978), den Besten & Edmondson (1981), Riemsdijk (1985), Haegeman & Riemsdijk (1986) – henceforth quoted as 'H&R' –,

Züritüütsch is similar to Dutch and standard German in having a rule commonly referred to as Verb Raising (VR). The analysis of verb clusters in terms of raising was first proposed by Evers (1975). The main effect of this movement rule is to create a cluster of verbs, traditionally called the "Verbal Field" (cf. Bech (1955/57)). Evers' rule of VR removes a verb from an embedded infinitival construction, thereby creating a headless clause which triggers a subsequent rule of tree pruning and clause union. Pruning of the embedded S-node reflects the fact that this type of complex construction is in many respects mono-clausal (cf. Grewendorf (1987)). Accommodating Evers' analysis into the framework of trace theory, his derivation of (1) will be represented by something like (2):

(1) da"s Johann arbeiten will
that John work wants

'that John wants to work'

(2) (a) da"s Johann [$_{S'}$[$_S$ PRO arbeiten]] will (D-structure)
(b) da"s Johann [$_{S'}$[$_S$ PRO t]] [arbeiten will] (V-raising)
(c) da"s Johann [arbeiten will] (pruning of S-labelled nodes)

In Dutch it is almost obligatory to reverse the order of verbs. In terms of V-raising, adjunction will not only be to the left of the matrix verb but in many cases also obligatorily to the right. The same holds in standard German if more than two verbs are involved; cf. (3a) which is derived from (3b):

(3) (a) da"s Johann wird/hat arbeiten wollen
that John will/has (to-)work wanted

(b) da"s Johann arbeiten wollen wird/*hat

Züritüütsch is unlike Dutch and German, however, in that the embedded constituent affected by the adjunction rule can be a projection of V, i.e. V′ or a VP. Hence, in the surface order of these Verb Projection Raising (VPR) constructions, indirect or direct objects may appear between the elements of the verbal cluster. Schematic examples are given in (4) and (5), where (4) represents the underlying source of the permutations shown in (5):

(4) COMP SUBJ [[IO [DO V_1]] V_2] V_3
das er em Karajan en arie vorsinge chöne wil
that he (to) K. an aria sing-for can wants

'that he wants to be able to sing an aria for Karajan.'

Koster (1987, ch. 5), or Cooper (1988). Our presentation will closely follow Riemsdijk (1985); the discussions in sections 2.3ff. are largely adopted from v. Stechow & Sternefeld (1988, ch. 12)).

(5) (a)	COMP	SUBJ	IO	DO	V_3			V_2			V_1
(b)	COMP	SUBJ	IO		V_3		DO	V_2			V_1
(c)	COMP	SUBJ			V_3	IO	DO	V_2			V_1
(d)	COMP	SUBJ	IO		V_3			V_2		DO	V_1
(e)	COMP	SUBJ			V_3	IO		V_2		DO	V_1
(f)	COMP	SUBJ			V_3			V_2	IO	DO	V_1

As an example of a derivation in terms of Verb Projection Raising (VPR), consider the generation of (5d). VPR will first adjoin the complex DO+V_1 to V_2, which yields (6a), where the newly formed constituent is marked by curly brackets:

(6) (a) COMP SUBJ IO [$_{V2}$ { V_2 DO V_1 }] V_3

The complex constituent V_2 = [V_2 DO V_1] will then be adjoined to the right of V_3. The result is (d), which is spelled out as (6b):

(6) (b)	das	er	em Karajan	{	wil [	chöne [	en arie	vorsinge]] }
	COMP	SUBJ	IO		V_3	V_2	DO	V_1

A purported difficulty for this analysis arises from (5b). The reader should verify for himself that rightward adjunction is not able to derive (5b) in the VPR-analysis. Hence, H&R propose a rule of reanalysis which first derives the clustering of verbs independently from the inversion of constituents: It is only in PF that inversion rules may permute the immediate constituents of a complex verbal constituent. As an illustration of their analysis, consider the derivation of (5b). In the first cycle, reanalysis applies to (7a) and yields the intermediate structure (7b), with newly formed constituents represented again by curly brackets:

(7) (a) COMP SUBJ [$_{CP}$ PRO [$_{CP}$ PRO IO DO V_1] V_2] V_3

(b) COMP SUBJ [$_{CP}$ PRO {IO {DO {V_1 V_2}}}] V_3

The exact mechanism of reanalysis seems to be the following: First one has to form the complex constituent (V_1 V_2), thereby erasing the projections of the verbs and the inner clausal structure of V_1. Next, the structure is rebuilt according to the principles of $\bar{X}$-theory (cf. also section 1.5).

The second application of reanalysis yields two further newly created constituents by bringing together V_3 and the first projection of [$V_1 V_2$]:

(7) (c) COMP SUBJ { IO {[DO [V_1 V_2]] V_3 }}

In the second cycle, reanalysis has formed a complex constituent out of V_3 and the former result of reanalysis [DO V_1 V_2] which had already been built up in (7b). Cyclic inversion in PF then yields the following representations:

(7) (d) COMP SUBJ [IO [[DO #[V_2 V_1]#] V_3]]
(e) COMP SUBJ [IO #[V_3 [DO [V_2 V_1]]]#] (=5b)

I have already discussed some of the problematic properties of this derivation in section 1.5. In the next section I go on to show that reanalysis can be dispensed with in favor of incorporation. I also attempt to show that such a theory is conceptually and empirically superior to the H&R theory of reanalysis.

2.2 The Koster-Riemsdijk Debate

The preceding analysis, if correct, presents a challenge for a mono-representational theory, because, in a sense, it is essentially derivational. Thus, "non-derivationalists" like Koster have to claim that (5b) does not pose any problem to an adjunction analysis à la Evers (1975) or den Besten & Edmondson (1981). Since adjoined structures could as well be base-generated directly, VPR constructions cannot give impetus to a derivational theory, if they could in fact be derived without reanalysis. In order to show that VPR *can* derive (5b), Koster (1987) proceeds as follows (for ease of exposition we will present his analysis in derivational terms). First, we apply VPR to the underlying structure (7a), repeated here as (1a).

(1) (a) COMP SUBJ [$_{CP}$ PRO [$_{CP}$ PRO IO DO V_1] V_2] V_3
(b) COMP SUBJ [$_{CP}$ PRO [$_{CP}$ PRO IO #*t*#] { #DO V_1# V_2 }] V_3

The output of adjunction is indicated by curly brackets; movement is indicated by #. At the intermediate cycle, we adjoin V_1 to V_2:

(1) (c) COMP SUBJ [$_{CP}$ PRO [$_{CP}$ PRO IO *t*] [DO #*t*# { #V_1# V_2 }]] V_3

We apply VPR again and adjoin the whole cluster to the matrix verb:

(1) (d) COMP SUBJ [$_{CP}$ PRO [$_{CP}$ PRO IO *t*] #*t*#] {#[DO *t* [$V_1$$V_2$]]# V_3}

Finally we apply inversion rules of PF:

(1) (e) COMP SUBJ [$_{CP}$ PRO [$_{CP}$ PRO IO *t*] *t*] [[DO *t* #[$V_2$$V_1$]#] V_3]
(f) COMP SUBJ [$_{CP}$ PRO [$_{CP}$ PRO IO *t*] *t*] #[V_3 [DO *t* [$V_2$$V_1$]]]#
(=5b)

This analysis shows that reanalysis can be dismissed in favor of movement. It should be noted, however, that (1) does not precisely report Koster's analysis as he does not assume the existence of a CP boundary between the verbs of a coherent construction. I will comment on this unusual feature of his analysis in the following sections. The crucial property of this analysis is independent from this aspect; it consists of separating VPR from inversion.

Given the trace theory of movement, we can easily generate (1d) or (1f) directly as surface structures. However, the analysis has an apparent disadvantage. Deriving these structures by movement would imply a violation of Chomsky's principle that intermediate projections are inaccessible for movement. Base-generation, on the other hand, will imply a violation of an extended version of $\bar{X}$-theory that allows adjunction of heads and phrases, but forbids adjunction of intermediate projections. In section 2.4, I show how to avoid these violations of otherwise well-motivated principles of UG.

In response to Koster, Riemsdijk (1985) argues against this proposal by pointing out some properties of adjunction which he takes to speak against VPR:

(2) (a) Reanalysis must be string-vacuous but adjunction must not.
(b) Reanalysis is cyclic but adjunction in (1) is not.
(c) Reanalysis is deterministic but adjunction is not.

All by itself the first alleged counter-argument does not have any force. It presupposes that a theory which blocks string-vacuous adjunction is more restrictive than one that does not. But anyone who argues against reanalysis, i.e. who argues in favor of a mono-representational VPR-theory, has to admit string-vacuous adjunction. So the real question should be whether such a theory is less restrictive than one which is derivational and employs reanalysis. In other words, we have to compare the following two theories:

(3) (a) derivational: no string-vacuous adjunction, (string-vacuous) reanalysis.
(b) representational: no reanalysis, (string-vacuous) adjunction.

At first sight, it appears as if both theories were on a par. Upon closer examination, however, one has to take into account that movement is narrowly restricted by the ECP, implying a number of empirical restrictions to the effect that incorporation cannot cross barriers. For illustration consider infinitival subjects as in (4). (4a) shows a D-structure source of reanalysis; (b) shows that the subject clause must be an island for scrambling. In (c) it is shown that – in contrast to the grammatical cases of complex predicates – the hypothetical verbal complex cannot undergo topicalization. Sentence (d) illustrates that negation cannot have scope over the matrix predicate. These effects could not be observed if reanalysis with the matrix predicate were possible.

(4) (a) da"s (ihr) [$_{CP}$ PRO den Schmuck zu besitzen] gefallen hat
that her the jewellery to own pleased has

(b) * da"s den Schmuck ihr zu besitzen gefallen hat

(c) * Zu besitzen gefallen hat (ihr) den Schmuck

(d) da"s (ihr) den Schmuck nicht zu besitzen gefallen hat

The movement theory correctly predicts that no verb can incorporate the predicate of an embedded subject clause, because movement would have to cross a barrier. No such restrictions have yet been formulated for reanalysis. Everything else being equal we must conclude that adjunction is more restrictive than an unrestricted mechanism of reanalysis.

Riemsdijk's second argument partially rests on a *petitio in principii.* It simply presupposes that a mono-representational theory has to embody some version of the principle of cyclicity. But for one thing, this cannot simply be presupposed, since the cycle is a *derivational* constraint; for another thing, a derivation that obeys the principle does indeed exist. The crucial point is illustrated by the step from (1b) to (1c), where adjunction takes place entirely within an already created verb cluster. This step violates the "strict cycle condition" as stated in Riemsdijk (1985):

(5) No rule may apply within a domain A, A minimal, when previously in the derivation a rule has applied within domain B, B minimal, and B contains A.

Even if something like the cycle were operative in a mono-representational theory, it is easy to see that Riemsdijk's criticism concerns just one particular derivation but not VPR in general. This immediately suggests a reversal of the order of rule application by first adjoining V_1 to V_2 in the lowest cycle and then adjoining the constituent [DO *t*] to the newly created verb cluster:

(6) (a) COMP SUBJ [$_{CP}$ PRO [$_{CP}$ PRO IO [DO V_1]] V_2] V_3

(b) COMP SUBJ [$_{CP}$ PRO [$_{CP}$ PRO IO [DO #*t*#]] #V_1# V_2] V_3

(c) COMP SUBJ [$_{CP}$ PRO [$_{CP}$ PRO IO #*t*#] #[DO *t*]# [V_1 V_2]] V_3

Since (6c) is identical with (1c), the derivation can proceed exactly as before. But this derivation clearly obeys the strict cycle condition. I conclude that the second objection doesn't bear any weight either.

The third objection is that Koster's method, i.e. string-vacuous VPR, will produce multiple derivations in many cases. Not surprisingly, however, the same can be shown for reanalysis. Suppose that inversion is optional, as it is the case for a number of control verbs in Dutch and Züritüütsch. The same string can be parsed ambiguously, depending on the option of applying reanalysis or not. What is even worse, reanalysis itself can be applied ambiguously, depending on which level of projection is reanalysed. Taking sentence (7) as an example from standard German, the structures in (8) are the outputs of reanalyzing different projections. These results may in turn serve as the underlying sources for different topicalizations in the verb-second main clauses (9):

(7) *D-structure source:*

weil der Jockel dem Karajan ein Lied vorsingen können wollen hat
because (ART) John (to) Karajan a song present be-able want has

(8) *different (re-)analyses:*

(a) weil der Jockel [dem Karajan ein Lied vorsingen können] wollen hat

(b) weil der Jockel dem Karajan [ein Lied vorsingen können] wollen hat

(c) weil der Jockel dem Karajan ein Lied [vorsingen können wollen] hat

(9) *different topicalizations:*

(a) [Dem Karajan ein Lied vorsingen] hat der Jockel können wollen.

(b) [Ein Lied vorsingen können] hat der Jockel dem Karajan wollen.

(c) [Vorsingen können wollen] hat der Jockel dem Karajan ein Lied.

If Riemsdijk agrees that scrambling is an adjunction rule, we immediately face another source of problems for this kind of determinism. For illustration consider the order DO IO which is usually derived via adjunction to VP. We may either move the DO across the IO or we may move both:

(10) (a) SUBJ DO_i $[_{VP}$ IO t_i V]

(b) SUBJ DO_i IO_j $[_{VP}$ t_j t_i V]

The second derivation could of course be blocked as it is string vacuous with respect to IO_j and t_j. However, consider a passivized sentence, i.e. a structure with no θ-marking of the subject position and no Case marking of the DO (if there is one). In German the DO may remain *in situ*, getting Case via coindexation with the empty subject. The DO may also move in front of an IO. The grammar will allow for three different analyses, two of them generated by scrambling and one by NP-raising:

(11) (a) SUBJ=[e] DO_i [$_{VP}$ IO t_i V] (scrambling to VP)
(b) DO_i [$_{IP}$ SUBJ=[e] [$_{VP}$ IO t_i V]] (scrambling to IP)
(c) [$_{IP}$ SUBJ_i=DO [$_{VP}$ IO t_i V]] (raising)

The DO may either adjoin to VP, to IP, or it may move into the subject position. Since movement is not string-vacuous in these cases, we end up with three possible structures but only one string.

These elementary examples suggest that it is more difficult to rule out a non-deterministic analysis on principled grounds than to accept it. Consequently, I cannot take it for granted (as Riemsdijk obviously does) that determinacy is a desirable goal or a criterion to test theories. Nor can I agree "that there are good reasons for excluding an analysis of the type Koster proposes on principled grounds." (ibid. p. 23)

2.3 Reanalysis: Its Place in a Derivational Theory

In this section, I report an argument by v. Stechow & Sternefeld (1988) which was designed to show that reanalysis defines a new level of representation. To establish this, it is sufficient to show that reanalysis can apply properly only after S-structure properties were checked. If reanalysis were to apply on the way from D-structure to S-structure, so the argument goes, we would give up the formal means for distinguishing between raising, control, and Exceptional Case Marking. For example, consider constructions with passivized control verbs. Unless one makes additional assumptions, there is no way to block the derivation from the D-structures (1) to the S-structures (2):

(1) (a) da"s [$_{IP}$ e [$_{VP}$[$_{CP}$ Hans arbeiten] gewollt wurde]]
that Hans work wanted was

(b) da"s [$_{IP}$ e [$_{VP}$[$_{CP}$ Hans zu arbeiten] gewünscht wurde]]
that Hans to work wished was

(2) (a) * da"s [$_{IP}$ Hans [$_{VP}$ arbeiten gewollt wurde]]
(b) * da"s [$_{IP}$ Hans [$_{VP}$ zu arbeiten gewünscht wurde]]

Reanalysis of (1) as (2) "raises" the D-structure subject *Hans*, this raising being induced either by movement or by projecting the subject GF onto the matrix position. Of course, movement in itself would not be allowed by the ECP, since it leaves an "ungoverned trace". As has been argued by Lasnik & Saito (1984), this property has to be checked within a level. But on the relevant level, which is shown in (2), the offending trace has been "deleted" by GF-projection.

One could object that GF-projection in (2) should be ruled out by the θ-criterion: The subject position must be a non-argument position qua subject of the passivized verb, but it must simultaneously be an argument position qua subject position of the embedded verb. The first requirement is violated since *Hans* is an argument. This reasoning is correct, but it does not prevail, however, if we look at the following derivations from (a) to (b):

(3)
(a) da"s *e* [*e* gearbeitet zu werden] gewünscht wurde (D-structure)
that worked to be wished was

(b) * da"s *e* [gearbeitet zu werden gewünscht wurde] (S-structure)

(4) (a) da"s Hans [PRO schnarchen] hört (D-structure)
that Hans snore hears

(b) * da"s Hans [schnarchen hört] (S-structure)

In (3) reanalysis has projected a non-argument position onto another non-argument position, whereas in (4) it has projected an argument-position onto another argument position resulting in a structure which should, if interpretable at all, mean that Hans hears *himself* snoring. In both cases the underlying D-structures are well-formed and so are the resulting S-structures. Nevertheless, the sentences are completely ungrammatical.

The ungrammaticality of (4) also shows that it is problematic to maintain the view advocated by Koster (1984) that coherent infinitives embed a governed PRO. If PRO could be governed by the matrix verb, this position could also be properly governed in ungrammatical raising constructions like (2), which now has to be analysed as (5):

(5) * weil Hans [$_{IP}$ *t* zu arbeiten] gewünscht wurde

It has been extensively argued in v. Stechow & Sternefeld (1988) and in v. Stechow (1989) that there is no straightforward way to distinguish this construction from grammatical cases of raising in non-control structures. As a result, we assumed that reanalysis must be a "late" rule that applies after S-structure conditions like the ECP, the θ-criterion or restrictions of Case theory have been checked. To see the effects of this proposal, assume that the derivations (3) and (4) have to pass through an intermediate level of representation between the levels shown in (3)/(4)(a) and (b):

(3) (c) * da"s [*e*] [$_{CP}$ PRO gearbeitet zu werden] gewünscht wurde

(4) (c) * da"s Hans$_i$ [$_{IP}$ PRO$_i$ schnarchen] hört

In (3c) the subject position is ungoverned and must be PRO. By definition PRO is an argument. The embedded passive cannot assign a θ-role to PRO, therefore this level of representation is ruled out by the θ-criterion. In (4c) $\bar{S}$-deletion has applied. Since both the matrix verb and the embedded verb assign a θ-role to their subject positions, these positions enter into one-element-chains. Applying standard definitions again, we can conclude from the argumenthood of the empty category that this element must be PRO. But as already presupposed above, we require PRO to be ungoverned. Only if PRO resists government will the construction be correctly blocked by the θ-criterion and by the definition of empty categories.

Koster (1984) comments upon the problem of control versus raising when discussing the ungrammaticality of *$John_i$ *was tried* t_i *to win*, which can be regarded as the English analogue of (2). He requires that governed PRO must be bound in its minimal governing category. "This means that there must be an obligatory c-commanding antecedent. *John* is the only NP that fulfills these conditions. But *John* is not the controller according to the independent theory of control, so the sentence is ruled out." (p. 431)

I cannot see how this explanation could work unless we presuppose that the empty element is PRO rather than trace. This must be a descriptive requirement which is bound to the presence of a control verb. The next step is to require an antecedent with an independent θ-role. In German, the analogue of *It was tried to win* is completely grammatical, so Koster's requirement that the antecedent must be explicit does not hold in general, rather it is an ad-hoc statement of the facts observed in the construction at hand. Furthermore, this kind of explanation does not carry over to examples like (4c); some additional lexical statement is called for. Lexical assumptions and construction specific ad-hoc statements must compensate for the loss of structure, and it seems that the reformulation of structural conditions can only be done in an unilluminating, hardly explanatory way. Moreover, it is shown in the next section that this explanation will lead to empirical problems when it comes to explain "long distance passives" in German.

H&R avoid these pitfalls because they adopt Huybregts' (1985) theory of "coanalysis", where both levels are represented as if they together represented an S-structure. Nevertheless, multi-dimensional representations increase the expressive power of UG and therefore require independent justification. The only motivation given in H&R seems to be that properties of quantifier scope should be read off from both representations. This theory encounters a number of difficulties, however, as has been pointed out by Haegeman (1988). We will see below that these problems can be solved in a theory that does not require multiple representations.

2.4 Incorporation and Dislocated VPs

In v. Stechow & Sternefeld (1988), H&R's theory was criticised as too complicated a description of the facts. The reason is that H&R did not take into account the possibility of scrambling in German and Züritüütsch. We conjectured that the order of objects in VPR-constructions is fairly free, so that it should be possible to derive more word order variants than shown in section 2.1. This prediction is fully borne out by the facts (cf. Cooper (1988) for a comprehensive description of the data). An alternative distribution of objects in Züritüütsch is shown in (1):

(1)	(a)	COMP	SUBJ	DO	IO	V_3			V_2			V_1
	(b)	COMP	SUBJ	DO		V_3		IO	V_2			V_1
	(c)	COMP	SUBJ			V_3	DO	IO	V_2			V_1
	(d)	COMP	SUBJ	DO		V_3			V_2		IO	V_1
	(e)	COMP	SUBJ			V_3	DO		V_2		IO	V_1
	(f)	COMP	SUBJ			V_3			V_2	DO	IO	V_1

In addition, it is possible to scramble objects in front of the subject. To derive the full range of data, one only has to assume that the base generated order [VP V] can be changed into [V VP]. Successive reordering derives the sequence of elements displayed in (1f). Subsequently, an independently motivated rule of Scrambling shifts objects to the left by adjunction to VP. Depending on which NP is scrambled to which VP, we can derive any of the grammatical variants attested by Cooper (1988).

Apart from being too restrictive, the H&R theory of reanalysis also makes wrong predictions not made by the scrambling account sketched above. Consider again the order of constituents in (1g):

(1) (g) COMP SUBJ IO V_3 DO V_2 V_1

The mechanism of H&R implies that the IO remains *in situ*, whereas the scrambling account claims that it has been adjoined to the matrix VP. As it is well-known from the literature on basic word order, NPs which are not scrambled can be stressed (cf. Lenerz (1977)). Therefore, the H&R theory would predict that the IO can receive stress because it has not moved. But as Geilfu"s (1989) pointed out with respect to similar examples in Yiddish, this prediction is incorrect. Lötscher (1978) observed that focus or stress can be on an object that precedes V_3 V_2 V_1, but he did not investigate the splitting of objects in (1g), where the most natural stress position is on the direct object. The impossibility of focussing the IO can therefore be explained by the assumption that IO has been scrambled (cf. Müller/Sternefeld (1990) for a derivation of this descriptive generalization from principles of UG). No such explanation is available in the theory of H&R.

If correct, this view could restore an adjunction analysis à la Evers. Assume that we proceed as in our earlier analysis of *tough* movement, i.e. we first move a VP to a SpecC position adjacent to the matrix predicate:

(2)

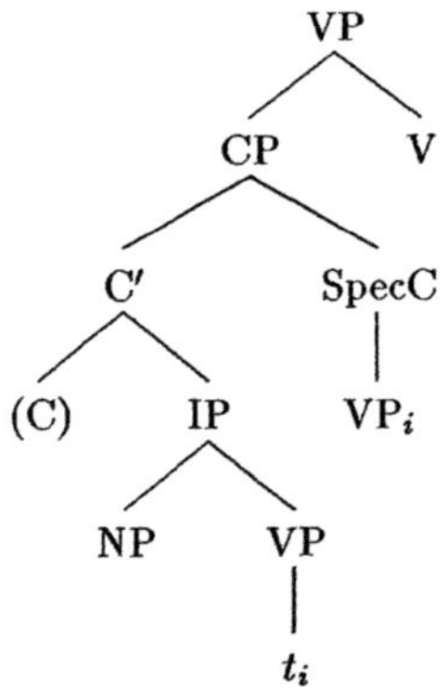

If V is a control verb, the CP has a "visible" head and the NP must be PRO, because it is protected from government by the joint presence of C, CP, and IP (cf. Baker (1988) and our discussion of *tough* movement). In contrast, the phonologically visible parts of the structure behave as if they were mono-clausal. We can therefore adjoin V to the V of the matrix clause, or we could move VP to the matrix VP, because CP is no barrier for anything within SpecC (cf. Chomsky (1986), Baker (1988)). The discussion of VPR has shown that in Züritüütsch both options are available. In Sternefeld (1990), I pointed out that it is even possible to move an object of the embedded verb to the matrix subject position, as in so-called "long-distance passives" in German:

(3) da"s der Wagen$_i$ [$_{CP}$ [$_{IP}$ PRO [$_{VP}$ t_j]] [$_{VPj}$ t_i t_k]]
that the car$_{NOM}$

[zu reparieren$_k$ versucht wurde]
to repair tried was

Zu reparieren has been incorporated into the passivized matrix verb. As a lexical (and somewhat marked) property of *versuchen* I assume that it can absorb the capacity of the trace of the incorporated *reparieren* to assign structural Case. Therefore, the object must move into the subject position of the matrix clause. In contrast to Baker, I assume that Case absorption is a marked property. It does not apply in other cases of V-movement in German such as verb second movement. If Case assignment is not blocked, we also have to revise Baker's theory in assuming that head movement cannot always remove a barrier for Case assignment. On the other hand, a number of languages (including German) exhibit Case absorption when V is incorporated into passive morphology, in which case the passive marker *werden* ('to be') absorbs accusative Case (with raising to subject as the usual consequence of Case absorption). Again, this seems to be a marked property of some languages. In many other languages passive morphology does not prevent a verb from assigning structural Case.

Returning briefly to Koster's (1984) account of coherent infinitives, we observe that in his analysis (reported in the last section) sentence (3) would either get the wrong meaning (with *the car* controlling PRO) or should not be interpretable at all. I conclude that his requirement that PRO must have an overt controller is in contrast to the facts. This destroys the basis for Koster's explanation of ungrammatical raising in control structures.

I now turn to H&R's motivation for allowing different dimensions of S-structure representations as inputs to LF. Basically, the reason for this is connected with the purported ambiguity of (4); the example is taken from West Flemish, cf. Haegeman (1988):

(4) da Jan Valère geen vlees liet eten
that Jan Valère no meet lets eat

It is claimed that *geen vlees* can have wide or narrow scope with respect to *liet*. Narrow scope can be read directly off a representation that "precedes" reanalysis, whereas wide scope can be read off the reanalysed structure, where the negated NP c-commands the matrix verb. In short, the theory rather naïvely presupposes that quantifier scope is a matter of (coanalysed) S-structure rather than LF.

In a mono-representational structure that presupposes VP movement, (4) can be represented as in (5):

(5) da Jan [$_{CP}$ [$_{IP}$ Valère t_i]][$_{VPi}$ geen vlees t_j]] liet eten$_j$

I assume that *eten* has been incorporated on the right side of *liet*. The command relations in (5) show that *geen vlees* c-commands t_j. By reconstruction of V-movement in LF, we predict that *geen vlees* can have scope over *eten*. Since *liet* c-commands *geen vlees*, it must have narrow scope. Wide scope can be derived by May's (1985) rule of quantifier raising (QR). QR can adjoin *geen vlees* to the matrix VP, so that *geen vlees* can gain wide scope over *liet* in LF. Alternatively, we could also assume that QR has applied "overtly" in S-structure, such that *Valère* and *geen vlees* are scrambled into the matrix clause. In the theory of QR, narrow scope is predicted when the negated NP adjoins only to the lower VP.

To get the effects of H&R's treatment of scope, we have to assume in addition that inverted material like the direct object in (6) is "frozen" for QR; it cannot be moved in LF to get wide scope:

(6) da Jan [$_{CP}$ [$_{IP}$ Valère t_i]][$_{VP}$ t_i]] liet [$_{VPi}$ geen vlees eten]

Geen vlees cannot be moved to get scope over *liet.* As has been pointed out in Lerner & Sternefeld (1984), this might be a consequence of Lötscher's (1978) observation that the extraposed material in VPR-constructions is focussed. In Lerner & Sternefeld (1984), a kind of freezing principle was employed to explain certain facts concerning the scope of negation in coherent infinitival constructions. The principle itself, namely, that the material within a focussed constituent must be interpreted *in situ* and resists movement out of the focussed constituent, cannot be explained by structural means but could be a consequence of functional considerations.

As a direct consequence of this assumption, we can also derive Haegeman's observation that the relative scope of the extraposed NPs in (7a) must be fixed, whereas it can be variable in (7b):

(7) (a) dan ze gingen al de studenten geenen boek geven
that they went all the students no book give
(b) dan ze al de studenten geenen boek geven
that they all the students no book give

In (a), *geenen boek* cannot get wide scope over *al de studenten. Prima facie*, these facts argue against a theory that treats inversion on the PF-side of the grammar. In the above analysis V incorporation or VP-raising applies on S-structure. Given the trace theory of movement, this account is essentially mono-representational. It does not require the dynamics of derivation nor does it imply additional levels of representation. The effects of "inversion" can therefore be read off the surface. We moreover predict that "inversion" will not be a rule of PF.

Up to this point we have not discussed the details of phrase structural configurations that result from inversion in S-structure. Current theories of VPR (now read: VP-raising) and Chomsky's (1986) generalized Structure-Preserving Constraint will yield a structure like (8) as a result of VPR, with the more "deeply" embedded VP now appearing adjoined to the right of the matrix VP:

(8)

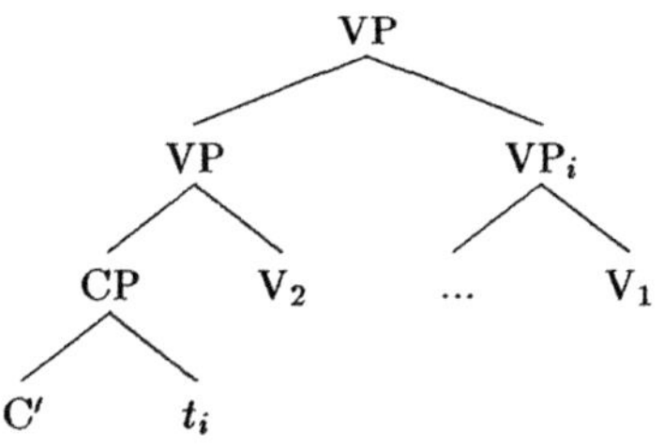

Above, we have seen that VP$_i$ must be transparent for movement; in particular it should be possible to move an NP directly from inside VP$_i$ to the operator position SpecC as in the following structure of a relative clause:

(9)

die$_j$ er h"at [$_{VP}$ [$_{VP}$ [$_{CP}$ ... t_i] welle] [$_{VPi}$ em Karajan t_j vorsingen]]
which he had wanted to Karajan sing-for

Since VP$_i$ must be transparent for movement, it must not constitute a barrier. The derivation of the required transparency of the embedded VP will lead to a number of problems, however.

First, the landing site of VP-movement is not selected or L-marked. Therefore, VP$_i$ should be a barrier for movement. This result is unexpected in the theories proposed in Sternefeld (1989) and M"uller & Sternefeld (1990), where operator movement cannot use adjunction to VP as an escape route. Next, VP is also a barrier by minimality. In our theory the only way to circumvent this barrier is head movement or incorporation. We therefore assumed that the head of VP$_i$ has to be incorporated into the head of the next maximal projection, in accordance with the head movement constraint (cf. Chomsky (1986)).

This process of incorporation can be either overt, as with V to I raising, or abstract, as in coherent infinitives in German. According to the considerations above we would expect that V$_1$ can be incorporated into V$_2$, which means that V$_2$ should actually be $V_{\underline{2}1}$ (cf.section1.8). But this kind of abstract incorporation seems to be blocked again by lack of L-marking or selection. This problem can be overcome, however, if it is assumed that L-marking of the trace of VP_i can be inherited by its antecedent in the process of rightward movement, as seems to be independently required in other cases of adjunction to VP, in particular in the case of extraposition of clausal complements.

Given this assumption, the VP can no longer be a barrier by lack of selection. However, VP still remains to be a barrier by minimality that has to be opened by head movement or abstract incorporation. But for this process the VP itself must not be a barrier for the head of VP. Given that no barrier can intervene between the two verbs, incorporation should be possible. Nevertheless, there still remains a problem which arises from the observation that overt incorporation into a verb from a postverbal position adjoined to VP must be blocked. This has been shown by reference to clitic movement in Italian:

(10) * pro^j [$_{VP}$ [$_{VP}$ [$_V$ ne_i telefonano]] [$_{NP}$ molti t_i]^j
of-them phone many

In order to block clitic movement out of an adjunct, Chomsky (1981) assumed some strict version of c-command for binding the trace t_i. Of course, one could wonder why the same restriction should not hold for abstract incorporation. V_2 in (8) does not even m-command V_1, therefore incorporation (whether overt or not) should be blocked by the same mechanism that blocks (10).

To solve the problem, one could assume that VPR is not adjunction to VP but must be adjunction to V. If this were true, we would have to give up the restriction that only heads can be incorporated into heads. A more interesting solution will avoid this conclusion while pertaining still to the above mentioned strict c-command requirement for the binding of traces.

In order to make VP_i transparent we presupposed that V_1 must incorporate into V_2. But this assumption is not really necessary. We can also take advantage of an option not mentioned so far, namely, that V_1 abstractly incorporates into another head higher up in the tree. This additional head is usually another V node or some tense or inflection node.

Incorporation into a c-commanding head will in most cases be abstract. In some cases, however, we also have evidence that something similar happens overtly in S-structure. A case in point is incorporation into *zu* (to) in standard German. In v. Stechow & Sternefeld (1988:380) we justified an analysis of German *zu*-infinitives which completely parallels the English type of construction in assuming an independent *to*-projection outside the VP. The verb then moves into the [+to]-tense node at the right periphery of the clause. The reason for adopting such an analysis was provided by the fact that German *zu* can appear in the "wrong place" after VP-internal reordering of the verbs. The same phenomenon can also be observed in Zurich German. The following example which involves incorporation into "to" and VPR in Züritüütsch is taken from Cooper (1989):

(11) Er h"at verschproche, d Chind la mediziin z schtudiere
he has promised the kids let medicine to study

The D-structure of the embedded infinitive is (12) with *z* (to) in the tense projection of the infinitive:

(12) $[_{CP}$ $[_{IP}$ PRO $[_{VP}$ $[_{IP}$ d Chind $[_{VP}$ mediziin schtudiere $]_{VP}$ $]_{IP}$ la $]_{VP}$ z]]

Here, the *z*-element would go proxy with the adjacent verb *la*. But VPR yields something like (13):

(13) $[_{CP}$ $[_{IP}$ PRO $[_{VP}$ $[_{VP}$ $[_{IP}$ d Chind t_i] la]$[_{VP}$ mediziin schtudiere $]_i]$ z]]

Finally, overt incoporation into *z* will move *schtudiere* into the Tense/INFL node which yields the surface structure (11). Note that in this structure *la* (let) is incorporated abstractly into *z* while *schtudiere* is incorporated overtly into *z*. Neither of these incorporations violates the HMC in the proposed structure. The proposed analysis exploits the possibility of "separate incorporation" (cf. Baker 1988: 362ff) which would be excluded if the structure of the embeddings were more hierarchical.

While coherent infinitives remain CPs, we showed above that this CP may be entirely empty, consisting only of traces and PRO in case of embeddings under control verbs. Although we observe some overt incorporation of verbs into matrix predicates, incorporation may also remain abstract. To see the difference, consider (14):

(14) (a) da"s er $[_{CP}$ $[_{IP}$ PRO t_1] $[_{VP1}$ mir ein Buch geben_1]]
that he to-me a book give
$\text{wollen}_{\underline{2}\ 1}$ wird
wants-to will

(b) da"s er $[_{CP}$ PRO mir ein Buch t_1] $[_{V\ \underline{2}\ 1}$ geben_1 wollen_2] wird

(c) da"s er $[_{CP}$ PRO mir ein Buch t_1] wird $[_{V\ \underline{2}\ 1}$ geben_1 wollen_2]

(d) $[_{VP1}$ mir ein Buch geben_1] wird er $[_{CP}$ PRO t_1] $\text{wollen}_{\underline{2}\ 1}$

In (a) the embedded VP was moved into the SpecC position, from where abstract incorporation into *wollen* can take place. In (b) *geben* is incorporated overtly. Both possibilities must exist in the grammar of German. Overt incorporation is required by examples like (c) where the complex verb is cyclically incorporated into *wird.* Overt incorporation as in (b) cannot be obligatory, however. This is shown in a verb second clause like (d), where the VP is moved into the *Vorfeld* position. Whereas abstract incorporation yields a grammatical structure, overt incorporation is not consistent with the topicalization of VP:

(15) * [$_{VP1}$ mir ein Buch t_1] wird er [$_{CP}$ PRO t_1] geben$_1$ wollen$_2$

This shows that the trace of head movement cannot be reconstructed through the trace of the VP, although (according to the theory of remnant topicalization; cf. den Besten & Webelhuth (1987)) some amount of reconstruction is required in (16), where scrambling has left a phrasal trace within a topicalized VP:

(16) [$_{VP1}$ t_i ein Buch geben$_1$] wird er mir$_i$ [$_{CP}$ PRO t_1] wollen$_{\underline{2}\ 1}$

Likewise, government of verbal Case cannot be transmitted through a trace. Consider (14a) again. In this structure, the matrix verb governs the embedded VP in SpecC and assigns verbal Case to it. Assignment is to the left of the matrix verb and percolates to the head of VP. In incoherent infinitival constructions the matrix verb does not govern a VP but selects an empty complementizer. As usual this means that assignment of relevant features is by government of CP and percolation of government to the head of CP. Consider now extraposition of CP. This process is grammatical in incoherent constructions; see above where (12) is an infinitive that has been extraposed in (11). Extraposition of CP is ungrammatical, however, with coherent infinitives:

(17) * da"s er t_i wollen wird [$_{CPi}$ PRO mir ein Buch geben]

The ungrammaticality of (17) now follows from our assumption about verbal government. The embedded VP must be governed. Above we assumed that government of the matrix verb is directed to its left. But there we find only the trace of CP. This could transmit government of its head, but it cannot reconstruct government of the VP, as would be required in coherent constructions. Therefore reconstruction of Case government must be excluded.

Above we saw that some relations like antecedent government and binding in (16) can be reconstructed via a trace, while this must be prevented for others. Why this should be the case is an open problem and must be left to future research.

3 The Economy of Levels

Let us now return to the more general issue of how levels arise. We will pursue the following questions: (a) How can levels of representation be defined? (b) Can the definition of levels distinguish between syntactic representations which are instantiated at a level, and representations which are not? (c) Does the characterization of levels have empirical impact on the description of certain phenomena of natural language? The answer to these questions will also take into account the results we attained in the preceding paragraphs.

In response to questions (a) and (b), a family of formal models will be developed that might help clarify the role of rules and constraints in defining levels of representation. It is shown that existing theories of UG define levels adequately only if the systems of UG "conspire" to yield a level with sufficiently "rich" properties which are able to distinguish this level from other levels. In particular, the answer to the second question – whether or not levels can be distinguished from representations that do not instantiate levels – will depend on the ability of rules and constraints to single out certain representations in a particular order. If levels are definable at all, this order must be a consequence of intrinsic properties of rules and constraints, which guarantee the uniqueness of levels and their intended place within a derivation.

Finally, I try to make clear that the definability of levels can only be achieved in a system of UG that does not recognize "too many" levels. In particular, it becomes difficult to define S-structure as soon as there is another level that precedes S-structure. Difficulties of this sort lead to the conclusion that the very nature of levels cannot be captured in terms of rules and constraints. Rather, levels are given as part of the biological organization of grammar; I speculate that they reflect properties of the branchings in a derivation.

3.1 Levels defined by Systems of Rules

According to an early discussion of the issue, levels can be characterized by an ordering of rules, with the "last application" of a certain rule defining a certain level. Lakoff & Ross (1967) seem to imply that the application of a single rule can give rise to a certain level. Taken literally, this conception is too restrictive, because it would imply a one-to-one-correspondence between levels and certain rules; nevertheless it is possible to generalize the idea by turning from rules to sets of rules. A meaningful notion of a level can be arrrived at by defining levels as generated by the last application of a rule within a set L_1, before another rule from a set L_2 can apply.

According to this informal characterization, we can define a level as a set L of rules that may or must apply during the derivation of that level. Given a collection $\mathcal{L}$ of levels – where each level in $\mathcal{L}$ consists of a set of rules L_i – we have to define a derivation with respect to $\mathcal{L}$ in such a way that it corresponds to the organization of levels given by $\mathcal{L}$. Intuitively, the subset property will hold among two elements of $\mathcal{L}$ iff one level comes "earlier" in a derivation than the other: If L_i is a subset of L_j, then any rule of L_j not in L_i must apply later than any rule in L_i. If the subset property between two sets does not hold, then these sets will give rise to a branching in a derivation.

For a set $\mathcal{L}$ to play the role of levels in a grammar, we have to impose a minimal amount of structure upon $\mathcal{L}$. The requirements on $\mathcal{L}$ are (partially) captured in the following definition:

Def. 1: By a grammar $G = \langle R, \mathcal{L} \rangle$ we mean a finite set R of rules and a set $\mathcal{L}$ of non-empty subsets of R such that

a. $\bigcup \mathcal{L} = R$

b. $\bigcap \mathcal{L}' \in \mathcal{L}$, for all $\mathcal{L}' \subseteq \mathcal{L}$.

The exact impact of these conditions on $\mathcal{L}$ can only become clear by considering the definitions of levels and derivations given immediately below. Intuitively, condition (a) will help to make rules of a derivation "level-specific": All rules belong to a certain level. Condition (b) will help to ensure that branchings in a derivation correspond to levels of representation.

In defining a derivation with respect to a grammar G, I make use of the following notational conventions: The yield relation "$y(\alpha, r, \beta)$" will hold if β is the result of applying rule r to α. "ι" will represent the iota operator: $(\iota r)(y(\alpha, r, \beta))$ denotes the unique rule that has been applied to α to yield β, where α and β are occurrences of representations in a tree τ. $(\iota r)(y(r, \beta))$ will be used to denote the rule that derives $\beta \in \tau$.

The following definition presupposes that derivations can be represented as trees of representations; in particular, no level of representation can be fed by more than one level of representation:

Def. 2: A derivation w.r.t. $G = \langle R, \mathcal{L} \rangle$ is a tree of representations such that

a. if α immediately dominates β, then $y(\alpha, r, \beta)$ for some $r \in R$.

b. if $(\iota r)(y(\alpha, r, \beta)) = r_i \in L_i$ and $(\iota r)(y(\alpha, r, \beta')) = r_j \in L_j$ then $r_i \notin L_j$ and $r_j \notin L_i$.

c. if $r_i \in L_i$ yields α (i.e., $r_i = (\iota r)(y(r, \alpha))$), α dominates β, and $r_j = (\iota r)(y(r, \beta)) \in L_j$, then $r_i \in L_j$.

Condition (a) interprets the dominance relation within a tree. Condition (b) describes a branching node α that immediately dominates β and β'. The condition states that a branching in a tree corresponds to subsets L and L′ of $\mathcal{L}$

such that neither one is a subset of the other: This condition on sets seems to be necessary and sufficient to induce a branching in a derivation. On the other hand, the conclusion from non-containment of levels to branchings in a derivation does not follow from the above definition. The reason is that one representation can, in principle, correspond to two or more levels. This point will be discussed further below.

Condition (c) connects the hierarchy imposed on $\mathcal{L}$ with dominance in a derivation: If r_j applies later than r_i, then r_i and r_j must be elements of the same set L_j. This condition reflects the role of the subset relation in $\mathcal{L}$: the system $\mathcal{L}$ is designed in such a way as to let its elements comprise *all* of the rules that can apply up to a certain point in a derivation.

The definition of a level is now straightforward:

Def. 3: α instantiates a level L in τ iff $(\iota r)(y(r,\alpha)) \in L$ and for all $\beta \in \tau$ dominated by α, $(\iota r)(y(r,\beta)) \notin L$.

I now go on to discuss the two requirements imposed on G by pointing out the consequences of dropping one of them while maintaining the other.

Dropping condition (b) of definition (1) would allow for two sets to intersect without giving rise to a level of interpretation. To see this, consider the intersection of L and L′. Suppose we remove this set from $\mathcal{L}$. The set of possible derivations will be the same as before, but the branching point in a derivation that contains the last application of $L \cap L'$ will no longer be a level of representation.

As another consequence of (b), we observe that $\cap\mathcal{L}$ is an element of $\mathcal{L}$. This means that the intersection of all "levels" is not empty and constitutes a level, traditionally called the level of deep structure. Within the *Aspects* model, $\cap\mathcal{L}$ is the set of base rules. Other types of rules that correspond to levels can easily be defined as follows:

Def. 4: r is an L-structure rule iff $r \in L$ and if $r \in L'$, then $L \subseteq L'$.

Intuitively, L-structure rules help to characterize L but do not characterize previous levels of representations. For example, S-structure rules will be all transformational rules that derive from D-structure the level characterized by the set that contains S-structure rules and D-structure rules.

Turning next to condition (a) of definition (1), suppose we were to drop this requirement on $\mathcal{L}$. From condition (a) of definition (2), we conclude that any rule r that does not belong to a set that characterizes levels can apply anywhere in a derivation. With regard to the definition of levels, this possibility would pose the question of whether a level can be reached by a level-unspecific rule.

Likewise we would have to ask whether these rules can induce branchings and whether they can derive end-points of a derivation.

A few considerations will show that there is some intuitive vagueness around these questions. Within the above model it is not clear how to decide the issues and which (empirical) consequences could be derived from any of the possible answers that could be given. The same holds if we were to modify the proposed model so as to allow for rules to be unspecific only with respect to a certain subset of $\mathcal{L}$. On the other hand, it has become standard practice to assume very general rules (like "move α") that connect more than two levels.

As a consequence of this shift from rules to representations, the interaction between levels and global rules is determined by constraints on representation. Rules have become more general by abstracting away from specifications in rules; these have to be compensated for in terms of specific constraints on the output of rule application.

As can be easily verified, levels of representation reflect rule orderings as they have been proposed in early periods of generative grammar (cf. Kayne (1975) for a relevant example that has a direct bearing on the discussion in section 1.6). Rule orderings of this kind are still operative in lexical phonology; they define different levels that constitute the input of different phonological and morphological rules. From our present point of view, however, orderings of *syntactic* rules are rejected on empirical and conceptual grounds (cf. Rizzi (1982) for an instructive discussion).

Another shortcoming of the above model emerges when language specific variation is taken into account. Let us restrict our attention to the micro-cosm of syntax, i.e. to the levels D-structure, S-structure and LF. Let us also adopt the following restriction on the "abstractness" of LF: Processes in LF must, in principle, be possible S-structure processes; i.e. there cannot be any principles of UG that prevent LF-processes from showing up overtly in the S-structure of some natural language. (Basically, this is the "Principle of Reversed Affability" to be found in Szabolcsi (1983).)

This hypothesis makes clear that different languages may require different organizations of rules to define their levels. According to the above model, levels are defined with respect to language specific grammars. Intuitively, however, the organization of levels should be definable on more universal grounds. If it is correct that the principles of UG allow a language whose scope relations can be read directly off the surface, we would like to say that S-structure and LF collapse. Formally, however, there is no way to express this intuition in terms of the organization of rules in a particular grammar. This problem can be taken as an indication that the characterization misses an important intuition concerning the role of levels in UG.

A somewhat related problem is the justification of non-branching levels in current syntactic descriptions. Consider the level of NP-structure as proposed by Riemsdijk and Williams (1981). Postulating a level between D-structure and S-structure imposes an extrinsic ordering on NP-movement and *wh*-movement. This ordering has empirical effects in blocking "improper movement" from $\bar{A}$-positions to A-positions. However, this effect is not what had been intended by stipulating an additional level. Rather than imposing an order on different types of movement, it was proposed that NP-structure should observe specific *constraints* that become operative before *wh*-movement can apply.

Likewise, it is proposed in the model of v. Stechow & Sternefeld (1988) that reanalysis requires a separate level of representation (cf. also Hornstein (1986) for a discussion of restructuring along similar lines). This requirement could not be expressed in terms of rule ordering, however, because no ordering of reanalysis with respect to other rules naturally suggests itself. As an illustration of this claim consider NP-movement. Before reanalysis, raising of PRO to the subject position in passivized infinitives is necessary to properly identify the empty category PRO. On the other hand, we have seen that in cases of long distance passives NP-movement applies after reanalysis. Therefore, NP-movement cannot be level-specific. The additional level of representation does not come in by rule ordering, rather it results from the requirement that a certain representation is subject to a set of certain constraints.

Within the syntactic theory of GB this observation generalizes to all levels of representation: If α is a level of representation, this level must be "justified" by being subject to level-specific constraints. As a result of making rules more and more general, specific constraints on representation must compensate for the expressive power of unconstrained rules. But as rules tend to become more general, rules alone cannot supply adequate means to distinguish levels. As it seems, we rather have to turn from rules to constraints on representations and should try to define levels in terms of constraints.

3.2 Levels Defined by Constraints

The idea of incorporating constraints into the model of grammar can be made precise in various ways. Let us take a radical position now by (a) restricting our attention to the levels of "syntax" proper and (b) restricting all rules to level-unspecific rules like "move α". The above requirement that the system of rules is just {R} implies that levels must be defined by constraints on representation.

A set C_i of constraints will induce a level of representation α only if α simultaneously satisfies all the constraints in C_i. Henceforth, I will assume that a grammar contains a system $\mathcal{L}$ of sets of constraints; any element of $\mathcal{L}$ is a subset of C and will be used to define a level (i.e. $\mathcal{L}$ is a subset of $\mathcal{P}(C)$). It is natural to assume that all elements of $\mathcal{L}$ exhaust C (i.e. $C = \cup\mathcal{L}$) which means that each constraint is attached to some level.

If C_1 and $C_2 \in \mathcal{L}$ overlap, the conditions in $C_1 \cap C_2$ must be met on both levels of representation represented by C_1 and C_2. In contrast, disjunctive applications of constraints (e.g. binding conditions in Belletti & Rizzi (1988)) will be excluded as a consequence of avoiding disjunctive statements in rules and conditions on rules.

Given a grammar $G = \langle R, C, \mathcal{L} \rangle$ a derivation can be defined as follows:

Def. 5: A tree τ is a derivation w.r.t. $G = \langle R, C, \mathcal{L} \rangle$ iff for all $\alpha, \beta \in \tau$:

a. If α immediately dominates β, then $y(\alpha, r, \beta)$ for some $r \in R$.

b. There is a (total) function f from $\mathcal{L}$ into τ such that

1. if $f(C_i) = \alpha$, then α satisfies all $c \in C_i$;
2. if α is a root node, a leaf, or a branching node, then α is in the range of f.

Condition (a) interprets dominance in a tree exactly as before. Clause (b) ensures the obligatoriness of constraints; furthermore, I simply stipulated that certain nodes in the tree must be levels. Perhaps we can (partly) derive this stipulation from universal properties of a derivation. Following Chomsky (1989), we could assume that derivations are as short as possible. As a consequence end points will be reached as soon as there is no more constraint that enforces the application of a rule. Reaching a leaf must be enforced by satisfying a constraint; therefore leaves will always represent levels.

As another global property of derivations, we might assume that branchings in a tree only occur if they are enforced by "contradicting levels", i.e. by sets of constraints that are not simultaneously satisfiable in one representation. All by itself, this does not guarantee that branchings correspond to levels, but in many cases the system of rules and constraints will have this effect.

Likewise, the system $\mathcal{L}$ by itself does not induce an ordering of levels. The intended ordering must be a consequence of intrinsic properties of rules and constraints. In other words, the ordering of levels must be induced by an "intrinsic ordering" of constraints. This seems to work fine with a number of levels and constraints that were proposed in the literature: D-structure can be defined as the level that restricts arguments to θ-positions. NP-structure has been defined as the level where Case is assigned and binding conditions (A) and (B) are checked. On this level, all Case bearing elements appear in positions to which Case can be assigned. The level of LF can be defined by the requirement that operators and quantifiers appear in operator and quantifier positions. A number of additional properties of grammar will conspire to fix the ordering of levels within a derivation: If operators have to bind variables and if variables have to be assigned Case, operatoı movement cannot precede Case assignment; if movement is only to non-θ-positions, NP-structure cannot precede D-structure, etc.

Somewhat surprisingly, however, it is difficult to see how the level of S-structure can be defined. Even if the level of NP-structure were real, most conditions of UG can be neatly divided into D-structure conditions, NP-structure conditions, and LF-condition. Perhaps the only condition that might universally characterize S-structure is subjacency. Within the model proposed above, this does not help, however, because subjacency cannot be used to pick out a level. Since NP-structure "vacuously" satisfies subjacency (perhaps as a consequence of subsuming NP-traces under antecedent-government as in Chomsky (1986a)), this constraint could be met on the "wrong level" without giving rise to a level different from NP-structure. Nor does it help to reintroduce a rule system as proposed in the last section and combine the models defined there with the definition given above. By the Principle of Reversed Affability we cannot neatly divide rules of UG into S-structure rules and LF rules.

In response to this problem, one could suggest that the mapping from constraints to representations must be injective. This requires a small change in the interpretation of dominance in a derivation. Previously, we allowed for a certain point in a derivation to be an S-structure and an NP-structure at the same time. But if the mapping from constraints to representations is injective, then this is no longer possible. We therefore have to change condition (a) of previous definitions to (a′):

(a′) If α immediately dominates β, then $\alpha = \beta$ or $\mathrm{y}(\alpha, \mathrm{r}, \beta)$ for some $\mathrm{r} \in \mathrm{R}$.

This move is not sufficient, however, to block inadequate applications of constraints at the wrong levels, even if we imposed an extrinsic ordering on $\mathcal{L}$ to the effect that derivations mirror the order of levels. Suppose that subjacency is ordered between NP-structure and LF constraints. Assume further that we have reached NP-structure during a derivation. By (a′) we can now move from NP-structure to a level that trivially satisfies subjacency without applying any rule (and before applying *wh*-movement). To ensure that subjacency fulfills its function, one has to characterize the level to which subjacency must apply independently from subjacency. But now we are back to the problem of characterizing S-structure on universal grounds.

The shift from rules to constraints cannot solve the problem of defining S-structure. There simply is no way to characterize this level on purely universal grounds. The conclusion must therefore be that S-structure can only be defined in a language specific way by taking into account *parameters* of rules or constraints.

Another difficulty arises for reanalysis. As we have seen above, it is crucial to block reanalysis before raising and control structures are checked. We have also seen that reanalysis should not be ordered with respect to other "S-structure"-rules. But if reanalysis is a level unspecific rule, reanalysis might apply "too early" so as to bleed the effects of constraints. Thus, we are back to the problem of defining levels by constraints. In v. Stechow & Sternefeld (1988), we simply defined the relevant level as the last representation *before* reanalysis applies. This is simply the opposite of what Lakoff and Ross had in mind when characterizing a level as the last representation that *follows* the application of a certain rule.

To summarize, the discussion has shown that the general problem of how levels should be defined has not been solved. Moreover, I even doubt that the methods proposed above will by themselves be able to do so. As soon as we stretch systems of rules and constraints in such a way that single levels are not "rich enough" and properties of $\mathcal{L}$ do no longer "conspire" to single out a level sufficiently distinct from other levels, we are lost in the realm of possible answers to the problem of how levels can be defined. Therefore, any multiplications of levels leading to difficulties of the kind described above should be avoided.

In particular, we have seen that it is doubtful whether reanalysis could justify a level, either in a derivational or in a multi-representational theory. On the other hand, we also pointed out that it is crucial for this kind of theory to be able to check properties of a representation before reanalysis can destroy relevant information. The solution proposed above is to reject reanalysis and adopt the mono-representational theory presented in 2.4.

3.3 Levels Defined as Branchings in a Derivation

The above considerations invite the inference that levels cannot be defined but must be taken as primitive entities in the organization of grammar. If this is the case, we still could ask how levels are made up and why they exist. It seems to me that levels arise from the need to connect different "mental organs". Phonological, morphological, semantical, and other "final" cognitive components (the leaves of a derivation tree) have to interact in some way or another. Within a modular system of grammar, the tree that displays the connection between these components can be interpreted as tying together informationally encapsulated systems (cf. Fodor (1983)); it displays which component has access to information encoded in another module of grammar.

Bringing together different modules can be done in a more or less efficient way. A direct connection between all modules would give us just one additional level. This "connectionistic" level would have to encode simultaneously all the information that is relevant for all modules. It seems that a direct connection of this kind will yield rather abstract representations; having just one representation and the rules that connect it with the "leaves" of the cognitive system could give rise to very complicated rules and structures; derivations cannot pass through intermediate levels and will be quite complex due to much irrelevant information in the "D-structure" level. One could imagine that the task of connecting modules is easier if intermediate levels help to simplify rules and representations.

By connecting the "leaves" of a cognitive system of language faculty in a more efficient and economical way, we derive the branching structure of a derivation. Each branching node defines a component of grammar where different information can be read off; thus, branching nodes represent "abstractions" from the levels immediately dominated by a branching. The rich intrinsic properties of the branching level induce certain limitations on the degree of abstraction from "later" stages that are closer to the "leaves" of cognition. Seen from this perspective non-branching levels do not make much sense. They simply should not arise, because they do not respect the economy of the system's organization.

It should go without saying that the above considerations are highly speculative. But if they are correct, we have found just another reason for rejecting D-structure in favor of a direct generation of S-structure. "By definition" S-structure is branching as is required by the economy of levels. Within the standard model of UG D-structure is not branching, in contrast to the demands of economy.

References

Adams, M. (1987) "From Old French to the Theory of pro-drop", *Natural Language and Linguistic Theory* 5, 1–32.

Baker, M. (1988) *Incorporation: A Theory of Grammatical Function Changing*, The University of Chicago Press, Chicago.

Baker, M. (1989) "Object Sharing and Projection in Serial Verb Constructions", *Linguistic Inquiry* 20.4, 513–554.

Baltin, M.R. (1982) "A Landing Site Theory of Movement Rules", *Linguistic Inquiry* 13, 1–38.

Barss, A. (1986) *Chains and Anaphoric Dependence*, PhD dissertation, MIT, Cambridge, Mass.

Barss, A. (1987) "Paths, Connectivity and Featureless Empty Categories", *GLOW Newsletter* 18, 13–14.

Bech, G. (1955/57) *Studien über das deutsche verbum infinitum* (=Det Kongeliege Danske Videnskabers Selskab; Dan. Hist. Filol. Medd. Bind 35, no. 2 (1955) & Bind 36, no. 6 (1957)). Also published by Niemeyer, Tübingen (1983).

Belletti, A & L. Rizzi (1988) "Psych Verbs and θ-Theory", *Natural Language and Linguistic Theory* 6, 291–352.

Belletti, A. (1988) "The Case of Unaccusatives", *Linguistic Inquiry* 19, 1–34.

Bennis, H. (1986) *Gaps and Dummies*, Foris, Dordrecht.

Bennis, H. & T. Hoekstra (1984) "Gaps and Parasitic Gaps", *The Linguistic Review* 4, 29–87.

den Besten, H. & J. A. Edmondson (1981) "The Verbal Complex in Continental West Germanic", *GAGL* 19, 11–61; also in W. Abraham (ed.) (1983) *On the Formal Syntax of the Westgermania*, Benjamins, Amsterdam.

den Besten, H. & G. Webelhuth (1987) "Remnant Topicalization and the Constituent Structure of VP in the Germanic SOV Languages", *GLOW Newsletter* 18, 15–16.

Chomsky, N. (1981) *Lectures on Government and Binding* (Studies in Generative Grammar 9), Foris, Dordrecht.

Chomsky, N. (1982) *Some Concepts and Consequences in the Theory of Government and Binding*, (Linguistic Inquiry Monograph 6), The MIT-Press, Cambridge, Mass.

Chomsky, N. (1982a) *The Generative Enterprise. A discussion with Riny Huybregts and Henk van Riemsdijk*, Foris, Dordrecht.

Chomsky, N. (1982b) "A Note on Non-Control PRO", *Journal of Linguistic Research* 1, 1–11.

Chomsky, N. (1986) *Knowledge of Language: Its Nature, Origin, and Use*, Praeger, New York/Westport/London.

Chomsky, N. (1986a) *Barriers*, (Linguistic Inquiry Monograph 13), The MIT-Press, Cambridge, Mass.

Chomsky, N. (1989) "Some Notes on Economy of Derivation and Representation", in I. Laka & A. Mahajan (eds.) *MIT Working Papers in Linguistics 10 (Functional Heads and Clause Structure)*, 43–74.

Cooper, K. E. (1988) *Word Order in Bare Infinitival Complement Constructions in Swiss German*, MA Thesis, University of Edinburgh.

Cooper, K. E. (1989) *Zurich German and Verb Raising Constructions*, Ms. Centre for Cognitive Science, Edinburgh.

Durie, M. (1988) "So-called Initial 1 Verbal Agreement in Kapampangan", *Linguistic Inquiry* 19, 147–154.

Emonds, J. E. (1985) *A Unified Theory of Syntactic Categories*, (Studies in Generative Grammar 19), Foris, Dordrecht.

Epstein, S. (1986) "The Local Binding Condition and LF Chains", *Linguistic Inquiry* 17, 187–205.

Evers, A. (1975) *The Transformational Cycle in Dutch and German*, Indiana University Linguistics Club, Bloomington & PhD dissertation. University of Utrecht.

Felix, S. (1983) "Parasitic Gaps in German", *GAGL* 22, 1–46.

Fodor, J. (1983) *The Modularity of Mind*, The MIT-Press, Cambridge, Mass.

Geilfu"s, J. (1989) "Yiddish as an SOV Language", Ms. University of Tübingen.

Grewendorf, G. (1987) "Kohärenz und Restrukturierung. Zu verbalen Komplexen im Deutschen", in B. Asbach-Schnitker & J. Roggenhofer (eds.) *Neuere Forschungen zur Wortbildung und Historiographie der Linguistik*, G. Narr, Tübingen, 123–144.

Haegeman, L. (1988) "Verb Projection and the Multi-Dimensional Analysis: Some Empirical Problems", *Linguistic Inquiry* 19, 671–684.

Haegeman, L. & H. van Riemsdijk (1986) "Verb Projection Raising, Scope, and the Typology of Rules Affecting Verbs", *Linguistic Inquiry* 17, 417–466.

Hornstein, N. (1986) "Restructuring and Interpretation in a T-Model", *The Linguistic Review* 5, 301–334.

Huybregts, M. A. C. (1985) "On Reanalysis and Covalency", Paper read at the Tilburg Workshop on Reanalysis, May 13, 1985.

Jaeggli, O. (1984) "Subject Inversion and the Null Subject Parameter", in C. Jones & P. Sells (eds.) *Proceedings of NELS* 14, Amherst, Mass., 132–153.

Kayne, R. (1975) *French Syntax: The Transformational Cycle*, Cambridge, Mass.

Kim, Y. & R. Larson (1989) "Scope Interpretation and the Syntax of Psych-Verbs", *Linguistic Inquiry* 20, 681–688.

Koster, J. (1982/83) "Enthalten syntaktische Repräsentationen Variablen?", *Linguistische Berichte* 80 (1982), 70–100 & 83 (1983), 36–60.

Koster, J. (1984) "On Binding and Control", *Linguistic Inquiry* 15, 417–459.

Koster, J. (1987) *Domains and Dynasties: The Radical Autonomy of Syntax*, Foris, Dordrecht.

Kuno, S. (1973) "Constraints on Internal Clauses and Sentential Subjects", *Linguistic Inquiry* 4, 363–385.

Lakoff, G. & J. Ross (1967) "Is Deep Structure Necessary?", Ms., published as: "Ist Tiefenstruktur notwendig?", in W. Abraham & R. J. Binnick (eds.) (1972) *Generative Semantik*, Athenäum, Frankfurt/Main, 66–70.

Lasnik, H. & M. Saito (1984) "On the Nature of Proper Government", *Linguistic Inquiry* 15, 235–289.

Lasnik, H. (1985) "Illicit NP-Movement: Locality Conditions on Chains?", *Linguistic Inquiry* 16, 481–490.

Lenerz, J. (1977) *Zur Abfolge nominaler Satzglieder im Deutschen*, (Studien zur deutschen Grammatik 5), Tübingen.

Lerner, J.-Y. & W. Sternefeld (1984) "Zum Skopus der Negation im komplexen Satz", *Zeitschrift für Sprachwissenschaft* 3, 159–202.

Lötscher, A. (1978) "Zur Verbstellung im Zürichdeutschen und in anderen Varianten des Deutschen", *Zeitschrift für Dialektologie und Linguistik* 45, 1–29.

May, R. (1985) *Logical Form*, The MIT-Press, Cambridge, Mass.

Müller, G. & B. Rohrbacher (1990) "Eine Geschichte ohne Subjekt", *Linguistische Berichte* 119, 3-52

Müller, G. & W. Sternefeld (1990) *Improper Movement*, Fachgruppe Sprachwissenschaft, Universität Konstanz, Arbeitspapier Nr. 26.

Müller, G. (1989) *Ā-Bewegung, Minimalitätsbarrieren & Kopfreanalyse.* Fachgruppe Sprachwissenschaft, Universität Konstanz, Arbeitspapier Nr. 13.

Müller, G. (forthcoming) "Abstrakte Inkorporation", to appear in G. Fanselow & S. Olsen: *DET, COMP und INFL*, Niemeyer, Tübingen.

Nanni, D. (1978) *The Easy Class of Adjectives in English*, PhD dissertation, University of Massachusetts.

Pesetsky, D. M. (1982) *Paths and Categories*, PhD dissertation, MIT Cambridge, Mass.

Platzack, C. (1986) "The Scandinavian Languages and the Null Subject Parameter", *Natural Language and Linguistic Theory* 5, 377–401.

Riemsdijk, H. van & E. Williams (1981) "NP-Structure", *The Linguistic Review* 1.2, 171–217.

Riemsdijk, H. van (1985) "Against Adjunction to the Head", unpublished Ms.

Rizzi, L. (1982) *Issues in Italian Syntax*, (Studies in Generative Grammar 11), Foris, Dordrecht.

Rizzi, L. (1982a) "Negation, Wh-movement and the Null Subject Parameter", in Rizzi (1982), 117–184.

Rizzi, L. (1986) "On Chain Formation", in H. Borer (ed.) *Syntax and Semantics 19: The Syntax of Pronominal Clitics*, Academic Press, New York, 65–96.

Rizzi, L. (1986a) "Null Objects in Italian and the Theory of pro ", *Linguistic Inquiry* 17, 501–557.

di Sciullo, A.M. & E. Williams (1987) *On the Definition of Word*. MIT-Press, Cambridge, Mass.

Sportiche, D. (1983) *Structural Invariance and Symmetry.* Ph.D. dissertation, MIT, Cambridge, Mass.

v. Stechow & W. Sternefeld (1988) *Bausteine syntaktischen Wissens. Ein Lehrbuch der generativen Grammatik*, Westdeutscher Verlag, Opladen.

v. Stechow, A. (1989) "Distinguo", *Linguistische Berichte* 122, 330–339.

Sternefeld, W. (1984) "On Case and Binding Theory", Diss., Universität Konstanz. Abbreviated version in: J. Toman (ed.) (1985) *Studies in German Grammar*, (Studies in Generative Grammar 21), Foris, Dordrecht, 231–288.

Sternefeld, W. (1989) "Extractions from Verb-Second Clauses in German", in: *Working Papers in Scandinavian Syntax*44, 119–140.

Sternefeld, W. (1990) "Scrambling and Minimality", in: G. Grewendorf & W. Sternefeld (eds.) *Scrambling and Barriers*, Benjamins, Amsterdam, 239–257.

Szabolcsi , A. (1984) "The Possessor that Ran Away from Home", *The Linguistic Review* 3, 89–102.

On Reconstruction and Coordination*

Tilman N. Höhle

0 Overview

This article is concerned with the evaluation of Ā-bound empty categories on the one hand, and with aspects of the theory of coordination on the other. As Koster (1987) urged, the way bound categories are evaluated should be deducible from the general principle 'Share Property' in conjunction with other universal principles (and, perhaps, learnable properties of particular languages). Clearly, this idea constitutes a research program rather than an articulated theory. The observations discussed in sections 3 through 6 are meant to contribute to this research program.

One main problem in the evaluation of traces are phenomena falling under the rubric of 'reconstruction'. When a clause contains a dislocated phrase, such as *this fool* in *this fool I can't stand*, certain conditions on well-formedness and/or interpretation seem to lead to incorrect predictions, or not be applicable at all when applied at S-structure. There are two approaches to this problem in the literature: (i) one may restrict the application of those conditions to a level of representation distinct from S-structure (true reconstruction), or (ii) one may extend the definition of those conditions in such a way that they can be applied correctly at S-structure (pseudo-reconstruction). Although (i) and (ii) are widely believed to be empirically equivalent, observations on coordination suggest that they are not, in that (ii) is incompatible with standard assumptions about how coordinate structures are translated into a semantic representation. Hence either (i) is correct, or the theory of translation must be modified.

The presentation proceeds as follows. As a general background the fundamentals of the theory of coordination are reviewed in section 1, and the results are used in section 2 to establish the most basic properties of German clause structure. In section 3 some observations on scope and binding properties of dislocated phrases such as alluded to above are displayed, and in section 4 the

*I am grateful to two anonymous referees and to the editors, who prompted me to rework an earlier version of this article ("Scope assignment and binding by reconstruction") that did not contain the discussion of section 6. Thanks are due to Werner Frey, Jürgen Pafel, Arnim von Stechow, and Craig Thiersch for important discussion.

H. Haider and K. Netter (eds.), Representation and Derivation in the Theory of Grammar, 139–197.

two approaches to reconstruction are spelled out. A discussion of coordination and its implications follows in section 5. On the basis of a number of considerations, among which parasitic gaps figure importantly, I conclude in section 6 that (i) – true reconstruction – cannot be correct.

1 Theory of Coordination

The theory of coordination that I assume is largely that of Neijt (1979: ch. 1). Its main characteristics will be recapitulated in the sections to follow.

1.1 Symmetric Coordination, Unreduced

Consider an S-structure configuration such as (1):

(1) $^{1}\mathrm{A} \ldots {}^{k}\mathrm{A}\ (\&)\ {}^{1}\mathrm{B} \ldots \&\ {}^{n}\mathrm{B}\ {}^{k+1}\mathrm{A} \ldots {}^{m}\mathrm{A}$

where each ^{i}B is a conjunct, each & is a coordinating element (e.g., a particle such as *und* 'and', *oder* 'or', *noch* 'nor') and each ^{i}A is an element external to the conjuncts ($m \geq 0$; $n \geq 2$). The fundamental principle is then (2):

(2) *Conservation Condition:*

Each ^{i}B is a constituent

(i) whose structure and whose combinatorial properties follow from general rules that are independent from coordination, or

(ii) which conforms to the coordination scheme (1).

In examples such as (3) the properties of the conjuncts indicated by brackets follow from rules independent from coordination, in accordance with (2i):

(3) (a) sie hofft, daß [Karl arbeitet] oder [Heinz nachdenkt]
she hopes that works or meditates
'she hopes that Karl works or Heinz meditates'

(b) sie hofft, daß weder [Maria arbeitet] noch [Hanna nachdenkt]
she hopes that neither works nor meditates
'she hopes that neither Maria works nor Hanna meditates'

In an example such as (4) the conjuncts themselves are coordinate structures in accordance with (2ii):

(4) sie hofft, daß weder [Karl arbeitet oder Heinz nachdenkt] noch [Maria arbeitet oder Hanna nachdenkt]

'she hopes that neither Karl works or Heinz meditates, nor Maria works or Hanna meditates'

Recursive embedding of coordinate structures within coordinate structures as seen here is naturally accounted for by the assumption that the string "(&) ^{1}B ... & ^{n}B" in (1) is a constituent, which I will refer to as a 'coordinate phrase'.

For symmetric coordination – which is the only type of coordination that we will consider here – also some principle like (5) holds:

(5) *External Homogeneity Condition:*

The combinatorial properties of each ^{i}B are satisfied by ^{1}A, ..., ^{m}A in the same way as the combinatorial properties of every other ^{j}B are.

We will not attempt to make this rather vague statement precise. Under appropriate specifications, it should follow from (5) that in the typical case all conjuncts are members of the same syntactic category and that each conjunct stands in the same grammatical relation to the external elements as every other conjunct. Specifically, the Coordinate Structure Constraint with its 'Across-The-Board exception' (6) should follow from (5):

(6) *CSC/ATB:*

If there is an ^{i}A in a $\bar{\text{A}}$-position that binds a trace in one ^{j}B, it binds a trace in every ^{k}B.

It should follow, then, that each single conjunct ^{i}B may be substituted for the whole coordinate phrase *salva grammaticalitate*. For example, (7) conforms to (6), and the substitutions in (8) are possible, whereas (9) does not conform to (6) and the substitutions in (10) are impossible:[1]

[1]There are some exceptions to substitutivity, the most conspicuous case being NPs coordinated by *and* in an environment requiring a plural NP, as in (i):

(i) (a) John and Bill may be brothers (*John may be brothers/a brother)

(b) John and Bill are nice (*John are nice)

(c) John and Bill will both be decorated (*John will both be decorated)

There are also some types of coordinate structures not conforming to (5) and its corollaries, which consequently are 'asymmetric' coordinations. See Höhle (1990) for asymmetric coordination in German, and Entjes (1972) on Dutch.

Split coordinations such as (ii) will not be considered here:

(7) (i) [den Vorschlag]$_i$ [[unterstützen viele t_i] und [lehnt kaum
the proposal support many and rejects hardly
einer t_i ab]]
one off
'many support the proposal and hardly anyone rejects it'

(ii) ich weiß nicht, [welchen Vorschlag]$_i$ [[viele t_i unterstützen]
I know not which proposal many support
und [kaum einer t_i ablehnt]]
and hardly one rejects
'I don't know which proposal is supported by many and rejected by hardly anyone'

(8) (i) (a) [den Vorschlag]$_i$ [unterstützen viele t_i]
(b) [den Vorschlag]$_i$ [lehnt kaum einer t_i ab]
(ii) (a) ich weiß nicht, [welchen Vorschlag]$_i$ [viele t_i unterstützen]
(b) ich weiß nicht, [welchen Vorschlag]$_i$ [kaum einer t_i ablehnt]

(9) (i) *[den Vorschlag]$_i$ [[unterstützen viele t_i] und [lehnt kaum einer ihn$_i$ ab]]
(ii) *ich weiß nicht, [welchen Vorschlag]$_i$ [[viele t_i unterstützen] und [kaum einer zuhört]]

(10) (i) *[den Vorschlag] [lehnt kaum einer ihn ab]
(ii) *ich weiß nicht, [welchen Vorschlag] [kaum einer zuhört]

1.2 Reductions

Naturally the Conservation Condition (2) and its corollaries are only true of a level of representation where no construction specific ellipsis has taken place. There are two types of ellipsis specific for (symmetric) coordination in German:

(11) *Right Periphery Ellipsis (RPE):*

In some ^{i}B a string at the right periphery is ellipsed at surface structure under phonological and sense identity with a string at the right periphery of the final conjunct ^{n}B.

(ii) sie hat gestern einen Hund gekauft oder eine Katze
she has yesterday a dog bought or a cat
'she bought a dog yesterday, or a cat'

(12) *Gapping:*

In some ^{i}B an independent verb is ellipsed (possibly together with certain other elements of the same conjunct) at surface structure under sense identity with corresponding elements in the initial conjunct ^{1}B.

RPE licenses examples such as (13):

(13) (a) [Heinz sollte den Hund ____] und [Karl sollte den Kater füttern]
should the dog and should the cat feed
'Heinz should feed the dog, and Karl should feed the cat'

(b) [Heinz hört dir ____] und [Karl hört mir zu]
hears you hears me to
'Heinz listens to you and Karl listens to me'

The conjuncts *Heinz sollte den Hund* in (a) and *Heinz hört dir* in (b) do not conform to clause (i) of the Conservation Condition (2), in that constituents like these are ungrammatical unless licensed by RPE.

Similarly for Gapping:

(14) (a) [gesungen hat Karl] und [geschrien ____ Heinz]
sung has and cried
'Karl has sung and Heinz has cried'

(b) [wen sollte sie suchen] und [wen ____ er ____]
whom should she seek and whom he
'whom should she look for and whom should he look for'

Again, constituents such as *geschrien Heinz* in (a) and *wen er* in (b) are ungrammatical unless licensed by Gapping (or as a kind of elliptical response in discourse). (Note by the way that there are two nonadjacent elision sites in (14b), as a consequence of the fact that a dependent (non-finite) verb may be gapped in tandem with the finite verb.)

Both RPE and Gapping are optional, of course. But in structures with multiple conjuncts an analogue to the External Homogeneity Condition (5) can be observed to hold:

(15) *Internal Homogeneity Condition:*

If in a conjunct ^{i}B there is an elision site licensed by an expression contained in a conjunct ^{j}B, then there is a corresponding elision site in each conjunct ^{k}B ($k \neq i$), where ^{k}B is a sister of ^{j}B.

Elision sites may be licensed by RPE or by Gapping. Consider first Gapping:

(16) (a) [Karl füttert den Hund], [Heinz ____ den Kater] oder [Walter ____ den Ochsen]
feeds the dog / the cat / or / the ox

'Karl feeds the dog, Heinz feeds the cat, or Walter feeds the ox'

(b) *[Karl füttert den Hund], [Heinz ____ den Kater] oder [Walter füttert den Ochsen]

(c) *[Karl füttert den Hund], [Heinz füttert den Kater] oder [Walter ____ den Ochsen]

If interpreted as a ternary coordination with *oder* 'or', all non-initial conjuncts must contain a Gapping site. Similarly for RPE:

(17) (a) [Karl füttert ____], [Heinz tränkt ____] oder [Walter streichelt den Hund]
feeds / waters / or / caresses the dog

'Karl feeds the dog, Heinz waters the dog, or Walter caresses the dog'

(b) *[Karl füttert den Hund], [Heinz tränkt ____] oder [Walter streichelt den Hund]

(c) *[Karl füttert ____], [Heinz tränkt den Hund] oder [Walter streichelt den Hund]

The two Homogeneity Conditions (5) and (15), taken together, account for restrictions on elision in conjuncts that are coordinate phrases. Consider (18a):

(18) (a) [Karl füttert den Hund] und [Heinz ____ den Kater] oder [Walter füttert den Ochsen]

(b) [[Karl füttert den Hund] und [Heinz ____ den Kater]] oder [Walter füttert den Ochsen]

'[Karl feeds the dog and Heinz feeds the cat], or Walter feeds the ox'

(c) *[Karl füttert den Hund] und [[Heinz ____ den Kater] oder [Walter füttert den Ochsen]]

'Karl feeds the dog, and [Heinz feeds the cat or Walter feeds the ox]'

This string of conjuncts can be interpreted as (18b), where no condition on elision is violated. But it cannot be interpreted as (18c): although the structure conforms to (12) and (15), it does not conform to (5), in that the combinatorial properties of the conjunct *Heinz den Kater* are dependent on the conjunct *Karl füttert den Hund*, whereas those of the conjunct *Walter füttert den Ochsen* are not. Consider also (19a):

(19) (a) [Karl füttert den Hund] und [Heinz füttert den Kater] oder [Walter ____ den Ochsen]

(b) [Karl füttert den Hund] und [[Heinz <u>füttert</u> den Kater] oder [Walter ____ den Ochsen]]

'Karl feeds the dog, and [Heinz feeds the cat or Walter feeds the ox]'

(c) *[[Karl <u>füttert</u> den Hund] und [Heinz füttert den Kater]] oder [Walter ____ den Ochsen]

'[Karl feeds the dog and Heinz feeds the cat], or Walter feeds the ox'

Here the interpretation (19b) does not violate any condition. The structure of (19c) conforms to (12), but it violates (15): there is an elision site in the last conjunct, licensed by *füttert* in the conjunct *Karl füttert den Hund*, but the sister of the latter conjunct does not contain an elision site. Finally, consider (20a):

(20) (a) [Karl <u>füttert</u> den Hund] und [Heinz ____ den Kater] oder [Walter ____ den Ochsen]

(b) [[Karl <u>füttert</u> den Hund] und [Heinz ____ den Kater]] oder [Walter ____ den Ochsen]

'[Karl feeds the dog and Heinz feeds the cat], or Walter feeds the ox'

(c) [Karl <u>füttert</u> den Hund] und [[Heinz ____ den Kater] oder [Walter ____ den Ochsen]]

'Karl feeds the dog, and [Heinz feeds the cat or Walter feeds the ox]'

As expected, (20a) is ambiguous between (b) and (c), since none of these violates any condition. When we compare (20c) with (18c) we can see that (5) induces a CSC/ATB effect on reductions. Comparing (20b) with (18b) and (19c) we can see that the reduction in the last conjunct *Walter den Ochsen* is parasitic upon the reduction in the conjunct *Heinz den Kater*, as required by (15). (For RPE similar sets of examples can easily be constructed.)

As long as only RPE or Gapping is applied within a coordinate structure, at least one conjunct (the final one or the initial one) must conform to the

Conservation Condition. But RPE and Gapping may act independently of one another with the result that no unreduced conjunct remains:

(21) [Karl hört dir ____], [Heinz ____ mir ____] oder [Walter ____ ihr zu]
hears you me or her to

'Karl listens to you, Heinz listens to me, or Walter listens to her'

Here the initial conjunct contains an RPE site licensed by *zu* in the final conjunct, and the final conjunct contains a Gapping site licensed by *hört* in the initial conjunct. Because of the Internal Homogeneity Condition the middle conjunct has to contain a Gapping site as well as an RPE site.

Despite considerable analytical efforts, the nature of the constraints that Gapping is known to obey has to a large degree remained something of a mystery; see, for example, Kohrt (1976) and Neijt (1979). RPE – which also goes under the names of Left Deletion, Shared Constituent Coordination, Backward Conjunction Reduction, Backward Gapping and Right Node Raising – is special in its own way. It allows parts of words to be ellipsed:

(22) [Karl suchte den Ein____] und [Heinz suchte den Ausgang]
seeked the in and seeked the outway

'Karl looked for the entry and Heinz looked for the exit'

(For details see Toman (1985: §4), Höhle (1985) and Neijt (1987).) It also allows non-constituents to be ellipsed. In (23), for example, the converb (the so-called 'separable verb prefix') *ein* and the N^0 *Lösung* are ellipsed, which can never form a constituent:[2]

[2] To be more exact, the converb here presumably is a sister of a verbal trace (cf. section 2) with which it forms a constituent, a verbal projection V^i. Since the count noun *Lösung* cannot function as an NP by itself, it cannot be a sister of that V^i. Rather it must be part of the NP *eine großzügige Lösung*, which in turn is part of a PP introduced by *für*.

Note incidentally that German has a null N^1 anaphor, similar to the English N^1 anaphor *one*, as in (i):

(i) die großen Hunde haben die kleinen ____ gebissen
the big dogs have the little bitten

'the big dogs bit the little ones'

Nevertheless, the elision of *Lösung* in (23) cannot be an instance of the null anaphor but must be a consequence of RPE. (23) can be used as an answer to the question "What proposals are being made?". In the same context also (ii), without RPE, could be used as an answer, but (iii), with a null N^1, would be uninterpretable:

(23) [Karl tritt für eine großzügige ____] und [Heinz tritt für eine sparsame Lösung ein]
steps for a generous and steps for a parsimonious solution in

'Karl pleads for a generous solution, and Heinz pleads for a parsimonious solution'

RPE in fact disobeys all (or nearly all) of the core constraints on movement rules; see Neijt (1979). In sum, RPE presumably is a process in the PF component, relating S-structure and surface structure.[3]

1.3 'Forward Conjunction Reduction'

Principles like (2) and (5) and reductions like (11) and (12) have, of course, been assumed ever since coordination has been a topic of theoretical scrutiny. The one assumption that distinguishes the present theory from most of its predecessors (as, for example, ch. 6 of Stockwell; Schachter & Partee (1973) and Terazu (1975)) and also from some more recent contributions (e.g., Oirsouw (1985) and Goodall (1987)) is (24):

(24) There is no type of elision specific to coordination other than those specified in (11) and (12).

This means, specifically, that there is no general rule of Forward Conjunction Reduction (FCR, alias Right Deletion, Coordinate Deletion or Left Peripheral Deletion), which has been hypothesized to be basically something like the mirror image of RPE in that it deletes a string at the left periphery of some conjunct ${}^{i}B$ under identity with a corresponding string in the initial conjunct ${}^{1}B$. The reason for not assuming FCR is simply that for a number of different types of phenomena, conditions of well-formedness and/or interpretation require (2), (5) and (24) jointly to be true. In particular, structures resulting from FCR – as opposed to RPE and Gapping structures – are syntactically well-formed

(ii) Karl tritt für eine großzügige Lösung ein, und Heinz tritt für eine sparsame Lösung ein

(iii) Karl tritt für eine großzügige ____ ein, und Heinz tritt für eine sparsame Lösung ein

[3]Possible targets of RPE must be flanked by strong morpheme boundaries, which in German coincide with syllable boundaries (Höhle 1985). Booij (1985) observes that RPE targets therefore are possible 'phonological words' (or rather, strings of phonological words). Hence, he argues, RPE is a rule operating on 'prosodic structure' in the PF component, not a rule of syntax proper.

only if they comply with the Conservation Condition (2), and their interpretations often do not accord to that of their unreduced sources. See, for example, Partee (1970), Partee & Rooth (1983), Lie (1982) and Neijt (1978, 1979, 1987, 1989) for ample demonstration.[4]

Part of the semantic evidence for (24) can be easily appreciated by comparing instances of RPE with putative instances of FCR.[5] Consider an example with a quantified NP such as *jedes Spielzeug* 'every toy':

(25) [Karl zeigt den Kindern ____] oder [Heinz zeigt den Eltern
shows the children or shows the parents
jedes Spielzeug]
every toy

This is synonymous with (26):

(26) [Karl zeigt den Kindern jedes Spielzeug] oder [Heinz zeigt den Eltern jedes Spielzeug]

'Karl shows every toy to the children, or Heinz shows every toy to the parents'

It does not mean 'for every toy, Karl shows it to the children or Heinz shows it to the parents'. Contrast this with (27):

(27) daß jeder Lehrer [den Kindern ein Buch zeigt] oder [den Eltern
that every teacher the children a book shows or the parents
einen Film zeigt]
a movie shows

'that every teacher shows a book to the children or shows a movie to the parents'

[4]Actually, FCR comes in two varieties in the literature, viz., as a deletion process and as an extraction-and-adjunction process. As an extraction process it is necessarily string vacuous w.r.t. the first conjunct and it results in adjunction structures that cannot be defended independently. Both varieties either undergenerate or overgenerate massively if they are not (i) very severely restricted and (ii) complemented by phrasal conjunction. But when phrasal conjunction is given, there is no point in having FCR in the first place. If it still turns out that some phenomenon can only be analyzed as the result of a conjunct initial elision process, care must be taken that this process be very narrowly constrained, otherwise gross misgeneration will be unavoidable. See Neijt (1979: 58f.) for a brief discussion, and Dowty (1988) for a different view, as well as Wesche (1989) for a critical appraisal.

[5]Part of the syntactic evidence for (24) is presently being rediscovered in the context of categorial grammar research, as in Houtman (1987).

This is not synonymous with what, according to FCR, would be its full form:

(28) daß [jeder Lehrer den Kindern ein Buch zeigt] oder [jeder Lehrer den Eltern einen Film zeigt]

'that every teacher shows a book to the children or every teacher shows a movie to the parents'

The difference between RPE structures such as (25) and putative FCR structures such as (27) is accounted for by assuming that (i) the interpretation of RPE structures proceeds from their unreduced form (which presumably is identical with S-structure), and (ii) that FCR does not exist, so that the interpretation of 'FCR structures' proceeds from an S-structure where the conjuncts and the coordinating particle are in the domain of the quantified NP *jeder Lehrer* 'every teacher'. Similar observations can be made for an indefinite NP such as *ein Buch* 'a book'. An instance of RPE such as (29) is synonymous with its unreduced form (30):

(29)	[Karl	zeigt	den	Kindern	____]	und	[Heinz	zeigt	den	Eltern
		shows	the	children		and		shows	the	parents

ein Buch]
a book

(30) [Karl zeigt den Kindern ein Buch] und [Heinz zeigt den Eltern ein Buch]

'Karl shows a book to the children, and Heinz shows a book to the parents'

That is, the book shown to the children need not be identical with the book shown to the parents.[6] Contrast this with a putative FCR structure such as (31):

[6]Both the full form and the RPE structure can also be understood to involve only one book. But while this interpretation is completely natural with the RPE structure, it has a ring of pedantry and lack of cooperativeness about it with the unreduced structure. We may account for this in terms of a Gricean theory of cooperative communicative behaviour. If a speaker knows that only one book is involved and has no reason to hide this fact from the listener, pronominalization provides him with a natural way of expressing this unambiguously, as in (i):

(i)	Karl	zeigt	den	Kindern	ein	Buch,	und	Heinz	zeigt	es	den	Eltern
		shows	the	children	a	book	and		shows	it	the	parents

'Karl shows a book to the children, and Heinz shows it to the parents'

Clearly, pragmatic principles of interpretation that depend on the form of an utterance proceed from surface structure.

(31) daß ein Lehrer [den Kindern ein Buch zeigt] und [den Eltern
that a teacher the children a book shows and the parents
einen Film zeigt]
a film shows

'that a teacher shows a book to the children and shows a movie to the parents'

This cannot be understood to involve two different teachers, one showing a book to the children and another showing a movie to the parents. But that would precisely be the preferred interpretation of its putative unreduced source (32):

(32) daß [ein Lehrer den Kindern ein Buch zeigt] und [ein Lehrer den Eltern einen Film zeigt]

'that a teacher shows a book to the children and a teacher shows a movie to the parents'

These facts are predicted by (24) but would be very difficult to account for under the assumption that FCR exists.

1.4 On θ-Theory

Given that FCR does not exist, coordinate structures that involve an NP trace are problematic for some versions of θ-theory. Consider the definition of chains (33), the principle of θ-role assignment (34), and the θ-criterion (35) from Chomsky (1982: 333ff.) in relation to the data (36):

(33) C = (α_1, ..., α_n) is a *chain* if and only if:

(i) α_1 is an NP

(ii) α_i locally A-BINDS α_{i+1}

(iii) for $i > 1$,

(a) α_i is a non-pronominal empty category, or

(b) α_i is A-free

(iv) C is maximal, i.e., is not a proper subsequence of a chain meeting (i–iii).

(34) Suppose that the position P is marked with the θ-role R and C = (α_1, ..., α_n) is a chain. Then C is assigned R by P if and only if for some i, α_i is in position P and C has case or is headed by PRO.

(35) *θ-Criterion:*

Given the structure S, there is a set K of chains, $K = \{C_i\}$, where $C_i = (\alpha_1^i, ..., \alpha_{n_i}^i)$, such that:

(i) if α is an argument of S, then there is a $C_i \in K$ such that $\alpha = \alpha_j^i$ and a θ-role is assigned to C_i by exactly one position P;

(ii) if P is a position of S marked with the θ-role R, then there is a $C_i \in K$ to which P assigns R, and exactly one α_j^i in C_i is an argument.

(iii) In case (i), α has the θ-role assigned by P.

(36) (a) John [may love Bill] and [may hate Mary]

(b) John_i [is loved t_i^1 by Bill] and [is hated t_i^2 by Mary]

(c) John_i [may love Bill] and [is loved t_i by him]

In (36a) the argument *John*, which occupies the subject position, is a member of the chain $C_1 = (John)$. The subject position is θ-marked (under predication) by the phrase *may love Bill* and it is θ-marked by the phrase *may hate Mary*. Hence, according to (34) two θ-roles are assigned to C_1, and *John* has two θ-roles, according to (35iii).

In (36b) *John* is a member of the chains $C_1 = (John, t^1)$ and $C_2 = (John, t^2)$. Both chains are maximal, according to (33iv). The position occupied by t^1 is θ-marked by *loved*, while the position occupied by t^2 is θ-marked by *hated*. Hence each chain has one θ-role assigned to it, and *John*, being a member of both chains, has two θ-roles.

In (36c) *John* is a member of the chain $C_1 = (John, t)$. Since chains must be maximal, there is no other chain that *John* is a member of. The subject position occupied by *John* is θ-marked by *may love Bill*, and the object position occupied by t is θ-marked by *loved*. Hence, both the subject position and the object position assign a θ-role to C_1, thus violating (35i).

We can see here that this version of the θ-theory induces an analogue of the CSC/ATB (6) for A-bound traces. The remarkable fact is that this analogue appears to be falsified by (36c). This, of course, is not particular to passive constructions, but is revealed by raising constructions just as well:

(37) (a) John_i [was likely t_i^1 to pass the exam] but [happened t_i^2 to flunk]

(b) John_i [may love Bill] and [is likely t_i to marry him]

Here again, (37a) is sanctioned by (35), as there are two chains with *John* a member of both, whereas (37b) is incorrectly ruled out by (35), since there is a chain two members of which occupy a θ-marked position.

There are a number of possible answers to this problem (which do not necessarily exclude one another). One could try to modify (35i) appropriately or one could replace 'NP movement', whose existence has been controversial at least since Shopen (1972), by rules operating on lexical entries. One could also question the assumption, presupposed in (36) and (37), that a subject phrase may originate in a position external to the VP. If it instead originates in a position contained in a projection of the verb (as a daughter of V^{max}), as argued by Fukui (1986), Kitagawa (1986) and others, then (36a, c) and (37b) have to be replaced by (38):

(38) (a) $John_i$ [may t_i^1 love Bill] and [may t_i^2 hate Mary]

(b) $John_i$ [may t_i^1 love Bill] and [is (t_i^2) loved t_i^2 by him]

(c) $John_i$ [may t_i^1 love Bill] and [is likely (t_i^2) to t_i^2 marry him]

Here *John* in each case is a member of two different chains and has two θ-roles, sanctioned by the θ-criterion.

One may also question two other assumptions. In (34) it is presupposed that a position can be θ-marked without being case-marked and furthermore, that a subject argument may get its θ-role by two different mechanisms, viz., by predication or by transmission mediated by NP trace. Suppose instead that a position can only be θ-marked if it is case-marked.[7] Then the position of an NP trace, not being case-marked, cannot be θ-marked. The unassigned θ-role will then have to be assigned in the way that external θ-roles standardly are assigned, namely, to a position external to the constituent that immediately dominates the θ-role assigner. Cf. Williams (1984, 1987) where a very similar set of assumptions is argued for. Under these assumptions the position occupied by *John* in (36) and (37) is the only position involved in the relevant chains that is θ-marked, and (35i) is always (trivially) met.[8]

---

[7]If this condition is to apply in full generality without any modification, the position of PRO must be case-marked. Otherwise, PRO must be treated as an exception, just as it is in (34).

[8]These assumptions would seem to be necessary, in fact, if it is true that the subject *keiner* 'no-one' in (i) is in its base position, as it appears to be:

(i) daß $keiner_i$ [den Hund streichelt] und [e_i gebissen wird]
that no the dog caresses and bitten becomes
'that no-one caresses the dog and is bitten'

Note that under these assumptions the S-structure position of the subject in English is a θ-position, and hence an A-position, even if the subject argument originates as a daughter of V^{max}, as in (38), because none of the trace positions in (38) could be θ-marked. See Höhle (1990) for an analysis of asymmetric coordination in terms of these assumptions.

2 German Clause Structure

Traditionally declarative sentences in German are hypothesized to conform to the (simplified) topological scheme (39):

(39) K – FIN – X – VK – Y

where K is one constituent, FIN the position of the finite verb, X a string of (possibly null) constituents and VK a string of (possibly null) verbs. For the most part we will disregard Y, which is a field reserved for extraposed elements. Examples such as (40) accordingly get the topological analysis (41):

(40)	(a)	den	Kindern	zeigt	Karl	ein	Buch	
		the	children	shows		a	book	
		'Karl shows a book to the children'						
	(b)	den	Kindern	wird	Karl	ein	Buch	zeigen
		the	children	will		a	book	show
		'Karl will show a book to the children'						

(41)	(a)	den Kindern	– zeigt	– Karl ein Buch	–	
		K	– FIN	– X	– VK	
	(b)	den Kindern	– wird	– Karl ein Buch	– zeigen	
		K	– FIN	– X	– VK	

This topological theory tells us next to nothing about the hierarchical structure of sentences, but the theory of coordination outlined in section 1, if correct, provides us with a means to inquire into constituent structure. Consider an example such as (42):

(42)	den	Kindern	zeigt	[weder	[Karl	ein	Buch]	noch	[Heinz	einen	Film]]
	the	children	shows	neither		a	book	nor		a	movie

'neither does Karl show a book to the children nor does Heinz show a movie to them'

Here, we can see that *Karl ein Buch* is an unreduced constituent: gapping cannot have been applied since the correlative coordinating particle *weder* 'neither' marks the beginning of the first conjunct and the finite verb *zeigt* 'shows' is outside that conjunct. But that conjunct would be an impossible kind of constituent if it would consist merely of *Karl* and *ein Buch*: neither of them stand in any grammatical relation to the other, but both may be said to stand in a grammatical relation to *zeigt*. (Analogously for the second conjunct *Heinz einen*

Film.) Such a violation of strict compositionality would be inconceivable. We must suppose, therefore, that each conjunct contains a phonologically empty verb in relation to which *Karl* functions as subject and *ein Buch* functions as object. Since verbs are situated in VK (as long as they are not in FIN or in K), we arrive at the conclusion that (40a) has the structure (43):

(43)	den Kindern	–	zeigt	–	[Karl ein Buch	–	[$_V$ *e*]	]
	K	–	FIN	–	[X	–	VK	]

The empty verb obviously must be related to the verb in FIN. I will assume here that FIN is a $\bar{A}$-position and that the empty verb is a trace bound by the verb in FIN.

In this way, coordination gives us a very simple argument that so-called verb-second clauses (and by analogous arguments 'verb-first' clauses) are properly speaking verb-final in S-structure, in that (i) FIN is not a verbal position proper but a position to be occupied by something bearing finite inflexion, and (ii) the true verbal position is clause-final. It is realized by a verbal trace if the verb bearing finite inflexion is attracted to the FIN position.[9] Furthermore, the theory of coordination – specifically hypothesis (24) – enforces the assumption that "FIN – X – VK" is a constituent. Consider an example such as (44):

(44)	den	Kindern	[[zeigt	Karl	ein	Buch]	oder	[zeigt	Heinz	einen	Film]]
	the	children	shows		a	book	or	shows		a	movie

'Karl shows a book to the children, or Heinz shows a movie to them'

Since FCR does not exist, *zeigt Karl ein Buch* must be an unreduced constituent (analogously for *zeigt Heinz einen Film*).

The K-position can be occupied by a constituent of virtually any type with any of a number of different functions. In (45a), for example, it is occupied by a direct object; in (45b) by an indirect object; in (45c) by a subject; in (45d) by a non-finite verb. In (45e) it is occupied by the pronominal *da* 'there' that originates in a 'pronominal PP' *davon* 'there-of, of that,' the preposition *von* 'of' being stranded in the X-field:

(45)	(a)	den Vorschlag	–	unterstützen	viele	(= (8ia))
		the proposal		support	many	

'many support the proposal'

[9]The theory of a clause-final verbal trace originated in the 20's of the 19th century in the work of the same authors who developed the first systematic theory of coordination and subordination (embedding). See Höhle (1986) for historical remarks.

(b) den Kindern – zeigt Karl ein Buch (= (40a))
the children shows a book
'Karl shows a book to the children'

(c) der Karl – sollte den Kater füttern (cf. (13a))
the should the cat feed
'Karl should feed the cat'

(d) gesungen – hat Karl häufig (cf. (14a))
sung has often
'Karl often sang'

(e) da – hat sie dir schon von erzählt
there has she you already of told
'she already told you about that'

Moreover, in varieties of German that make use of 'long extractions' the K-position serves as a landing site for long extracted expressions of just the same types:

(46) (a) den Vorschlag – glaube ich nicht, daß viele unterstützen
the proposal believe I not that many support
'I do not believe that many support the proposal'

(b) den Kindern – hoffen wir, daß Karl ein Buch zeigt
the children hope we that a book shows
'we hope that Karl shows a book to the children'

(c) der Karl – denke ich, daß den Kater füttern sollte
the think I that the cat feed should
'I think that Karl should feed the cat'

(d) gesungen – fürchte ich, daß Karl häufig hat
sung fear I that often has
'I am afraid that Karl often sang'

(e) da – behauptet Karl, daß sie dir schon von erzählt hat
there claims that she you already of told has
'Karl claims that she already told you about that'

(In these examples the embedded clauses introduced by *daß* 'that' are situated in the Y-field of their matrix clauses.) From (45) and (46) we must conclude that the K-position is a $\bar{A}$-position and that the constituent which occupies the K-position $\bar{A}$-binds a trace in its original position. In (45b), for example, the indirect object *den Kindern* '(to) the children' that occupies the K-position certainly is a dislocated constituent, its normal position being in the X-field after the subject. So, we have to assume that there is a trace in X that is $\bar{A}$-bound by *den Kindern*, as in (47):

(47) [den Kindern]$_i$ [zeigt$_j$ [Karl t_i ein Buch – t_j]]
K [FIN [X – VK]]

Embedded clauses typically (but not invariably) are 'verb-final'; they conform to the (simplified) topological scheme (48):

(48) CMP – X – VK – Y

where the CMP-field in Standard German is very similar to what used to be called the 'COMP-position' in English (except that in finite clauses CMP cannot be empty) and where X, Y and VK are characterized exactly as in (39). Of course, VK cannot in general be empty here, since there is no other position in the clause that a finite verb could move to. Here again coordination data such as (49) lead to the conclusion that "X – VK" is a constituent:

(49) (a) daß [weder [Maria arbeitet] noch [Hanna nachdenkt]]
that neither works nor meditates
(cf. (3b))

(b) welchen Vorschlag [[viele unterstützen] und [kaum einer ablehnt]]
which proposal many support and hardly one rejects
(cf. (7ii))

Clearly there is a phrasal Ā-position (exactly one such position) in the CMP-field that serves as a landing site for (short or long) extractions, (49b) being an instance of short extraction of a direct object. The structure of a simple (non-coordinate) example of this type is accordingly as shown in (50):

(50) [welchen Vorschlag]$_i$ [viele t_i – unterstützen werden]
which proposal many support will
CMP [X – VK]
(cf. (8ii))

Summarizing these observations (and ignoring the Y-field), 'verb-second' clauses are structured as in (51a) and 'verb-final' clauses are structured as in (51b):

(51) (a) $[_\alpha$ K $[_\beta$ FIN $[_\gamma$ X VK]]]
(b) $[_\delta$ CMP $[_\epsilon$ X VK]]

As to the category types, we certainly may identify δ with S′, where presumably S′= C^{max}. It is plausible to assume that $\epsilon = \gamma =$ S, but it is not obvious whether S = I^{max} or S = V^{max} with the subject position a daughter of V^{max}. We may naturally assume that β and α are projections of FIN, but again it is not obvious whether FIN $= C^0$ (so that $\beta = C^1$ and $\alpha = C^{max} = \delta$) or rather FIN $= I^0$, in any of the current conceptions of I (so that $\beta = I^1$ and $\alpha = I^{max}$, but certainly $\alpha \neq \gamma$), or even FIN = CONFL^0, i.e., the unification of I^0 and C^0.[10] FIN is a $\bar{A}$-position such that a verb in FIN binds a trace in the VK-field of its own clause. K is a $\bar{A}$-position, and there is a phrasal $\bar{A}$-position in the CMP-field. They both serve as landing sites for (short or) long extractions such that the extracted expression binds a trace in some S ($= \gamma = \epsilon$).[11]

3 On $\bar{A}$-Binders

We will now have a look at constituents occupying a $\bar{A}$-position, specifically, the K-position and the FIN-position of German declaratives. We will see that

[10]If FIN $= I^0$, (51b) should perhaps be replaced by (i), with I^0 empty, as suggested by Kathol (1989) (cf. Höhle 1990):

(i) $[_\delta$ CMP $[_{I^{max}}$ I^0 $[_\epsilon$ X VK$]]]$

[11]There are also $\bar{A}$-positions in the X-field, such as the positions of *da* (extracted from a PP whose remnant is *von*, cf. (45e) and (46e)) in (i):

(i) (a)

sicherlich	–	hat	–	da	mein	Kollege	schon	jemand	von	–	erzählt
certainly	–	has	–	there	my	colleague	already	someone	of	–	told
K	–	FIN	–				X			–	VK

'my colleague certainly told someone about that already'

(b)

ob	–	mein	Kollege	da	schon	jemand	von	–	erzählt	hat
whether	–	my	colleague	there	already	someone	of	–	told	has
CMP	–				X			–	VK	

'whether my colleague told someone about that already'

However, $\bar{A}$-positions in X, as opposed to the $\bar{A}$-position in CMP and to K, do not serve as landing sites for long extractions; i.e., they conform to the properties that are characteristic of 'clitic-movement' (cf. Aoun 1985).

It appears that reflexives and weak pronouns may also undergo clitic-movement. Just like A-binders, they are not subject to the CSC/ATB, even though they $\bar{A}$-bind a trace:

(ii) (a)

wenn	Karl	sich$_i$	weder	[t_i	um	die	Kinder	kümmert]	noch		
if		-self	neither		about	the	children	worries	nor		
									[seine	Arbeit	erledigt]
									his	work	executes

'if Karl neither sees to the children nor does his work'

(b)

daß	mich$_i$	jeder	[t_i	nur	anstarrt]	und	[mir	nicht	hilft]
that	me	every		only	stares-at	and	me	not	helps

'that everyone only stares at me and does not help me'

some of them behave as if they occupied the position of the trace they bind.

3.1 Scope

3.1.1 True Quantifiers

Consider an example with a quantified NP in the K-position such as (52), read with normal (falling) declarative intonation:

(52) alle Politiker haben nicht zugehört
all politicians have not listened

It means: 'For all politicians x, x did not listen'; i.e., the negator *nicht* 'not' is in the scope of the quantified NP *alle Politiker* 'all politicians'. This is just as we would expect, given that in German scope relations are typically determined by the s-command relations[12] at S-structure. See Jacobs (1982, 1983) and Pafel (1988) for ample demonstration and discussion.[13]

The scope relations are reversed, however, under 'I-Topic intonation', i.e., when a special bipartite intonation pattern is used such that there is rising intonation on a first stressed constituent (indicated by " / ") and falling intonation on a second stressed constituent (indicated by " \ "), as in (53):[14]

(53) ALLE / Politiker haben NICHT \ zugehört

This means: 'It is not the case that all politicians listened'; i.e., *alle Politiker* is in the scope of the negator. This reversal of scope cannot be accounted for by assuming that with I-Topic intonation *nicht* is raised at LF so that it s-commands the K-position. Compare (54a) and (54b):

[12]In a tree T, α s-commands β if and only if β is contained in a sister of α. The only difference between s-command and c-command (under its most usual definition, where it is the converse of 'in construction with' (Klima 1964: 294)) resides in the 'first branching node' condition that is built into c-command. That condition has never been argued for, and in those few cases where it has a chance to apply nontrivially, it appears to have unfelicitous consequences.

[13]It is often argued that examples such as (i) falsify the claim that in the unmarked case scope is determined by s-command at S-structure, in that (i) has a reading with *someone* outside the scope of *everyone*:

(i) everyone loves someone

While the observation is correct, it does not show that there is an ambiguity of scope. What is at stake here, rather, is the specific reading versus the non-specific reading of the indefinite NP, and the specific reading cannot be adequately represented by the mechanisms of quantifier scope. See Kasher & Gabbay (1976) and Fodor & Sag (1982) for discussion.

[14]Jacobs (1982) introduced the term 'I-Topikalisierung' for the intonation pattern under discussion, where "I" is short for 'intonation'.

(54) (a) ALLE \ Politiker hat so mancher nicht verstanden
all politicians has such some not understood
'for all politicians x, there are several people y such that it is not the case that y understood x'
($\forall$x $\exists$y NEG)

(b) ALLE / Politiker hat so mancher NICHT \ verstanden
'there are several people y such that it is not the case that, for all politicians x, y understood x'
($\exists$y NEG $\forall$x)

In (a) as well as in (b) the indefinite *so mancher* 'several people' is outside the scope of *nicht* 'not'. In (a) *alle Politiker* has widest scope (over *so mancher* and over *nicht*); in (b) it has narrowest scope (*so mancher* and *nicht* are outside its scope). If *nicht* were raised, we would get the reading 'it is not the case that, for all politicians x, there are several people y such that y understood x' (NEG $\forall$x $\exists$y). But this is not the reading of (b); rather, (b) is synonymous with (55):

(55) es hat so mancher nicht alle Politiker verstanden
'several people did not understand all politicians'
($\exists$y NEG $\forall$x)

It is not true, then, that the scope reversal that we observe with I-Topic intonation is a result of LF raising.

Neither is I-Topic intonation by itself able to induce scope reversal. Consider (56), where the quantified NP bearing rising intonation is not in the K-position but in the X-field:

(56) trotzdem haben ALLE / Politiker NICHT \ zugehört
still have all politicians not listened
'it is still the case that, for all politicians x, x did not listen'

To the extent that (56) is acceptable at all, only the normal scope relations in accordance with s-command are available. Although the intonation and the linear precedence relations are the same in (56) and (53), no reversed scope interpretation is available.

There is, of course, one obvious difference between (53) and (56): in (53) *alle Politiker* Ā-binds a trace in the X-field, whereas there is no reason to assume that it does in (56). Hence I will assume that (57) is true:

(57) With I-Topic intonation a quantified expression E1 that bears rising intonation is in the scope of exactly those expressions E2 that have scope over a trace *t* that is Ā-bound by E1 (for E2 $\neq$ E1).

We may naturally assume that (53) has the structure (58a) and that (54b) has the structure (58b):

(58) (a) [ALLE Politiker]$_i$ [haben [NICHT t_i zugehört]]
(b) [ALLE Politiker]$_i$ [hat [so mancher [NICHT t_i verstanden]]]

In both cases t_i is s-commanded by, and in the scope of, *nicht*; hence the Ā-binder *alle Politiker* is in the scope of *nicht* too.

There might also be another possible analysis. Suppose that scope can be extended upwards so that the primary s-command domain is properly included in the extended scope domain, as long as the extension does not include any expression that is sensitive to scope. For example, the extended scope domain of *nicht* in (59) will include the definite NPs *du* 'you' and *den Hund* 'the dog', although they are not s-commanded by *nicht*:[15]

(59) vielleicht hast du den Hund nicht gehört
perhaps have you the dog not heard
'perhaps you did not hear the dog'

Assume furthermore that a Ā-bound trace behaves like a definite NP in that it can lie in an extended scope domain. Cf. Basri & Finer (1987), who argue on morphological grounds for the definiteness of trace. Under this assumption (58) may be replaced by (60):

(60) (a) [ALLE Politiker]$_i$ [haben [t_i [NICHT zugehört]]]
(b) [ALLE Politiker]$_i$ [hat [so mancher [t_i [NICHT verstanden]]]]

Now the trace t_i can be considered to be in the (extended) scope of *nicht*, hence, by (57), *alle Politiker* is in the scope of *nicht*.

There is evidence that some mechanism like this must indeed be available in German. Jacobs (1980) exemplified and discussed in detail examples such as (61):

[15]It is a remarkable fact that indefinite non-specific NPs can lie in an extended scope domain, as in (iB), although they are evidently sensitive to scope, provided they are contextually 'given' (explicitely or by implicature):

(i) A: wir müßten einen Zuschuß haben
we should a grant have
'we should have a grant'

B: ich bin sicher, daß ihr einen Zuschuß gar nicht benötigt
I am sure that you a grant not need
'I am sure that you are not in need of a grant'

(61) (a) ALLE / Lehrer haben mir KEIN \ Buch empfohlen
all teachers have me no book recommended
'it is not the case that all teachers recommended a book to me'
(NEG ∀x ∃y)

(b) BEIDEN / Ärzten sollte Luise KEINE \ Spieldose vermachen
both doctors should no musical box will
'Luise should not will a musical box to both doctors'
(NEG 2x ∃y)

Here the phrases *alle Lehrer* 'all teachers' and *beide Ärzte* 'both doctors' are understood to be in the scope of negation. Yet, this cannot be accounted for by giving maximal scope to the negatively quantified phrases *kein Buch* 'no book' and *keine Spieldose* 'no musical box'. This would give us the readings 'there is no book that all teachers recommended to me' (NEG ∃y ∀x) and 'there is no musical box that Luise should will to both doctors' (NEG ∃y 2x), and these readings are unavailable for (61). At the same time the reading that (61) has is not available in (62) (with or without I-Topic intonation):

(62) (a) mir haben alle Lehrer kein Buch empfohlen
'for all teachers x, x did not recommend a book to me'
(∀x NEG ∃y)

(b) Luise sollte beiden Ärzten keine Spieldose vermachen
'for both doctors x, Luise should not will a musical box to x'
(2x NEG ∃y)

Hence it appears necessary to assume that in (61) the negation contained in the negatively quantified NP extends its scope over a trace to its left:

(63) (a) [ALLE Lehrer]$_i$ [haben [mir t_i [KEIN Buch empfohlen]]]

(b) [BEIDEN Ärzten]$_i$ [hat [Luise [t_i [KEINE Spieldose vermacht]]]]

There is also some doubt whether the structures given in (58) can be adequate for (53) and (54b). Pafel (1989) observed that examples such as (64) are bad although their presumed 'sources' (65) are unobjectionable:

(64) (a) ??VIELE / Schwestern bewundern NICHT \ den Arzt
many nurses adore not the doctor

(b) ??ALLE / haben NICHT \ einen Hund gesehen
all have not a dog seen

(65) (a) trotzdem bewundern nicht viele Schwestern den Arzt
'still, not many nurses adore the doctor'
(b) trotzdem haben nicht alle einen Hund gesehen
'still, not everyone saw a dog'

This is difficult to understand if (58) is correct. But it can be accounted for if we make two assumptions. First, the focal NP of a focus sensitive logical element (such as negation and scalar particles) can never be extracted out of this element's s-command domain; hence (64) cannot 'derive' from structures such as (65), but only from structures such as (66):

(66) (a) trotzdem bewundern viele Schwestern nicht den Arzt
(b) trotzdem haben alle nicht einen Hund gesehen

Second, the placement of *nicht* before the objects as in (66) is felicitous only if its s-command domain contains a focal NP. This condition is not observed in (64). I assume, therefore, that the structures (60) and (63) are the only correct ones.

3.1.2 Indefinites and Clauses

Consider an example with an indefinite NP in the K-position such as (67), read with normal declarative intonation:

(67) ein Politiker hat nicht zugehört
a politician has not listened

This has a reading where the NP is in the scope of the negation *nicht*: 'It is not the case that a politician listened'. Similarly for (68):

(68) einen Politiker haben viele Leute verehrt
a politician have many people adored

Here the indefinite NP *einen Politiker* 'a politician' can be understood to be referentially dependent on (i.e., in the scope of) *viele Leute* 'many people': 'there were many people who adored a politician'. The S-structures of (67) and (68) can be assumed to be as shown in (69):

(69) (a) [ein Politiker]$_i$ [hat [t_i [nicht zugehört]]]
(b) [einen Politiker]$_i$ [haben [viele Leute [t_i verehrt]]]

In these readings, then, the scope relations that the phrase in the K-position enters into are determined by the position of the trace that it Ā-binds.

Indefinite NPs, however, differ significantly from quantified NPs with regard to the role played by intonation. The scope relations of truly quantified NPs seem to be unambiguous. With normal intonation they are strictly determined by their S-structure position, as in (52) and (54a). With I-Topic intonation they are determined by the position of their trace, as in (53), (54b) and (61). But the scope relations of indefinite NPs are ambiguous with normal intonation: there is one scope reading determined by the position of their trace, as in (67) and (68); and there is another scope reading determined by their S-structure position, such that they are outside the scope of any element s-commanded by them.[16]

Sometimes it is not obvious a priori whether a given NP should be expected to behave like a quantified NP as in (52) or rather like an indefinite NP as in (68). Consider (70), read with normal declarative intonation:

(70) viele Politiker haben die meisten nicht verstanden
many politicians have the most not understood

This has a reading with *viele Politiker* 'many politicians' in the scope of *die meisten* 'most people' and outside the scope of the negation: 'For most people x there are many politicians y such that x did not understand y' (MOSTx MANYy NEG). Hence, the scope relations are determined according to the position of the trace:

(71) [viele Politiker]$_i$ [haben [die meisten [t_i nicht verstanden]]]

(The negation can extend its scope over the trace, but it need not.)

Similarly for (72):

(72) vielen Politikern ist auch KARL nicht begegnet
many politicians is even not met

This has a reading with *vielen Politikern* in the scope of *auch Karl* 'even Karl' and the negation: 'Even Karl did not meet many politicians'. Here we may assume that the trace is in the extended scope of *nicht*:

(73) [vielen Politikern]$_i$ [ist [auch KARL [t_i nicht begegnet]]]

[16]This seems to be a genuine ambiguity of scope, independent of the specific/non-specific ambiguity. See Pafel (1988) for arguments to this effect.

Ordinarily NPs of the form "*viele (N)*" 'many (N)' are thought to be truly quantified, but here we can see that they behave like indefinites.[17] This observation is corroborated by left dislocation structures. Definite NPs as well as indefinite NPs can participate in such constructions, whereas truly quantified NPs are strictly excluded:[18]

(74) (a) deinen Vorschlag, den versteht keiner
your proposal the understands no
'no-one understands your proposal'

(b) einen Porsche, den hat sie früher mal besessen
a the has she earlier once owned
'earlier, she owned a Porsche'

(c) wilden Tieren, denen gehe ich aus dem Weg
wild animals the go I out the way
'I avoid wild beasts'

(75) (a) *jedes wilde Tier/jedem wilden Tier, dem gehe ich aus dem Weg
'I avoid every wild beast'

(b) *kein Vorschlag/keinen Vorschlag, den verstehe ich
'I do not understand any proposal'

(c) *fast alle Leute, die mußte ich nach Hause schicken
'I had to send away almost all people'

But *viele (N)* does occur in left dislocation:

(76) (a) viele Vorschläge, die verstehe ich nicht
'there are many proposals that I do not understand'

(b) viele Leute, die mußte ich wegschicken
'there are many people that I had to send away'

(c) viele Lehrer/vielen Lehrern, denen gehe ich lieber aus dem Weg
'there are many teachers that I rather avoid'

---

[17]This has been independently observed by Pafel (1989). Example (70) is adapted from him.

[18]This fact is important for the general theory of scope reversal. According to Kiss (1987) scope reversal in Hungarian is dependent upon an intonation pattern that seems to be very similar to I-Topic intonation in German. She argues that in Hungarian this is an instance of left dislocation, implicating that this assumption may somehow contribute to an explanation of scope reversal. But while it is true that left dislocation shows various 'connectedness phenomena', scope reversal with quantified NPs as in (53) and (54b) cannot be an instance of left dislocation in German, given that quantified NPs are not allowed in left dislocation structures.

Hence, *viele (N)* cannot be considered to be necessarily quantificational in the way that *jed-/kein-/alle (N)* 'every/no/all (N)' are. In those cases where *viele (N)* does show distributive effects, as in (68), this may be caused by the plural, just as plural definites can be distributive:

(77) die Leute benutzten ein Stäbchen zum Essen

'the people used a chopstick for eating'

A similar question arises with regard to clauses in the K-position. The preposed clause in (78) contains the negative polarity item *jemals* 'ever' that is bound to be in the scope of the negation:

(78) (a) daß du jemals so etwas tun könntest, hat manch einer nicht geglaubt
that you ever such some do could has many one not believed

'many did not believe that you would ever be able to do something like that'

(b) [daß du jemals so etwas tun könntest]$_i$ [hat [manch einer [t_i nicht geglaubt]]]

Although there does not seem to be any a priori reason to expect this, complement clauses seem to behave like indefinite NPs in that they may enter into scope relations according to the position of the trace bound by them, without the help of I-Topic intonation.

3.1.3 Verbs

It has often been observed that finite verbs in the FIN-position behave exceptionally with regard to scope. When the finite verb is in VK, as in (79), scope is assigned in accordance with the usual s-command condition:

(79) daß Karl irgendjemand kein Buch zeigen möchte
that someone no book show wants

'that there is a person x such that Karl does not want to show a book to x'

The indefinite *irgendjemand* 'someone' is outside the scope of the negatively quantified NP *kein Buch* 'no book', and in the reading considered here, *möchte* 'wants' is in the scope of the negation. Remarkably, in a corresponding clause with the finite verb in FIN, exactly the same scope relations are found:

(80) Karl möchte irgendjemand kein Buch zeigen

That is, *kein Buch* still has scope over *möchte* but does not have scope over *irgendjemand.* This is less surprising, though, than it seems to be, since we know (i) that the verb in FIN Ā-binds a trace in VK, and (ii) that scope relations may be determined by the position of such a trace:

(81) Karl [möchte$_i$ [irgendjemand kein Buch zeigen t_i]]

This effect is independent of intonation.[19]

One might entertain the assumption (i) that the scope relations of the verb are determined at D-structure, not S-structure; or (ii) that movement of the verb to the FIN-position is a PF phenomenon. However, there is rather direct evidence from Verum focus ('polarity focus') that both assumptions are incorrect. Under appropriate contextual conditions, stress on the finite verb in the FIN-position, as in (82), can be understood to emphasize that the assertion is true:

(82) er HÖRT mir zu
he hears me to
'he does listen to me'

This effect is absent when the finite verb is in VK, as in (83):

(83) (a) du siehst doch, daß er mir zuHÖRT
you see that he me to-hears
(b) du siehst doch, daß er mir ZUhört

In (83a), *zuHÖRT* 'listens' may be in contrast to *zuSTIMMT* 'agrees'; in (83b), *ZUhört* may be in contrast to *WEGläuft* 'runs away'. But neither of them can have an effect even remotely similar to (82). I assume, therefore, that the FIN-position is associated with a meaning component symbolized by "VERUM".

[19]It would be natural, therefore, to assume that this effect is optional, and so it seems indeed to be in certain cases. In general, however, it appears to be obligatory. An example such as (i) apparently cannot have the meaning of (ii), but must be understood as in (iii):

(i) Karl füttert den Hund nicht
feeds the dog not

(ii) There is a relation of feeding such that it does not hold between Karl and the dog.

(iii) There is no relation of feeding such that it holds between Karl and the dog.

By stressing phonetic material (i.e., the verb) in FIN that component can be emphasized. Importantly, the Verum component can be in the scope of a negation to its right. In a context such as (84a) an utterance of (84b) can have the effect of an emphatic denial of the truth of (84c):

(84) (a) wir hoffen, daß dir alle zuhören
'we hope that everyone listens to you'

(b) aber es HÖRT mir keiner zu
but it hears me no to
'but no-one does listen to me'

(c) es hört mir jemand zu
'someone listens to me'

As VERUM is associated with FIN and FIN is not s-commanded by *keiner* 'no-one', we must assume that VERUM is in the scope of negation by virtue of the fact that the verb in FIN $\bar{A}$-binds a trace that is s-commanded by negation. Cf. Höhle (1988).

We may extend these observations by considering verb projections in the K-position. In (85) the indefinite *einen Hund* 'a dog' is referentially dependent on *viele Kinder* 'many children':

(85) einen Hund gefüttert haben viele Kinder
a dog fed have many children
'many children fed a dog'

Similar observations hold with regard to negation. In (86) the negative polarity item *jemals* 'ever' must be in the scope of the negatively quantified phrase *keiner von euch* 'none of you':

(86) jemals gearbeitet hat wohl keiner von euch
ever worked has presumably no of you
'presumably none of you has ever worked'

The structures shown in (87) allow these observations to be accounted for by the assumption that the verb projections are in the scope of those expressions that s-command their trace:

(87) (a) [einen Hund gefüttert]$_i$ [haben [viele Kinder t_i]]
(b) [jemals gearbeitet]$_i$ [hat [wohl keiner von euch t_i]]

3.2 A-Binding

The observations that we have made with regard to scope assignment are paralleled by observations concerning A-binding. In order to appreciate the data to follow it is important to recognize that 'binding' – specifically A-binding – as used here is an undefined notion the elucidation of which is a topic of current research. By its very nature binding is an irreflexive asymmetric relation, and it is an open question whether it should be construed as being transitive. Although the device of coindexing, a symmetric and transitive relation by definition, is a truly misleading means of representing binding relations, I will use it in the conventional way.

3.2.1 Overt Anaphoric Expressions

Consider an example with a verb projection in the K-position containing a reflexive:

(88) (a) sich rasieren sollte sie
-self shave should she
'she should shave herself'

(b) [sich$_i$ rasieren]$_j$ [sollte$_k$ [sie$_i$ [t_j t_k]]]

The reflexive *sich* '-self' (3rd person, no gender or number distinctions) is understood as being A-bound by *sie* 'she', although it is not s-commanded by its antecedent. The usual formulations of the binding theory, relying strictly on s-command, cannot account for a case like (88) at S-structure. We note, however, that *sich* is bound by an antecedent that s-commands the trace that is Ā-bound by *sich rasieren*, as shown in (88b).

In (89a) the reflexive *sich* in the K-position (to which the emphatic particle *selbst* 'self' may be added) is A-bound by an antecedent that s-commands the trace that is Ā-bound by the reflexive:

(89) (a) sich (selbst) sollte sie rasieren
-self (self) should she shave
'she should shave herself'

(b) [sich (selbst)]$_i$ [sollte [sie$_i$ [t_i rasieren]]]

Note that this configuration is different from a strong crossover configuration (which will be discussed in section 6.1). The reflexive must be bound, and *sie* is the only possible antecedent. From the asymmetry of binding it follows that *sie* cannot be bound by *sich*, hence there is no chance for a strong crossover effect to ensue.

In (90) and (91) we observe A-bound possessives:

(90) (a) seinen Hund gefüttert hat wohl keiner
his dog fed has presumably no
'presumably, no-one fed his dog'

(b) [seinen$_i$ Hund gefüttert]$_j$ [hat$_k$ [wohl keiner$_i$ [t_j t_k]]]

(91) (a) seinen Hund hat wohl keiner gefüttert
his dog has presumably no fed
'presumably, no-one fed his dog'

(b) [seinen$_i$ Hund]$_j$ [hat [wohl keiner$_i$ [t_j gefüttert]]]

Under the relevant reading the possessive *seinen* 'his' is A-bound by *keiner* 'no-one', which s-commands the trace of the phrase that contains the possessive.

The same configuration is found in complement clauses:

(92) (a) zugeben, daß er krank ist, würde wohl keiner
admit that he ill is would presumably no
'presumably, no-one would admit that he is ill'

(b) [zugeben, daß er$_i$ krank ist]$_j$ [würde$_k$ [wohl keiner$_i$ [t_j t_k]]]

(93) (a) daß er krank ist, würde wohl keiner zugeben
that he ill is would presumably no admit
'presumably, no-one would admit that he is ill'

(b) [daß er$_i$ krank ist]$_j$ [würde [wohl keiner$_i$ [t_j zugeben]]]

Under the relevant reading *er* 'he' is A-bound by *keiner*, which again s-commands the trace of the phrase that contains the bound pronoun.

3.2.2 Pronominal Coreference

Let us try to replace the binding relations seen in (88)–(93) by coreference:

(94) (a) [den Kerl dort drüben]$_i$ rasieren sollte er$_j$
'shave the guy over there, he should'

(b) [den Kerl dort drüben]$_i$ sollte er$_j$ rasieren
'the guy over there, he should shave'

(95) (a) den Hund von [dem Kerl dort drüben]$_i$ gefüttert hat er$_j$ selten
'feed the dog of the guy over there he seldom has'

(b) den Hund von [dem Kerl dort drüben]$_i$ hat er$_j$ selten gefüttert
'the dog of the guy over there he seldom fed'

(96) zugeben, daß [der Kerl dort drüben]$_i$ krank ist, würde er$_j$ kaum

'admit that the guy over there is ill, he hardly would'

The examples are perfectly grammatical, and since pronouns usually pick up a referent introduced earlier in the text, we would expect that the pronoun *er* 'he' may be understood as being coreferential with the definite NP *d– Kerl dort drüben* 'the guy over there' to its left. But this reading is as difficult to get here as it is in (97):

(97) (a) trotzdem sollte er$_j$ [den Kerl dort drüben]$_i$ rasieren

(b) trotzdem hat er$_j$ den Hund von [dem Kerl dort drüben]$_i$ gefüttert

(c) trotzdem würde er$_j$ kaum zugeben, daß [der Kerl dort drüben]$_i$ krank ist

In (97) well-known restrictions against coreference make a disjoint reference reading nearly obligatory (i.e., $i \neq j$). Obviously the same is true of (94)–(96). It appears, then, that with verb projections and definite NPs in the K-position coreference relations are obligatorily computed with respect to the trace that is $\bar{A}$-bound by them.

With clauses the situation is slightly different. While (93) shows that binding in accordance with the position of the trace is possible, coreference is not excluded in the same configuration:

(98) (?)daß [der Kerl dort drüben]$_i$ krank ist, würde er$_i$ kaum zugeben

'that the guy over there is ill, he would hardly admit'

While judgements vary somewhat, there is no doubt that a coreference reading is far more accessible here than in examples like (96).

3.2.3 Empty Categories

Given that A-binding of non-empty anaphoric expressions may involve the position of a $\bar{A}$-bound trace, we may expect empty categories to behave similarly.

There is in fact evidence in English that traces of 'NP-movement' (passive and subject-to-subject raising) may be bound by an antecedent they are not s-commanded by, as long as they are lexically governed (data from Thiersch (1985) and personal communication):

(99) (a) [criticized t_i by his boss]$_j$ John$_i$ has never been t_j

(b) [likely t_i to succeed]$_j$ though John$_i$ may be t_j

(c) [likely t_i to be fired t'_i]$_j$ John$_i$ certainly is t_j

In each case t_i is A-bound by *John*. This is possible because *John* s-commands t_j, which is Ā-bound by the phrase containing t_i.[20] Equivalent examples can be found in Italian:[21]

(100) [tradito t_i da sua moglie]$_j$ [credo che Mario$_i$ non sia mai stato t_j]
'betrayed by his wife, I believe that Mario has never been'

Traces of clitic-movement behave just the same:

(101) [offerte t_i a sua moglie]$_j$ [credo che Mario ancora non le$_i$ abbia t_j]
'offered t_i to his wife, I believe that Mario them$_i$ has not yet'

Although such traces are Ā-bound by their antecedent (t_i is Ā-bound by *le*), they are known to comply with the conditions on A-bound traces (Aoun 1985). Therefore (101) does not come as a surprise, given that (100) is possible.

In German there is at least one obvious candidate for 'clitic-movement', viz., structures such as (102a) related to (102b):

(102) (a) er hat da$_i$ oft [t_i von] gesprochen
he has there often of spoken
'he often talked about that'

(b) er hat oft davon gesprochen

Cf. note 11. Whereas *davon* 'there-of' can be contained in a phrase in the K-position (103), the trace of *da* cannot (104):

(103) (a) [davon gesprochen]$_i$ [hat er oft t_i]
thereof spoken has he often

[20]However, M. Baltin (cited by Saito (1989: 199)) observed that in raising structures the binder cannot be a non-argument:

(i) *[how likely t_i to be a riot]$_j$ is there$_i$ t_j

(ii) *[how likely t_i to be taken t_i of John]$_j$ is advantage$_i$ t_j

This seems also to be true of pure passive structures:

(iii) *[made t_i by John]$_j$ [considerable headway]$_i$ has been t_j

(iv) *[kept t_i on John]$_j$ though tabs$_i$ will be t_j

It appears, then, that the preposed phrase must be a predicative category (assign an external θ-role), for reasons unknown.

[21]In this paper, Italian data are taken from Longobardi (1985).

(b) davon$_i$ [hat er oft t_i gesprochen]

(104) (a) ?*[[t_j von] gesprochen]$_i$ [hat er da$_j$ oft t_i]

(b) *[t_j von]$_i$ [hat er da$_j$ oft t_i gesprochen]

I assume that the trace t in (102a) is not lexically governed but antecedent-governed. If this is correct, we may assume that t_j in (104) fails to be antecedent-governed (whereas t_i in (101) is lexically governed). This would mean, then, that for antecedent-government to be possible, binding must be determined by s-command at S-structure.

Italian allows extraction much more freely than English. It thereby offers an opportunity to observe the behaviour of Ā-bound traces. As it turns out, traces of wh-movement (105) and topicalization (106) must be s-commanded by their antecedent at S-structure:[22]

(105) *[a sposare t_i]$_j$ [non so proprio [[quale ragazza]$_i$ [Gianni sarebbe disposto t_j]]]

'to marry t_i, I really do not know [which girl]$_i$ Gianni would be ready'

(106) *[a comprarti t_i per il compleanno]$_j$ [penso [che [solo questo regalo]$_i$ [potrei convincere tua moglie t_j]]]

'to buy you t_i for your birthday, I think that [only this present]$_i$ I might be able to persuade your wife'

But in the same configuration parasitic gaps are much better:

(107) ?[senza conoscere e_i prima bene]$_j$ [non so proprio [[quale altra ragazza]$_i$ [Gianni sarebbe disposto a sposare t_i t_j]]]

'without knowing e_i well beforehand, I really do not know [which other girl]$_i$ Gianni would be ready to marry t_i'

This differential behaviour of wh-traces and parasitic gaps poses important questions which will be taken up in section 6.4.

[22]In this respect so-called scrambling in Japanese (at least, non-local scrambling) behaves like wh-movement and topicalization in Italian; see Saito (1989: 190). Note that scrambling in Japanese (as opposed to 'scrambling' in German) also behaves as wh-movement does in some variants of English w.r.t. A-binding, discussed in section 6.3; see reference in note 31.

4 Reconstruction

We have seen that in a number of cases scope assignment and binding of expressions contained in a phrase that Ā-binds a trace may or must consider the position of the trace. How can these facts formally be accounted for?

As to the observations on scope, it seems natural to account for them by mechanisms used in the translation from the syntactic form into a semantic representation. Suppose that a constituent containing a Ā-bound trace is translated in such a way that a variable replaces the trace and a lambda operator binds the variable, as in (108):

(108) (a) XP_i [... YP ... t_i ...]

(b) XP'_σ λ Z_τ (... YP′ ... Z_τ ...)

In the semantic representation (108b) the Ā-binder XP is represented by an expression XP′ of type σ, and the variable Z corresponding to the trace is of type τ. If σ is a higher type than τ, XP′ will have scope over the lambda expression; if $\sigma = \tau$, YP′ will have scope over XP′. Depending on properties of XP and on intonation, the translation mechanism will fix τ equal to σ or lower than σ.

Unfortunately this simple idea cannot account for the observations on binding, for elementary reasons. If XP contains an expression that is understood to be bound by YP and XP is translated in the usual way, i.e., without taking YP into account, then XP′ will contain a free variable that cannot become bound by lambda conversion; cf. Engdahl (1986: 29–32). At the same time it seems obvious that the grammatical principles governing scope and binding are essentially similar. That is, in those cases where the position of the trace must be considered in order for the trace binder to be treated properly, the trace cannot be evaluated by lambda conversion. Rather there must be a different mechanism that is able to account for scope as well as for binding.

The question of how to adequately account for binding phenomena of the kind we have discussed has a long history. One traditional answer is that A-binding relations must be determined at a level (or: at levels) of representation more abstract than S-structure (and surface structure). Proposals differ as to how this level is to be characterized precisely. For concreteness, we may define a level of R-structure as in (109):

(109) *R-structure:*

(i) The theories of scope and A-binding apply only at R-structure.

(ii) If at S-structure some phrase D occupies a Ā-position Pa and binds a trace *t* in an A-position Pb, then at R-structure a representation of D may occupy Pb while Pa is empty. Otherwise, R-structure and S-structure are identical.

(iii) Clause (ii) is subject to certain conditions to be specified separately.

If a phrase D is in position Pb at R-structure while it is in position Pa at S-structure, according to clause (ii), I will say that D is 'reconstructed'. (In a moment, "reconstruct" will acquire a second, though related, meaning.) The conditions that (109ii) is subject to may then be tentatively stated as in (110):

(110) *Conditions on reconstruction:*

(i) Indefinite NPs and clauses are optionally reconstructed.

(ii) Verbs and verb projections are obligatorily reconstructed.

(iii) Definite NPs are obligatorily reconstructed.

(iv) Truly quantified expressions are reconstructed if and only if they bear rising intonation within an I-Topic intonation pattern.[23]

(v) There is no other case of reconstruction.

This set of conditions seems to give correct results over a fairly broad empirical domain, as the reader may verify by reconsidering section 3. Naturally there remain many questions of descriptive detail on the one hand, and of theoretical rationalization on the other, which we cannot follow here.[24] Rather, we will explore some consequences of an alternative account for reconstruction phenomena.

There have been various attempts to account for binding facts like those we have seen in section 3.2 directly at S-structure. To this end, the binding theory must be modified in such a way that A-binding may be mediated somehow by a Ā-bound trace. Proposals to this effect have been made, e.g., by Guéron (1984), Roberts (1985), Williams (1986) and works cited there. For our purpose we may follow Williams's suggestion of generalizing the notion of c-command domain:

---

[23]The fall must be on a scope inducing expression (scalar particle, negation, distributive quantifier etc.) or on the focus of such an expression, as in (i):

(i) JEDEN / Hund hast auch DU \ dem Kater nicht zeigen können
every dog have even you the cat not show can
'even you were not able to show every dog to the cat'

Here *du* 'you' is the focus of the scalar particle *auch* 'even'.

[24]This remark applies in particular to the treatment of coreference, which on the whole is much less straightforward than section 3.2.2 makes it appear.

(111) *R-domain:*

(i) The theories of scope assignment and binding apply at S-structure.

(ii) (a) In the unmarked case, X is in the domain of Y if and only if X is s-commanded by Y.[25]

(b) X can be in the scope of Y or X can be A-bound by Y only if X is in the R-domain of Y.

(c) If X is in the domain of Y, then X is in the R-domain of Y.

(iii) If some phrase D $\bar{A}$-binds a trace t and t is in the R-domain of some A ($A \neq D$), then any B contained in D may be in the R-domain of A.

(iv) Clause (iii) is subject to the conditions on reconstruction.

Note that the clauses in (ii) are simply reformulations of the standard assumptions for the normal case. Clause (iii) corresponds to clause (ii) of (109). Accordingly, if a phrase D is in the R-domain of A according to (111iii) I will say that D is 'reconstructed'. Hence the conditions (110) apply in this case. To distinguish between the two senses of "reconstruct", I will speak of 'true reconstruction' in the case of (109) and of 'pseudo-reconstruction' in the case of (111).

As it stands, (111) is not exactly equivalent to (109) as long as the characterization of the Opacity Domain (OD, or Governing Category or Binding Category) for A-binding is not modified accordingly. Without such a modification ungrammatical examples such as (112) and (113) would be admitted alongside with their grammatical counterparts (114) and (115):

(112) (a) *Karl$_i$ wollte wissen, welche Scherze über sich$_i$ ich liebe
wanted know which jokes about -self I love
'Karl wanted to know which jokes about him(self) I like'

(b) *sich$_i$ glaubt Karl$_i$, daß ich liebe
-self believes that I love
'Karl believes that I like him(self)'

(c) *sich$_i$ glaube ich, daß Karl$_i$ hofft, daß du liebst
-self believe I that hopes that you love
'I believe that Karl hopes that you love him(self)'

---

[25]The extension of the scope domain of negation that we observed in (61) and (63) is an exception to the unmarked case. Other types of exceptions will be discussed in sections 6.4 and 6.5.

(113) (a) *wir wissen, welche Scherze über ihn$_i$ niemand$_i$ liebt
we know which jokes about him nobody loves
'we know which jokes about him(self) nobody likes'

(b) *ihn$_i$ (selbst) meine ich, daß jeder$_i$ rasieren sollte
him (self) mean I that every shave should
'I think that everyone should shave him(self)'

(114) (a) Karl$_i$ wollte wissen, welche Scherze über ihn$_i$ ich liebe

(b) ihn$_i$ glaubt Karl$_i$, daß ich liebe

(c) ihn$_i$ glaube ich, daß Karl$_i$ hofft, daß du liebst

(115) (a) wir wissen, welche Scherze über sich$_i$ niemand$_i$ liebt

(b) sich$_i$ (selbst) meine ich, daß jeder$_i$ rasieren sollte

Hence we have to revise the binding theory (for German) along the lines of (116):

(116) *Binding theory for R-domains:*

(i) X is the Opacity Domain (OD) of Y if and only if X is the smallest constituent that contains a SUBJECT β such that Y is in the R-domain of β.

(ii) An anaphor δ must be A-bound by a phrase α that is contained in the OD of δ.

(iii) A personal pronoun π must not be A-bound by a phrase α that is contained in the OD of π.[26]

With this modification (112) and (113) are correctly ruled out, and (111) is equivalent to (109) with regard to the kind of examples we have discussed so far. We will now turn to coordination in order to see whether and how differences between true reconstruction and pseudo-reconstruction may arise there.

[26]In German only third person pronouns are subject to (116iii). There is no OD for possessives or for first or second person pronouns. This is a natural state of affairs, as the existence of an OD for a pronominal is induced by the existence of a corresponding lexical anaphor. There are no reflexive possessives and no first or second person reflexives in German. Alternatively, possessives and first/second person pronominals may be considered to be systematically ambiguous in having the OD of a pronoun or the OD of an anaphor.

5 Reconstruction in Coordination

5.1 Scope

Consider an example such as (117) read with normal intonation:

(117) (a) fast jeden Hund hat Karl gefüttert oder hat Heinz gestreichelt
almost every dog has fed or has caressed
'for almost every dog x: Karl fed x or Heinz caressed x'

(b) [fast jeden Hund]$_i$ [[hat Karl t_i gefüttert] oder [hat Heinz t_i gestreichelt]]

Although *fast jeden Hund* 'almost every dog' functions as the direct object of two different verbs (and therefore binds two traces in (b)), the phrase has scope over the entire coordinate phrase. This fact immediately confirms one aspect of the conditions on reconstruction given in (110): in accordance with (110iv), *fast jeden Hund* is not reconstructed. If it were, (117) would be synonymous with (118), at least under true reconstruction:

(118) Karl hat fast jeden Hund gefüttert oder Heinz hat fast jeden Hund gestreichelt

'Karl fed almost every dog, or Heinz caressed almost every dog'

We may conclude that also in a simple (non-coordinate) case such as (119a) there is no reconstruction, even though (a) and (b) are logically equivalent here:

(119) (a) fast jeden Hund hat Karl gefüttert

(b) Karl hat fast jeden Hund gefüttert

The situation is different in (120). This example has a reading equivalent to (121):

(120) (a) einen Hund haben viele gestreichelt oder hat jeder gefüttert
a dog have many caressed or has every fed

(b) [einen Hund]$_i$ [[haben viele t_i gestreichelt] oder [hat jeder t_i gefüttert]]

(121) es haben viele einen Hund gestreichelt, oder es hat jeder einen Hund gefüttert
it have many a dog caressed or it has every a dog fed

'many people caressed a dog, or everyone fed a dog'

That is, *einen Hund* 'a dog' in the K-position can be understood to be in the scope of both *viele* 'many people' and *jeder* 'everyone'.

In a formal sense this is predicted by true reconstruction (109) as well as by pseudo-reconstruction (111), but there is an important difference. Under true reconstruction, R-structure is the level of representation where scope and binding is determined, hence semantic interpretation proceeds off this level, and in particular the interpretation of coordinate structures proceeds from R-structure. The R-structure representation of (120) is similar to (121) in that the positions of the two traces in (120b) are each occupied by *einen Hund* in (121); hence there is one occurrence of *einen Hund* in the domain of *viele*, and there is another occurrence of *einen Hund* in the domain of *jeder*.

Under pseudo-reconstruction, semantic interpretation proceeds from S-structure. In S-structure there is just one occurrence of *einen Hund*. It is in the R-domain, hence in the scope, of *viele* and of *jeder* – but that is either nonsensical or false. The problem presents itself lucidly when we make use of Skolem functions. Suppose that *viele* is represented by the variable "x" bound by some suitable quantifier and that *jeder* is represented by the variable "y" bound by the universal quantifier. Being in the scope of *viele*, *einen Hund* must be represented by "$f_1(x)$"; being in the scope of *jeder*, it must be represented by "$f_2(y)$". But for the translation of one and the same expression to be represented in these two ways, it must be the case that $f_1(x) = f_2(y)$. But this is empirically false: (120) is understood in the same way as (121), i.e., $f_1(x)$ and $f_2(y)$ are independent of each other.

The same problem presents itself from a different angle in an example such as (122), which in one reading is equivalent to (123):

(122) (a) einen Hund hat Karl gefüttert und hat Heinz gestreichelt
a dog has fed and has caressed

(b) [einen Hund]$_i$ [[hat Karl t_i gefüttert] und [hat Heinz t_i gestreichelt]]

(123) es hat Karl einen Hund gefüttert, und es hat Heinz einen Hund gestreichelt

'Karl fed a dog, and Heinz caressed a dog'

True reconstruction maps (122) into an R-structure representation similar to (123), the translation of which immediately represents the relevant reading of (122), where there may be two different dogs involved. But pseudo-reconstruction seems to be unable to generate this reading. Although (111) allows *einen Hund* to be 'reconstructed', it is not obvious which effect pseudo-reconstruction may be supposed to have in this case: *einen Hund* is neither A-bound by, nor in the scope of, any other expression. By usual assumptions the interpretation of the coordinate phrase will result in an expression roughly indicated by (124), where "x" is a variable of type e:

(124) ((HAS (FED (KARL, x))) & (HAS (CARESSED (HEINZ, x))))

Since *einen Hund* in (122) must be translated as being existentially quantified, this quantifier will have to bind both occurrences of "x" in (124). But this is not the reading we are interested in. Under the assumptions we made in section 4 it does not seem possible to get the correct interpretation, as long as we stick to standard assumptions about how to translate coordinate structures semantically (e.g., Partee & Rooth 1983).

A particularly interesting instance of the phenomenon seen in (122) can be observed in (125), which in one reading is equivalent to (126):

(125) ein Affe hat den Hund gefüttert und hat den Kater gefüttert
an ape has the dog fed and has the cat fed

(126) ein Affe hat den Hund gefüttert, und ein Affe hat den Kater gefüttert
'an ape fed the dog, and an ape fed the cat'

That is, the ape that fed the dog need not be the ape that fed the cat. This reading is unavailable in (127):

(127) (es ist wahr) daß ein Affe den Hund gefüttert hat und den Kater gefüttert hat
(it is true) that an ape the dog fed has and the cat fed has
'(it is true) that there is an ape that fed the dog and fed the cat'

From an observational point of view, this difference seems surprising. But it fits naturally into the general picture, given the structures of (125) and (127) as shown in (128):

(128) (a) [ein Affe]$_i$ [[hat t_i den Hund gefüttert] und [hat t_i den Kater gefüttert]]
(b) daß ein Affe [[den Hund gefüttert hat] und [den Kater gefüttert hat]]

In (128b) the subject *ein Affe* is not subject to reconstruction as there is no trace that is Ā-bound by it; hence it has scope over the entire coordinate phrase. In (128a), by contrast, *ein Affe* Ā-binds two traces, and true reconstruction yields a representation that is translated into a semantic representation equivalent to the translation of (126). (Pseudo-reconstruction faces the same problem here as it did with (122), of course.)[27]

Let us finally look at (129) under the reading it shares with (130):

[27]The reading we observed in (125) is less readily available, although not impossible, in (i):

(129) (a) einen Hund hat mancher gefüttert, aber keiner gestreichelt
a dog has some fed but no caressed

(b) [einen Hund]$_i$ [hat [[mancher t_i gefüttert] aber [keiner t_i gestreichelt]]]

(130) mancher hat einen Hund gefüttert, aber keiner hat einen Hund gestreichelt
some has a dog fed but no has a dog caressed

'some people fed a dog, but no-one caressed a dog'

Here, *einen Hund* is in the scope of *mancher* 'some people' on the one hand, and in the scope of *keiner* 'no-one' on the other hand. This much is correctly predicted by true as well as by pseudo-reconstruction. But true reconstruction generates two occurrences of *einen Hund*, so that the semantic interpretation of the coordinate structure is straightforward at R-structure. Pseudo-reconstruction, by contrast, must do with one occurrence, on which it imposes conflicting demands by requiring it to be at the same time in the scope of negation and outside the scope of negation.

5.2 A-Binding

As we would expect, the observations on scope are paralleled by observations on binding. Consider (131), which is synonymous with (132):

(131) (a) sich im Spiegel betrachtet hat Heinz selten und hat Karl häufig
-self in-the mirror viewed has seldom and has often

(b) [sich im Spiegel betrachtet]$_i$ [[hat Heinz selten t_i] und [hat Karl häufig t_i]]

(i) ein Affe hat den Hund gefüttert und den Kater gefüttert
an ape has the dog fed and the cat fed
'an ape fed the dog and fed the cat'

Note that (i) can be analyzed in two ways, viz., according to (ii), where there is only one trace bound by *ein Affe*, or according to (iii):

(ii) [ein Affe]$_i$ [hat [t_i [[den Hund gefüttert] und [den Kater gefüttert]]]]

(iii) [ein Affe]$_i$ [hat [[t_i den Hund gefüttert] und [t_i den Kater gefüttert]]]

It is plausible that the human parser avoids building up traces as far as possible; hence the preference for (ii).

(132) Heinz hat sich selten im Spiegel betrachtet, und Karl hat
has -self seldom in-the mirror viewed and has
sich häufig im Spiegel betrachtet
-self often in-the mirror viewed

'Heinz seldom viewed himself in the mirror, and Karl often viewed himself in the mirror'

True reconstruction maps (131) into an R-structure representation similar to (132), so that one occurrence of *sich* '-self' can be A-bound by *Heinz* and a second occurrence can be A-bound by *Karl*, which is a correct result. According to pseudo-reconstruction, *sich* in (131) must be A-bound by *Heinz* as well as by *Karl.* This correctly accounts for the ungrammaticality of (133):

(133) *sich im Spiegel betrachtet haben die Jungen häufig und haben
-self in-the mirror viewed have the boys often and have
wir selten
we seldom

The reflexive *sich* must be bound, and *die Jungen* 'the boys' is a possible binder under reconstruction. As a consequence of the External Homogeneity Condition (5), reconstruction must apply to each conjunct if it applies to any conjunct; hence *sich* must also find a binder in the second conjunct. As *sich* (3rd person) cannot be bound by *wir* (1st person), the example is ungrammatical. But semantically it is a fault that *sich* is at the same time bound by *Heinz* and by *Karl* in (131). This could make sense if and only if *Heinz* is identical with *Karl* – an incorrect result.

A similar observation holds for (134), which shares a reading with (135):

(134) (a) seinen Hund hat jeder selber gefüttert und hat kaum einer
his dog has every self fed and has hardly one
schlecht behandelt
bad treated

(b) [seinen Hund]$_i$ [[hat jeder t_i selber gefüttert] und [hat kaum einer t_i schlecht behandelt]]

(135) es hat jeder$_i$ seinen$_i$ Hund selber gefüttert, und es hat kaum
it has every$_i$ his$_i$ dog self fed and it has hardly
einer$_j$ seinen$_j$ Hund schlecht behandelt
one$_j$ his$_j$ dog bad treated

'everyone$_i$ fed his$_i$ dog by himself, and hardly anyone$_j$ treated his$_j$ dog badly'

By pseudo-reconstruction, there is one occurrence of *seinen Hund* 'his dog' that is relevant for the determination of A-binding and for semantic interpretation. The possessive *seinen* 'his' can be A-bound by *jeder* 'everyone' and by *kaum einer* 'hardly anyone'. It must, in fact, be bound by each of them; but semantically this is nonsense. R-structure, on the contrary, is similar to (135) in that there are two occurrences of *seinen (Hund)*; consequently the first occurrence can be bound by *jeder* and the second one by *kaum einer*, in accordance with the facts.[28]

5.3 Discussion

While true and pseudo-reconstruction seem to be empirically indistinguishable in simple cases, their effects differ markedly in coordinate structures. The predictions of true reconstruction are consistently correct, whereas the predictions of pseudo-reconstruction are nonsensical or false. Let us briefly reflect on why this is so.

To say that an expression D is 'reconstructed' means that D behaves to a large degree as if it occupied the position of a trace t that it Ā-binds. True reconstruction generates a level of R-structure where D does in fact occupy the position of t. Consequently, in coordinate structures an occurrence of D is available in each conjunct. By applying the theories of A-binding, of scope determination and of semantic interpretation at R-structure, D is translated correctly as a part of each conjunct. Pseudo-reconstruction, in contrast, seeks to achieve the same results at S-structure by allowing the expression D to be in the R-domain of expressions it s-commands. However, the notion of R-domain, by itself, does not suffice. Rather an appropriate translation of D must be available in each conjunct of a coordinate structure. The translation of (136a) (= (122)), for example, must have a translation of *einen Hund* 'a dog' as part

[28]Nevertheless, there is a problem. As there are two occurrences of the possessive at R-structure and any given possessive is ambiguous between a bound and a referential reading, (134) should be at least four-ways ambiguous; but in fact it is only two-ways ambiguous: the possessive may be referential (referring to one fixed referent), or it may be bound in the way we have discussed. There is no 'mixed' reading. The same observation holds of pronouns, as in (i), where either $j = l = h$, or $j = i$ and $l = k$:

(i) daß er gerne trinkt, würde fast jeder leugnen und würde kaum einer zugeben
that he gladly drinks would almost every deny and would hardly one admit
'almost everyone$_i$ would deny that he$_j$ likes drinking, and hardly anyone$_k$ would admit that he$_l$ likes drinking'

Presumably NPs must be determined as being referential or non-referential before reconstruction applies. (Notice that the conditions on reconstruction (110) also rely on a partial semantic characterization of the Ā-binder.) The consequences of this fact remain to be explored.

of the translation of each conjunct. The translation of (136b) (= (134)), again, must have a translation of *seinen Hund* 'his dog' as part of the translation of each conjunct, and each of them must contain a different variable:

(136) (a) einen Hund hat Karl gefüttert und hat Heinz gestreichelt
'Karl fed a dog, and Heinz caressed a dog'

(b) seinen Hund hat jeder selber gefüttert und hat kaum einer schlecht behandelt
'everyone$_i$ fed his$_i$ dog by himself, and hardly anyone$_j$ treated his$_j$ dog badly'

If we wish to obtain these results not at R-structure but at S-structure, we have to introduce the assumptions singled out in (137):

(137) *Translation according to pseudo-reconstruction:*

(i) In a coordinate structure each conjunct ^{i}B is separately evaluated with respect to the elements ^{j}A that are external to the conjuncts (cf. (1)).

(ii) Under reconstruction the expression D is translated during the evaluation of a phrase P that is s-commanded by D, so that an appropriate translation of D is part of the translation of P.

Note that condition (ii) does not seem to introduce problems of a formal nature. We have been supposing throughout that the relation of the trace t contained in P to its Ā-binder D can be recognized at S-structure, hence D can be made accessible for the purpose of evaluating P.[29] In accordance with (i), then, the expression D will be translated as many times as there are conjuncts containing a trace Ā-bound by D. But condition (i) seems problematic. Although it resembles the way the External Homogeneity Condition on coordinate structures was put in (5), it contradicts the way that semantic interpretation of coordinate structures is standardly thought to be done (e.g., by Partee & Rooth 1983). The standard assumption is that the translation of the external elements ^{j}A combines with the translation of the entire coordinate phrase, whose translation in turn results from combining the translations of the conjuncts ^{i}B. We have seen that this method of interpretation can be successfully applied at R-structure but not at S-structure. It is not obvious, though, whether there are strong reasons to prefer the standard assumption over (137i).

[29] In this regard an S-structure representation from which Ā-binding relations can be retrieved would seem to be equivalent to a phrase linking grammar representation such as is used by Engdahl (1986). The evaluation of P cannot be done strictly compositionally at S-structure, in any case.

In the next section we will turn to some considerations that might help in deciding between true and pseudo-reconstruction and, by implication, between the standard assumptions about coordination and (137i).

6 Pseudo-Reconstruction or True Reconstruction?

6.1 Ā-Binding: Strong Crossover

As a possible argument for true reconstruction, consider strong crossover:

(138) (a) *who$_i$ does he$_i$ like e_i

(b) *he$_i$ likes who$_i$

It seems natural to relate the impossibility of (138a) to the impossibility of (138b). In the latter, *who* cannot A-bind *he* since it is s-commanded by *he*, and *who* cannot be bound at all; cf. Wasow (1979) and Riemsdijk & Williams (1981). For this kind of explanation to be successful, however, it would have to be necessary that Ā-binding of *he* by *who* in (138a) is theoretically excluded. But why should Ā-binding of *he* be excluded? It is true that English does not favour Ā-binding of pronominals, but it does occur in weak crossover constructions (which are incomparably better than strong crossover constructions, as Wasow (1979) takes pains to demonstrate). Also, there are languages such as Swedish that even require resumptive pronouns under certain conditions, although they disallow strong crossover configurations just as English does. The same question arises with parasitic gap constructions: why is (139a) impossible although Ā-binding of a secondary gap is possible in (139b)?

(139) (a) *who$_i$ do you think e'_i likes e_i

(b) Bill is the kind of person whom$_i$ everyone who knows e'_i dislikes e_i

It seems that a principle such as (140) must be stipulated:

(140) *Restriction on multiple binding:*

If an A-position P_1 is in the unmarked (i.e., s-command) domain of an A-position P_2 and the category in P_2 is bound by some category E, then a category in P_1 cannot be bound by E.[30]

[30] It follows that the relation of binding is intransitive, at least insofar as it observes s-command. I will in fact assume that it is always intransitive, even if s-command is not observed.

By (140), *e* in (138a) and (139a) cannot be bound by *who* since, by assumption, *he* and *e'* are. As an empty category can occupy the position of *e* only if it is Ā-bound, configurations like these are ruled ungrammatical at S-structure. If this account is correct, reconstruction does not have anything to contribute to an explanation of strong crossover.

6.2 Verum Focus

In section 3.1.3 we considered examples such as (141) (= (84b)):

(141) es HÖRT mir keiner zu

'no-one does listen to me'

There we concluded (i) that a meaning component symbolized as 'VERUM' is associated with the FIN-position and (ii) that VERUM can be in the scope of the negation because *hört* Ā-binds a trace that is in the domain of the negation. If this is to be accounted for by true reconstruction, VERUM must somehow be picked up by the verb *hört* and taken along into the position of the trace. But why and how should the verb be able to do that? It is the FIN-position that VERUM is associated with, and there is no independent reason for assuming that this situation may change during the derivation. It seems more adequate, hence, to assume that the scope of negation with respect to VERUM is accounted for by pseudo-reconstruction.

6.3 Lexical anaphors

In section 4 we noted that for pseudo-reconstruction to work properly in German, the characterizations of the Opacity Domain of anaphors and pronominals had to be adjusted as in (116). For many speakers of English just the same considerations apply. However, a number of authors have observed that a subset of speakers do allow lexical anaphors to be bound in exactly those configurations that are impossible in German:[31]

(142) (a) Mary wonders which picture of herself John will prefer *t*

(b) which picture of herself does Mary think that John will prefer *t*

(c) which picture of herself do you think that Mary wants me to buy *t*

[31]See Weisler (1983). Furthermore, see Reed (1978) for (142b,c); Jacobson & Neubauer (1976), Rouveret & Vergnaud (1980) and Williams (1986) for (142a); Langendoen & Battistella (1982) and Guéron (1984) for (142b), and also Engdahl (1986: 112) for Swedish and Kitagawa (1986: ch. 4.3.8) for Japanese.

In the system of those speakers who accept (142) the reflexive contained in the phrase D (*which picture of herself*) can be bound by any phrase α that s-commands the reflexive or the trace of D, as long as α does not s-command an accessible SUBJECT that s-commands the reflexive.

If we wish to account for these data by true reconstruction, we must allow an expression D that contains a lexical anaphor (but not a pronoun) to optionally replace an intermediate trace in a $\bar{A}$-position, rather than a trace in an A-position.

Under pseudo-reconstruction the characterization of the OD of lexical anaphors, repeated in (143), must be modified as in (144):

(143) X is the OD of a lexical anaphor δ if and only if X is the smallest constituent that contains an accessible SUBJECT β such that δ is in the R-domain of β. (Cf. (116i).)

(144) (i) X is the OD of a lexical anaphor δ if X is the smallest constituent that contains an accessible SUBJECT β such that δ is in the domain of β, if there is such a constituent.

(ii) Otherwise, the whole sentence is the OD of δ.

In (144i) "R-domain" of (143) is replaced by "domain", and in (144ii) the OD gets a default characterization. The effect is that the OD is directly determined by the s-command relations, without any appeal to the base position of D. In this sense (144) can be viewed as a natural generalization of (143). This is as we would expect, given that the system exemplified in (142) constitutes the marked case in relation to the more restricted versions of English and German, and that marked extensions of the unmarked case should be rationalizable in terms of generalization and simplification.

The extensions required for true reconstruction, by contrast, do not seem equally natural. If there is reconstruction, we expect the base position of D to be involved, as this position is naturally relevant for semantic interpretation. But reconstruction into an intermediate $\bar{A}$-position seems an artificial consequence of the initial assumptions, rather than a natural generalization of the unmarked system. Conceptually, then, the accounts given for (142) by pseudo-reconstruction and by true reconstruction are very different, with true reconstruction looking distinctly suspicious.

6.4 Ā-Binding: Parasitic Gaps

We noted in section 3.2.3 that a trace of ordinary wh-movement must be bound under s-command at S-structure, while a parasitic gap need not;[32] cf. (145) (=(105)) and (146) (=(107):

(145) *[a sposare t_i]$_j$ [non so proprio [[quale ragazza]$_i$ [Gianni sarebbe disposto t_j]]]

'to marry t_i, I really do not know [which girl]$_i$ Gianni would be ready'

(146) ?[senza conoscere e_i prima bene]$_j$ [non so proprio [[quale altra ragazza]$_i$ [Gianni sarebbe disposto a sposare t_i t_j]]]

'without knowing e_i well beforehand, I really do not know [which other girl]$_i$ Gianni would be ready to marry t_i'

With respect to a true wh-trace there do not seem to be technical problems. At S-structure the checking mechanism takes a phrase occupying a Ā-position and looks for a trace s-commanded by it. In (145) a trace (viz., t_j) corresponding to *a sposare* is found, but there is no trace s-commanded by *quale ragazza*; hence this configuration is ungrammatical. In (146) a trace (t_j) corresponding to D_j (*senza conoscere prima bene*) as well as a trace (t_i) corresponding to D_i (*quale altra ragazza*) is found; hence this configuration is grammatical w.r.t. binding of traces of true wh-movement.[33] But how is the parasitic gap e_i in (146) formally licensed?

With true reconstruction the phrase D_j containing e_i must be reconstructed into the position of the trace t_j that it Ā-binds, in order for e_i to be s-commanded by a Ā-binder. This will work as long as the Ā-binder D_i that licenses the parasitic gap is not reconstructed by itself. But suppose it must be reconstructed, for example, if it contains a reflexive. In this case the parasitic gap cannot be licensed at R-structure. But by hypothesis, binding relations that are relevant for parasitic gaps are determined at R-structure. (If they

[32] Unlike Italian, English strongly resists extraction from wh-interrogatives, in particular extraction of adjuncts. The initial adverbial in (i), therefore, cannot result from extraction (cannot bind a trace):

(i) after visiting Bill, who did you hire

We consequently expect English examples corresponding to (146) to be distinctly bad, and in fact E. McNulty observed that they are:

(ii) *without reading, which report did you file

See Lasnik & Uriagereka (1988: 75).

[33] A similar mechanism must apply for the determination of antecedent-government, if the account proposed for (104) is correct.

were determined at S-structure, (146) should be ungrammatical in the same way as (145).)

The point may also be illustrated by examples adapted from K. Kearney (cited by Chomsky (1986b: 60)):

(147) (a) which books about himself did John file *t* before Mary could read *e*

(b) *which books about herself did John file *t* before Mary could read *e*

While (147a) may be slightly marginal for some speakers, (147b) is impossible. Under true reconstruction, the binding relations of both *himself* and *e* must be determined at R-structure. But if the antecedent of *t* is reconstructed, as in (148), it can no longer license *e*:

(148) *John filed which books about himself before Mary could read *e*

We must conclude that parasitic gaps are licensed at S-structure. But at S-structure, true reconstruction cannot license (146) or (147a). Hence true reconstruction must give way to pseudo-reconstruction.

The examples (147) show more than this. The binding relations of the reflexive must be determined (by pseudo-reconstruction) with reference to *t*, not to *e*. Although *e* is licensed by D (*which books about himself*), D is not reconstructed with respect to *e*. The same fact is apparent from the meaning of the sentences. (147a) corresponds to (149), but not to (150):

(149) (a) which books about himself did John file *t* before Mary could read them

(b) John filed some books about himself before Mary could read them

(150) John filed some books about himself before Mary could read some books about herself

That is, the parasitic gap in (147a) as well as the pronoun *them* in (149) is anaphoric to the phrase *which/some books about himself*, with *himself* bound by *John*. In this regard, *e* does not behave like a trace $\bar{A}$-bound by D, but like a pronoun A-bound by *t*. In fact, although the position of *e* (presumably) is not s-commanded by the position of *t*, it is in its domain, as shown by (151):

(151) (a) John filed [every book]$_i$ before Mary could read it$_i$

(b) John filed [no book]$_i$ before Mary could read it$_i$

Here *it* is A-bound by the quantified phrase in the object position of *filed*.[34]

Note also that (149a) does not show any weak crossover effect. Such an effect would be expected if *them* were Ā-bound by D in the way that *t* is. In parasitic gap constructions of the type shown in (152a) substitution of a pronoun for the empty category in fact yields the typical weak crossover effect, see (152b). With this type, binding from the position of *t* into the position of *e* is not possible, as shown by (152c):

(152) (a) he is the kind of person whom$_i$ everyone who knows e_i dislikes t_i

(b) ??he is the kind of person whom$_i$ everyone who knows him$_i$ dislikes t_i

(c) *many people who know him$_i$ dislike everyone$_i$

Clearly the properties of parasitic gap constructions like (147) and their difference from those like (152a) call for some elaboration of theoretical assumptions.

We may begin by distinguishing two different aspects of binding. First, binding has a purely syntactic aspect which need not have any semantic counterpart; call this s-binding. It appears that pure s-binding holds in constructions with obligatory reflexives that are often found in Slavic and Germanic languages (other than English):

(153) (a) Karl weigert sich, das zu tun
refuses -self that to do
'Karl refuses to do that'

(b) Karl kümmert sich um die Kinder
worries -self about the children
'Karl sees to the children'

It can be demonstrated that these reflexives are semantically empty (they do not bear a θ-role).

Second, binding typically has a semantic (or 'functional') aspect in that the possible semantic value of a bound expression is determined by its binder; call this f-binding.[35] The pronoun *it* in (151) is f-bound by the object of *filed*. By the same token, I will assume that *them* in (149) and *e* in (147a) are f-bound by the object of *file(d)* (the trace in (149a) and (147a)).

I will assume, furthermore, that for proper binding to be possible, the bindee must be s-bound and if it bears a θ-role, it must also be f-bound. In (147a) and (149a) the trace *t* is s-bound and f-bound by D (*which books about himself*).

[34]See Engdahl (1986: 300) for similar observations on Swedish.

[35]It seems that virtually the same distinction between two aspects of binding has been made by Chomsky (1986a: 85).

The pronoun *it* in (151) is s-bound (and f-bound) by *every book/no book*. In (149a) *them* is s-bound (and f-bound) by the trace. But in (147a) I assume the parasitic gap e is not s-bound by t (although it is f-bound by t). Rather I propose that e is s-bound by D, the Ā-binder of t. That is, I assume that in this type of construction s-binding and f-binding of one category (viz., e) can be exercised by different binders.[36] In (152), by contrast, it is obvious from (152c) that the object position of *know* cannot be s-bound by the object position of *dislikes*. Hence *him* in (152b) must be s-bound by *whom*. English strongly disfavours s-binding of an anaphoric expression by a Ā-binder, hence the marginality of (152b). In (152a) both t and e are s-bound by *whom*; t is f-bound by *whom*, and e presumably may be too.

Let us now return to the Italian case (154a) (= (146)) with the schematic structure (154b):

(154) (a) ?[senza conoscere e_i prima bene]$_j$ [non so proprio [[quale altra ragazza]$_i$ [Gianni sarebbe disposto a sposare t_i t_j]]]

(b) [...e_i...]$_j$ [...[E$_i$ [...t_i t_j]]]

This is a parasitic gap construction of the type seen in (147). The f-binding of e_i is naturally accounted for under pseudo-reconstruction, as it is a case of A-binding (by t_i), assuming that the preposed adverbial clause falls under (110i). We must also allow s-binding of e_i by E_i to be possible under reconstruction. This is somewhat surprising, given that traces of true wh-movement are not licensed by reconstruction. The conclusion seems to be that a Ā-binder is not allowed to have its f-binding relations determined by reconstruction.

6.5 Ā-Binding: Weak Crossover

To broaden the view on s-binding and f-binding, we may add some observations on weak crossover. Consider (155) and (156):

(155) (a) ?wem$_i$ würden seine$_i$ Eltern t_i ein Auto schenken
whom would his parents a car donate
'for whom is it true that his parents would give him a car?'

[36]But naturally if β is s-bound by α, the semantic value of β must be determined by α. Hence either α f-binds β, or α f-binds δ and δ f-binds β. I continue assuming that binding is intransitive (cf. note 30), but I now restrict this assumption to any given type of binding (s-binding/f-binding). Hence in (147a), both t and e may be s-bound by D, as long as e is not s-bound by t. Notice that (147a) does not violate (140), since binding of e by t does not observe s-command.

(b) ?[fast jeden Lehrer]$_i$ haben seine$_i$ Schüler schon mal t_i reingelegt
almost every teacher have his students already once cheated

'it is true of almost every teacher that his students cheated him at least once'

(156) (a) ?*dann würden seine$_i$ Eltern jemandem$_i$ ein Auto schenken
then would his parents somebody a car donate

'then his parents would give a car to someone'

(b) ?*deshalb haben seine$_i$ Schüler [fast jeden Lehrer]$_i$ schon mal reingelegt
therefore have his students almost every teacher already once cheated

'therefore his students cheated almost every teacher at least once'

While the judgements on (155) vary considerably with speakers and types of Ā-binders, the crossover effect is in any case weak, and many speakers find examples like these perfectly unobjectionable. (156) on the other hand is decidedly marginal. It appears, then, that the possessive (*seine* 'his') in (155) can be bound because it is s-commanded by its semantic antecedent at S-structure. That is, the weak crossover configuration is a kind of parasitic Ā-binding much like parasitic gap configurations are. We must also assume that German disfavours Ā-binding of possessives (and pronominals) to a much smaller degree than English does.

We must ask, then, what kind of binding is involved. The possessive can hardly be both s-bound and f-bound by its Ā-binder. If it were, – i.e., if a pronominal expression could be s-bound and f-bound by a Ā-binder just like empty categories can – we would expect resumptive pronominals to be possible in German at least to the extent that they are, for example, in Swedish. However, resumptive pronominals are possible in German at best to the degree that they are in English. Hence we have to choose between s-binding and f-binding, and the possessive must have different binders for s-binding and f-binding, just as parasitic gaps may have two different binders. We may conjecture that in cases like these it is always s-binding that is determined by s-command. If so, we must assume that the possessive is f-bound by the trace that is Ā-bound by the s-binder of the possessive.

This assumption finds some support in long extractions such as (157) and (158):

(157) (a) wem$_i$ würden deine Eltern sagen, daß du t_i unter die
whom would your parents say that you under the
Arme greifen sollst
arms grip should
'for whom is it true that your parents would say that you should help him'

(b) *wem$_i$ würden seine$_i$ Eltern sagen, daß du t_i unter die Arme greifen sollst

(158) (a) [fast jeden Lehrer]$_i$ haben deine Kollegen gesagt, daß du
almost every teacher have your colleagues said that you
schon mal t_i reingelegt hast
already once cheated have
'it is true of almost every teacher that your colleagues said that you cheated him at least once'

(b) *[fast jeden Lehrer]$_i$ haben seine$_i$ Kollegen gesagt, daß du schon mal t_i reingelegt hast

The (a)-cases, with a second person possessive (*deine* 'your') contained in the matrix subject, are fully acceptable (for speakers who make use of long extractions). In the (b)-cases the third person possessive (*seine* 'his') should be able to be bound by the preposed phrase; however, the bound reading is judged to be very bad even by speakers who judge (155) and the (a)-cases of (157), (158) to be impeccable. This state of affairs is not surprising under the assumption that the possessive must be f-bound by the trace. For this to be possible at all, we have to assume that f-binding – as opposed to s-binding – may rather liberally disregard s-command, perhaps in the way that quantifier scope does (in the marked case). But we would not expect f-binding to extend upwards out of its clause, just as scope typically does not. Consequently, the possessive can be f-bound by the trace in (155) but not in (157b) and (158b). The binding relation in (155), then, is similar to the one argued for in connection with (154) and (147), namely, it is determined by s-binding from a $\bar{A}$-position and f-binding from an A-position.

These results lead us to reconsider (159) (= (152a)):

(159) he is the kind of person whom$_i$ everyone who knows e_i dislikes t_i

In section 6.4 we assumed that e here may be f-bound by *whom*. But now it seems probable that e is f-bound by t. In fact the long extraction in (160) appears to be significantly worse than (159):

(160) ?*he is the kind of person whom$_i$ everyone who knows e_i believes that many students admire t_i

If these speculations are correct, an interesting generalization emerges:

(161) *Conjectures about $\bar{A}$-binding:*

(i) Only real traces can be f-bound by a $\bar{A}$-binder.

(ii) F-Binding by a $\bar{A}$-binder must conform to s-command.

(iii) A $\bar{A}$-binder can be subject to reconstruction only w.r.t. a trace that it f-binds (i.e., a real trace).

7 Conclusion

In the course of the main discussion we considered two ways of construing 'reconstruction': true reconstruction, which involves an abstract level of representation, R-structure; and pseudo-reconstruction, which tries to do without such an extra level. Coordination showed that pseudo-reconstruction must be bought at a price: the standard view of the way coordinate structures are translated into the semantics must be abandoned. Although the translation mechanism that is needed under pseudo-reconstruction does not seem to pose extraordinary technical problems, one would not like to give up the standard view if not forced to. Consideration of some further kind of data – in particular, certain parasitic gap constructions – led us to conclude that true reconstruction cannot consistently achieve the results it is designed for. If these conclusions are correct, reconstruction is done at S-structure, and consequently the theory of semantic translation for coordinate structures must be revised in the way indicated in (137).

Conceptually this is an interesting result. Natural intuition would lead us to expect phenomena to fall into one of two classes: they should either be typical of S-structure or of reconstruction. Hence, many observers feel that true reconstruction is the natural way to account for reconstruction phenomena, and that pseudo-reconstruction, while technically possible, may be a descendant of ideological preconception rather than of open-minded inquiry. However, parasitic $\bar{A}$-binding characteristically involves S-structure and reconstruction at the same time, and hence, pseudo-reconstruction.

The reason why parasitic $\bar{A}$-binding can have its somewhat paradoxical properties seems to reside in the fact that under certain conditions two aspects of binding – viz., f-binding and s-binding – that normally go hand in hand can to some extent be dissociated from each other. If f-binding were necessarily coupled with s-binding, there would presumably be no parasitic binding at all, and we would not have been able to see as clearly that true reconstruction is not available in natural language.

References

Aoun, Joseph (1985) *A grammar of anaphora.* – Cambridge, Mass.: MIT Press.

Basri, Hasan & Finer, Daniel L. (1987) The definiteness of trace. – *Linguistic Inquiry* 18. pp. 141–147.

Booij, Geert E. (1985) Coordination reduction in complex words: a case for prosodic phonology. – In: *Advances in nonlinear phonology.* Ed. by Harry van der Hulst and Norval Smith. – Dordrecht: Foris. pp. 143–160.

Chomsky, Noam (1982) *Lectures on government and binding. The Pisa lectures.* 2nd revised ed. – Dordrecht: Foris.

Chomsky, Noam (1986a) *Knowledge of language: its nature, origin, and use.* – New York: Praeger.

Chomsky, Noam (1986b) *Barriers.* – Cambridge, Mass.: MIT Press.

Dowty, David (1988) Type raising, functional composition, and non-constituent conjunction. – In: *Categorial grammars and natural language structures.* Ed. by Richard T. Oehrle, Emmon Bach and Deirdre Wheeler. – Dordrecht: Reidel. pp. 153–197.

Engdahl, Elisabet (1986) *Constituent questions. The syntax and semantics of questions with special reference to Swedish.* – Dordrecht: Reidel.

Entjes, H. (1972) Nog eens die glibberige samentrekking. – *De Nieuwe Taalgids* 65. pp. 385–389.

Fodor, Janet Dean & Sag, Ivan A. (1982) Referential and quantificational indefinites. – *Linguistics and Philosophy* 5. pp. 355–398.

Fukui, Naoki (1986) *A theory of category projection and its applications.* – PhD dissertation, MIT, Cambridge, Mass.

Goodall, Grant (1987) *Parallel structures in syntax. Coordination, causatives, and restructuring.* – Cambridge: Cambridge University Press.

Guéron, J. (1984) Topicalisation structures and constraints on coreference. – *Lingua* 63. pp. 139–174.

Höhle, Tilman N. (1985) On composition and derivation: the constituent structure of secondary words in German. – In: Toman (ed.). pp. 319–376.

Höhle, Tilman N. (1986) Der Begriff 'Mittelfeld'. Anmerkungen über die Theorie der topologischen Felder. – In: *Akten des 7. Internationalen Germanisten-Kongresses Göttingen 1985. Band 3.* – Tübingen: Max Niemeyer. pp. 329–340.

Höhle, Tilman N. (1988) VERUM-Fokus. – In: *Sprache und Pragmatik.* Arbeitsberichte. No. 5. – Lund: Germanistisches Institut der Universität Lund. pp. 2–7.

Höhle, Tilman N. (1990) Assumptions about asymmetric coordination in German. – In: *Grammar in progress. Glow essays for Henk van Riemsdijk.* Ed. by Joan Mascaró and Marina Nespor. – Dordrecht: Foris. pp. 221–235.

Houtman, Joop (1987) Condities op nevenschikking. – *GLOT* 10. pp. 437–457.

Jacobs, Joachim (1980) Lexical decomposition in Montague-grammar. – *Theoretical Linguistics* 7. pp. 121–136.

Jacobs, Joachim (1982) *Syntax und Semantik der Negation im Deutschen.* – München: Wilhelm Fink.

Jacobs, Joachim (1983) *Fokus und Skalen. Zur Syntax und Semantik der Gradpartikeln im Deutschen.* – Tübingen: Max Niemeyer.

Jacobson, Pauline & Neubauer, Paul (1976) Rule cyclicity: evidence from the Intervention Constraint. – *Linguistic Inquiry* 7. pp. 429–461.

Kasher, Asa & Gabbay, Dov M. (1976) On the semantics and pragmatics of specific and non-specific indefinite expressions. – *Theoretical Linguistics* 3. pp. 145–190.

Kathol, Andreas (1989) V2 and licensing in German. – draft of ms.

Kiss, Katalin É. (1987) *Configurationality in Hungarian.* – Dordrecht: Reidel.

Kitagawa, Yoshihisa (1986) *Subjects in Japanese and English.* – PhD dissertation, University of Massachusetts, Amherst, Mass.

Klima, Edward S. (1964) Negation in English. – In: *The structure of language. Readings in the philosophy of language.* Ed. by Jerry A. Fodor and Jerrold J. Katz. – Englewood Cliffs, NJ: Prentice-Hall. pp. 246–323.

Kohrt, Manfred (1976) *Koordinationsreduktion und Verbstellung in einer generativen Grammatik des Deutschen.* – Tübingen: Max Niemeyer.

Koster, Jan (1987) *Domains and dynasties: the radical autonomy of syntax.* – Dordrecht: Foris.

Langendoen, D. Terence & Battistella, Edwin L. (1982) The interpretation of predicate reflexive and reciprocal expressions in English. – In: *Proceedings of NELS* 12, 1982. Ed. by James Pustejovsky and Peter Sells. – Amherst, Mass.: GLSA UMass. pp. 163–173.

Lasnik, Howard & Uriagereka, Juan (1988) *A course in GB syntax. Lectures on binding and empty categories.* – Cambridge, Mass.: MIT Press.

Lie, Svein (1982) Combinatory coordination in Norwegian. – In: *Papers from the sixth Scandinavian conference of linguistics.* Ed. by Thorstein Fretheim and Lars Hellan. – [Dragvoll:] Tapir. pp. 84–89.

Longobardi, Giuseppe (1985) Connectedness, scope, and c-command. – *Linguistic Inquiry* 16. pp. 163–192.

Neijt, Anneke (1978) Marked coordination in conjunction with the SOV – SVO problem. – In: *Linguistics in the Netherlands 1974 – 1976.* Ed. by Wim Zonneveld. – Lisse: Peter de Ridder. pp. 188–195.

Neijt, Anneke (1979) *Gapping. A contribution to sentence grammar.* – Dordrecht: Foris.

Neijt, Anneke (1987) Coordination reduction in Dutch morphology. – *Grazer Linguistische Studien* 28. pp. 91–101.

Neijt, Anneke (1989) [Review of] R. R. van Oirsouw, The syntax of coordination, London, Croom Helm, 1987. – *Lingua* 78. pp. 343–356.

Oirsouw, Robert R. van (1985) A linear approach to coordinate deletion. – *Linguistics* 23. pp. 363–390.

Pafel, Jürgen (1988) *Die Parameter des relativen Quantorenskopus im Deutschen.* – Stuttgart: IBM Deutschland. (LILOG-Report 48.)

Pafel, Jürgen (1989) "ALLE haben NICHT gelacht". Zum Phänomen des diskontinuierlichen negativen Quantors. – draft. [unpubl.]

Partee, Barbara Hall (1970) Negation, conjunction, and quantifiers: syntax vs. semantics. – *Foundations of Language* 6. pp. 153–165.

Partee, Barbara & Rooth, Mats (1983) Generalized conjunction and type ambiguity. – In: *Meaning, use, and interpretation of language.* Ed. by Rainer Bäuerle, Christoph Schwarze and Arnim von Stechow. – Berlin & New York: Walter de Gruyter. pp. 361–383.

Reed, Ann M. (1978) Picture noun reflexives and promotion. – In: *Proceedings of the eighth annual meeting of the North Eastern Linguistic Society.* Ed. by Mark J. Stein. – Amherst, Mass. pp. 167–177.

Riemsdijk, Henk van & Williams, Edwin (1981) NP-structure. – *The Linguistic Review* 1. pp. 171–217.

Roberts, Craige (1985) On the assignment of indices and their interpretation in binding theory. – In: *Proceedings of NELS* 15, 1985. Ed. by Stephen Berman, Jae-Woong Choe and Joyce McDonough. – Amherst, Mass. pp. 362–376.

Rouveret, Alain & Vergnaud, Jean-Roger (1980) Specifying reference to the subject: French causatives and conditions on representations. – *Linguistic Inquiry* 11. pp. 97–202.

Saito, Mamoru (1989) Scrambling as semantically vacuous A'-movement. – In: *Alternative conceptions of phrase structure.* Ed. by Mark R. Baltin and Anthony S. Kroch. – Chicago & London: University of Chicago Press. pp. 182–200.

Shopen, Tim (1972) *A generative theory of ellipsis. A contribution to the linguistic use of silence.* – IULC.

Stockwell, Robert P.; Schachter, Paul & Partee, Barbara H. (1973) *The major syntactic structures of English.* – New York: Holt, Rinehart and Winston.

Terazu, Noriko (1975) Coordinate deletion, gapping, and right node raising. – *Studies in English Linguistics* 3. pp. 19–65.

Thiersch, Craig (1985) VP and scrambling in the German Mittelfeld. – draft of ms. [unpubl.]

Toman, Jindřich (ed.) (1985) *Studies in German grammar.* – Dordrecht: Foris.

Toman, Jindřich (1985) A discussion of coordination and word-syntax. – In: Toman (ed.). pp. 407–432.

Wasow, Thomas (1979) *Anaphora in generative grammar.* – Ghent: Story-Scientia.

Weisler, Steven (1983) Generalized binding. – In: *University of Massachusetts Occasional Papers in Linguistics*, vol. 8. Ed. by Toni Borowsky and Dan Finer. – Amherst, Mass. pp. 131–176.

Wesche, Birgit (1989) Spurious ambiguities – on the syntax-semantics relation in C(U)G. – In: *Views of the syntax/semantics interface. Proceedings of the workshop 'GPSG and semantics' TU Berlin, Feb. 22 to 24, 1989.* Ed. by Stephan Busemann, Christa Hauenschild, and Carla Umbach. (KIT – Report 74) – Berlin: Technische Universität. pp. 185–193.

Williams, Edwin (1984) Grammatical relations. – *Linguistic Inquiry* 15. pp. 639–673.

Williams, Edwin (1986) A reassignment of the functions of LF. – *Linguistic Inquiry* 17. pp. 265–299.

Williams, Edwin (1987) NP trace in θ-theory. – *Linguistics and Philosophy* 10. pp. 433–447.

An Argument for Movement

Katalin É. Kiss

0 Introduction

The paper will argue for the necessity of maintaining the distinction between movement rules and rules of construal (taken for granted in the standard version of the Government Binding Theory, e.g., in Chomsky (1981), but denied in Koster (1987)). It will identify a distinguishing property of movement rules not taken into account so far: the capability of creating scope.

Evidence for the claim that movement rules create scope, while rules of construal do not do so, will be provided by the comparison of two Hungarian constructions: Operator Movement, and Left Dislocation. First (in sections 1 and 2) it will be demonstrated that in the framework of standard Government Binding Theory, Operator Movement has to be analyzed as a movement rule, and Left Dislocation has to be analyzed as a base-generated construction interpreted by a rule of construal – independent of scope considerations. Then (in sections 3 and 4) scope relations in the output of Operator Movement, and in the output of Left Dislocation will be compared. It will be shown that Operator Movement assigns scope to the preposed operator, while Left Dislocation, when involving an operator, does not affect scope at all. That is, in $\bar{A}$-chains resulting from Operator Movement, the scope of the operator extends over the c-command domain of the head of the chain, while in $\bar{A}$-chains resulting from Left Dislocation, the scope of the operator heading the chain extends over the c-command domain of the root of the chain. Finally (in section 5), two potential counter-arguments to the claim that movement determines scope will be discussed and dismissed.

1 Operator Movement: an Instance of "move wh"

Section 1 will examine whether Operator Movement is, indeed, an instance of "move α", by checking whether it displays the defining property of movement rules, i.e. whether it observes the Subjacency Condition.

H. Haider and K. Netter (eds.), Representation and Derivation in the Theory of Grammar, 199–215.

As a background to the analysis of Operator Movement, first the Hungarian sentence structure will be briefly outlined.

As is argued e.g. in É. Kiss (1988), the Hungarian sentence is the realization of a predication relation between a VP, and one (or more, or null) pre-VP arguments, functioning as the topic of the sentence. The topicalized constituents bind empty argument positions in the VP. All the arguments of the V, including the subject, are generated inside the VP, as right hand sisters to the V. Arguments of operator function, i.e. the focus, the PreV functioning as an aspectual operator, wh-phrases, and quantified phrases undergo Operator Movement, being preposed into the left periphery of the VP, into positions from which they c-command their domain. That is:

(1)

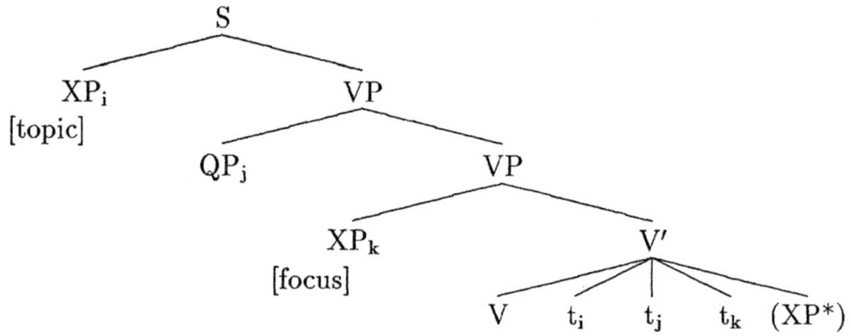

The specifier position of VP is the landing site of the focus, or the aspectual operator, or, in interrogative sentences, of the interrogative phrase (in multiple questions, one of the interrogative phrases). E.g.[1]

(2) (a) [$_T$ János] [$_{VP}$ kit$_i$ [$_{V'}$ kérdezett meg t$_i$]]
John who-acc asked pref.
'Who did John ask?'

(b) [$_T$ János] [$_{VP}$ Marit$_i$ [$_{V'}$ kérdezte meg t$_i$]]
John Mary-acc asked pref.
'John asked Mary.'

Quantified phrases in Hungarian undergo Q-Raising in syntax: they are iteratively adjoined to VP. Cf.[2]

---

[1]Although we assume that the topic also binds an empty argument position in the VP, we will not denote its trace – for perspicuity's sake.

[2]The particle *is* 'even' serves to turn a phrase containing a numeral which is interpretable referentially too into a quantified, i.e. operator phrase.

It is debated whether preverbal particles such as *meg*, when occurring preverbally in complementary distribution with the focus, actually occupy the specifier position of the VP, as

(3) (a) [$_T$ János] [$_{VP}$ mindenkit$_i$ [$_{VP}$ kétszer is$_j$ [$_{VP}$ meg
John everybody-acc twice even pref.
[$_{V'}$ kérdezett t$_i$ t$_j$]]]]
asked

'John asked everybody twice.'

(b) [$_T$ János] [$_{VP}$ kétszer is$_j$ [$_{VP}$ mindenkit$_i$ [$_{VP}$ meg
John twice even everybody-acc pref.
[$_{V'}$ kérdezett t$_i$ t$_j$]]]]
asked

'On two occasions, John asked everybody.'

In Government Binding Theory, the defining property of movement rules is that they are subject to the Subjacency Condition (cf. Chomsky 1981, pp. 80–85). Hungarian Operator Movement does observe various manifestations of the Subjacency Condition. Namely, it observes the Complex-NP-Constraint:

(4) (a) *Melyik jelöltet$_i$ hallottad [$_{NP}$ a hírt
which candidate-acc heard-you the news-acc
[$_{CP}$ hogy megválasztották t$_i$]]
that elected-they

'Which candidate did you hear the news that they had elected?'

(b) Melyik jelöltet$_i$ hallottad [$_{CP}$ hogy megválasztották t$_i$]
which candidate-acc heard-you that elected-they
'Which candidate did you hear that they had elected?'

Operator Movement from an embedded clause is also blocked by a pronoun in the matrix clause coindexed with the embedded sentence:

(5) (a) *[Senkit sem]$_i$ hallottam azt$_j$ [hogy megválasztották-volna t$_i$]$_j$
nobody-acc not heard-I it-acc that they-had-elected

'Nobody have I heard it to have been elected.'

(b) [Senkit sem]$_i$ hallottam, hogy megválasztottak-volna t$_i$.
nobody-acc not heard-I that they-had-elected
'Nobody have I heard to have been elected.'

indicated in (3), or whether they are part of the V and are postponed in the presence of a focus by some adjacency requirement between the focus and the V stem. If we assume, as I do in (3), that *meg* occupies the Specifier of VP slot, then the functional characterization of the Specifier of VP slot, naturally, has to be extended: it is the landing site of the focus, the interrogative wh-phrase, or the aspectual operator.

The ungrammaticality of (5a) also appears to be a consequence of the Complex-NP-Constraint. The pronoun, bearing a case corresponding to the θ-role of the embedded sentence and occupying a position corresponding to its communicative (i.e. topic, focus, or neutral) role, is in all probability a nominal head to which the embedded sentence serves as a complement. The relative positions of the pronoun and the embedded sentence also confirm this claim: the sentence either immediately follows the pronoun (see 6a), or occupies a peripheral position – obviously as the result of Extraposition (see 6c).

(6) (a) Elmondta [$_{NP}$ [$_{NP}$ azt] [$_{CP}$ hogy pontosan mi
told it-acc that exactly what
történt]] valaki neked?
happened somebody to-you
'Did somebody tell you what exactly had happened?'

(b) ?? Elmondta, hogy pontosan mi történt, azt valaki neked?

(c) Elmondta [$_{NP}$ azt t_i] neked valaki [$_{CP}$ hogy pontosan mi történt]$_i$?

Operator Movement can only take place from a governed complement clause. In Hungarian, the most obvious symptom distinguishing object clauses introduced by *hogy* 'that' and adjunct clauses introduced by *hogy* is that object clauses trigger object-V agreement; i.e. they require the same agreement marker on the V as definite objects do, while adjunct clauses require an indefinite agreement marker used in the absence of a definite object. Compare, for instance, the suffix on the V *dicsekszik* 'brag', taking an adjunct clause, with the suffix of the V *hall* 'hear', taking an object clause:

(7) (a) Dicsekede-tt, hogy az ő jelöltjét
bragged-3.sg-past-indef. that the his candidate-acc
választották meg.
elected-they pref.
'He was bragging that his candidate had been elected.'

(b) Azt hallo-tta, hogy az ő jelöltjét
it-acc heard-3.sg-past-def. that the his candidate-acc
választották meg.
elected-they pref.
'He heard that his candidate had been elected.'

The adjunct clause in (7a) is an island for movement, as predicted by the Adjunct Condition subsumed by Subjacency:

(8) *Kit$_i$ dicsekedett, hogy megválasztottak t$_i$?
whom bragged-he that elected-they
'Whom did he brag that they had elected?'

The fact that the object clause of *hall* 'hear' is a possible source of extraction is illustrated by (4b) and (5b).

Operator Movement is impossible from an embedded complement clause with an empty complementizer – in spite of the fact that the presence or absence of the complementizer *hogy* 'that' as the head of governed complement clauses is often optional. E.g.

(9) (a) Azt mondta, (hogy) a független jelöltet választották meg.
it-acc said-he (that) the independent candidate-acc elected-they pref.
'He said (that) they had elected the independent candidate.'

(b) *A független jelöltet$_i$ mondta, megválasztották t$_i$.
the independent candidate-acc said-he elected-they
'It was the independent candidate that he said they had elected.'

We propose the following explanation for this phenomenon: the complementizer *hogy* L-marks the S node dominating the XP-VP predication structure. In lack of a complementizer, the S node is a barrier, and the CP immediately dominating it also inherits barrierhood from S – i.e. two barriers are crossed by the extracted operator in violation of the Subjacency Condition. (Notice that the analysis of IP in Chomsky (1986) cannot be adopted directly to Hungarian as in Hungarian the sentence is not a projection of I. In fact, it is not a projection at all, but is an exocentric category, the realization of a predication relation between the topic and the VP (cf. É. Kiss 1988)). Naturally, in the absence of independent evidence showing the L-marking capability of the complementizer *hogy*, our explanation remains tentative.

In the course of long Operator Movement, the case of the moved operator is reassigned on every cycle by the V currently governing it. Of the case inherited by the operator and the one assigned to it in the given cycle, the more marked one is transmitted to the antecedent (assuming the markedness hierarchy Oblique > Accusative > Nominative). E.g.

(10) Kit$_i$ akarsz [$_{CP}$ t$'_i$ hogy [$_S$ elnök legyen t$_i$]]
whom want-you that chairman become
'Whom do you suggest shall be the chairman?'

The question word, functioning as the subject of the embedded clause, bears accusative case in (10). The accusative is presumably assigned by the V *akarsz* 'want-you' to t'_i, the chain-link in its government domain. In addition to being assigned accusative case by *akar*, t'_i also inherits nominative case from t_i. The more marked one of the two conflicting cases, i.e. the accusative wins and is transmitted to the antecedent *kit* 'whom'. As is claimed in É. Kiss (1985–86), the process of cyclic case-reassignment to links of movement chains is by no means specific to Hungarian. Similar phenomena have been attested for example in French (cf. Kayne (1980)), Greek (cf. Groos & van Riemsdijk (1981)) and in fact in English too. Consider, for instance, (11), the English equivalent of (10), with the embedded subject assuming accusative case when moving into the government domain of the matrix transitive V:

(11) Whom$_i$ do you suggest [$_{CP}$ t'_i [$_{IP}$ t_i shall be the chairman]]

In constructions like (11), *whom* is preferred to *who* in certain British dialects and is not ungrammatical, merely stylistically marked as pompous in American English either. The process of case assignment in (10) and (11) is evidence of cyclic movement satisfying the Subjacency Condition because in the chain *kit*$_i$/*whom*$_i$ t'_i t_i it is only t'_i, the intermediate link, that is in the government and case assignment domain of a potential accusative assigner.

2 Left Dislocation: A Base-Generated Construction

The goal of section 2 is to prove that Left Dislocation, unlike Operator Movement, does not observe the Subjacency Condition, hence it cannot involve movement. Left Dislocation constructions contain a left peripheral phrase binding an empty position in the VP pronounced as an independent phonological phrase with a particular, rising intonation contour (to be indicated by the letters L(ow) and H(igh) under the corresponding vowels). The phrase in Left Dislocation is optionally followed by a demonstrative or, marginally, a personal pronoun cliticized to it and coreferent with it. E.g.

(12) Jánost$_i$ (azt$_i$ / ?őt$_i$) nem hívtuk meg e$_i$.
L H
John-acc that-acc / him not invited-we pref.
'As for John, we didn't invite him.'

The demonstrative presumably forms an appositive construction with the NP in Left Dislocation. In any case, it cannot originate in the VP and move via

Topicalization, as it is inseparable from the NP in Left Dislocation; i.e. whenever the NP-gap relation violates Subjacency, the demonstrative-gap relation also violates it. If a quantified phrase appears in Left Dislocation, the demonstrative has to be omitted – presumably because it is necessarily referential.

(13) Mindegyik kollégánkat$_i$ (??azt$_i$) nem hívtuk meg e$_i$.
L H
every colleague-ours-acc that-acc not invited-we pref.
'Every colleague of ours, we did not invite.'
[We didn't invite every colleague of ours.]

The phrase in Left Dislocation constitutes an independent phonological phrase certainly because it is outside CP, the maximal sentence projection.

The phrase in Left Dislocation and the empty VP-internal position coindexed with it form an $\bar{A}$-chain. This chain, however, does not observe the Subjacency Condition of movement. Therefore, it must be a chain resulting from a rule of construal, i.e. from the coindexation of two base-generated entities. Thus, a Left Dislocation construction does not satisfy the Complex-NP-Constraint; that is, the empty category – left dislocated phrase relation can cross the boundary of either a complex NP with a lexical head (see (14a)) or of a complex NP with a pronominal head (see (14b)).

(14) (a) Sok szavazatot$_j$, [$_{NP}$ azt a hírt t$_i$] hallottam,
L H
many votes-acc that the news-acc heard-I
[$_{CP}$ két jelölt kapott e$_j$]$_i$
two candidates-nom received
'Many votes, I heard the news that two candidates had received.'
[I heard the news that two candidates had received many votes.]

(b) Sok szavazatot$_j$, [$_{NP}$ azt t$_i$] hallottam, [$_{CP}$ két
L H
many votes-acc it-acc heard-I two
jelölt kapott e$_j$]$_i$
candidates-nom received
'Many votes, I heard it that two candidates had received.'
[I heard it that two candidates had received many votes.]

In Left Dislocation constructions, the empty category – left dislocated phrase relation does not observe the Adjunct Condition: the empty category can be located in adjunct and complement clauses alike. Compare with the ungrammatical (8):

(15) A legtöbb szavazatot$_i$, dicsekedtek, hogy az ö
L H
the most votes-acc bragged-they that the their
jelöltjük kapta e_i.
candidate-nom received

'The largest number of votes, they were bragging that their candidate had received.' [They were bragging that their candidate had received the largest number of votes.]

If in a complex sentence the complementizer *hogy* of the embedded clause can be omitted, it can also be omitted if the sentence involves Left Dislocation. E.g.

(16) Elegendő szavazatot$_i$, azt hallottam [$_{CP}$ (hogy)
L H
sufficient vote-acc it-acc heard-I that
[$_S$ egyik jelölt sem kapott e_i]]
neither candidate-nom not received

'Sufficient votes, I heard (that) neither of the candidates had received.' [I heard (that) neither of the candidates had received sufficient votes.]

As discussed in connection with (9b), in our interpretation the complementizer *hogy* L-marks the category S. If *hogy* is omitted in (16), the empty category – left dislocated phrase relation crosses two barriers (S and CP, a barrier by inheritance). Since no movement is involved, no Subjacency violation arises.

In a Left Dislocation construction, the case of the left dislocated constituent cannot be reassigned by the matrix V. Cf.

(17) *Mindenkit$_i$, úgy hallottam, nem szavazott e_i.
L H
everybody-acc so heard-I not voted
'Everybody, so I heard, had not voted.'
[I heard not everybody had voted.]

The explanation of the ungrammaticality of (17) is straightforward: the $\bar{A}$-chain *mindenkit*$_i$ e_i, not being a movement chain, has no intermediate links and neither its root nor its head is in the government domain of the accusative assigner *hallottam* 'heard-I'.

As a result of our analysis of Hungarian Operator Movement and Left Dislocation from the point of view of Subjacency in sections 1 and 2, we identify Operator Movement as a movement rule, and Left Dislocation as a base-generated construction, interpreted by a rule of construal. The difference between the outputs of Operator Movement and Left Dislocation can, naturally, also be expressed in a representational framework: Operator Movement results in a chain the links of which locally bind each other, while Left Dislocation results in a chain which is not constrained with respect to locality. The distinction between local and non-local Ā-chains, however, amounts to reintroducing the movement rule – rule of construal distinction under a different terminology.

3 Scope Relations in the Output of Operator Movement

In sections 3 and 4, we will examine how Operator Movement and Left Dislocation, respectively, affect the scope of the operators involved.

An operator preposed by Operator Movement has scope over the domain it c-commands. (The c-command notion involved in Hungarian scope interpretation is the stricter c-command notion of Reinhart (1976), according to which a category A c-commands a category B if neither dominates the other, and the first branching node dominating A also dominates B.) Thus, a focus or a wh-phrase in the specifier of VP takes scope over V′ (see structure (1)), and is inside the scope of a quantified phrase adjoined to VP. E.g.

(18) [$_S$ [$_{VP}$ Mindenkinek [$_{VP}$ János [$_{V'}$ vette az ajándékot]]]]
everybody-dat John-nom bought the present-acc
'Everybody was bought the present by John.'
[In the case of everybody, it was John who bought him the present.]

(In the English glosses of the examples, the surface order of operators is intended to express their scope order as well.)

(19) [$_S$ [$_{VP}$ Sokan [$_{VP}$ három verset [$_{V'}$ tanultak meg könyv nélkül]]]]
many three poem-acc learnt perf. by heart
'Many (persons) learnt three poems by heart.'

An operator preposed into the Specifier of VP, naturally, also has scope over the sentence negating particle adjoined to V′. E.g.

(20) [$_S$ János [$_{VP}$ kinek [$_{V'}$ nem [$_{V'}$ vett ajándékot]]]]
John whom not bought present-acc
'(As for) John, who didn't he buy a present?'

In case the sentence contains, for instance, two QPs adjoined to VP, both QPs have scope over the segment of the VP they minimally c-command. For example in (21), QP_j has scope over VP2 including QP_k, the focus and V′, while QP_k has scope over VP3 including the focus and V′.

(21) (a)

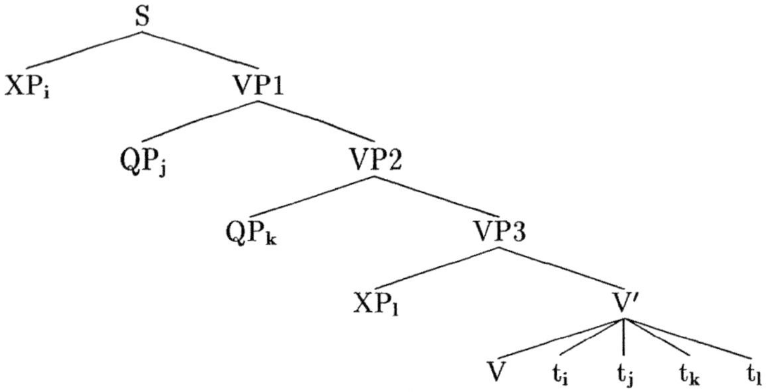

(b) [$_S$ János [$_{VP}$ mindenkit [$_{VP}$ kétszer is [$_{VP}$ le [$_{V'}$ győzött]]]]]
John-nom everybody-acc twice even perf. beat
'John has beaten each person twice.'

A change in the surface order of QPs naturally leads to a change in interpretation:

(22) [$_S$ János [$_{VP}$ kétszer is [$_{VP}$ mindenkit [$_{VP}$ le [$_{V'}$ győzött]]]]]
John twice even everybody-acc perf. beat
'On two occasions, John beat everybody.'

(May (1985) predicts QP_i and QP_j in (21) to have identical scope and thus predicts sentences (21) and (22) to have identical meanings. The Hungarian data clearly contradict this theory and support the scope interpretation theory of May (1977).)

If a QP is intended to have narrower scope than the focus, then instead of being adjoined to V′ it is left in V′, where its scope extends over V′, its c-command domain. (Adjunction of a maximal projection to a non-maximal projection is excluded in Chomsky (1986).) E.g.[3]

[3]It is crucial that the QP in V′ be pronounced without a primary stress. A heavily stressed QP in V′ has wide scope, i.e. scope extending over the VP. Stressed post-verbal QPs are shown in É. Kiss (1987) to first undergo Operator Movement, i.e. adjunction to VP, and then to be scrambled back into V′ by a stylistic rule.

(23) [$_S$ [$_{VP}$ János [$_{V'}$ győzött le mindenkit]]]
John beat perf. everybody-acc
'It was John who beat everybody.'

Here is an example with two QPs left in their base-generated positions in V′. Both QPs are in the scope of the focus, but their scope relative to each other is not fixed; they have identical domains (V′):

(24) [$_S$ [$_{VP}$ János [$_{V'}$ győzött le mindenkit kétszer]]]
John-nom beat perf. everybody-acc twice
'It was John who beat everybody twice.'
or:
'It was John who, on two occasions, beat everybody.'

Our observations concerning scope relations in the output of Operator Movement can be summarized in the form of the following generalization:

(25) An operator preposed by Operator Movement c-commands its scope.

4 Scope Relations in Left Dislocation Constructions

When Left Dislocation involves a QP, the QP obligatorily has narrow scope with respect to the operators preposed by Operator Movement into the left periphery of VP; its scope extends over V′. E.g.

(26) Mindenkinek$_i$ [$_S$ [$_{VP}$ János [$_{V'}$ vett ajándékot e$_i$]]]
L H
everybody-dat John bought present-acc
'It was John who bought everybody a present.'

(27) Sokan$_i$ [$_S$ [$_{VP}$ három verset [$_{V'}$ tanultak meg könyv nélkül e$_i$]]]
L H
many three poem-acc learnt perf. by heart
'It was three poems that many (persons) learnt by heart.'

(28) Mindenk$_i$ ellen$_i$ [$_S$ János [$_{VP}$ kétszer [$_{V'}$ győzött e$_i$]]]
L H
everybody against John-nom twice won
'It was on two occasions that John won against everybody.'

The sentence in (29a) would be ungrammatical if the universally quantified phrase had been preposed by Operator Movement – as a universally quantified phrase (in Hungarian) cannot have wider scope than sentence negation – see (29b).

(29) (a) Mindenkit$_i$ [$_S$ [$_{VP}$ [$_{V'}$ nem győzött le János e$_i$]]]
H L
everybody-acc not beat perf. John-nom
'John didn't beat everybody.'

(b) *[$_S$ [$_{VP}$ Mindenkit$_i$ [$_{V'}$ nem [$_{V'}$ győzött le János e$_i$]]]]
'Everybody was not beaten by John.'

That a QP in Left Dislocation has scope over V′, the c-command domain of the empty argument coindexed with it, becomes especially clear when the sentence also contains another narrow scope QP left in V′. In this case the scope relation of the QP in Left Dislocation and the QP in V′ is vague; either of them can be understood as having scope over the other. Cf.

(30) Kétszer is$_i$ [$_S$ [$_{VP}$ János [$_{V'}$ győzött le mindenkit e$_i$]]]
L H
twice even John beat perf. everybody-acc
'It was John who, on two occasions, beat everybody.'
or:
'It was John who beat everybody twice.'

(31) below is ungrammatical because the QP in Left Dislocation cannot take scope over VP although it is not subordinated to another operator (it does not enter into a scope relation with the perfectivity operator in the Specifier of VP). It has to have scope over V′ only, the c-command domain of the empty argument coindexed with it.

(31) *Mindenkit$_i$ [$_S$ [$_{VP}$ le [$_{V'}$ győzött János e$_i$]]]
L H
'John beat everybody.'

Our observations concerning the scope of operators in Left Dislocation can be generalized as follows:

(32) An operator in Left Dislocation has scope over the c-command domain of the empty argument coindexed with it.

That is, the comparison of the scope relations in Operator$_i$ ... t$_i$ chains resulting from Operator Movement, and the scope relations in Operator$_i$ ... e$_i$ chains resulting from a rule of construal coindexing a phrase in Left Dislocation with an empty argument position has shown that in Operator$_i$ ... t$_i$ chains created by movement the operator has scope over the c-command domain of the head of the chain, while in Operator$_i$ ... e$_i$ chains created by construal the operator has scope over the c-command domain of the root of the chain. These data confirm the necessity of the distinction between rules of movement and rules of construal, as they demonstrate that movement rules involving operators (i.e. "move wh"-type rules) assign scope to the moved element, while rules of construal do not do so.

5 Two Apparent Counter-Arguments

The claim that movement rules of the "move wh"-type create scope has been dismissed several times in the literature – cf. van Riemsdijk and Williams (1981), Cinque (1982), Haik (1984), or Koster (1987). There are two types of apparent counter-examples. Example (33) is said in Haik (1984) to demonstrate that the scope of a wh-phrase is always the minimal S containing the trace of the wh-phrase.

(33) Which men$_i$ did someone say that Mary likes t$_i$?

In (33) *someone* is indeed outside the scope of the wh-phrase; however, other quantified phrases replacing *someone* would fall within the scope of the wh-phrase. E.g.

(34) Which men$_i$ did everyone say that Mary likes t$_i$?

(34) means in its preferred interpretation: 'For which men is it true that everyone says that Mary likes them?' That is, the scope of the wh-phrase is determined not by the position of its trace but by the position of the operator itself. The wh-phrase has scope over the matrix sentence in (33) too. Merely *someone* in the given construction must be interpreted referentially, for reasons unclear to me.

An apparent counter-argument against the claim that wh-movement fixes the scope of the wh-moved element is based on a construction existing both in German and in Hungarian. Koster (1987) claims, relying on the work of van Riemsdijk (1983) and de Meij and Marácz (1986), that in German and Hungarian constructions represented by the Hungarian (35) the wh-phrase in the most deeply embedded clause has scope over the whole complex sentence.

Its scope is extended outside its c-command domain by the wh-phrases in the superordinate clauses, functioning as scope markers.

(35) Mit gondolsz hogy mit mondott Vili hogy
what-acc think-you that what-acc said Bill that
ki látta Jánost?
who saw John-acc
'What do you think, what did Bill say, who saw John?'

That is, (35) is claimed to be the equivalent of (36):

(36) Kit gondolsz hogy Vili mondott hogy látta Jánost?
whom think-you that Bill said that saw John-acc
'Who do you think that Bill said saw John?'

The existence of structure (35) actually cannot disprove the claim that wh-movement creates scope. At the very best it can show that the scope created by wh-movement can be further extended by a series of c-commanding wh-phrases. However, the construction represented by (35) – at least its Hungarian version – does not support even this weaker claim. According to the native speakers' intuitions, (35) is not a complex sentence but a series of non-embedded questions. This is how de Meij and Marácz (1986) paraphrase it:

(37) What is your opinion on the following question: What is it that Bill said with respect to the following issue: Who saw John?

Another fact indicating the lack of proper embedding is that (35) with the complementizer *hogy* 'that' spelled out in the second and the third clauses is marginal; it should be marked by ?. The fully grammatical version of (35) involves no complementizer at all:

(38) Mit gondolsz, mit mondott Vili, ki látta Jánost?

Furthermore, (35) cannot involve simple embedding because the matrix verbs *gondol* 'think' and *mond* 'say' do not allow interrogative complement clauses. The analysis proposed for German in van Riemsdijk (1983), and adopted for Hungarian in Marácz (1987) accounts for the apparent violation of the selectional requirements of *mond* and *gondol* as follows: (35) involves a single question: *Ki látta Jánost*? 'Who saw John?'. In LF, where the selectional requirements are checked, *ki* 'who' moves up to the topmost wh-position – hence *gondol* 'think' and *mond* 'say' do not have an interrogative operator within their domain anymore. In Hungarian, however, there is reason to doubt the LF-movement of *ki* in (35) – as the construction is also grammatical if some of the verbs in the path of movement are non-bridge verbs. E.g.

(39) Mit gondolsz, mire célzott Péter, miért ment-át
what think-you what-at hinted Peter, why passed
János a vizsgán?
John the exam
'What do you think, what did Peter hint at, why did John pass the exam?'

The V *céloz* 'hint', a non-bridge verb, blocks syntactic Operator Movement from its complement clause:

(40) **Miért$_i$ céloz Péter, (hogy) János átment a vizsgán t_i?
why hints Peter that John passed the exam
'Why$_i$ does Peter hint that John passed the exam t_i?'

The complement clause of *céloz* may be an island because *céloz* assigns oblique case to it (cf. Chomsky 1986:36). Whatever the reason is that makes the CP dominating the embedded clause a barrier, it should also prevent the proper government of the trace of *miért* in the case of LF-movement – if LF-movement were indeed involved in (39).

A further piece of evidence indicating that constructions (35) and (36) are not logical equivalents of each other is provided by sentences involving both interrogation and negation, and a modal matrix V. E.g.

(41) Mit akarsz, (hogy) Mari kivel ne találkozzék?
what want-you that Mary whom not meet
'What do you wish, who shouldn't Mary meet?'

Cf. also:

(42) Kivel$_i$ nem akarod, hogy Mari t_i találkozzék?
whom not want-you that Mary meet
'Who don't you wish that Mary should meet?'

In such constructions interrogation and negation must apparently have scope over similar domains; i.e. if the interrogative phrase is raised into the matrix sentence, in front of the modal, the negative particle must be raised too. Consider the highly marginal (43) with only the scope of interrogation extended over the matrix modal:

(43) ??Kivel$_i$ akarod, hogy Mari t_i ne találkozzék?
whom want-you that Mary not meet
'Who do you wish that Mary should not meet?'

If the wh-phrase *kivel* in (41) indeed ends up in the matrix wh-position in LF (as it does in (43)), it is not clear what prevents the raising of the negative particle into the matrix clause too:

(44) *?Mit nem akarsz, (hogy) Mari kivel találkozzék?
what not want-you that Mary whom meet
'What don't you wish, who should Mary meet?'

The interrogative phrase, the negative particle, and the modal in (41) in fact must occupy the same relative positions as they would occupy in two consecutive, non-embedded questions – cf.

(45) Mit akarsz? Mari kivel ne találkozzék?
what want-you Mary whom not meet
'What do you wish?' 'Who shouldn't Mary meet?'

In view of these considerations, the alleged pieces of evidence refuting the scope assigning potential of movement rules, a property distinguishing them from rules of construal, lose their force.

References

Chomsky, N. (1981) *Lectures on Government and Binding*, Foris, Dordrecht.

Chomsky, N. (1986) *Barriers*, MIT Press, Cambridge, Mass.

Cinque, G. (1982) "Constructions with Left Peripheral Phrases, 'Connectedness', Move Alpha and ECP", unpublished, University of Venice.

Groos, A. and H. van Riemsdijk (1981) "Matching Effects in Free Relatives: A Parameter of Core Grammar", in A. Belletti, L. Brandi, L. Rizzi, eds., *Theory of Markedness in Generative Grammar*, Scuola Normale Superiore, Pisa.

Haik, I. (1984) "Indirect Binding", *Linguistic Inquiry* 15, 185–223.

Kayne, R. (1980) "Extensions of Binding and Case Marking", *Linguistic Inquiry* 11, 75–96.

É. Kiss, K. (1985–1986) "Parasitic Chains", *The Linguistic Review* 5, 41–74.

É. Kiss, K. (1987) *Configurationality in Hungarian, Studies in Natural Language and Linguistic Theory*, Reidel, Dordrecht.

É. Kiss, K. (1988) "Eliminating the Configurationality Parameter", unpublished, Linguistics Institute of the Academy of Sciences, Budapest.

Koster, J. (1987) *Domains and Dynasties*, Foris, Dordrecht.

Marácz, L. (1987) "Connectedness and Correspondence Effects in Hungarian", *GLOW Newsletter* 18, 43–45.

Marácz, L. and S. de Meij (1986) "On Question Sentences in Hungarian", in W. Abraham and S. de Meij, eds., *Topic, Focus, and Configurationality*, John Benjamins, Amsterdam.

May, R. (1977) *The Grammar of Quantification*, Ph.D. dissertation, MIT, Cambridge, Mass.

May, R. (1985) *Logical Form: its Structure and Derivation*, MIT Press, Cambridge, Mass.

Reinhart, T. (1976) *The Syntactic Domain of Anaphora*, Ph.D. dissertation, MIT, Cambridge, Mass.

Riemsdijk, H. van (1983) "Corresepondence Effects and the Empty Category Principle", in Y. Otsu et al., eds., *Studies in Generative Grammar and Language Acquisition*, Editorial Committee, Tokyo.

Riemsdijk, H. van and E. Williams (1981) "NP-structure", *The Linguistic Review* 1, 171–217.

Barriers and the Theory of Binding*

Gisbert Fanselow

0 General Remarks and Overview

In the past ten years, considerable progress has been made towards the goal of unifying the locality conditions of various subsystems of UG. At present, three major approaches may be distinguished within this research programme: while the theories developed by Kayne (1983), Koster (1984a, 1987) and Pesetsky (1982) express generalizations about local domains in terms of quasi-geometric properties of tree configurations and directionality of government, local domains are fixed in terms of specific properties of subtrees in the two approaches implicit in the Barriers-framework, viz. the status of L-marking of a given category (cf. Chomsky 1986a), and extensions of a relativized concept of minimality (cf. Rizzi 1990, Fanselow 1988a, 1989a).

The goal of this paper is to argue that the local domain for anaphoric binding is reducible to a relativized and feature-based concept of minimality as well. The discussion will lead to a question that arises in the context of recent proposals such as Aoun (1985), Bouchard (1984) or Chomsky (1986a,b): is it possible to find a uniform formulation for the principles of UG? The paper argues that this question can be answered positively, at least for the ECP, Binding Theory's Principle A, the Case Filter, and the identification conditions for *pro* and PRO. Such a unification, however, appears to presuppose a principled distinction of three levels of representation (D-structure, S-structure and LF) and might also have to rely on a strictly derivational concept of certain syntactic rules.

In section 1, the status of Principle A of the binding theory in Chomsky (1986a,b) will be discussed briefly. section 2 identifies a number of problems that arise in any attempt to subsume the local domain of anaphoric binding under the 'traditional' concept of barriers. In section 3, these observations will be related to further problems of the L-marking account of barriers. It will be argued in sections 4 and 5 that these problems can be overcome in terms

*This article is a completely rewritten version of the talk presented at the Oberkirch workshop. For helpful comments, I am indebted to Sascha W. Felix, Peter Staudacher, and two anonymous reviewers for the present volume. A more elaborate treatment of anaphoric binding in terms of relativized minimality can be found in Fanselow (1990b).

H. Haider and K. Netter (eds.), Representation and Derivation in the Theory of Grammar, 217–250.

of a relativized and feature-based minimality condition. section 6 deals with some 'long-distance-binding' phenomena in Icelandic, while section 7 argues that data from Italian and German necessitate a reformulation of the ECP in terms of a Principle of Full Specification. We relate this principle to the Case Filter and the identification conditions for PRO and *pro* in section 8. The final section is dedicated to a discussion of the implications the approach developed here will have for a number of issues such as the nature of the relation between levels of representation.

1 The ECP and Principle A in the 'Barriers'-Framework

Chomsky (1986a:68–80) has demonstrated that reference to lexical or θ-government can be eliminated from the definition of the term 'proper government', which is central for the ECP (2):

(1) α properly governs β iff α antecedent-governs β.

(2) ECP: A non-pronominal NP must be properly governed.

Subject and adjunct WH-traces depend on antecedent-government for obvious reasons, so the elimination of lexical or θ-government from (1) does not have any consequences for these. Object WH-traces as in (3) are antecedent-governed by a trace adjoined to VP which is motivated on independent grounds (cf. Chomsky 1986a:7f).

(3) who$_i$ did [$_{IP}$ you [VP t$_i$ [$_{VP}$ invite t$_i$]]]

The situation is more complex for NP-traces. According to the definition of barrierhood given in (4)–(7), the subject *John* cannot antecedent-govern its trace in (8) directly, as the VP-node intervening between the two categories constitutes a barrier.

(4) *Barrier* (by L-Marking)
For any maximal projections Σ, ϕ, Σ is a barrier for α if

a) Σ is a blocking category that includes α, with $\Sigma \neq$ IP
or

b) Σ immediately dominates ϕ, ϕ a blocking category for Σ.

(5) *Barrier* (by Minimality)
β does not govern α in the structure $[\phi \cdots \beta \cdots [\Sigma \cdots \delta \cdots \alpha \cdots]]$ if Σ is a projection of δ excluding β (and if b) Σ immediately dominates δ).

(6) Σ is a *blocking category* (BC) for α if

a) Σ includes α, and,

b) Σ is not L-marked.

(7) α *L-marks* β if

a) α is a lexical category

b) α assigns a θ-role to Σ

c) α and Σ are sister nodes.

(8) [$_{IP}$ John$_i$ [$_I$ was$_j$] [$_{VP}$ t$_j$ invited$_k$ t$_i$]]

Adjunction to VP being restricted to $\bar{A}$-movement, the NP-trace t$_i$ in (8) cannot satisfy the ECP in the way just outlined for WH-traces. However, one may assume that *was* is moved to I in structures such as (8),[1] and that verbs are generally coindexed with each other. Consequently, the indices j and k of (8) are identical. Furthermore, by subject-I agreement the indices i and j are identified as well. In other words, (8) is indexed as in (9), a structure in which the verb *invite* counts as an *antecedent*-governor for t$_i$, since the two categories in question share indices.[2]

(9) [$_{IP}$ John$_i$ [$_I$ was$_i$] [$_{VP}$ t$_i$ invited$_i$ t$_i$]]

As Chomsky (1986a:68–80) has pointed out, the distribution of NP-traces follows from the ECP if proper government is restricted to antecedent government. Consider, for example, the following data:

(10) a. John$_i$ was$_j$ [$_{VP}$ expected$_k$ [$_{IP}$ t$_i$ to win]]

b. John$_i$ was$_j$ [$_{VP}$ laughed$_k$ [$_{PP}$ at t$_i$]]

(11) a. *John$_i$ was$_j$ [$_{VP}$ expected$_k$ [$_{IP}$ Mary$_l$ [$_{VP}$ to kiss$_m$ t$_i$]]]

b. *John$_i$ was$_j$ [$_{VP}$ preferred$_k$ [$_{CP}$ for [$_{IP}$ t$_i$ to win]]]

c. *John$_i$ was$_j$ [$_{VP}$ expected$_k$ [$_{CP}$ that [$_{IP}$ t$_i$ wins]]]

d. *John$_i$ was$_j$ [$_{VP}$ expected$_k$ [$_{CP}$ that [$_{NP}$ pictures of t$_i$] will be for sale]]

---

[1] This technical detail of Chomsky (1986a) conflicts with recent results of Chomsky (1988) and Pollock (1989), but there are other ways in which coindexation of V and I may be guaranteed.

[2] This idea can be made precise in terms of the notion 'extended chain', cf. chapter 11 of Chomsky (1986a).

We have already seen why the transitivity of coindexation ensures that the NP-trace in (9) satisfies the ECP. For similar reasons, the indices i, j and k in (10a) are identical, so *expected* is a potential antecedent-governor for t_i. Furthermore, the IP-node intervening between the trace and *expected* is L-marked. Therefore, it cannot constitute a barrier, and (10a) is correctly predicted to be well-formed. (10b) differs from (9) only insofar as a PP node separates t_i from its potential antecedent-governor *laughed*, but as PP is L-marked, no problems arise.

(11a) is an instance of illicit long-distance NP-movement from object-position. By (4), (6), and (7) the VP of the lower clause is a barrier for external government, so $kiss_m$ is the only potential governor for t_i. But as *kiss* shares indices with its own subject only, indices m and i won't be identical,[3] so *kiss* cannot antecedent-govern t_i. This will imply an ECP-violation for (11a).

In (11b,c), a subject has been extracted from a CP. t_i is included in the IP-node of the embedded clause, which is not L-marked. By (4) and (6), the dominating CP-node is a barrier for potential antecedent-government by the c-commanding verb. In addition, *for* and *that* block government by the minimality condition (5). In (11d), t_i is embedded in a subject-NP, which is not L-marked, hence a barrier. To sum up, the ECP blocks all ungrammatical instances of NP-movement.

In this framework, Principle A of the Binding Theory applies to NP-traces in a vacuous fashion only. While this does not imply any technical problems, the resulting system is conceptually unsatisfactory. As Chomsky (1981) has stressed, the distributions of NP-traces and lexical anaphors are nearly identical, so it would be quite a surprise if two distinct subparts of UG, the ECP and barriers on the one hand, and Principle A and Governing Categories on the other, would make near-identical predictions. It is necessary to find a common formulation for the ECP and Principle A. Indeed, a number of ideas for such a unification can be found in the literature: while Aoun (1985) tries to reduce the ECP to a generalized version of Principle A, Chomsky (1986b) suggests an approach in which the ECP is the basic principle.

Chomsky observes that (certain types of) anaphors have to be moved to I at S-structure in languages such as Italian or French. Note, furthermore, that rules which apply at S-structure in certain languages frequently turn out to be LF-processes in others. For example, all WH-phrases within a clause are

---

[3] m is identical with i if the subjects of the two clauses are coindexed:

(i) *$Mary_i$ was_i $expected_i$ $herself_i$ to $kiss_i$ t_i

(i) satisfies the ECP, but is ruled out on independent grounds: As Rizzi (1982) and Roberts (this volume) have suggested, there is a locality requirement on A-chain formation that implies that the local binder of a trace t_i must be part of the A-chain of t_i. Consequently, *herself* and t_i must be links of a single chain, which is θ-marked twice. In other words, (i) violates the θ-criterion.

moved to Spec-CP in Bulgarian or Rumanian (cf. Rudin 1988), a process that is mirrored by LF-movement in Japanese and Chinese (cf. Huang 1982), and a combination of processes at both levels in English. Similarily, English quantifier raising at LF (cf. Hornstein 1984 and May 1985) has an S-structure equivalent in German (cf. Fanselow 1988b, 1990a) or Hungarian (cf. for example, Kiss 1986). It is not unlikely, then, that Italian S-structure anaphor movement is mirrored by an LF-process in English. Consequently, Chomsky suggests that anaphors have to be adjoined to the I node they are coindexed[4] with at LF. This movement process creates a trace that is subject to the ECP. Along these lines, effects of Principle A of the binding theory may be (partially) derived from the ECP, as Chomsky (1986b:175–177) shows.

While the systems of principles in Chomsky (1986a) and (1986b) are not fully compatible, it nevertheless seems possible to push the reduction of Principle A to the ECP further than in Chomsky's original proposal. Thus, consider the data in (12), and their corresponding LF-representations (13):

(12) a. John_i will invite himself_i

b. John_i will laugh at himself_i

c. John_i will expect himself_i to win

d. *John_i will expect Mary to kiss himself_i

e. *John_i will expect that himself_i wins

(13) a. John_i $[_I$ himself_i $[\text{will}_i]]$ $[_{VP}$ invite_i $t_i]$

b. John_i $[_I$ himself_i $[\text{will}_i]]$ $[_{VP}$ laugh_i $[_{PP}$ at $t_i]]$

c. John_i $[_I$ himself_i $[\text{will}_i]]$ $[_{VP}$ expect_i $[_{IP}$ t_i to win$]]$

d. *John_i $[_I$ himself_i $[\text{will}_i]]$ $[_{VP}$ expect_i $[_{IP}$ Mary $[_{VP}$ to kiss $t_i]]]$

e. *John_i $[_I$ himself_i $[\text{will}_i]]$ expect_i $[_{CP}$ that t_i wins$]$

Himself is adjoined to the I-node it is coindexed with in the LF-representations (13). VP is a barrier in (13a–c), so *himself* cannot be the antecedent-governor for its LF-trace. However, coindexation of V and I and subject-I-agreement guarantee that the V-head of the VP bears the index of the subject, and therefore the index of the trace of the anaphor. Consequently, V is the antecedent-governor for the trace of the anaphor. Notice that both the PP and the IP nodes dominating the traces in (13b,c), respectively, are L-marked. No barrier will therefore intervene between the trace and the antecedent-governing verb.

[4]Coindexation of the anaphor with I is a consequence of subject-I agreement for subject-bound anaphors. We will disregard non-subject bound anaphors for the moment.

The ungrammaticality of (12d,e) follows from the ECP, since in (13d) *kiss* does not bear the index of *himself*, and the VP that *kiss* projects constitutes a barrier that blocks antecedent government of t_i by *expect* or *himself*. The LF (13e) is ruled out for the reasons we have already discussed in the context of the parallel structure (11c). It seems as if the basic distribution of anaphors can be deduced from LF-raising of anaphors and the ECP.

2 Some Problems

The account outlined above has a number of serious problems, however. The first difficulty stems from a rather general problem of the Barriers-theory: it is unclear why P should not block antecedent government in examples such as (10b) or (12b) due to the minimality condition (5).

Another difficulty lies in the fact that the contexts in which NP-traces are grammatical are just a subset of the constructions that allow lexical anaphors:

(14) a. *$John_i$ was expected that $[_{NP}$ a picture of $t_i]$ will be for sale

b. $John_i$ expects that $[_{NP}$ a picture of $himself_i]$ will be for sale

c. John $himself_i$ expects that $[_{NP}$ a picture of $t_i]$ will be for sale

(14a) is correctly blocked by the ECP: the subject of the embedded clause is not L-marked, hence a barrier. By (4b), the IP node of the embedded clause inherits barrierhood from the subject-NP. The IP itself is a BC by its own right, so the CP dominating it inherits barrierhood as well. Consequently, three barriers intervene between the trace and the next potential antecedent governor, *expects*. By the same reasoning, three barriers should stand between the trace and its potential antecedent governor in the LF (14c) of (14b). Therefore, (14b) should constitute a rather severe violation of the ECP, which it does not.

This fact is an instance of a general point: lexical anaphors are licensed in categories that are not L-marked, and which therefore should be barriers for antecedent government for a trace created by LF-movement. This fact is illustrated by examples such as (15), or German data such as (16).

(15) they saw snakes $[_{PP}$ near each other]

(16) $John_i$ arbeitet für $sich_i$
John works for himself

Similarily, many languages tolerate 'long distance anaphors' (cf. for example, Everaert (1986) or Manzini & Wexler (1987) for a detailed discussion), where the extension of the domain of binding is not mirrored by a comparable extension of barriers for antecedent-government. Furthermore, the analysis of anaphoric binding in Italian by Belletti & Rizzi (1988) suggests that in some languages, the well-formedness of anaphoric binding is determined prior to S-structure, a fact that is incompatible with an explanation of anaphoric binding in terms of LF-movement.

Finally, the importance of the presence of a specifier for the constitution of binding domains is not captured by a reduction of Binding Theory's Principle A to antecedent-government. As *Bill's picture of herself* is L-marked in (17), the corresponding LF-representation (18) does not violate the ECP, a fact that incorrectly predicts (17) to be well-formed.

(17) *Mary$_i$ saw Bill's picture of herself$_i$

(18) Mary$_i$ herself$_i$ saw [$_{NP}$ Bill's picture of t$_i$]

3 Against L-Marking

The problem noted in the context of (14)–(16) is not confined to the behavior of lexical anaphors: LF-processes typically affect categories embedded in subjects or adjunct-PPs, i.e. projections that are not L-marked and should therefore constitute barriers. This appears to hold for LF-WH-extractions (cf. Fanselow 1988a, 1989a for a discussion) and can also be illustrated by data involving quantifier-raising such as (19) and (20):

(19) everyone's$_i$ mother likes him$_i$

(20) a. daß der Direktor von jedem Institut da war
that the director of every institute there was

b. daß ein Polizist vor jedem Gebäude steht
that a policeman in front of every building stands

(21) [$_{IP}$ everyone$_i$ [$_{IP}$ t$_i$'s mother likes him$_i$]]

(22) a. for every institute [$_{IP}$ the director of t$_i$ was present]

b. for every building [$_{IP}$ a policeman stands [in front of t$_i$]]

In (19) and (20a), the quantifier embedded in the subject may have scope over the whole clause, as the (translated) LF-representations (21a) and (22) illustrate. The LF-structures (21) and (22a) imply, however, that subject NPs are not barriers for LF-movement.[5] In the preferred reading of (20b), the quantifier *jedem Gebäude* 'every building' has scope over the subject *ein Polizist* 'a policeman', a fact that is expressed by the (translated version of) the LF (22b). (22b) can be well-formed, however, only if quantifiers may be extracted from non-L-marked adjunct categories at LF.

There are several ways in which these observations might be explained. One might suggest, for example, that L-marking is not relevant for barrierhood at LF, which would predict both (14b) and (19–20) to be well-formed. This account is, however, incompatible with the fact that the status of adjunct traces with respect to proper government is not determined prior to LF (cf. Lasnik & Saito 1984) and seems to crucially involve (4).

Another option that relates to the theory of May (1985) would be to license adjunction to arguments at LF. Nothing would change for movements at S-structure, while the data in (19–20) would be connected to LFs like (23):

(23) a. $[_{IP}\ \alpha_i\ [_{IP}\ [_{NP}\ t_i'\ [_{NP}\ t_i\ N]]\ INFL']]$
b. $[_{IP}\ \alpha_i\ [_{IP}\ NP\ INFL\ [_{VP}\ VP\ [_{PP}\ t_i'\ [_{PP}\ P\ t_i]]]]]$

Not being L-marked, the subject-NP in (23a) would still be a barrier, which, however, could be overcome by adjunction. There is no barrier between t_i and t_i' in (23a), since t_i' is not excluded from NP. Since t_i' is not included in NP, only the dominating IP node could be a potential barrier for antecedent government, but due to the special status of IPs in (4), IP is a BC, and not a barrier here. For similar reasons, no barriers intervene between α_i and t_i' and t_i' and t_i in (23b).

While this approach would capture the LF-processes discussed so far, it cannot cope with the fact that, under specific conditions, subjects and adjuncts do not block antecedent-government even at S-structure. Consider, for example, a parasitic gap construction like (24), discussed by Kayne (1983):

(24) which man_i do [close friends of e_i] admire t_i

As parasitic gaps do not differ from real gaps with respect to the ECP, the question arises of how e_i is properly governed in (24). Notice that in contrast

[5] Cf. Fanselow (1988a, 1989a) for more details. May (1985) suggests a different treatment for (19): he proposes that the quantifier is adjoined to the subject-NP rather than to the IP-node. In connection with an extension of the notion 'c-command', which implies that the scope of an operator is restricted by the first maximal projection including the quantifier, correct predictions about scope seem to be made. Notice that this type of approach presupposes two major changes in the theory of grammar: adjunction to argument expressions must be allowed at LF, and the notion of c-command must be redefined. We will discuss the first change in the main text below. Furthermore, there is no way in which May's proposal could be extended to the other problems we discuss below.

to examples such as (25),[6] no empty operator can be assumed to properly govern e_i in (24): the subject-NP does not provide an $\bar{A}$-position to which an empty operator could be moved, and the operator cannot be adjoined to NP (at S-structure), since NP is an argument-expression.

(25) a. which articles$_i$ did you file t_i [OP$_i$ without PRO reading e_i]

b. a man who everybody [$_{CP}$ OP$_i$ [$_{IP}$ who knows t_i] [$_{VP}$admires t_i]]

Consequently, there is no way to escape the conclusion that it is *which man* itself that properly governs e_i, a fact that is incompatible with the assumption that subjects are barriers for government due to the lack of L-marking. A similar conclusion may be drawn for extractions of PPs or pro-PPs[7] from subjects in German examples like (26), which seem to correspond to similar data for *dont* extraction in French (Pollock, p.c.).

(26) a. das Kind, [von dem]$_i$ gestern [der Vater t_i] anrief
the child of who yesterday the father called

'the child, whose father rang up yesterday'

b. da haben mich [deine Argumente [$_{PP}$ t_i gegen] nicht überzeugt
there have me your arguments against not convinced

'your arguments against that didn't convince me'

The same observation can be made for adjunct-PPs in German: PP-pro-forms like *da*, *hier* or *wo* may be extracted from adjuncts:

(27) da$_i$/hier$_i$/wo$_i$ kriegst Du einen furchtbaren Kopf [t_i nach]
there/here/where get you a terrible head after

'after this you'll get a terrible headache/ after what will you get a terrible headache?'

We have to conclude, it seems, that L-marking is not the correct parameter to determine the barrierhood of a given XP. As we will see below, a relativized concept of minimality is however able to account for the data we have discussed.

---

[6]In (25b), the specifier of the relative clause CP may host the empty operator since, due to the Vacuous Movement Hypothesis, *who* does not have to move to Spec-CP at S-structure, cf. Chomsky (1986a:48–54) for details.

[7]It is not all too clear whether *da* should be categorized as a pro-form for PPs in constructions like (25b), as its phonetic shape would suggest, but we won't go into further details here (cf. Fanselow (1990b) for a more elegant solution). Hans den Besten (p.c.) observes that (26b) is not accepted by all native speakers of German, a fact I do not have an explanation for.

4 Relativized Minimality

At the beginning of section 2 we remarked that (28) is not fully compatible with the Barriers-framework, since the minimality condition (5) predicts that *at* blocks antecedent government of t_i by *laughed* and the adjunct trace, respectively.

(28) a. $John_i$ was_i $laughed_i$ $[_{PP}$ at $t_i]$

b. who_i did he $[_{VP}$ t_i $[_{VP}$talk $[_{PP}$ about $t_i]]]$

Obviously, potential relations of government should not be blocked by *any* type of intervening governor, i.e., a relativization of the minimality condition in the sense of Rizzi (1990) is necessary. Since *at* and *about* are lexical governors, while t_i or *laughed*$_i$ are antecedent governors (in the sense of Chomsky 1986a), a first idea would be to relativize (5) with respect to the lexical/antecedent distinction: lexical government is blocked by minimal lexical governors only, and antecedent government by minimal antecedent governors. Accordingly, *at* and *about* will not block antedecent-government in (28).

If this distinction is introduced into the minimality condition, correct predictions follow for the majority of data discussed in sections 2 and 3 without any reference to L-marking. Consider, first, anaphors in non-subject positions. The LF-traces of anaphors dominated by V' must be antecedent-governed within VP, since V is a minimal antecedent governor by virtue of being coindexed with I. Consequently, an LF-trace of an anaphor in object position or embedded in a complement PP must be antecedent-governed by V, i.e. it must bear the index of V, I, and therefore of the subject. We thus derive a major prediction of Principle A from relativized minimality. Notice that similar results follow if obligatory V-I-coindexation is eliminated from UG: Since we argued that L-marking is not the right concept for fixing barrierhood, VP is not a barrier *per se*, and V will exert minimality effects only on those relations of government that it enters itself. If V bears no index, it is not a potential antecedent governor, so VP won't block antecedent government. Only the c-commanding I will have such effects. But as I will bear the very same index V would have if it were coindexed with I, nothing will change. By a relativization of the minimality condition, it will be predicted that e_i must be antecedent-governed within IP.

(29) $[_{CP}$ α_i $[_{IP}$ β_i $[_{I'}$ I $[_{VP}$ V ($[_{PP}$ P) $[_{NP}$ $e_i]$ (])]]]]

As we have already noted, this is the right prediction for NP-movement, antecedent government of traces of anaphors at LF, and for quantifier raising,[8]

[8]i.e., it will correctly capture the observation made in Hornstein (1984) and May (1985) that the scope of a complement quantifier never goes beyond the clause the quantifier is

but, incorrectly, antecedent government of a WH-trace e_i by an operator α_i in Spec-CP appears to be blocked. The problem can be overcome in several ways: a further relativization of the minimality condition in terms of the distinction between $\bar{A}$ and A-positions in the sense of Rizzi (1990) might be introduced, or we might follow ideas developed by Aoun (1985): If e_i were coindexed with I in (29), a violation of Principle C would ensue if e_i is a WH-trace, since I is obligatorily coindexed with the subject β_i, which would therefore A-bind a variable. Thus, we might say that I is able to antecedent-govern those positions only with which it could be coindexed without a violation of other subsystems of UG, principle C, in particular.[9] If the anaphor is embedded in an adjunct-PP, the next c-commanding I node will also count as a minimal antecedent governor, so again, the LF trace of an anaphor must bear the index of the subject.

If we assume LF-movement of anaphors, the grammaticality of anaphoric binding is thus determined by properties of intervening I-nodes that count as minimal antecedent-governors. This type of explanation of anaphoric binding with reference to I has a number of advantages over Principle A as formulated in Chomsky (1986b), which defines the local domain of anaphoric binding with respect to the presence of a subject (cf. the notion 'complete functional complex'). A number of languages, German among them, possess a type of construction such as (30) which lacks a structural subject position, as Haider (1988) has demonstrated:[10]

(30) Hans glaubt, daß mir geholfen wird
Hans believes that me_{dat} helped is
'Hans believes that people are helping me'

(31) a. *$Hans_i$ glaubt, daß $sich_i$ geholfen wird
Hans believes that himself helped is
'Hans believes that people are helping him'

b. $Hans_i$ glaubt, daß ihm_i geholfen wird
Hans believes that him helped is (=31a)

Nevertheless, a finite clause without a structural subject functions as a barrier for anaphoric binding, as the contrast between (31a) and (31b) illustrates. This

embedded in. In German, however, it seems as if quantifiers in object position of ECM-clauses may have scope over the embedding clause. Cf. Fanselow (1990b) for a detailed treatment.

[9]Or rather the θ-criterion, if strong crossover-effects are to be explained in terms of chain formation in the sense of Rizzi (1982), as Roberts (this volume) suggests.

[10]I.e., in contrast to, for example, Icelandic, the dative NP *mir* 'me' does not have any subject properties. Furthermore, Haider (1988) argues at length that the assumption of an expletive *pro* subject in (30) and a set of related constructions would lead to a number of unsurmountable problems. Cf. Fanselow (1990b) for further arguments corroborating with Haider's view.

fact is predicted if an *I node* triggers minimality effects on antecedent government for the anaphor's LF-trace, but it would require a number of changes[11] in the concept of a complete functional complex.

A similar problem for an explanation of anaphoric binding with reference to subjects would arise in the context of data such as (32):

(32) They$_i$ [$_{VP}$ gave$_j$ [$_{VP}$ the books [$_{V'}$ e$_j$ to each other$_i$]]]

Larson (1988) has argued that *the books* is the specifier of a second VP projection in (32). If anaphoric binding of complements were restricted by specifiers, the lower VP should block the coindexation in (32), which it does not. Again, a number of modifications would have to be added to the definition of a CFC, while a minimality-based account will work without any further stipulations if, as we have argued above, V does not bear indices.

Let us turn now to data such as (33), which illustrate that NPs function as barriers for anaphoric binding if a subject is present:

(33) a. she saw [$_{NP}$ a picture of herself]

b. *she saw [$_{NP}$ Bill's picture of herself]

(33a–b) illustrates the familiar pattern of anaphoric binding affecting complements of NP. The data in (33) would be predicted, if the process of (abstract) specifier-head agreement applies within NPs only if the specifier is syntactically realized. But only if specifier-head agreement has been applied, the head bears an index that counts as a potential antecedent-governor for a category in complement position.[12] The same appears to hold for non-finite clauses as well:

[11] For example, the notion SUBJECT of Chomsky (1981) might be reintroduced, or the complement clauses in (30–31) might be considered to be functionally complete, since the θ-criterion excludes a thematic subject, and no true expletive subjects exist in German.

[12] One might wonder why the argument index that each NP bears and that percolates down to the nominal head, does not count as a potential minimal antecedent-governor. Again, an answer may be found in Aoun (1985): if a complement were coindexed with the nominal head, a violation of the i-within-i condition would ensue. If α is a potential antecedent governor for β only if α and β could be coindexed without a violation of other principles of UG, it will follow that N cannot antecedent-govern a category in the complement position of NP. We have to assume that indices derived by Spec-head-agreement are invisible for the i-within-i condition. This assumption is motivated on independent grounds, however: otherwise, each finite structure [$_{IP}$ NP$_i$ INFL$_i$ VP]$_i$ would violate the i-within-i-condition.

(33) c. *er$_i$ liess [$_{IP}$ mich [$_{VP}$ sich$_i$ schlagen]]
he let me himself beat
'he let me beat him'

d. er$_i$ liess [$_{IP}$ [$_{VP}$ den Wagen sich$_i$ reparieren]]
he let the car himself repair
'he made someone repair the car for him'

The contrast in (33c–d) was first discussed by Reis (1976). She observed that object anaphors in ECM-constructions can be bound from outside if the verb of the ECM-clause is either ergative or if its external argument is not expressed syntactically. Grewendorf (1989) relates this behavior to the presence of a structural subject in the ECM-clause of (33c), and its absence in (33d). Consequently, non-finite I seems to behave like N: it bears an agreement index (and will act as a minimal antecedent-governor) only if a specifier is syntactically realized. There is a fundamental difference, then, between finite I and N: N (DET) and non-finite I bear agreement indices only if specifier-head agreement has applied, whereas indices are intrinsic to finite I.

Bearing this observation in mind, let us turn to anaphors in subject positions or embedded therein. If we interpret the minimality condition in the sense of Chomsky (1986a:42–48), i.e. if we assume that a governor has minimality effects for categories dominated by its first projection only, the well-formedness of anaphoric binding in (34), of parasitic gaps as in (35), and of quantifier raising data as in (36), is predicted, since neither I nor NP-internal agreement will have minimality effects for the specifier position:

(34) a. they hope that each other's pictures [$_{I'}$ will be for sale]

b. they like each other's [$_{I'}$ pictures]

c. they would prefer for each other [$_{I'}$ to win]

d. they expect each other [$_{I'}$ to win]

(35) who$_i$ do [$_{NP}$ close friends of e$_i$] admire t$_i$

(36) a. everyone's mother likes him

a′. [$_{IP}$ everyone$_i$ [$_{IP}$ [$_{NP}$ t's mother] likes him]]

b. Somebody expects every Republican to be elected

b′. [$_{IP}$ every Republican [$_{IP}$ someone expects [$_{IP}$ t$_i$ to be elected]]]

Incorrect predictions are made for subjects of finite clauses, which should not be affected by I-based minimality effects. i.e., (37a–c) should be well-formed, and (37d–e) should have the LF-representations (38a–b), respectively:

(37) a. *They expect that each other will win

b. *Who$_i$ do they expect that t$_i$ will win ?

c. *John$_i$ seems that t$_i$ will win

d. Someone expects that every Republican will be elected

e. *Who expects that who will win

(38) a. *[$_{IP}$ every Republican$_i$ [$_{IP}$ someone expects that [$_{IP}$ t$_i$ will be elected]]]

b. *who$_j$ who expects that [$_{IP}$ t$_j$ will win]

There is some irony in this state of affairs since relativized minimality seems to be unable to account for just those data that Chomsky (1986b) related to the ECP, i.e. to minimality effects interpreted in terms of Chomsky (1986a). Nevertheless, our result is in line with Chomsky (1980), (1981), (1986b) insofar as the data in (37) turn out to be rather unrelated to overall conditions on anaphoric binding. We have already observed another difference between finite IP-structures and other construction types above, so it would be desirable to reduce the two observations to a single factor.

5 Feature-Based Relativized Minimality

Relativized minimality in the sense of section 4 still does not answer an important question: why is NP-movement more restricted than anaphoric LF-movement to I, or, more generally, why do S-structure movements (WH, scrambling, etc.) normally lead to ungrammaticality if the phrase is extracted from a subject or an adjunct, while LF movements do not? A consideration of contrasts at S-structure such as those in (39) turns out to be helpful:

(39) a. da$_i$ habe ich nicht [$_{PP}$ t$_i$ für] gestimmt
there have I not for voted
'I didn't vote for that'

b. *ihn$_i$ habe ich nicht [$_{PP}$ für t$_i$] gestimmt
him have I not for voted
'I didn't vote for him'

As (39b) shows, German PPs are islands for S-structure movement in general, but a class of expressions, which are homophonous to PP-pro-forms (*da* 'there', *wo* 'where', and *hier* 'here'), can be extracted from PP, cf. (39a). If these expressions are pro-PPs, the difference between (39a) and (39b) may be related to Case Theory: being an NP, *ihn* has to derive a case feature from t$_i$ in (39b) since otherwise a violation of the Case Filter would ensue. This requirement does not hold for *da* in (39a), as PPs do not need case.[13] The contrast in (39) can be derived, then, if case transmission, but not antecedent-government, is blocked for the empty category in (39b). As we shall see, restrictions on S-structure movement as compared to LF-movement can always be explained in terms of blocked case transmission. In order to make this idea precise, compare (39b) with (39c):

(39) c. ihn$_i$ haben wir [$_{VP}$ t$'_i$ [$_{VP}$ nicht t$_i$ gewählt]]
him have we not elected

'we didn't vote for him'

Which category blocks case transmission in (39b)? Relativized minimality implies that the item in question must be a case assigner, so the preposition *für* is a likely candidate. But if, in general, case assigners block case transmission, why can objects be extracted from a VP, the head of which *is* a case assigner? In contradistinction to PPs, which are arguments, VPs are possible targets for adjunction, so no problem will arise for case transmission in (39c): Although, in principle, *gewählt* will exert minimality effects on case transmission, t$'_i$ is not excluded from VP, so the case assigned by V to the root trace can be transmitted to the intermediate trace. t$'_i$ is not included in VP either, so V won't block case transmission between t$'_i$ and *ihn*. The situation is different with PPs: the WH-phrase cannot adjoin to PP, so minimality effects triggered by the case-assigning P will be effective; *ihn* cannot derive a case feature in (39b), and the structure is ruled out.[14]

There is an apparent problem, though: case transmission is an instance of case sharing via coindexation, while case assignment by V or P is an instance of case government by a lexical category, and in the light of the discussion in the preceding section, we should expect that the two processes do not interfere with respect to (5), the minimality condition. Data such as (39a–b) suggest, however, that the partitioning of government relations should be drawn in a different fashion for the purposes of the minimality condition: it is not the nature of the governor that is relevant, but rather the type of feature that is transmitted. Thus, minimal case governors block government relations for case in general.

For antecedent government, a slight reformulation is necessary. The ECP requires that an empty category must find an antecedent with a certain index in a local domain. As indices are connected to φ-features (person, number,

[13]Cf. Fanselow (1988a, 1989a) for a more detailed discussion of this contrast, and Fanselow (1990b) for possible alternatives within a framework of relativized minimality.

[14]We will disregard INFL-triggered Case minimality here.

gender, etc.), the effects of the ECP can be rephrased as follows: A trace must have an antecedent-governor, since it needs φ-features that it will derive from its antecedent. In other words, antecedent-government may be construed as an assignment of φ-features. If this is correct, we expect antecedent government, i.e. transmission of φ-features, to be blocked by exactly those X^0-categories that have φ-features, i.e. that bear an index – but this is exactly what we found out to be true in the preceding section. To sum up, the ECP and the minimality condition can be rephrased as in (40) and (41):

(40) ECP: a non-pronominal empty category must have φ-features.

(41) Relativized feature-based minimality condition:

α cannot enter a relation of government for the feature f with β at the level L in

$$[_\phi \cdots \alpha \cdots [_\Sigma \cdots \delta \cdots \beta \cdots]]$$

if Σ is a projection of δ that excludes α, and if δ governs β for f at L (and if δ c-commands β).[15]

As P does not have or govern φ-features, no problems for φ-feature transmission into PPs arise. By (41), P blocks case feature transmission, a fact that is unproblematic for the pro-PP in (39a), but triggers a Case Filter violation for *ihn* in (39b). In this way, extractions of NPs from PPs are blocked at S-structure in German. Notice that P – like any other lexical category – assigns case at S-structure only, so no case minimality effects arise at LF. Consequently, PP cannot be a barrier for case and φ-feature transmission (=antecedent government) at LF. (42) thus implies, without any further stipulation, that NPs can be extracted from PP in the course of WH-movement, quantifier raising, or anaphor movement at LF, but not at S-structure (cf. the data discussed above).

Incorrectly, however, (42) is ruled out, so some mechanism of domain extension in the sense of Koster (1987) is called for:

(42) who did you laugh $[_{PP}$ at $t_i]$

[15]The c-command requirement in brackets corresponds to Chomsky's restriction of minimality effects on the category immediately dominating δ. Notice that there is a certain danger of circularity with (41) since we define the notion government by refering to government itself, but this problem can be overcome quite simply: we first define a notion α GOVERNS β for f that holds if α m-commands β and if α is an f-assigner or transmitter. The minimality condition could then roughly be formulated as follows: α governs β for the feature f iff α GOVERNS β for f, and if there is no δ closer to β in the sense of (41) that GOVERNS β for f.

Following ideas originally proposed by Kayne (1981), the contrast between English on the one hand, and other Germanic and Romance languages on the other, with respect to preposition stranding might be described as follows: in English, but not in French or German, V and P assign case in the same fashion. If a clause such as (43) is added to (41), minimality effects will be triggered by *laugh* in (42) only, and can be avoided by adjunction to VP, cf. above. Fanselow (1988a, 1989a) presents additional evidence that shows why (43) should be preferred to a statement in terms of tree geometry:

(43) Unless the next category τ c-commanding δ that could govern β for f governs f in the same way as δ would.

Notice that (43) already predicts the generalization noted by Hornstein & Weinberg (1981) that P-stranding is impossible for adjunct PPs without reference to L-marking. In contrast to the complement PP in (44a), the next case assigner for an adjunct-PP in (44b) is not V but I, since the case assignment domain of V appears to be restricted to V′ in English. Obviously, I and P do not govern case the same way, so no domain extension in the sense of (43) applies, and the structure is ruled out as a violation of the Case filter due to relativized minimality.

(44) a. WH_i $[_{IP}$ ..INFL $[_{VP}$ V $[_{PP}$ P $t_i]]]$

b. *WH_i $[_{IP}$ ..INFL $[_{VP}$ V′ $[_{PP}$ P $t_i]]]$

Consider now the contrast in (45a–b):

(45) a. who_i do $[_{NP}$ close friends of $e_i]$ INFL $[_{VP}$ t_i $[_{VP}$admire $t_i]]$

b. *who_i do $[_{IP}[_{NP}$ close friends of $e_i]$ INFL admire Bill$]$

In (45a), t_i transmits case to WH_i, as minimality effects of *admire* can be overcome in the way discussed for (39c). Consequently, case transmission between *who*$_i$ and e_i is unnecessary. As a result of the preceding section, we also know that I cannot block transmission of φ-features (=antecedent government) between *who* and t_i and e_i, so (45a) is grammatical.

In principle, NPs may be extracted from NP: the preposition *of* could trigger case minimality effects, but as N does not govern case to the right in English, it is the category that embeds NP that determines if domain extension applies. If NP is a complement, the next case assigner is V, which governs case in the same way as the preposition *of*, so VP is the relevant minimality barrier for case, which can be overcome by adjunction. If, as in (45b), NP is a subject, the next potential case assigner is I, so domain extension won't apply. As there is no other category present in (45b) from which *who* could derive its case features, and as the subject is a case barrier, (45b) falls victim to the Case Filter. The contrast between a real and a parasitic gap embedded in English subjects thus turns out to follow from the Case Filter. In section 4, we also observed that subjects are not barriers for LF-movement. This fact is predicted without any further stipulation since I – like any other X^0-element – does not govern case at LF, and therefore cannot trigger case minimality effects at this level.

At a first glance, our approach does not relate to NP-movement: in NP-movement, the moved NP is case marked in its landing site, so no problem seems to arise if a case barrier intervenes between the antecedent and its trace. The solution to this problem is quite simple, however. Root WH-traces are directly case marked, and intermediate traces inherit case features in the same way as the WH-phrase does. So WH-traces satisfy the Case Filter. If we impose the same requirement, viz. the Case Filter, on NP-traces, it will follow that NP-traces must derive case features from their antecedents, since root positions of NP-movement are, in general, not case marked directly. In this way, we predict that no case barrier may intervene between the antecedent and its trace. Let us consider briefly (46):

(46) a. John was [$_{VP}$ invited t_i]

b. John was [$_{VP}$ laughed at t_i]

c. John seems [$_{IP}$ t_i to win]

d. *John was expected that pictures of t_i are for sale

VP cannot be a barrier for case transmission in (46a), since V is passivized[16] and has thus lost its ability to assign case. In (46b), *at* might be a potential trigger for case minimality effects, but as Hornstein & Weinberg (1981) observe, a certain type of reanalysis must be asssumed to apply for prepositional passives for independent reasons. (46b) contains a complex verb *laugh at*, which also loses its case assignment properties by passivization. In (46c), neither *seem* nor the infinite I[17] assign case. The situation is a bit more complex in (46d): no case agreement relationship can be established between *John* and its trace: as we saw for (45b), the PP embedded in the subject is a case barrier. This alone does not guarantee that (46b) is ill-formed, since the trace might be case marked by *of*. But Chomsky (1986b) has argued that chains may not be case marked twice. Consequently, either two cases are assigned to the chain ⟨John, t_i⟩, which violates the constraint just mentioned, or t_i is not case marked by *of*. As case transmission from *John* is blocked, t_i will be left without case, and violates the constraint suggested in the above paragraph, which can be formulated as

[16] Again, the situation is a bit more complex here, cf. Fanselow (1990b) for details.

[17] This assumption will be revised below.

in (47). (47) may be combined with (41), our reformulation of the ECP: Case and φ-features are the only feature complexes any NP must have. (48) thus implies (40) and (47).

(47) A non-pronominal empty category must have a case feature.

(48) The features of a non-pronominal empty category must be specified completely.

(49) a. they hope that pictures of each other [$_{I'}$ are for sale]

b. they each other$_i$ hope that pictures of t$_i$ are for sale

(46d) contrasts with (34a), repeated here as (49a) for convenience. The reason for this difference in grammaticality is already predicted, however: anaphor movement is an LF process, so the case minimality effects triggered by I that rule out (46d) are irrelevant for the LF (49b). The question that we posed at the beginning of this section thus seems to find a satisfactory answer in terms of feature-based relativized minimality.

6 Some Remarks on Long Distance Binding

Before we turn to the consequences of (48) for the overall conception of UG, anaphoric binding in languages such as Icelandic should be discussed. In conjunction with (48), the minimality condition (41) restricts anaphoric binding to a rather small set of structures that characterizes English, but not languages such as Icelandic. Properties of long distance anaphors have been studied in detail by Everaert (1986) and Manzini & Wexler (1987), among others, and it is helpful to summarize some major points:

a) Anaphors of a given language may differ with respect to the local domain in which they have to be bound.

b) 'Long distance anaphors' are always bound by a *subject.*

c) Options for long distance binding (ldb) seem to be parametrized in terms of I-features: some languages allow ldb into (tenseless) ECM-constructions only, other tolerate ldb in infinitives in general, further languages (Icelandic) restrict ldb to subjunctive and infinite complements, and (perhaps) languages such as Japanese do not impose any restrictions on ldb.

(50) Jon$_i$ segir aδ Maria elski sig$_i$
John says that Mary loves-subj refl.

In the framework described above, two accounts for ldb phenomena as exemplified in (50) come to mind. A first idea would be to assume that *sig* may be moved at LF to the I-node of the matrix clause of (50), i.e. for some reason I-triggered minimality effects for φ-government might be less severe in Icelandic, so that *sig* might antecedent govern its LF trace even if it is adjoined to the matrix I. This approach faces a fundamental problem, however: as far as we know, options for ldb are not mirrored by similar extensions for processes like WH-movement, quantifier raising or NP-movement.

There appears to exist, however, one domain that is loosely correlated with long distance binding phenomena. As Fanselow (1985) observes, languages with ldb tend to have surprising case properties as well: Languages with long distance anaphors like Icelandic, Middle High German or Ancient Greek also show 'long distance case agreement' in predicative constructions, exemplified in (51) for Icelandic: the case features of the adjective are either determined locally by PRO (nominative) or by the controller *hann* of PRO (accusative). Ldb languages may also tolerate case conflicts in relative clauses (e.g. Gothic, Ancient Greek).

(51) hun$_{nom}$ baδ hann$_{acc}$ aδ PRO INFL vera goδan$_{acc}$/goδur$_{nom}$
he asked her to be good

Another striking pecularity of Icelandic is that finite and non-finite clauses may be complements of prepositions (cf. Andrews 1982):

(52) Eg vonast til aδ verδa vitjaδ
I hope towards COMP to-be invited

Stowell (1981) accounts for the ungrammaticality of the English counterpart of (52) by a Case Resistance Principle, which forbids case assignment to a category that is itself a case assigner. While details of this condition turn out to be quite problematic,[18] it seems reasonable to say that I is inherently nominative, and would have two case features if it received case from outside. In the unmarked case, double specifications of features should be forbidden, so $[_{PP}$ P $[_{CP} \cdots$ I $\cdots]]$ is ruled out if we assume, following Stowell (1981), that a case feature assigned to CP percolates down to I.

The well-formedness of (52) suggests that case feature conflicts on I are marginally possible in Icelandic. This assumption implies a strictly local account for (51). (51) is a control structure, i.e. the φ-features of the embedded clause's subject (and consequently the φ-features of the infinite I-node) are

[18]Notice that, for example, N is a case assigner in German although it will inherit the case feature assigned to NP.

determined by the controller of PRO. In the unmarked case, this feature determination may not be accompanied by a sharing of case features: if we assume that non-finite (controlled) INFL bears inherent nominative case as well (see below), a case conflict on I would follow. If Icelandic tolerates such conflicts to a certain limit, nothing prevents the controller *hann* from copying its accusative case onto PRO and I. The predicative adjective may then choose between the two case features present on I, accusative and nominative. Thus, a situation will arise in which case conflicts on I give the impression of 'long distance' agreement.

Under this perspective, it is not unreasonable to suspect that feature conflicts are tolerated in other domains as well. In infinitives and subjunctive clauses, certain features (mood, etc.) of the embedded I are determined by the matrix I. If feature conflicts are ruled out in a given language, no φ-features can be transmitted between the governing and the governed I positions. Languages like Icelandic which are somewhat liberal with respect to double specification of features may, however, allow a transmission of φ-features, which will give rise to an indexation like (53) for (50):

(53)	Jon_i	$INFL^i$	segir	aδ	$Maria_j$	$INFL^{j,i}$	elski	sig_i
	John	says		that	Mary		loves-subj	refl.

For (53), a very simple account for 'long distance binding' can be developed: the subjunctive I node of the embedded clause already bears the (parasitic) index and φ-features of the matrix subject, so *sig* will fulfill the condition that it must be adjoined to an I it is coindexed with at LF, even if it moves to the lower I. But as the features of an embedded I are determined by a governing I only, and as the governing I is coindexed with its subject only, parasitic features of the lower INFL will be φ-features of subjects. In other words: if 'long distance binding' results from parasitic features on INFL, it is predicted that only subjects are possible antecedents for 'long distance bound' anaphors (= generalization b).

Generalization c) can be expressed as well: Icelandic does not allow, for example, long distance case agreement with indicative clauses, so the question of whether a given instantiation of INFL may bear a parasitic feature seems to be correlated with some metric of 'strength' for I. I is a composite of a set of features,[19] which may partially be determined from 'outside': an infinitive does not have an independent specification of φ-features, a subjunctive does not specify 'MOOD' independently, etc. In this sense, a given feature f may not be specified in two different ways for an I node beyond a specific degree of 'independence'. A parasitic case feature thus appears to be incompatible with an

[19]It might be more appropriate to speak of different projections of TENSE, MOOD, AGR, etc., in the sense of Pollock (1989) and Chomsky (1988) instead of one INFL node.

indepedent specification of φ-features (=subjunctive, indicative) in Icelandic.[20] In a given language, then, the strength of I seems to determine if parasitic φ-features are licensed, i.e., it determines if the I node may carry φ-features of a governing I/subject that trigger 'long distance' binding effects for anaphors. Finally, different types of anaphors within a language may or may not be able to refer to parasitic features. Along these lines, the effects of generalization a) may be captured which would otherwise have to be expressed as different governing categories for different anaphors. To sum up, an approach that explains long distance binding as a strictly local process in terms of parasitic φ-features on I predicts generalizations b) and c).

7 Direct φ-feature assignment to anaphors

So far, we have formulated our account of anaphoric binding strictly in terms of the LF-movement approach proposed in Chomsky (1986b). On the basis of a contrast such as (54), Belletti & Rizzi (1988) argue that the effects of Principle A might have to be checked as early as at D-structure in Italian; the same facts hold for German, as (55) illustrates:

(54) a. questi pettegolezzi su di sé$_i$ preoccupano Gianni$_i$
these gossips about himself worry Gianni
più di ogni altra cosa
more than every other thing

b. *questi pettegolezzi su di sé$_i$ descrivono Gianni$_i$
these gossips about himself describe Gianni
più di ogni biografia ufficiale
more than every biography official (official b.)

(55) a. die Geschichten über sich$_i$ gefallen Hans$_i$
the stories about himself please Hans

b. *die Geschichten über sich$_i$ charakterisieren Hans$_i$
the stories about himself characterise Hans

On the basis of independent evidence, Belletti & Rizzi (1988) demonstrate that *questi pettegolezzi su di sé* is a D-structure object in (54a), but not in (54b). At D-structure, *Gianni* will therefore c-command the anaphor in (54a), a fact that seems to predict the well-formedness of (54a) if Principle A is checked at D-structure. While data such as (54) and (55) are not strictly incompatible with

[20]It would be more appropriate to say that these parasitic features are grammatically invisible beyond a certain degree of independence of INFL, since it seems that Stowell's Case Resistance effects are absent for any type of INFL in Icelandic.

an LF-approach to anaphoric binding,[21] they seem to favor a solution which does not generally involve LF-movement. Above, we have suggested that the ECP may be rephrased as in (41), repeated here as (56):

(56) ECP: a non-pronominal empty category must have φ-features.

Notice that empty categories fall under locality restrictions just because they do not have φ-features intrinsically, and must therefore derive these from an antecedent. If lexical anaphors lack intrinsic specification of φ-features as well, they would be subject to the very same locality restriction without a recourse to LF-extractions. Note that lexical anaphors differ from lexical pronominals in a rather important respect which is somewhat obscured by specific idiosyncrasies of English. Generally, α may bind a category β just in case α and β share φ-features. These include person, number and grammatical gender in German, as (57)–(59) demonstrate:

(57) a. die Glühbirne fehlt an ihrem/* seinem Platz
the bulb$_{\text{feminine}}$ misses at her/ its place
'the bulb is missing in its place'

b. der Wagen fehlt an seinem/* ihrem Platz
the car$_{\text{masculine}}$ misses at his her place
'the car is missing in its place'

(58) a. man$_i$ denkt, daß man$_i$/ *er$_i$ intelligent ist
One$_{\text{arb}}$ thinks that one$_{\text{arb}}$/ he$_{\text{3person}}$ intelligent is
'People believe they are intelligent'

b. du$_i$ denkst, daß du$_i$/*er$_i$ kommen kannst
you believe that you/he come can
'you believe that you are able to come'

(59) alle Männer$_i$ hoffen, daß sie$_i$/*er$_i$ kommen
All men hope that they/he come
'All men hope that they will be coming'

[21]One could, for example, move the phrase *questi pettegolezzi su di sé* back to its D-structure position at the level of LF. This is not without problems, since in a German sentence like (i), anaphoric binding is okay even if *die Geschichten über sich* is not in the scope of *scheinen*, i.e. if it should not be moved back at LF.

(i) die Geschichten über sich scheinen Hans zu beunruhigen
the stories about himself seem Hans to worry
'the stories about him$_i$ seem to worry Hans$_i$'

Problems like these might be avoided with a concept of connectedness.

If we turn to lexical anaphors, however, there are no morphological differences with respect to number and gender, and anaphors are morphologically restricted to 3rd and arbitrary person specification. A similar situation holds for Romance languages, cf. (60) and (61).

(60) a. der Mann liebt sich
the man loves refl.
'the man loves himself'

b. die Männer lieben sich
the men love refl.
'the men love themselves'

c. die Frau liebt sich
the woman loves refl.
'the woman loves herself'

d. man liebt sich
one loves refl.
'one loves oneself'

e. *ich liebe sich
I love refl.

(61) a. El hombre se quiere
the man refl. loves =(60a)

b. Los hombres se quieren =(60b)

c. La mujer se quiere =(60c)

d. Uno se quiere =(60d)

e. *Yo se quiero =(60e)

The situation exemplified by (60) and (61) suggests that German and Romance anaphors lack inherent specification of φ-features. A survey covering about 30 languages from different parts of the world carried out by one of my students, Ildiko Szakacs, showed that a majority of at least the languages included in the sample patterns with German and not with English, i.e., there is no morphological indication of the inherent presence of φ-features with lexical anaphors. Consequently, we may assume that the difference between *himself*, *oneself*, *themselves*, etc. is just a morpho-phonological "spell-out" of φ-features that have, nevertheless, been assigned to lexical anaphors by their syntactic antecedents.

If lexical NPs in general have to possess φ-features, i.e. if (62) holds, and if lexical anaphors do not have them inherently, as (60–61) suggests, an anaphor must derive φ-features in a process that the minimality condition predicts to be confined by φ-feature bearing minimal governors.

(62) A lexical NP must have φ-features.

Let me illustrate this briefly with (63):

(63) *he$_i$ expects Mary$_j$ INFL$_j$ to like himself$_i$

Being an anaphor, *himself* must derive φ-features in (63). Due to I-triggered minimality effects, this process has access only to elements included within the $\bar{I}$ projection of the embedded clause, i.e. *himself* can only derive its φ-features from I_j, i.e. *Mary*, and not from *he*. But as binding is connected to sharing of φ-features (see 57–59), *he* cannot bind *himself*, and the structure is predicted to be ungrammatical. In general, LF-movement and direct φ-identification will have the same effects for English (at least in the standard cases we have discussed), but direct φ-identification allows for a parametrization that is not open to the LF-account: if certain languages like Italian or German allow that φ-features may be copied onto an anaphor at D-structure already (or rather between D-structure and S-structure), data such as (54) and (55) are no problem.

There is a further advantage of direct φ-feature specification for anaphors: Since nothing has been specified to the contrary, the anaphor may, in principle, derive its φ-features from *any* category not excluded from the minimality barrier, in particular, it may derive its φ-features from an object. Object bound anaphors are no problem, then, for our account while they seem to resist a satisfactory treatment in terms of LF-movement that adjoins the anaphor to an I node coindexed with the anaphor (since there is none in the case of object bound anaphors).

(62) can be generalized in an obvious way: having a phonetic matrix, lexical anaphors must fulfill the Case Filter as well, i.e. they must be specified for all features defined for NPs. On the other hand, all other sort of lexical NPs possess φ-features inherently, and are subject to the Case Filter. We may summarize what we have so far in (64):

(64) The features of a non-pronominal empty category or an NP with a phonetic matrix must be specified completely.

8 The Principle of Full Specification

(64) is a rather powerful principle: on the one hand, it subsumes the effects of the Case Filter (for obvious reasons), and, on the other hand, it allows to

derive both the ECP and Principle A of the Binding Theory, as we have argued above. Nevertheless, the formulation of (64) appears to be rather strange: why should there be a principle that applies exclusively to traces and lexical NPs? An obvious move would be to push the generalization further and replace (64) by the Principle of Full Specification:

(65) Principle of Full Specification (PFS)

An NP must be specified completely !

pro and PRO are the only categories not yet captured by (64), so we may confine our discussion on these two types of empty categories. The generalization of (64) to *pro* is rather unproblematic: *pro* is subject to the condition (66) (cf. Chomsky 1982) and appears in case marked positions only, so it already fulfills (65) in standard GB theory.

(66) *pro* must be identified for its φ-features.[22]

The role of PRO with respect to PFS seems to be less clear, however. If PRO is subject to PFS, it must have a Case feature, which could be assigned by (tensed) non-finite I. If standard GB-theory is modified in this respect, two questions arise: why are lexical NPs excluded from the subject position of infinitives, and how could case be assigned to PRO if PRO must be ungoverned, as the so-called PRO-theorem seems to require?

According to the PRO-theorem, PRO must be ungoverned because a) PRO is both a pronoun and an anaphor, which will imply that b) it can fulfill the requirements of Principle A and Principle B only if it lacks a governing category which is the case only if c) PRO is ungoverned. Notice that the PRO-theorem does not follow under the approach developed in the preceding section (since we do not assume a concept such as governing category).

The PRO-theorem has a number of problems, however. First, if we follow Chomsky (1986b) in postulating a PRO-subject for the NP in (67), we have to give up the PRO-theorem anyway.

(67) They$_i$ heard [$_{NP}$ PRO$_j$ stories about them$_i$]

Giving up the PRO-theorem does not make harm to other parts of grammar, since, as Chomsky (1981:217f.) shows, the presence of a governor in the definition of Governing Category is postulated just to derive the PRO-theorem. In

[22]Normally φ-features of *pro* are identified by the I node *pro* is coindexed with. Even in those cases (e.g., arbitrary *pro* in object position in Italian) in which *pro* is not identified by inflection, there must still be a rule for the language in question that assigns content to *pro*.

other words, nothing will change for binding (apart from the behavior of PRO) if we drop reference to a governor in our account of binding, as we already have done implicitly above by eliminating Principle A. Furthermore, rejecting the PRO-theorem allows us to give up another stipulation: since PRO is m-commanded by the non-finite I node, one would have to stipulate that non-finite INFL does not govern (unmotivated otherwise) in order to prevent the m-commanding INFL from governing PRO. Finally, if we do not need to derive the PRO-theorem from binding theory, the only reason why one would still need a Principle B in UG (in the light of the discussion in Koster (1987) and Fanselow (1989b)) will disappear.

If these considerations are on the right track, we have to reconsider the connection between I and PRO. For the following discussion, it is important to keep in mind that additional specifications do not make the overall grammatical system more complex than standard GB-theory is, since these new statements replace (otherwise unmotivated) stipulations about the relevance of an additional governor for binding, the failure of non-finite I to govern, etc.

Taking up the idea, developed by Koster (1984b), that obligatorily controlled PRO is an anaphor, we can observe that PRO and lexical anaphors are in complementary distribution: lexical anaphors show up in all positions in which they are not case-marked by I, whereas PRO occurs only in those positions in which it would have to be case-marked by I in line with the requirements imposed by PFS. If we assume that PRO's φ-features are determined by the infinite I node, i.e. if control affects I rather than PRO, this observation may be phrased as follows: only if both φ-features and case are determined by the same category (i.e. I), an empty category can be chosen. Similar observations appear to hold for the other expressions without phonetic content: *pro* is case-marked and identified by I,[23] and an NP-trace depends on its antecedent both for case and φ-features in the approach developed above. The situation appears to be different for WH-traces, since we assumed that in (68), t_i maps its case feature (determined by V, for example) onto WH_i, but derives φ-features from WH_i:

(68) WH_i [.... [$_{VP}$ V t_i]]

A slight reformulation, however, allows to extend our observations to WH-traces. If case marking is a process that may apply at any time between D- and S-structure, WH_i may be case-marked *before* it is moved. By PFS, WH_i and t_i still must enter into a relation of case transfer, since otherwise, t_i could not receive the required case feature. In other words, the results of sections 3 and 4

[23]This statement is too general: if Rizzi (1986) is correct, pro_{arb} is licensed in object position in Italian, where it is case marked by V. As this type of pro_{arb} is confined to object position, it is not unreasonable to suspect that the arb-φ-feature is governed by V as well. This way, the correlation stated above still holds.

are preserved under this reformulation. So a new empty category principle (69) may be formulated, which does not replace the ECP but the PRO-theorem:

(69) $[_{NP}\ \alpha]$ may lack a phonetic matrix only if its features are determined by a single category.

From (69), the fact that PRO may appear only in positions governed by I follows. We have to explain, then, why lexical anaphors may not show up in the context where PRO would be licensed by (70):

(70) *he tries himself to win

The answer is obvious: similar restrictions hold for the distribution of *pro* and lexical pronominals, as Montalbetti (1984) and Rigau (1988) have observed for Spanish and Catalan:

(71) a. los estudiantes creen que pro_i son inteligentes

b. *los estudiantes creen que $ellos_i$ son inteligentes

As (71) illustrates, lexical pronouns cannot be bound in a position Σ if an empty pronoun with the same index is licensed in Σ. Since the set of positions, where *pro* is licensed is a subset of the position that would, in principle, tolerate a lexical pronoun with the same index, the contrast in (71) may be derived from a Proper Inclusion Principle that states that, if two otherwise identical expression types have a nested distribution, the expression with the bigger domain is not licensed in the contexts where its restricted counterpart may be used. This principle, inspired by suggestions of Chomsky & Lasnik (1977) and Koster (1987) obviously relates to Proper Inclusion Precedence in Phonology, and seems to account for Principle B effects as well, cf. Fanselow (1989b). By (69), however, the empty anaphor PRO has a more restricted domain than lexical anaphors, so Proper Inclusion Precedence will enforce PRO in the context of (70).[24]

This account makes an interesting prediction: In English the binding of a lexical pronoun in structures such as (71b) in not blocked. As *pro* is not licensed in English, the Proper Inclusion Principle cannot apply. We should expect, then, that languages which do not license PRO possess nominative anaphors. This prediction seems to be borne out in Modern Greek: the language does not license the category PRO (cf. Philippaki-Warburton 1987), and has nominative anaphors (cf. Campos 1989).

[24]The relation between PRO and a lexical anaphor is, thus, parallel to the complementary distribution of *pro* and *ell, ella* in Catalan as described by Rigau (1988), and not to what apparently holds for certain dialects of Spanish in the sense of Montalbetti (1984).

Obviously, this is only half of the story: we still must explain why non-anaphoric lexical NPs are illegitimate in the subject position of infinitives, and why PRO is not licensed in the subject position of a finite clause. Somehow, any approach has to characterize the difference between finite clauses and non-finite ones, and we might try (72), which replaces the stipulation that non-finite I does not govern its subject.

(72) If I is coindexed with Σ, I is finite if and only if Σ DERIVES its φ-features within the clause of I from a category different from I.

The clause of INFL α is the biggest CP/IP projection that does not contain another c-commanding INFL. Σ DERIVES φ-features if Σ derives φ-features or possesses them inherently. By (72), a non-finite I may not be coindexed with a category that either has independent φ-features, or derives these within the immediately dominating CP/IP node. If the subject can derive case from a position Σ different from I, i.e. in ECM contexts, (72) imposes no restrictions, but by (69) PRO will be excluded from ECM-clauses since V or P but not I case-mark PRO here. In normal infinitives, ECM is impossible, so the subject must be coindexed with I, if it is to satisfy the Case Filter part of PFS. By (72), this is possible, however, only if the subject does not DERIVE its φ-features within CP, i.e., if it is not a lexical NP except for an anaphor (since non-anaphors possess φ-features inherently) nor a WH-trace (which derives its φ-features from the trace in Spec-CP). In other words, only NP-traces, PRO, and lexical anaphors are licensed by (72), but lexical anaphors are excluded by the overriding Proper Inclusion Principle.

If I is finite, ECM is impossible in general, so any category Σ in subject position (in English, and most other languages) must be coindexed with I. By (72), this is possible if and only if Σ DERIVES its φ-features within the dominating CP, i.e. if and only if Σ is lexical and not an anaphor, or a WH-trace under certain conditions. In other words, lexical anaphors, traces and PRO may not show up in finite clauses if coindexed with INFL. WH-traces will be licensed only if they are identified within the CP-projections, i.e., if there is a binding WH-trace in Spec-CP. If some principle like the doubly filled COMP filter excluded this option for *that* clauses in English, we can derive the Nominative Island Condition effects *in toto*.

Notice that (72) does not refer to subject positions, but to the class of NPs that are coindexed with INFL, i.e., nominative NPs. Icelandic clearly favors this formulation: dative subjects may be bound from outside in Icelandic subjunctive clauses (73), as Maling (1984) observes, while nominative anaphors are excluded in general. Consequently, no configurational solution will be possible, an explanation must crucially refer to case theory, as Everaert (1988) argues.

(73) $\text{h\'un}_i$ $\text{sag}\delta\text{i}$ $\text{a}\delta$ $\text{s\'er}_i$ θatti vænt un mig
she said that herself_{dat} was fond of me

(72) does not take into account pro-drop languages on the one hand, and nominative subjects of infinitives in languages such as Latin, Italian or Spanish, on the other, so a reformulation is necessary that will make reference to the notion of an 'independent' INFL. I decline to make this explicit here for reasons of space, cf. Fanselow (1990b) for a full treatment.[25]

9 Conclusions

The main objective of the paper has been to argue for two claims:

a) Locality restrictions for various processes reduce to a relativized and feature-based minimality condition.

b) Several principles of UG, viz. the ECP, the Case Filter, Principle A of the binding theory, and the identification condition for *pro*, can be replaced by a single principle, the Principle of Full Specification.

As far as a) is concerned, we have argued that L-marking is not the correct notion for barrierhood, and that the concept of minimality has to be relativized. Relativized minimality might have to be combined with some quasi-geometrical restriction on domain extension; we have discussed only in passing why tree geometry in the sense of Kayne (1983), Koster (1987) and Pesetsky (1982) is not a sufficient concept; cf. Fanselow (1990b) for some further discussion.

As a consequence of the unification of local domains, we have seen that various principles of UG have found a common formulation. It can be argued that the simplification of UG may be pushed further: subjacency reduces to Full Specification as well (cf. Fanselow, 1990b), Principle B is a consequence of a more encompassing general restriction, Proper Inclusion Precedence or some different version of this concept (cf. Koster (1987), Fanselow 1989b), and effects of Principle C may be related to θ-theory and general principles on chain formation (cf. Roberts, this volume). Consequently, UG would consist of $\bar{X}$-theory, θ-theory and the Principle of Full Specification. There are some clouds that cast a gloom over this otherwise quite bright picture: as we have seen in the preceding section, we need two additional specifications to account for the behavior of PRO. While it is clear that more work is called for in this

[25] In this paper, we also take up the issue of arbitrary PRO: we may assume that non-finite INFL may freely take up the feature 'arb' if it is not in a control context and map this feature into the subject position. In this way, we can derive the results obtained for controlled PRO in the case of PRO_{arb} as well.

domain, it should be noted that the standard theory needs the same number of stipulations for PRO, as we have argued above.

Two more general points seem to follow from our discussion. With the notable exception of Muysken & Riemsdijk (1985), feature theory has played a rather unimportant role within GB-theory,[26] in contrast to the GPSG- or LFG-accounts.[27] The present article has argued that a deeper analysis of feature determination will, indeed, lead to welcome consequences.

Our approach also heavily depends on feature assignment processes located at different levels of representation, and perhaps, between different levels of representations, as we argued in the final section for case features of WH-phrases. If the approach developed here has any merits, it seems as if a derivational concept of grammar is superior to the purely representational account.

References

Abraham, W., & S. de Meij, eds. (1986) *Topic, Focus, and Configurationality.* Amsterdam, Benjamins.

Andrews, A. (1982) 'The representation of Case in modern Icelandic'. In: J. Bresnan (1982): 427–503.

Aoun, J. (1985) *Generalized Binding.* Dordrecht: Foris.

Belletti, A. & L. Rizzi (1988) 'Psych-Verbs and θ-Theory'. *Natural Language and Linguistic Theory* 6: 291–352.

Bouchard, D. (1984) *On the Content of Empty Categories.* Dordrecht: Foris.

Bresnan, J., ed. (1982) *The Mental Representation of Grammatical Relations.* Cambridge, Mass.: MIT-Press.

Campos, H. (1989) 'Modern Greek and CP transparency'. *Linguistic Inquiry* 20: 321–327.

Chomsky, N. (1980) 'On Binding'. *Linguistic Inquiry* 11: 1–46.

Chomsky, N. (1981) *Lectures on Government and Binding.* Dordrecht: Foris.

Chomsky, N. (1982) *Some Concepts and Consequences of the Theory of Government and Binding.* Cambridge, Mass.: MIT-Press.

[26]Recent investigations on the nature of functional category have changed the situation, however.

[27]There is also an obvious relation between the Principle of Full Specification and a somewhat liberalizable restriction on feature conflicts in the present approach, and the principles of functional completeness, coherence and uniqueness in LFG. If the approach developed here has any virtues, the demonstration that there are quite deep connections between standard GB-theory, GPSG and LFG (and Koster's approach) might be among them.

Chomsky, N. (1986a) *Barriers.* Cambridge, Mass.: MIT-Press.

Chomsky, N. (1986b) *Knowledge of Language.* London: Praeger.

Chomsky, N. (1988) 'Some Remarks on the Economy of Derivation and Representation'. Ms., MIT.

Chomsky, N. & H. Lasnik (1977) 'Filters and Control'. *Linguistic Inquiry* 8: 425–504.

Everaert, M. (1986) *The Syntax of Reflexivization. Dordrecht*, Foris.

Everaert, M. (1988) 'Nominative Anaphors in Icelandic: Morphology or Syntax?'. Ms., Univ. Tilburg.

Fanselow, G. (1985) *Deutsche Verbalprojektionen und die Frage der Universalität konfigurationaler Sprachen.* Diss., Univ. Passau.

Fanselow, G. (1988a) 'Kasusminimalität und L-Markierung'. *Groninger Arbeiten zur Germanistischen Linguistik* 29: 114–136.

Fanselow, G. (1988b) 'German Word Order and Universal Grammar'. In: U. Reyle & C. Rohrer (1988): 317–355.

Fanselow, G. (1989a) 'Features, parameters, and relativized minimality'. Paper, presented at the 1989 GLOW conference, Utrecht, April 1989.

Fanselow, G. (1990a) 'Scrambling as NP-movement'. In: G. Grewendorf & W. Sternefeld (1990): 113–140.

Fanselow, G. (1989b) 'Konkurrenzphänomene in der Syntax: eine nicht-pragmatische Reduktion der Prinzipien B und C der Bindungstheorie'. *Linguistische Berichte* 124: 385–414.

Fanselow, G. (1990b) *Minimale Syntax.* Habilitation Thesis, Univ. Passau.

Grewendorf, G. (1989) *Ergativität im Deutschen.* Dordrecht: Foris.

Grewendorf, G., & W. Sternefeld, eds. (1990) *Scrambling and Barriers.* Amsterdam: Benjamins.

Haider, H. (1988) 'Pro pro-drop Drop'. *Wiener Linguistische Gazette* 42/43: 57–78.

Hornstein, N. (1984) *Logic as Grammar.* Cambridge, Mass.: MIT-Press.

Hornstein, N. & A. Weinberg (1981) 'Case Theory and Preposition Stranding'. *Linguistic Inquiry* 12: 55–91.

Huang, J.T. (1982) 'Move WH in a Language without WH-movement'. *The Linguistic Review* 1: 369–415.

Kayne, R. (1981) 'On Certain Differences between French and English'. *Linguistic Inquiry* 12: 349–371.

Kayne, R. (1983) 'Connectedness'. *Linguistic Inquiry* 14: 223–249.

Kiss, K.É. (1986) 'The Order and Scope of Operators in the Hungarian Sentence'. In: Abraham & de Meij (1986): 181–214.

Koster, J. (1984a) 'Global Harmony'. *Tilburg Papers in Language and Literature* 61. Tilburg.

Koster, J. (1984b) 'On Binding and Control'. *Linguistic Inquiry* 15: 417–459.

Koster, J. (1987) *Domains and Dynasties.* Dordrecht: Foris.

Larson, R.K. (1988) 'On the Double Object Construction'. *Linguistic Inquiry* 19: 335–391.

Lasnik, H. & M. Saito (1984) 'On the nature of proper government'. *Linguistic Inquiry* 15: 235–289.

Maling, J. (1984) 'Non-Clause Bound Reflexives in Icelandic'. *Linguistics & Philosophy* 7: 211–241.

Manzini, R., & K. Wexler (1987) 'Parameters, Binding Theory, and Learnability'. *Linguistic Inquiry* 18: 413–444.

May, R. (1985) *Logical Form: its Structure and Derivation.* Cambridge, Mass., MIT-Press.

Montalbetti, M. (1984) *After Binding: On the Interpretation of Pronouns.* PhD-diss., MIT.

Muysken, P. & H. v. Riemsdijk (eds.) (1985) *Features and Projections.* Dordrecht, Foris.

Pesetsky, D. (1982) *Paths and Categories.* PhD-diss., MIT.

Philippaki-Warburton, I. (1987) 'The Theory of Empty Categories and the Pro-Drop-Parameter in Modern Greek'. *Journal of Linguistics* 23: 289–318.

Pollock, J.-Y. (1989) 'Verb movement, UG, and the structure of IP'. *Linguistic Inquiry* 20: 365–424.

Reis, M. (1976) 'Reflexivierung in deutschen AcI-Konstruktionen. Ein transformationsgrammatisches Dilemma.' *Papiere zur Linguistik* 9: 5–82.

Reyle, U., & C. Rohrer, eds. (1988) *Natural Language Parsing and Linguistic Theory.* Dordrecht: Reidel.

Rigau, G. (1988) 'Strong Pronouns'. *Linguistic Inquiry* 19: 503–511.

Rizzi, L. (1982) *Issues in Italian Syntax.* Dordrecht: Foris.

Rizzi, L. (1986) 'Null Objects in Italian and the Theory of pro'. *Linguistic Inquiry* 17: 501–557.

Rizzi, L. (1990) *Relativized Minimality*, MIT-Press, Cambridge, Mass..

Roberts, I. 'NP-Movement, Crossover and Chain-Formation', this volume.

Rudin, C. (1988) 'On multiple questions and multiple WH-fronting'. *Natural Language and Linguistic Theory* 6: 445–502.

Stowell, T. (1981) *Origins of Phrase Structure*. PhD-diss., Cambridge, Mass., MIT.

Levels and Empty Categories in a Principles and Parameters Approach to Parsing

Hans-Peter Kolb & Craig Thiersch

Abstract

This paper* discusses some basic problems of the implementation of a principles and parameter based linguistic theory. In the first part it outlines the distinguishing features of such a model, exemplified by its best known variety, Government and Binding (G/B) Theory (cf. Chomsky 1981, 1982, 1986a-b). Part 2 discusses some implications of preserving these properties for the design of a parser. Part 3 goes into several relevant issues in linguistic theory in more detail.

1 Introduction

G/B theory departs in several important respects from traditional models. Its main properties relevant for an implementation are

(1)
- The well-formedness of a structure depends on the interaction of general principles rather than specific rules.
- All structure is "projected" from the lexicon.
- There exists a "Universal Grammar". The grammar of a particular language is derived from UG by parameter setting.
- UG itself has a modular structure.

Let's look at each of these claims a bit more closely:

1.1 Principles vs. Rules

Most linguistic theories characterize the speaker's linguistic competence through a set of language specific rules, such as phrase structure rules or transformations, conflating the notions "grammatical construction" and "rule of

*Based on previous work implementing a prototype G/B parser in Prolog. Thanks to all our friends at the University of Tilburg and elsewhere who have commented over the years on rough drafts, as well as to the Dutch organizations N.W.O. and the K.N.A.W. for funding this research.

H. Haider and K. Netter (eds.), Representation and Derivation in the Theory of Grammar, 251–301.

grammar". These rules are highly specific and complex objects which generally describe the phenomena more or less adequately, but fail to capture a lot of important generalizations, both intra- and inter-lingual.

As an example, consider the following sentences and, at the risk of beating a dead horse, the (highly simplified) rules employed by early transformational grammar to analyze them:

(2) a. (John said that) Jill kissed Jack.

b. (John said that) Jack was kissed by Jill.

(3) • PS-rules:

$S \rightarrow$ NP AUX VP

VP $\rightarrow$ V NP

(...)

• Transformation:

SD:	NP,	[+V,+Aux]*,		[+V,-Aux],		NP
	1	2		3		4
SC:	4	2	BE+EN	3	by	1

The passive transformation performs several operations simultaneously: It reverses the arguments of the verb, adjusts the inflection, adds two words, and in most versions, builds structure. But since the only connection between these operations is this not further analysable rule, it has nothing to say about the fact, that all the elements of "passive" also occur independently:

(4) • Movement of the logical direct object:

The destruction of Rome vs. *Rome's destruction*

• The passive morphology: *A beaten man...*

• The *by*-phrase for agent: *A book understandable by non-specialists...*

Moreover, there are phenomena with "passive" properties in many languages, but even in closely related languages they can't be described by the same rules, mostly for reasons that don't have anything to do with the construction in question, such as the different underlying constituent order in Dutch:

(5) a. (Kees zei dat) Jan Marie kuste
K. said that J. M. kissed
'Kees said that Jan kissed Marie.'

b. (Kees zei dat) Marie door Jan gekust werd.
K. said that M. by Jan kissed was
'Kees said that Marie was kissed by Jan'

Now assume that the notion of rule as sketched above is in fact a derived one, i.e. that grammatical constructions are not generated by specific rules, but are rather a function of the interaction of very simple, atomic declarative statements like the following:

(6) a. i. An argument has exactly one θ-role.
ii. An overt NP has Case.
iii. A NP can move.

b. i. A verb assigns a θ-role to each of its arguments.
ii. A transitive verb assigns Case to its object.
iii. Finite inflection assigns Case to the subject position.
iv. Passive morphology absorbs both the Subject- ("external") θ-role and Case-assignment to the object (Burzio's Generalization).
v. A preposition assigns Case and θ-role to its complement.

These statements (strongly simplified as they are) are enough to account for the relevant ("passive-like") properties not only of (2), but of (4) and (5), too: In the active cases of (2), (5) there is no problem. Both the subject and the object get a θ-role from the verb, and Case is assigned to the object by the verb and to the subject by the finite inflection (cf. **Jack (to) kiss Jill*, **Jan Marie kussen*). In the corresponding passive sentences no Case is assigned to the object and no θ-role to the subject. The only way to save the structure w.r.t. (6) is for the object to move to a position where Case, but no θ-role is assigned, i.e. the subject position, while the external argument can either not be realized at all (*Jack was kissed*, *Marie werd gekust*) or be provided with the necessary Case and θ-role by a preposition (whose special meaning links its complement to the absorbed agentive argument of the head, i.e. in this case the verb).

Obviously there is a fundamental difference between (3) and (6) only if the conditions of (6) apply blindly to any structure, i.e. if they are overall structural conditions on well-formedness. But if they do, then they are extremely powerful. Just adding the assumption that verbs like *seem* don't have an external argument, for example, is then sufficient to explain the following paradigm:

(7) a. It seems that Jack is happy.

b. Jack seems to be happy.

c. * It seems Jack to be happy.

d. * Jack seems that it is happy.

Moreover, if pretheoretic notions such as subject, object, assignment of θ-roles and Case, etc., are defined in general structural terms (*dominance*, *precedence*, *c-command*, *government*, etc.), it should be possible to do away with structure-building rules entirely, syntactic structure being completely determined by the interaction of the general conditions.

1.2 Projection from the lexicon

Only the conditions in (6a) state truly syntactic principles, while the statements in (6b) have a distinctly lexical flavour. In fact, the properties of lexical items seem to determine to a large extent the syntactic structure of a given string of words. This suggests a very strong stance of the lexicon in a principles based theory.

This extensive influence is expressed in the $\overline{\mathrm{X}}$-hypothesis of GB-theory,[1] i.e. the axiom that all syntactic structure is endocentric and ultimately projected from a lexical head.[2] Hence a typical constituent structure is

(8)

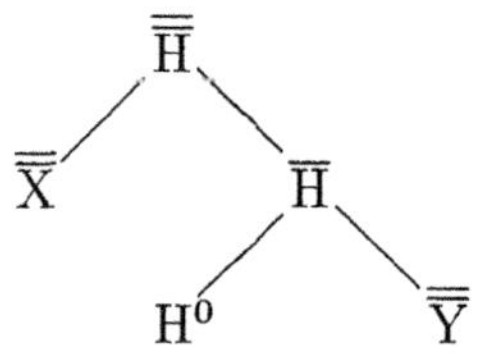

(left-right order irrelevant
binary-branching accidental)

In a particular version of $\overline{\mathrm{X}}$-theory we might now call the constituents in position $\overline{\overline{\mathrm{X}}}$ Specifiers, and $\overline{\overline{\mathrm{Y}}}$ Complements, whose actual realization would depend upon the lexical properties of the head.

The only configuration which is not lexically determined (but highly constrained by syntactic conditions) is an adjunction structure like

---

[1]This hypothesis is not specific to GB-theory. It dates back to early "EST"-times of Transformational Grammar (Chomsky 1970) and plays a major role in many current linguistic theories such as GPSG. In most formulations, however, it is used as a constraint on possible *rules* rather than as a direct structural condition.

[2]But cf. discussion in §3.

(9)

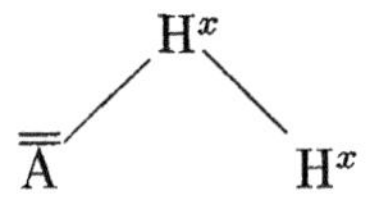

which, however, still obeys endocentricity.[3]

Note, however, that in a principles based approach the $\bar{X}$-hypothesis itself is to a large extent a derived notion. At least the argument structure of a constituent (cf. 8) will be determined by the structural conditions on Case and θ-role assignment.

1.3 Parametrizability

How, then, do we account for the differences between languages? Obviously it would be neither desirable nor necessary to construct a complete set of structural conditions for every language. The conditions in (6), for instance, seem to be sufficient to explain the characteristic aspects of "passive" phenomena (*inter alia*) in a large set of different languages. What distinguishes (2) from (5) is the fact that the internal arguments ("objects") of a verb appear on its right in English, but on its left in Dutch. As it is θ-theory that determines where arguments can appear in a structure, one way to express this is to say that verbs may assign their internal θ-roles to the right or to the left.[4]

Since θ-role assignment etc. is structurally constrained to government configurations, we can reduce this statement even further: Verbs may govern to the left or to the right, but they do it uniformly in a language. What we end up with is an example of a parameter which determines under what circumstances a universal condition on human language applies: Let's assume that Universal Grammar (i.e. the set of universally valid structural conditions) contains the statement

(10) **A verb governs to the 'dir'**
where *dir* is a variable ranging over {left, right}

---

[3]Such an account, of course, renders the venerable sentential structure $[_S$ NP VP $]$ malformed, but the idea that the sentence is actually a projection of the verb or of some inflectional element is neither new nor a special GB invention. Keeping these qualifications in mind, we will continue using S to label the sentential node.

[4]The matter is somewhat more complicated; cf. for example discussion of Chinese in Travis (1984), where it is suggested that θ-assignment is to the left but Case-assignment to the right, resulting in the variable position of objects to the left and right of the verb, with and without accompanying preposistions, respectively.

One of the differences between English and Dutch, then, is the choice of value for *dir*, the parameter setting.

A different type of parameter is exemplified by (11):

(11) a. (Jan zei dat)
Kees Marie de kinderen wilde helpen leren zwemmen.
K. M. the children wanted help teach swim
'Jan said that Kees wanted to help Marie teach the children to swim.'

b. (Hans sagte daß)
Karl Marie die Kinder schwimmen lehren helfen wollte.
... swim teach help wanted

It is not hard to show that both sentences have identical underlying structures (cf. Evers 1975, Haegeman&vanRiemsdijk 1986) and that the main difference between Dutch and German w.r.t. this construction is the presence or absence, respectively, of an inversion mechanism operating on the verb cluster. Parameter setting in such a case would indicate whether a specific option is employed by a particular language at all.[5]

This feature of a principles and parameters based theory is, of course, not only theoretically (learning theory), but also commercially interesting: A principles-and-parameters-parser would by definition be a universial parser, i.e. it could be used for different languages by just exchanging the lexicon and fixing the parameters. Unfortunately the theory of parameters is, maybe not so surprisingly, still very much a *terra incognita.* There have been proposed interesting parameters accounting for various differences between languages, but the set is clearly far from complete, and even the discussion as to what counts as a parameter (as opposed to plain stipulation) has barely started yet. So, whatever the fate of the various GB/PP-parsing projects, the truly universal parser will remain in a visionary state for quite some time.

1.4 Modularity

GB-theory has a modular organization in several respects:

First there is a methodological point: Lexicon, morphology, and syntax are claimed to form a self-sufficient unit which can be studied and explained independently of other modules of cognition. It is not obvious how this sense of modularity could have much impact on the design of a parser — unless

[5] In this particular case, however, it may well be the case that we just have yet not reached a sufficient level of abstraction, i.e. the inversion facts may follow from the interaction of even more abstract conditions which in turn could be parametrized.

modelling of human processing is part of the motivation of doing it, a topic to which we return.

Two other aspects of modularity, however, do inevitably influence the setup of an implementation:

The conditions of UG are not an unstructured set, but are grouped together in subtheories, modules. The canonical modules of GB are

(12)
- θ-theory, which, as we have seen, insures that arguments have a unique thematic role, and thereby determines where in a structure constituents with argument status may appear;
- Case-theory, indicating which elements assign and receive Case, thereby restricting the visibility of certain constituents;
- Binding-theory, dealing with constraints on referential dependency among constituents;
- Control-theory, which is concerned with the choice of antecedent for "understood subjects", i.e. with contrasts such as *Jack promised Jill [e] to leave* vs. *Jack persuaded Jill [e] to leave*;
- Bounding-theory, which specifies certain locality conditions, mainly on movement;
- the Empty Category Principle (ECP), which imposes additional constraints on empty categories, in particular, on traces; and
- $\overline{\text{X}}$-theory.

These subtheories may share basic notions such as c-command which, in fact, plays a role in all modules, or government, relevant in θ-, Case- and Binding-theory, or co-indexing, pertaining to Binding- and Control-Theory, but they are conceptually independent in the sense that no module requires (the output of) another one to apply. They interact, but they don't depend on each other. Eliminating one or more of the modules doesn't cause the whole system to crash, it just makes it less restrictive. (Try that with a phrase structure rule...!)

This is definitely a property of the theory one would like to preserve in a parser: It means that every module can be developed and tested independently and even changes in the final program can be confined to the module(s) they relate to.

The third form of modularity, the assumption of different levels of syntactic representation, however, spells trouble, as we will see shortly.

According to this hypothesis there exists a level of representation, D-structure, which contains the interface between syntax and the lexicon. It is a pure reflection of $\overline{\mathrm{X}}$- and θ-theory as well as the lexical properties of the words employed. It is mapped via a general movement rule ("move α", "move-anything-anywhere") onto S-structure, whose well-formedness is determined by the ECP, Case-, Bounding- and again θ-theory. This structure is in turn mapped on the one hand via stylistic rules, post-lexical phonology, etc. onto Phonetic Form, roughly corresponding to Surface Structure in vintage Transformational Grammar, and on the other via another instance of "move α" (Quantifier Raising) and other processes onto Logical Form, the interface to other modules of cognition, such as semantics, pragmatics, etc. Hence LF is also checked by a set of subtheories.[6]

We end up with the well-known T-model of the organization of grammar:

(13)

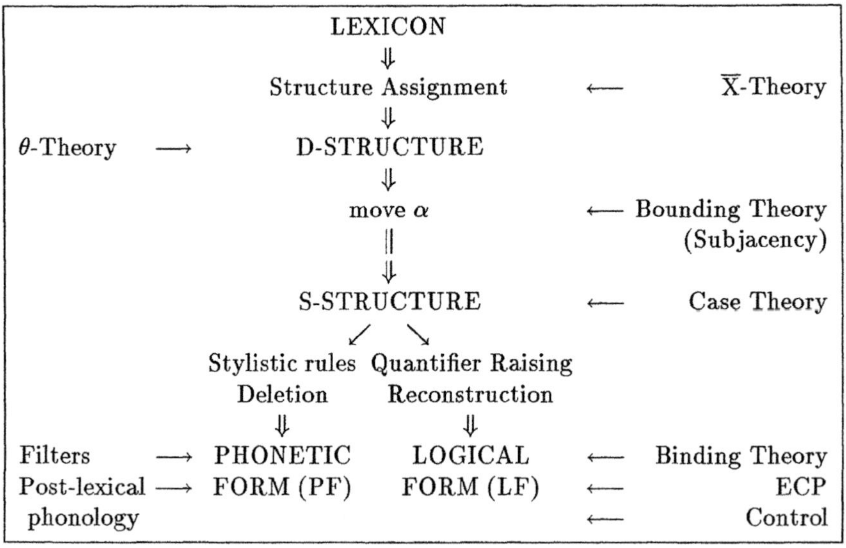

2 Principles based parsing

In general, a parser is a device which takes a string of words as input and returns some — preferably finite — time later either a structural description of that string or the message that it is not a well-formed string of the language. Highly simplified, it consists of three components — a grammar: G, a procedural interpretation of G: P, and a lexicon: D.

[6]The attentive reader may note some discrepencies between the text and the diagram; precisely which conditions apply to which levels is a matter of some controversy, and we take, for the most part, no stand here.

In a traditional parser, G consists of a uniform set[7] of rules — usually phrase structure rules "augmented" in some way or other — which constitutes a more or less adequate generative description of (some fragment of) some language L, D is an arbitrary list of <word, category> pairs,[8] and P can be understood as a procedural metagrammar[9] for G which uses G and D on a particular string of symbols S to decide whether S is a well-formed string of L, and, if so, assigns a structural description it.

While P determines the structural properties of G, its relation to L is very indirect[10] as is the one between D and L;[11] all relevant structural information about L is contained in G — which has to be written from scratch for every new language to be dealt with by the system. Insights into the universal properties of natural languages are not represented, not even representable, in the parser.[12]

In an abstract model of a universal parser based on a principles and parameters approach on the other hand the relations among G, P, D and L are very close, but considerably more intricate than in the traditional approaches: there is no set of rules which would define the structural properties of L. Instead, G consists of a set of universal conditions on possible structures of human language, i.e. *UG*. It determines the structure of a particular L in the same indirect sense in which the laws of statics plus the set of all communal building regulations in the world determine the structure of a particular building. P is a set of instructions (some of them parametrizable, in which cases P also contains the default settings) as to whether (under what circumstances) and how to apply the conditions of G.

P and G together define the notion "possible human language":

(14) Any language which — given an appropriate lexicon — is describable by a subset of G in a configuration permitted by P is a PHL.

---

[7] or a small number of such sets, c.f. the set of PS-base rules plus the set of transformations in classical transformational grammar.

[8] ...and where they aren't just this, as in GPSG, the additional lexical information is just a shorthand for more G-rules, as in all actual implementations of GPSG we are aware of.

[9] We disregard the differences between rule interpreters and compiled parsers as no theoretical issues seem at stake there.

[10] Generally P may restrict the type of L by imposing more or less rigid constraints on the weak generative capacity of G (cf. Tomita 1986), but most existing formalisms (ATNs, DCGs, Unification Grammar,...) have Turing power, anyway. Direct constraints on the structure of L can, however, be explicitly built into the formalism, as in Marcus (1978).

[11] Exemplified by lexical insertion (into full-fledged syntactic trees!) in early transformational grammar.

[12] This is one of the reasons why there are quite a few prototypes of parser schemes with rather impressive performance, i.e. Ps designed to work for any G written in a certain formalism (cf. Karttunen (1986), v/d Steen (1987) and many others), but so few parsers for natural languages which really deserve the name.

Note, by the way, that the question as to what is the structurally unmarked language determined purely by P and UG is not well defined (although some of the work in the field seems to suggest American English as a good candidate...). Obviously it is the learnability of deviant settings for every single parameter, rather than the consistency of the whole set, which has to determine the initial parameter settings. Thus consistency, i.e. the existence of some "unmarked language", would be a rather uninteresting possibility following from nothing but the laws of pure chance.

The individual differences between languages are encoded in a highly complex D which not only contains categorial information for the terminals of L, but also any idiosyncratic parameter settings. Thus the structural properties of some particular language L are a function of the interaction of P, G, and D. Given that P and G stay constant for all languages, the parser may be regarded as an interpreter of the lexicon rather than an interpreter of (language-)specific phrase-structure (and movement) rules.[13]

While anyone designing a parser for a rule-based model can draw on a large variety of well-understood methods,[14] it is obvious that retaining the relevant features of a principles and parameters based approach in a parser implies a major departure from the common scope as well as from the traditional techniques of natural language parsing. What, then, could a parser designed along the lines of such a theory look like?

As the answer to this question will largely depend on the final goal of an implementation, a short digression on possible motivations for such an enterprise seems in order.

2.1 Motivations and non-Motivations

If we ignore commercial applications for the moment, which are by definition uninteresting from the linguistic (though not necessarily from the computational) point of view because they depend on efficiency in the strong sense, which in turn implies heuristics, cutting corners, the supremacy of execution speed over theoretical aptness, we are left with two possible motivations: trying

[13]This property is claimed to be shared by quite a number of theories of grammar (GPSG, LFG, etc.). A discussion of these claims would exceed the scope of this paper. There is, however, one more major principles based approach, which shares it by definition: Generalized Categorial Grammar. (cf. Steedman 1987, Moortgat 1987, ...) A GCG with a general type raising rule, however, abandons (syntactic) structure: *all* relevant properties are lexically coded, structural considerations play no role in parsing (though they may play a role in the design of the lexicon). This avoids some of the problems discussed in the following paragraphs and allows for a strict left-to-right, "on-line" parsing strategy, but it is hard to imagine how strongly structurally constrained phenomena, such as the binding theory facts, could be integrated into such a system.

[14]cf., for example, Aho&Ullmann (1972) for a collection of algorithms.

to simulate the "human parser"[15] or just writing a "theory development/testing tool".

On the background of the strong claims of G/B-type theories about the cognitive/psychological reality of Universal Grammar, modeling human processing seems to be an especially captivating option. Note, however, that, just as in early generative grammar, we are dealing with a theory of linguistic competence here, a fact that is particularly emphasized by its declarative setup. The common assumption (e.g. in Chomsky 1981) is that a child starts out with an innate "zero state" of linguistic knowledge, i.e. a representation of Universal Grammar with the default parameter settings, and some, again innate, language acquisition device (LAD). The LAD then uses *inter alia* linguistic experience to map the zero state onto a "steady state" of knowing and being able to use a particular language. While it is not obvious that the zero state is (part of) a parsing device at all, and the LAD still has very much the status of a "black box", the steady state has to contain, maybe even consist of, an efficient, robust, and highly specific parser. Is it this device that would have to be modelled in a psychologically relevant implementation? Apart from the fact that modeling the latter would set an end to any ambitions of universality, it also presupposes a matching computational theory of performance[16] accounting not only for the grammatical factors, but also for the rôle of semantics, pragmatics, and extragrammatical knowledge in general in human language processing.

But even if we neglect the complex and notoriously badly understood interaction between the various modules of cognition, two empirical questions have to be solved before anyone can embark on the task of simulating the human parser:[17]

(15) a. **What kind of a machine is the human brain?**
Is it a simple serial van Neumann computer, just incredibly fast and with no practical limits on space? Is it a parallel machine, maybe one whose processors are highly specialized special purpose inference machines? Or is the secret just "more of the same", including redundancies in the information structure, precompilation of patterns, heuristics, in short all the dirty things that a scientist carefully tries to avoid when setting up a theory?

b. **How are the modules/conditions/parameters reflected in**

[15]...a motivation which, in fact, hardly anyone working on this matter fails to stress — no matter how implausible the actual system proposed may be in this respect.

[16]...which, as Marcus (1978) has claimed, might even serve to explain some of the primitives of the theory of competence.

[17]Marcus' Parsifal (1978) is a good example of an ingenious but premature step in this direction.

the parser?
Is the parser just an interpreter of UG and lexicon, as in our abstract model in the last section, i.e. is the learning of a language nothing more than the setting of parameters in the "database"? Or is it in fact the learning device which creates the parser by input driven deduction on UG and compilation of the theorems, in which case the parsing device proper would only very indirectly reflect UG? Or is it a combination of both?

These lists are certainly not exhaustive. But note that even if we had a conclusive description of performance phenomena, they could be mimicked in any computational model employing any random pair from (15a) and (15b). And this implies that even psycholinguistics is of only very limited help as long as there are no answers to these questions, which have barely been tackled up to now.

Hence, if we want to avoid pure speculation we have to fall back on the apparently least attractive option: the formalization and algorithmization of the theory. But as this is a necessary prerequisite of any further developments, the results stand a good chance to serve as starting points for more ambitious projects.

2.2 Investigating the model

Abstracting away, then, from the overload of "psychologically real" parsing, designing a Principles-and-Parameters parser reduces to the task of making explicit the trinity introduced in section 2, i.e.:

(16)
- design of the lexicon, including the problem of lexical derivation.
- axiomatization of G, i.e. explicitly formalizing the modules of UG. As there doesn't exist a complete, coherent and fully explicit version of a G/B-type theory, this is basically a linguistic problem, and a non-trivial one, too.[18]

[18]Where the theory *is* explicit, however, formalization is not a very demanding task: Most of the notions are defined in a semi-formal way which can be easily translated into, for instance, a PROLOG definition. Consider as an example the following notion of 'c-command':

Node A c-commands node B,
if neither A nor B dominates the other and
if the minimal branching node dominating A also dominates B.

In order to write a working PROLOG definition we only have to make explicit the implicit reference structure 'A c-commands B in structure N':

```
c-commands(_A, _B, _N) :-
    not(dominates(_A, _B)),
```

- design of P, i.e. the development and formalization of a parsing strategy, of a "driver". Given the theoretical objectives any principles and parameters based theory must meet, this can be done, though not finally implemented, independent from G.

It is this last point, where the basic problems of a G/B parser lie, even if we neglect the additional complications of on-line parsing and psychological reality. For the rest of this section we will therefore focus on the this topic.[19]

Remember that the G/B modules are considered as conditions on arbitrarily assigned structures, active on different levels of representation. In its pure form, then, the G/B parsing problem looks suspiciously hard, NP-hard[20] to be exact: Structural descriptions are easy to verify, but hard to get at. The undesirable consequences of this property become clear immediately when we ask ourselves what an appropriate driver could look like:

When starting a parse, all we have to work on is the input-string, roughly corresponding to PF in (13). According to (13) the only interface to the lexicon is located at D-structure. So if we want to stick strictly to the setup of the theory, we have exactly one option: We can generate well-formed strings starting at D-structure until we arrive at one that matches the input.[21] The disadvantages of such a procedere, however, are just too obvious. Without spe-

---

```
          not(dominates(_B, _A)),
          minimal_branching_node_dominating_A(_C, _A, _N),
          dominates(_C, _B).
dominates(_node, _node1) :- daughter_of(_node1, _node).
dominates(_node, _node1) :- daughter_of(_node2, _node),
          dominates(_node2, _node1).
minimal_branching_node_dominating_A(_C, _A, _N) :-
                    node(_C, _N),
                    branching(_C),
                    dominates(_C, _A),
                    not(node(_D, _N), branching(_D),
                         dominates(_D, _A), dominates(_C, _D)).
node(_node, _node).
node(_node, _tree) :- dominates(_tree, _node).
branching(_node) :- daughter_of(_daughter1, _node),
          daughter_of(_daughter2, _node),
          _daughter1 /= _daughter2.
```

The definition of *daughter_of* obviously depends on the preferred representation of syntactic trees, but is in any case trivial.

[19]For a discussion of a range of further linguistic problems, cf. §3.

[20]I.e., "as hard as" any problem in $\mathcal{NP}$, the set of problems solvable by a non-deterministic automaton in polynomial time. A formal proof of this property has been worked out in E.Ristad (1988).

[21]This strategy is the starting point of Mark Johnson's (1987) G/B-parser.

cial provisions[22] we even end up with a halting problem, if the language to be parsed is not finite — and the infinity of natural language seems to be a pretty well established fact...

A much less obviously intractable strategy would allow access to the lexicon from PF, using the lexical information on sub-categorization and selection as well as the only module interpretable as an *overall* structural condition, $\overline{\text{X}}$-theory,[23] to assign structure to the input. That is, we would generate all $\overline{\text{X}}$ compatible structures, and use the other modules at the appropriate levels to filter the bad ones out. This leads to the following, "naive" parsing adaptation of (13):

(17)

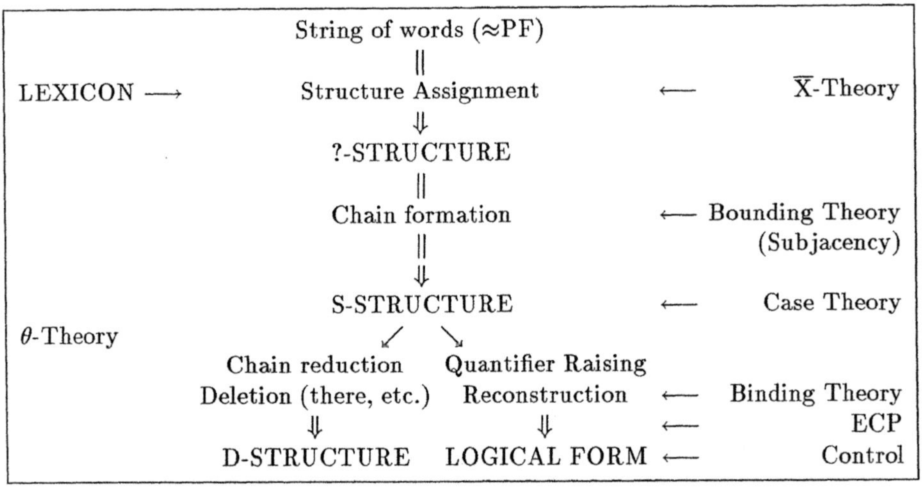

This scheme introduces a new intermediate level of representation *?-STRUCTURE* consisting of a labelled bracketing possibly including empty categories, but stating no relations between parts except precedence and dominance. "Move α" is split into two sub-processes, chain-formation deriving S- from ?-STRUCTURE, and chain-reduction deriving D- from S-structure.

But again we are faced with a halting problem: since ?-STRUCTURE may contain empty categories, without the modules constraining empty categories being available at this level, we end up with infinitely many possible

[22]Restricting lexical access to the words occurring in the input string or making the width of the structure tree a fucntion of the input string would be obvious options to take — and pretty much the only ones, too.

[23]All other modules only involve relations between specific subparts of the structure, i.e. a binder and a bindee, a θ-assigner and an argument, a Case-assigner and an NP, etc...

Note that this step implies the theoretical, and linguistically relevant decision that $\overline{\text{X}}$-theory apply not only at D-structure.

?-STRUCTUREs for any given string. Even if we employ *ad hoc* restrictions, such as allowing gaps only in argument positions[24] (which can be derived from lexical information), we get an intractable number of possibilties. A version of $\overline{\text{X}}$-theory along the lines briefly sketched above, for example, with Chomsky-adjunction permitted at any bar-level, but restricted to binary branching, will allow more than 35000 *different* ?-STRUCTUREs for the simple German subordinate clause ... *dass der Karl den Hund schlug* ('... that Karl beat the dog').[25]

The conclusion is clear: Bad structures must be kept from being generated in the first place. But the generation of a faulty structure is only preventable, if all relevant conditions are checked as soon as possible already during structure building, i.e. they must be reinterpreted as conditions on structure assignment.

Aside from G/B-theory, the equivalence between the declarative and the procedural view on structural conditions is, for all practical purposes, a straightforward fact.[26] What complicates matters in our case, however, is that in the standard formulation of GB-theory the relevant conditions don't refer to the same levels, i.e. structures. Hence a procedural re-interpretation of the modules alone isn't enough. The interconnection of the levels, and their contribution to the grammatical well-formedness of a sentence, also have to be captured in an incremental way.

It is to date a matter of debate whether the relation between the linguistic levels is a truly derivational one, i.e. if there exist specific mappings to derive S- from D-structure and LF and PF from S-structure, with the modules purely functioning as filters on these derivations but too weak to define the levels by themselves; or whether the levels are, in fact, *constituted* by sets of modules, i.e. if they exist in parallel, connected only by the overlap of the conditions that are operative on them.[27] It is obvious that the first view causes great problems for an incremental parsing model. In the absence of conclusive linguistic evidence for the necessity of a derivational approach, we will therefore adhere to the second, more declarative view.

We seem to be left with two options, then: On the one hand we could try to construct all levels in parallel. Such a setup would mean to parse what is in fact an S-strucure, but to use the interaction of modules and lexical information to predict for every substructure to be built a corresponding D-structure and LF, whose availability in turn determine the well-formedness of the S-structure.

[24]... which would practically ban movement of adjuncts from grammar, provided this sort of movement leaves traces. See discussion in § 3.3

[25]Assuming, of course, that initially *no* conditions apply to Chomsky-adjunctions via "move α".

[26]cf. the interpretation of phrase structure rules as node admissibility conditions in GPSG.

[27]In the standard formulations for example, specified by the Projection Principle.

Alternatively, we could compile the modules to constrain a single "annotated S-structure", which contains all the information of the original levels, leading to the following scheme:

(18)

		String of words LEXICON		
		↘ ↙		
$\overline{\text{X}}$-Theory	⟶	Incremental (*'Cyclic'*)	⟵	Bounding Theory
θ-Theory	⟶	structure assignment	⟵	Binding Theory
Case Theory	⟶	incl. Chain formation,	⟵	ECP
		Scope assignment	⟵	Control
		⇓		
		Annotated S-STRUCTURE		

This is a pseudo-alternative, however: Already in a canonical S-structure all properties of D-structure are trivially represented, except for the one fact that every argument has to start out from a θ-position. But this requirement[28] can easily be formulated as a condition on chain formation:

(19) For every chain C (which is a complete linear ordering $<$ on a set of syntactic nodes) and every node $n_i \epsilon C$, if n_i is a θ-position, then there does not exist a node $n_j \epsilon C$ such that $n_i < n_j$

i.e. if a chain contains a θ-position, then it must be its last element. It can be argued that this condition is just a descriptive statement while the assumption of a level of D-structure provides us with an explanation of the facts, but it seems reasonable to assume that the "backwards-move-α" mechanism of the polystratal variant would use exactly the same constraint to construct D-structure.

An equally perspicuous relationship holds between any given LF and its corresponding S-structure.[29] What makes LF special in the canonical case is the fact that there may be more than one LF per S-structure.

Both the poly- and the monostratal option referred to above, however, treat a derivation (including LF/Scope assignment) homogenously, i.e. to different readings, whether purely structural or scope ambiguities, correspond to different derivations, and each derivation represents exactly one D-, one S-structure

[28] As observed by Goldsmith, ca. 1972, as quoted in Chomsky (1975), pp.115-17; cf. also Koster(1978), etc. Basically it boils down to traces (and phonetically realized morphemes like the preposition *by*) encoding the DS positions in SS.

[29] The intuitive difference in status between the two pairs reduces to the fact that we generally take S-structure for a true, in fact *the* primary structural level, while the status of LF is much less lucid in this respect. (cf. the presumable structural ambiguity of *Who did you promise to leave* vs. the scope ambiguity of *Some woman is loved by every man*; that the difference turns on structure vs. scope is less than straightforward in some cases; cf. discussion in §3.3, for example.) Cf. also footnote 38.

and one LF, either directly, or trivially derivable. Hence the options are theoretically indistinguishable: If the levels can be constructed in parallel, then they can be conflated, too.

In any case we end up with one single condition on the combinability of two nodes:

(20) Nodes A^i and B^k can be combined to form node $\alpha = [_{A^j} A^i B^k]$ if B^k is licenced as a satellite of A^i in the configuration α, i.e., if the structure α fulfills all modules relevant to B^k (left-right order irrelevant; cf. discussion in § 3 as to the bar-level values of i, j, k.)

2.3 Locality

Such an approach reduces parsing to problem solving, where structure building is driven by a grammatical "expert system", a very desirable result given the declarative setup of the underlying theory. Its success, however, largely depends on the size of the local domains in which the modules can, in fact, be checked locally, in the linguistic as well as in the procedural sense.

Linguistically, a module M applies locally to some structure N, if N contains all the information needed to decide whether it is well-formed according to M.

It is easy to see that a module such as $\overline{\text{X}}$-theory can be checked locally in this sense within the smallest possible domain: any node. The same applies to θ-theory[30] under a bottom up strategy of tree construction.

(21) a. A structure N is well-formed according to $\overline{\text{X}}$-theory[31] iff N is of category C and bar-level B and there exists a node D in N of category C and bar-level $B1$ such that D is a daughter of N and $B \geq B1$ or N is a terminal.

b. N is well-formed according to θ-theory iff for every argument (= NP or complement clause) daughter A of

[30] At least if we limit ourselves for the time being to the canonical formulations which have nothing to say about sentences like

Schlagen	wollte	Hans	den	Hund	eigentlich	nicht
beat	wanted	Hans	the(acc.)	dog	actually	not

'H. did not really want to beat the dog'

where the θ-(and Case-)assigner of the object has been preposed. In an A-chain $(x_1, x_2, \ldots, x_n)$, the distance between the Case-position x_1 and the θ-position x_n can presumably be indefinitely long; in §3.2 we look more closely at the locality requirement between links x_i and x_{i+1}.

[31] This is the most liberal version of $\overline{\text{X}}$-theory possible. More restrictive formulations can be obtained by adding the appropriate conditions to the consequens of the definition.

N there exists a chain[32] (possibly of length 1) which contains *A* and a θ-position.

But not all modules have this property. Consider the following data:

(22) a. ... Jack to have seen Jill

b. ... Jack had seen Jill

c. ... Jack to have been seen *e* (by Jill)

d. ... Jack had been seen *e* (by Jill)

e. ... Jack to seem that Jill had seen him

f. ... Jack seems that Jill had seen him

When the S-node is being built in (22), the θ-module will accept the structures (a-d): (a, b) directly, and (c, d) via a non-trivial chain headed by *Jack* and including a θ-position. It will reject (e, f). A local Case-module designed along the lines of (21b) on the other hand would accept (b, d, f), but would not only correctly reject (e) but also — prematurely, at least — (a) and (c), which can be saved by becoming the complement of an exceptional case-marking verb like *believe*. The best we can do, in terms of locality, is to accept all the clauses, but to place a constraint on further processing, in this case the requirement for the resulting structure to get Case and transmit it to the subject-NP.

Note that while this example, as well as the entire discussion in this section, presupposes a bottom up parsing strategy, the locality problem is not restricted to, or even an artefact of, such an approach. As Chain formation is not an immediate option with a top down method, both Case and θ-theory cause problems when parsing *Jack*: If the clause is not embedded under an exceptional case-marking verb, Case theory has to restrict INFL to [+ tense]. In the case of θ-theory we even end up with a disjunctive constraint on the remainder of the sentence: either INFL assigns an external θ-role or the VP contains a gap in theta-position (i.e. some sort of GPSG-like slash mechanism).

A similar problem returns in the case of Binding theory:

(23) A structure *N* is well-formed according to Binding theory iff *N* has an indexing *I* such that

a. for every anaphor *A* in *N*,
if there exists a governing category *G* for *A* in *N*[33]
then *A* is bound in *G*;

---

[32] ...of the proper specifications, the spelling out of which would lead us too far astray here.

[33] *X* is bound if it is co-indexed with a c-commanding element (in argument position). *X* is free if it is not bound.

b. for every pronominal P in N,
either there exist a governing category G for P in N
and A is free in G, or A is free;

c. for every "referential expression" R in N, R is free.

The conditions in (23) can only give a definitive answer locally if the structure checked contains a governing category for every anaphor in it, i.e. the locality domain of (23a) is not any node, but rather any governing category, a much weaker notion.

But (23) also scores extremely low on locality in the *procedural* sense: Verifying it means exhaustive search of the complete (possibly deeply embedded) tree structure, one of the computationally most ineffective operations possible.[34]

Further complications arise with empty categories as in

(24) a. Who do you believe [*e* to be funny] *referential expression*

b. Jack is believed [*e* to be funny] *anaphor*

c. Jack tries [*e* to be funny] *PRO ("pronominal anaphor")*

not even the status of the NP *e* with respect to Binding Theory can be determined locally.[35]

Having noted some of the computational problems involved, let us now turn to the question of whether some revisions of linguistic theory might partly ameliorate the problem.

3 Some theoretical issues

As argued in the preceding section, in implementing a theory of the sort envisaged by the most common version of the principles and parameters approach, G/B theory, one immediately runs into a problem weeding out the multitude of possible structures[36] early on in the parse, caused in part by the structure of a theory which claims that certain conditions which license structure can only be "checked" by transforming, or rearranging, the structure. While we cannot review all of the arguments for and against a multi-leveled theory here, we would like to suggest some theoretical revisions which make a monostratal approach seem more promising, in that they limit still further the locality of

[34]While there are fairly obvious short-cuts for (23a, b), no such option exists for (23c).

[35]Cf. Kolb (1989) for additional discussion of a possible solution involving constraint propagation.

[36]quite aside from the problem more often discussed in the parsing literature of deciding which of two alternate structures for a genuinely ambiguous string is the correct one on the basis of, say, semantic considerations.

the domain in which conditions must be checked. First, however, some preliminaries: beyond the general claim that language specific constructions result from the interaction of universal principles with language specific parameters (defaults) and lexical idiosyncracies, various versions of G/B theory (or the Principles and Parameters approach in general) make certain specific claims about the nature of Universal Grammar[37], the truth of which is an empirical matter, but which bear on the form of a "universal parser". In particular, the precise manner in which constituents are licensed will in some cases determine the locality of the licensing relationship as well as bearing on the question of whether a separate "level" of representation is necessary for the licensing to be checked.

Hence we begin by discussing the uniform constituent hypothesis and its relation to licensing in the next section (cf. §1.1 above); followed by a look at some areas where the proliferation of ambiguous structures can (possibly) be stemmed locally in building up S-structure: A-chains and Adjuncts.[38]

3.1 Uniform Constituent Hypothesis

One part of the Universal Grammar Hypothesis that has received renewed attention recently is the uniform constituent hypothesis (partially embodied in X-bar theory). As noted above in §1.2, all constituents project from a lexical head[39] according to universal principles and any idiosyncracies of constituent

[37]Several of which have been touched upon above in section 1.

[38] There are many other sources of proliferation of ambiguous structures, such as a Chomsky-adjunction (e.g. in scrambling languages and for extraposition), but to discuss them all here would take us beyond the scope of this article, and we limit ourselves to these two cases.

While it is in theory possible to imagine cases where an LF structure would influence the building up of an S-structure, e.g., *if* one were to assume Q-raising, one could imagine that for a particular string S-structure S_1 would permit quantifier movement to creating LF_1 giving the intended scope, whereas S-structure S_2 would create an ECP violation and hence the only reading would be a non-sensical, or unintended one; but this seems rather similar to the much-discussed attachment problem for PPs (cf. footnote 94 in §3.3.), which must rely on extra-grammatical factors to decide the upon the correct structure, and hence we have nothing to say about it here.

On the other hand, it *has* been suggested in recent work (Chomsky (1989), based on the analysis in Pollock (1989)), that checking conditions head movement in LF is crucial for determining the grammaticality. If so, this would be such a case. This article notes the computational problems this entails and hence takes a rather pessimistic view of the relationship grammar/parser. An alternative, at least for English, is sketched in Thiersch (1989; *forthcoming*).

[39]Of course, under a theory including "predication" as a basic concept, exocentric constituents could be allowed — e.g. the structure [$_S$ NP VP] would be licensed if VP is "predicated" of NP. We try in the following to justify the endocentric approach, for reasons which we hope will become clear in the following sections.

structure result from lexical properties plus (presumably simple) language-specific parameters. Of particular importance is the concept of "licensing"[40]: i.e., the idea that a constituent appears when and only when it is required by some independent module of the grammar. Hence PS-rules are otiose and, if we are lucky, nothing needs to be stipulated regarding phrase-structure as it follows from principles of independently motivated modules. In this spirit, let us take a particularly strong version of "X-bar" theory, and see how much can be derived:

(25)
- all lexical items[41] head a projection, including "little words" like conjunctions;
- that branching is strictly binary[42];
- that the bar-levels are represented by exactly two binary features, which indicate (1) whether a node dominates a Maximal projection of the head, and (2) whether a node is a Lexical item. (non-branching in the syntax)[43];
- all constituents have the same functional structure, consisting of a Specifier, Complement and (optional) Adjuncts, and these in fact have "typical" semantic interpretations, simplifying the semantic analysis of the constituents[44].

So for example, let us consider the canonical X-bar structure in (8), repeated here:

[40]Cf. Abney (1985). An early attempt to work out the details of the X-bar hypothesis understood as condition on possible structures appeared in Stowell's (1981) dissertation, and subsequent refinements and attempts to eliminate inconsistences have appeared in Muysken (1982), Pesetsky (1982), Gazdar and Pullum (1982), Thiersch (1985), Cann (1986) and Chomsky (1986b), Fukui and Spaes (1986) among many others.

[41]We leave open the (important) question as to whether strictly non-lexical items such as a hypothetical INFL have full projections. There is nothing crucial to parsing involved which is particular to INFL; cf. comments below in section 3.1.1 about bound morphemes and the instantiation of features.

[42]This leads to certain theoretical consequences which are discussed in the literature; cf. Kayne (1984).

[43] Cf. Muysken (1982) and Thiersch (1985) among others.

[44]Details in Thiersch (1985) and Cann (1986) among others.

(8)

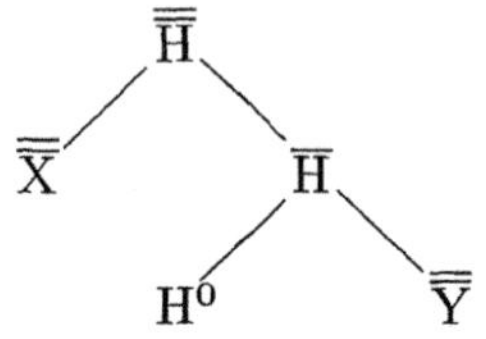

(left-right order irrelevant
binary-branching intentional)

where $\overline{\overline{H}}$ is [+max, −min], $\overline{H}$ is [−max, −min], and H^0 is [−max, +min]; $\overline{\overline{X}}$ is generally referred to as the Specifier and $\overline{\overline{Y}}$ as the complement. The representation of bar-levels as features can be exploited to eliminate vacuous (non-branching) projections, leading to structures like the following:

(26)

(a)

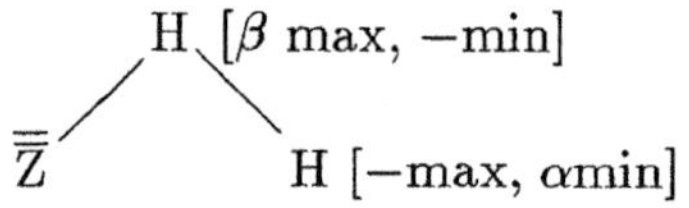

(b) $\overline{\overline{H}}$ (i.e., [+max, +min])

Where the (a) structure is ambiguous, i.e. doesn't suffice to decide whether $\overline{\overline{Z}}$ is a Specifier or a Complement, and will be disambiguated by other modules such as θ-theory; (b) is, of course, a lexical word which functions syntactically as a maximal projection, such as *he* and *down* in *he fell down.* The structure in (26a) could be viewed as a filter on tree-admissibility, and (26b), as well as the full $\overline{\overline{X}}$ with Specifier and Complement are subcases thereof.

If adjuncts (modifiers of the head) appear at the $\overline{X}$ level, and only this level is recursive (the "traditional" view), this would indeed also be a subcase of (26a) and we would need to say no more about the phrase-structure. However, there are two reasons for relaxing this: Firstly, if we allow Chomsky adjunction to maximal categories, e.g., in "scrambling" structures:[45]

(27) a. Er meint, daß seinen Sohn ein toller Hund gebissen hat.
he means that his son a mad dog bitten has
'He says a mad dog bit his son.'

b. *presumable structure*:
daß [S [$_{\text{NPacc}_i}$ seinen Sohn] [S ein toller Hund [e_i] ...]]

[45]Nearly everyone does, although for different constructions – e.g. to VP in Chomsky (1986b), to S in Saito (1985), etc.

then at S-structure we have a violation of (26a). Secondly, we might want to allow adjunction directly to minimal categories, e.g., for the "unmarked" order of the arguments in German:

(28) ... daß er den Hund mit einem Stock geschlagen hat
that he the dog with a stick beaten has
'... that he beat the dog with a stick'

often referred to in the literature as the tendency for the direct object to be "left-peripheral".[46] We could relax the condition (26a) on phrase structure to allow identity operators, if properly licensed, yielding the structure in (9), repeated here:

(9)

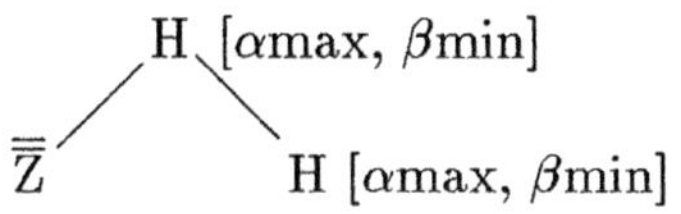

where the $\overline{\overline{Z}}$ is *either* a "true" adjunct (modifier), licensed as indicated below in section 3.3, or a "scrambled" element, licensed as part of an A-bar chain.[47]

3.1.1 Licensing

Clearly not all constituents have the canonical structure, which after all is only a skeleton, or admissibility condition. From the above discussion, it should be clear why the constituent structure is different for different heads: the satellites appear only when properly licensed. Implicit in the preceding discussion, as well as in much of the literature,[48] is that the basic licensing relationship is between head and satellite.[49] Let us look at a specific proposal for the interpretation/licensing of the canonical Complement, Adjunct, and Specifier positions.

---

[46]It should be noted, however, that the issue is more complicated that this - cf. Czepluch (1988) for more complex data.

[47]Under a non-scrambling approach we would lose "parasitic gap" effects noted in Felix (1983), Bennis and Hoekstra (1985) and Thiersch (1985) which would arise under a scrambling analysis; cf. Huybregts and van Riemsdijk (1985) for an alternative. The issue may be a red herring under other analyses of case-marked θ-positions. Chomsky (1986b) contains a somewhat different proposal. Also see footnote 57 for a reinterpretation of the bar-level features...

[48]Cf. similar proposals of this nature in the work of Abney, Fukui, and Spaes cited in the bibliography.

[49]Strongly implying, although not *a priori* necessitating, binary branching; see discussion of small-clause in § 3.2.2 and of double object constructions in footnote 85.

The Complement The standard assumption about argument positions like the complement is that assignment of θ-role licenses a potential position, and assignment of Case allows lexical material to appear in the position. (If no lexical material appears then the resulting empty category must be A-bar bound.)

This leaves other kinds of relationships between items which presumably stand in a *head:complement* relation unaccounted for. Hence let us assume that there are basically two kinds of heads,[50] namely true "content" predicates (such as main verbs, prepositions, nouns, etc.) and operators, such as modal verbs and complementizers: in the first case, the complement is an argument of the head in the usual sense, and in fact the one usually[51] referred to as the internal argument of the predicate; in the second, the complement is itself a predicate.[52]

The Specifier Let us further assume that the Specifier is always the "other" (i.e., external) argument, or, more precisely, receives the compound thematic role determined by the head and its complement (and adjuncts) as noted in the literature. In the case of a simple predicate head, it is the external argument, and in the operator case it is the undischarged argument of the complement.[53] For example, take the sentences *John beat the dog* and *John was beating the dog*[54]:

[50]For example, cf. Abney (1985); the idea itself is ancient, e.g. the notion of "full" and "empty" categories in Chinese grammar ...

[51]But cf. § 3.2 and especially § 3.2.3.

[52]Assuming here the analysis of auxiliaries argued for in Gazdar, et al. (1982) and elsewhere, where each is the complement of the preceding verb, and the verbal inflections are discharged in the same manner as Case. Cf. references therein. While this analysis might seem to create a proliferation of "maximal" projections which could cause problems for various parts of the binding/bounding theory, only certain of them will "count" (e.g. [+tense]).

[53]Cf. footnote 39 as well as Williams (1981) and others for details of a somewhat different view of the external argument. Alternatively, one can assume that the $(n\text{-}1)^{th}$ projection of the head is always predicated of the Specifier. The latter needs to be developed, but the idea seems promising; cf. recent work by J.-R. Vergnaud and several others.

[54]While we believe that the proper analysis for noun-phrases (traditionally NP) is really a DetP, i.e. the determiner is an operator which takes an $\overline{\overline{\mathrm{N}}}$ as its complement (at least for some languages), nothing crucial to this paper hinges on the distinction, and we have hence left the alternating notations NP/DP or $\overline{\mathrm{N}}/\overline{\mathrm{D}}$ etc. unchanged. Cf. the articles by Abney, Corver, Fukui, and Spaes cited in the bibliography for discussion.

(29)

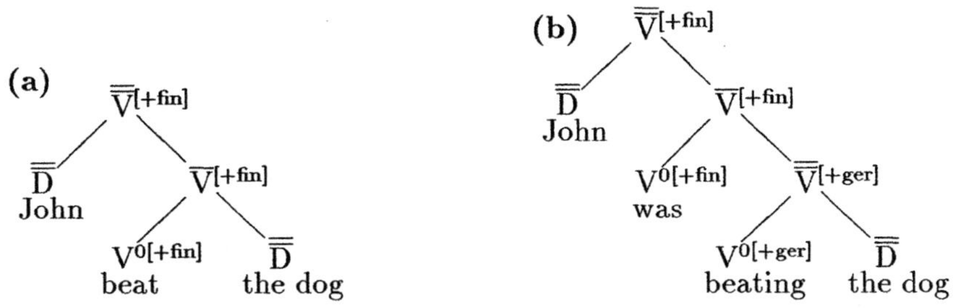

The verb *beat* assigns its direct object Case (e.g., accusative) to the right in both cases; but in (29a), the verb is [+tense] and hence can assign the subject Case, nominative, to the left, licensing this positon and allowing it to be assigned the thematic role of subject. In (29b) however, the verb *beating* is [−tense] and hence cannot assign nominative Case to its left. Thus the projection ends with the structure

(30) $[_{V[+max]}\ [_{V[+min]}$ beating$]\ [_{DetP}$ the dog$]]]$

since no specifier is licensed and therefore there is no "subject". In the next projection, however, *was* is [+tense] and can assign nominative Case, licensing the specifier position, but has no θ-role of its own to assign. Its lexical specification includes a complement of, say, [+V, +ING], which is fulfilled by (30) above. Since (30) is an open predicate, and the verb *be* links the nominative NP to the open argument position of its complement, the DetP *John* is assigned to the "dangling" argument position.[55] (The [+V, +fin] head of course has an additional semantic contribution, minimal in the case of BE, but considerable in the case of modals, for example). It is easy to see how this applies to the other auxiliaries, embedded auxiliaries (which are subcategorized by their complements just as "main" verbs are by *their* objects), and to other complement types: *John is very tall*, *John is in the kitchen*[56] as well as, possibly, in other kinds of projections: e.g. the DetP where the DET *'s* assigns Case: *John* 's

[55]Cf. details in § 3.2.

[56] Assuming the preposition in this example is a two-place predicate. This suggests that what characterizes adjunct modifiers such as

the man [with the hat]	P-max
a student [sick of the exams]	A-max
a man [to fix the sink]	V-max
the cat [which Fred saw]	C-max

is that they are all *syntactically* open predicates with the unsatisfied argument position in the Specifier position and is coindexed with an appropriate referent within a certain domain, an idea which will will be taken up and discussed in more detail in § 3.3

beating the dog. This has some consequences for the formation of A-chains and will be considered below again in § 3.2.[57]

Note that in (29) there is no separate INFL projection; it seems unnecessary in light of the above discussion, and stems from a more general consideration: if we consider elements such as DET, INFL, COMP to be operators in the sense of Abney (1985), Fukui and Spaes (1986), then in some languages they will be realized on the surface as independent morphemes (the article in English, German, or INFL in Warlpiri) and in other cases as a bound morpheme (e.g., the [definite] article in Skandanavian, Bulgarian, or INFL in many European languages.) Presumably its effects can be redefined as effects of the features such as [+tense]. That is, features which themselves play a crucial role may nevertheless be instantiated independently in some languages and as inflections in others.[58]

It should be noted that in addition to the constructions discussed here and in the references which do adhere to the canonical structure, there are many which remain problems: for example, clitic and clitic-doubling constructions, or languages with purported multiple wh-extraction, like Polish and Romanian.[59]

---

[57] Note that under this interpretation the features no longer have the interpretation usually associated with them in the works cited above (such as "projection", "word", "lexical", "maximal"), but come close to meaning something like [±Spec, ±Compl]:

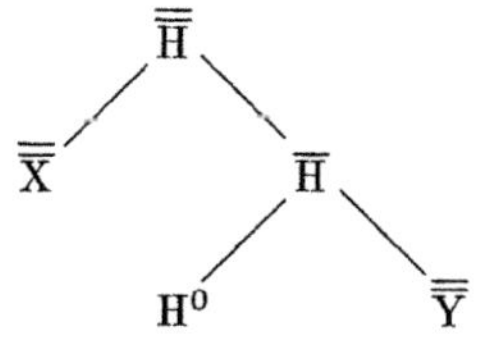

= H[−Spec, −Comp]

= H[+Spec, −Comp]

= H[+Spec, +Comp]

i.e., [+Comp] would mean the head still needs to discharge a complement; [−Compl], that the H (or its projection) either *has* a complement (which may be a Case-marked empty category) or does not subcategorize for one, and the "condition" on X-bar structure is simply the familiar one that, if there are both an internal and external argument, the "internal" one must be discharged first; cf. discussion in Burzio (1981/86) and § 3.2. Since adjuncts (see § 3.3) are not arguments of the H-projection, they fall outside of this system and hence can be freely adjoined if they are (a) properly licensed and (b) violate no other constraints (including directionality of headedness). We will nevertheless continue to refer to the features as [max] and [min].

[58] In the case of *English*, as opposed to, say, Icelandic (Holmberg 1986) or French (Pollock 1989) — it is far from clear that there is head-movement into an INFL position — evidence consists primarily in "do-support", which in Subject-Aux inversion is movement into COMP, as in other Germanic languages; before *so* where it applies equally to other inflections (..., *and John might be doing so, too*); and before certain cases of *not*, the only real evidence. But the latter has a rather more plausible non-movement analysis. For discussion of the evidence, cf. Thiersch (1989; *forthcoming*).

[59] The latter is particularly instructive, as the framework described in the body of the paper does not countenance $[_{\text{Spec(COMP)}}\ wh_1\ wh_2\ \ldots wh_n]$; Toman (1982) and Cichocki

Clearly we cannot discuss all such cases in a short article.[60]

Let us first look more closely at the status of empty-categories which result from "movement" in the usual sense and are cases of A-binding, where we will suggest that they are more locally bound (and licensed) than empty categories resulting from A-bar bound movement. We then turn our attention the proper treatment of adjunct modifiers, another source of structural proliferation.

3.2 A-chains

In § 3.1.1 above, we suggested that, in the case of a complement which is not a semantic argument of the head (i.e., grammatical object) but rather an open predicate (such as the complements of modal verbs or the copula) the undischarged argument of the Complement (generally the "external" one), or rather the corresponding compound θ-role, is assigned to the (potentially

(1983) have shown that in the Slavic case, only the first 'wh' is in COMP and the rest are "scrambled" to the front; Comorovski (1986), on the other hand, shows this is not the case in Romanian, as all wh-words are subject to long-distance extraction. Her solution, however, namely adding an *ad hoc* PS-rule for Romanian COMP is clearly unacceptable in the Principles and Parameters approach in which language-specific PS-rules are eliminated in favor of licensing and parameters. In her paper there are a myriade of tantalizing details suggesting more principled avenues of approach...

[60] We should note for completeness, however, that there are two cases deserving special attention: first, if we assume that the function of some operators is (among other things) to change the categorial status of their complement, e.g., the argument $COMP_a$ takes an assertion ($\overline{V}$[+tense]) and allows it to function as an argument, or the relative $COMP_r$ which allows its complement to have an empty argument position so that the assertion can function as an unsaturated predicate (modifier). (That they are different is easier to see in languages where they are morphologically distinct, e.g. Bavarian *daß* vs. *wo*.) The Specifier of COMP in these cases, of course, does not get a compound θ-role as described above, but just the θ-role assigned to the A-bar chain.

The other case is coordination: assuming the analysis of coordination suggested elsewhere (for example in Thiersch 1985), the conjunction, an operator, is a *defective* head, underspecified for features, which unifies its categorial and bar-level features with those of its satellites (corresponding to the usual Specifier and Complement positions). Hence coordinated $\overline{\overline{V}}$'s form a $\overline{\overline{V}}$ and N's form an N, etc. So, for example, in

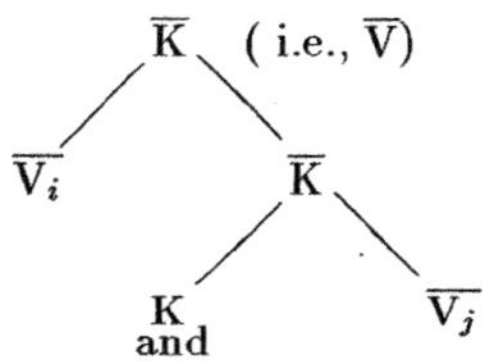

the whole projection is also a $\overline{V}$. Here the positions do not have the canonical interpretaton just alluded to, and furthermore can iterate. Aside from the details, discussed elsewhere, this is basically the minimal assumption we need to make about coordination.

unrealized) specifier of the next head:

(31) $[_{\overline{\overline{V}}_{[+fin]}}$ John$_i$ is $[_{PP}\ \theta_i$ [in the kitchen]]]

Hence, in a sequence of embedded structures (Complements) with unrealizable specifiers, the θ-role of the potential "Specifier" or external argument position of each Head, can be assumed to be the undischarged one from *its* respective Complement:

(32) [John$_i$ might [e_i have [e_i been [θ_i beating the dog]]]]

in this case the external argument of *beating*. (The e_i's only serve to indicate how the chain is formed and are not intended to indicate empty categories in the G/B sense.[61]) This looks suspiciously like the cases discussed in the literature under the rubric of "A-chains": a category "moves" from its base position (a θ-position) because there is no Case assigned, in a series of steps through θ-less and Case-less position until it ends in a Case position:

(33) John$_i$ seems $[_\alpha\ t_i$ to have been beaten $t_i]$

where the locality of the operation is guaranteed by the binding theory, which requires that the empty categories each be bound in their governing category, appropriately defined. Since one needs to say something about the former case (e.g., auxiliaries) anyway, one might ask whether they are both part of the same process, in which case A-binding is automatically strictly local, since it is always mitigated by a head. We would like to maintain a structural requirement limiting the linking of the "A-chain" arguments to the strictly local structure:

(34)

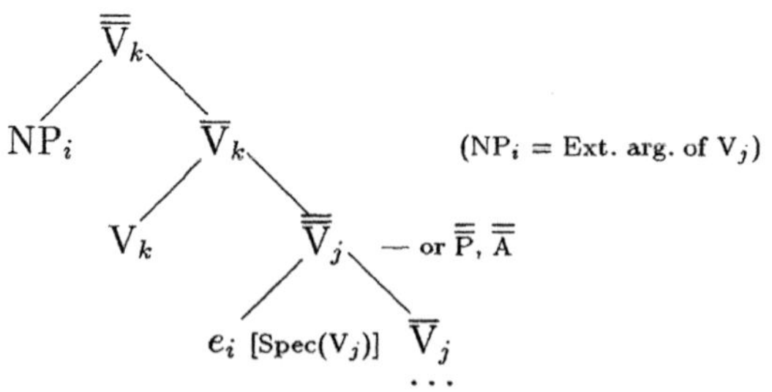

[61] Although one might countenance a revision of the theory in which they were. In fact, there is some evidence that these Specifier positions do have empty category status and are part of a chain in some sense: cf. discussion in §3.2.1 below as well as recent work: e.g., Koopman and Sportiche (1988), Sportiche (1988).

where V_k is the operator which transmits the θ-role.

This has both advantages and disadvantages: On the one hand it captures both the intuition and the facts about the strict locality of A-binding, and loses the parallel to the binding of overt anaphors, which seems spurious in view of cases like *They believed that picture of each other were on sale* which have no parallel in the case of empty anaphors. That is, the extensive discussion as to why there is no "super-raising" is spurious.[62]

On the other hand, there are (at least) two problematic considerations: One is the case of infinitival complements as in (33) above, or

(35) John tried [PRO to leave]

where the complement has often been assumed to be an $\overline{\mathrm{S}}$, i.e., $\overline{\overline{\mathrm{C}}}$, preventing Case assignment to the position of the PRO/trace. If it is true in the case of *seem*, as well as other cases discussed below, that the arguments are really transmitted by intervening heads in the same way as in (31) and (32), then we need to assume that α in (33) consists of only one projection, too, and not a vacuous double, i.e., $\overline{\overline{\mathrm{INFL}}}$ or $\overline{\overline{\mathrm{V}}}$ inside $\overline{\overline{\mathrm{C}}}$,[63] as we would not otherwise have strict locality for the passing of the θ-role (cf. details in §3.2.2). However, as has been noted in the literature, these putative $\overline{\overline{\mathrm{C}}}$'s nevertheless have to be transparent for government in certain cases like (33) or else an ECP violation would result from the trace of movement not being governed, but not in the other case: (35). Furthermore, we have the case of *believe*, discussed below, where Case *is* assigned to the DP, and something like $\overline{\mathrm{S}}$-deletion must be stipulated. Rather than this unsatisfactory state of affairs, let us observe that two things must in any case be specified idiosyncratically in the lexicon: the assignment of Case[64] and categorial subcategorization: e.g., whether a verb takes as complement a DP, CP or both. Crucial to the latter is that we differentiate the categories more finely on the basis of their feature composition; for example, the complement of the auxiliary verb *have* is not just any VP but the maximal projection of [+V, −fin, +part.]. Suppose we assume that *seem* no more assigns Case here than does the auxiliary verb *might*, so the $\overline{\overline{\mathrm{C}}}$ is not necessary to block Case assignment.[65] That is, there are some (Case-assigning) verbs that take a CP type of *to*-projection,

(36) a. He knows that fact.

[62]as are some ECP cases, as well. See ensuing discussion, and § 3.3.1 as well.

[63]Unless we are willing to except a dummy phonetically null COMP which acts as a quasi copula, a move which seems unnecessary in view of the discussion in the text ...

[64]Obvious for so-called lexical case, e.g., Dative vs. Genetive; cf. further discusssion in §3.2.3

[65]If Burzio's hypothesis, $-\theta_{ext} \rightarrow -$Acc., is true, *seem* could not possibly assign object Case. Modals in certain languages seem to present a problem: *Das*$_{[\mathrm{acc.}]}$ *kann er doch!*.

b. He knows [what$_i$ [PRO to do e_i]]

c. * He knows John to leave.

some which do not

(37) * It seemed [who to visit]

and some which take both

(38) a. John discovered [how [PRO to solve the problem]]

b. John discovered [the problem to be unsolvable]

Evidently *discovered* assigns Case (*John discovered the solution*), which is assigned in (38b) but blocked by the intervening C-projection in (38a); cf.

(39) * John discovered why the problem to be unsolvable

It is then no longer necessary to invoke the ECP to rule out the A-chain in (40b):

(40) a. [the problem]$_i$ was discovered [$_S$ [e]$_i$ to be unsolvable]

b. *[the problem]$_i$ was discovered [$_{S'}$ why [$_S$ [e]$_i$ to be unsolvable]]

as the chain is simply not local in the sense of (34).

The raising cases like (33) would then in fact work the same way as (31), but the "empty category" in the specifier position would be the same as whatever is indicated by the θ_i's and e_i in (31) and (32). That is, *seem* will also function rather like a modal, assuming that *all* modals take projections with propositional content and it is only chance (parametric variation) that some of them subcategorize for a $\overline{\overline{\mathrm{C}}}$ as well as a $\overline{\overline{\mathrm{to}}}$, or $\overline{\overline{[+\mathrm{V},-\mathrm{fin}]}}$[66]: for example, in English *want* is infelicitous with *that S* complements, but acceptable with *for* infinitivals (with or without realized subject, depending on Case assignment); German *wollen* on the other hand *does* take a *daß*, i.e., *that* complement, but only a bare infinitival (*Er wollte gehen*; **Er wollte zu gehen*); nevertheless all of the complements are propositional in nature, involving a full argument structure.[67]

Before we attempt a partial formalization of these ideas, we need to discuss some of the problems related to the passive construction.

[66]That is, the maximal projections of *to* and [+V,−fin.].

[67]This suggests, by the way, that what is distinctive about the *try* (control PRO) cases is that the *to*-projection has an empty element which may be *referentially* independent, and it is not θ-independence, as has often been assumed, which distinguishes PRO. If we consider cases like

i. John$_i$ wanted [e_i to sing a song]

3.2.1 Passive

Suppose for the moment that A-chains are *always* constructed by linking the available argument of the Complement with the Specifier as suggested above, rather than by "move α" as is the case of $\overline{\text{A}}$-bar chains. As noted above, in the normal case it is the "external" argument which is linked, as in *John was beating the dog.* In the case of the past-participle, however, no Case is assigned to the complement position.[68] If its projection is embedded under an auxiliary which assigns accusative Case, such as *have*, the Case is exceptionally passed down, and the object can be realized *in situ*; if not, then it cannot be phonetically realized[69]:

(41) a. Fred *had* beaten the dog.

b. The dog *was* beaten — .

This can also be seen from the fact that the past participle always has the passive interpretation in isolation

(42) a. [$_{NP}$ the boy [beaten (by the police) yesterday]]

b. * [$_{NP}$ the boy [beaten the dog yesterday]]

cf. [$_{NP}$ the boy [beating the dog]]

---

ii. daß Hans$_i$ [e_i ein Lied singen] wollte (*lit.* '...a song sing wanted')

iii. daß Hans$_i$ [e_i das Lied singen] kann (*lit.* '...a song sing can')

iv. John$_i$ can [e_i play the piano] =

v. John$_i$ is able [e_i to play the piano]

it is hard to imagine any difference in the θ-roles in the PRO versus the modal cases; if there are two θ-roles for the coindexed categories in (i) and (v), then there surely are in (ii)–(iv). Referential independence, however, is suggested by the contrast

vi. Fred wanted PRO$_{arb}$ to meet at 5pm.

vii. * Fritz wollte e_{arb} um 5 Uhr zusammenkommen.
(*lit.* '...wanted at 5 o'clock together come')

[68]There seems to be no justification for assuming that there are two distinct forms, the past participle and the passive participle. Unlike, for example, the simple past tense and the past participle, where some forms are identical and some are not, and hence the language learner could posit different forms, the former are *always* identical. This has been noted elsewhere, e.g. Höhle (1978).

[69] Cf. discussion in Thiersch (1985), for example, and for a suggestion of how the Case is exceptionally assigned, Vergnaud (1985). Note that *accusative* Case is necessary to realize the internal argument in this position, and the Case (nominative in English, instrumental in Russian, etc.) assigned in predicative constructions doesn't count, for whatever reasons. Cf. Vergnaud (*op cit.*) for discussion.

Hence if we imagine the arguments to be on a stack, with the *internal* argument on top, i.e., with the highest priority,[70] then *it* is the only one available for being linked to the subject in this case, hence the passive construction. If Burzio's hypothesis is true,[71] then the *have* in example (41a) has assigned its accusative Case (exceptionally), and therefore must assign a θ-role to its subject position; presumably the possessive role is not available (different *have*) and so the "next" one available is the external one of the participle. Since the accusative Case is presumably being assigned by the *have* and not the participle, the object does not need to be governed by the participle and could just as well appear in the Specifier position of the participle, giving the "small clause" reading[72]:

(43) John had [[his car]$_i$ stolen e_i]

This gives us a possible answer to the question posed in footnote 61: are the e_i's in each intervening (auxiliary) verb in (32) real positions which form part of a chain? In (43) the presence of *his car* in this position evidently blocks the realization of the external θ-role of *stolen*, but the *have* still needs to discharge a θ-role, and the only θ-role left for the *have* to assign to *John* is the "patient/benefactive" one. In other words, the intermediate e_i's apparently must be unoccupied for the θ-role to be passed up. Thus we may be able to maintain the structural requirement for the linking of the "A-chain" arguments suggested in (34). In this way we can generalize the account of auxiliary verbs and A-chains above to cover passive as well, by referring to the "first available non-discharged argument".[73] However, there is a problem for all accounts: assuming that the external θ-role is unavailable outside of the local domain (bottom-most V-projection), the stack-model taken literally (as in the next section) would imply that the external θ-role is *truly* unavailable in passives. Yet it seems to be "picked up" by the by-phrase, and, contradictorily, available nevertheless. We present a solution in § 3.3.2 after examining the status of adjunct (modifier) phrases.

[70] Cf. footnote 57 where it was suggested that the features correspond rather directly to the argument structure.

[71] I.e. the contrapositive of $-\theta_s \rightarrow -\text{Acc.}$: If a verb assigns Case to its object, it must assign a θ-role to its subject. Note that while this may play a role in the construction discussed in the text, passive is no longer a subcase, as it results from removal of Case, under this analysis, and the absense of subject θ-role then follows as discussed in the text. Perhaps the arrow goes both ways, although there is some evidence that the generalization may be spurious; cf. Napoli (1988) and the discussion in §3.2.3.

[72] Probably *should* be considered a small clause. Cf. subsequent discussion, esp. § 3.2.2.

[73] Assuming, as is standard, that an argument which gets Case is discharged and must be realized by a true syntactic position – either phonetically realized or A-bar bound. Cf. further discussion of details in §3.2.2 below.

Recall that the other case of argument reduction, true intransitives such as *eat* must be done in the lexicon, as they are highly idiosyncratic, as has often been noted in the literature: *John ate yesterday* versus **John devoured yesterday*.

Before dealing with some potential problems, let us look more closely at some details of Case- and θ-assignment, and attempt to (partially) formalize this.

3.2.2 θ-linking and Case assignment.

Let us suppose for concreteness that we have associated with each head three *ordered* lists[74]: a Case-list, θ-list, and a category (subcategorization) list, each consisting of not more than two elements.[75] So, for example, the θ-list for all forms of BEAT would be $(\theta_{int},\ \theta_{ext})$,[76] whereas the θ-list for an auxiliary verb, such as HAVE would contain a variable in the second position: $(\theta_{int},\ \_\theta_{ext})$.[77] The Case-list for *beats* would be (Acc., Nom.), for *beating* (Acc., $\_x$) and for *beaten* ($\_x$, $\_y$).[78] Further, we need to indicate which elements are Case-requiring (DetP) and which are Case-resistant (CP). Suppose for the sake of argument, that part of the Case specification of a DetP contains a variable $< +,\ -,\ \ldots,\ \_\mathrm{C},\ \ldots >$ in the place where a Case-resistant item would contain a constant; consequently the Case resistant element will not unify with a specification containing Case and hence can only appear outside the domain of the Case-assigner, as required; the "Case-filter" can be simulated by requiring that the variable _C be unified with a constant (from the Case-assigner) at some point.

We can now translate the simplex cases discussed earlier into this formalism: in *John beats the dog*, for example, the partially complete Case feature list of *the dog* is unified with that of *beats* creating a list of constant features (no variables) and the (internal) θ-role can be popped from the list. In *John is [* e_i *beating the dog]*, the external θ-role is "next" on the list (the internal one having been already discharged by the accusative Case) and is available to be associated with the specifier position of *beating* and can be unified with the external argument of *is*. Notice then what happens to the Case in the so-called small clause constructions:[79] If we unify a DP, *Fred*, with a non-Case assigning element, like *clever* or *in her hands*, then the variable _C in the DP remains a

[74]Lists in the computational sense, i.e. pushdown stacks, not just enumerations.

[75]Clearly the choices for the elements are not arbitrary, i.e., the lists are to some extent related to one another lexically as well by the syntax, but this plays only a minor role in the following discussion.

[76]N.B. internal argument first (i.e. on top), for the reasons suggested above.

[77]Where the underline indicates a variable. This formalization, although clearly inspired by Prolog unification, is only given for the sake of concreteness to make the following discussion more specific and is not intended *per se* to make any theoretical claim about unification as a cognitive process.

[78]Of course to be more accurate the Case-list is a function of the root lexeme and the inflectional morphology: for example, *beat-* itself is marked only for accusative, *-s* (or rather [+Tense]) adds nominative, and the participle deletes the accusative.

[79]A misnomer, as should be clear from the discussion herein.

variable and is unified with the Case specification in the resulting constituent, which then also becomes a Case-requiring entity.[80] If this projection is then further combined with a Case-assigning element then the variable _C can be unified with a constant, and the Case-filter is satisfied by unification, as the DP Fred now also contains the constant, as in

(44) a. Susan considered Fred clever.

b. Susan had Fred in her hands.

c. Susan believed Fred to have left.

The auxiliary verb *had*, however, is different in that its internal Case, for whatever reason,[81] may be unified not only with the specifier (external) Case, but the internal Case as well. That is, if we unify *beaten* with an (accustive) DP *John*, so that $[_{VP_{part}}$ *beaten John*] itself becomes a Case-requiring entity, as indicated above, the accusative Case of *have* may be unified with the internal Case specification, giving *had beaten Fred.* We can see this is exceptional by

(45) a. * Susan considers beaten Fred

b. * Susan believes beaten Fred

As noted above, we need to require in any case that the next available θ-role is added to the θ-list of the auxiliary by unifying it with the variable θ-role; in this case (where *beaten DP* is embedded under *have*), this will be the external θ-role of *beaten*, the internal one already having been bound to the DP and popped from the list. If there is no object present, unification producing the constant in the Case-list of *beaten* makes it a Case assigner, and hence its internal θ-role has the usual status of a true syntactic variable. If embedded under a form of *be*, whose Case-list presumably is something like (QC, Nom.), where QC = 'quirky case' whose morphological realization varies with language, the assignment is incompatible to an overt NP governed by the participle[82]; if there is no object, the "next" θ-role is unified upward, and in this case the internal one still heads the stack. Note that unification with the "next" θ-role is via the

[80]That is, after unification its Case-list will also include the incomplete specification <+ − ... _C ...>, for example.

[81]Exactly why *have* has this property is not clear. Cf. Verngaud (1985) for a suggestion, based among other things, on clitic climbing in Romance languages. See also discussion below.

[82]Precisely why this cannot be assigned to a DP under a participle is a serious, and unsolved, problem, as noted in footnote 69. For example, QC in Russian may be realized as instrumental, *On byl studentom* = 'he was a student', but **On byl uviden studentom* = 'He was seen a student' is out in the intended sense, just as in English, etc. Cf. further discussion of "QC" cases below. Suggesting that BE "weakly" assigns this case just displaces the problem.

specifier position, since realizing the internal argument in this position blocks the unification with the θ-position of the upper verb, as pointed out in (43) above.

Let us now look at the small-clause/ECM structures with *believe* more carefully. Suppose we have a projection which assigns no Case to its Specifier, like a *to*-projection [*to have left*] or a participle *beaten*, with a DP to their left under *believed*. If we unify the DP *John* with the projection of *to* forming [*John to have left*] or [*John beaten*] by the same mechanism, then the specification of the *to*-projection or $VP_{[+part]}$ will also contain a variable on its Case-list and be a Case-requiring element in the sense above. Again, the participle *believed* is not a Case-assigner *per se*, and combining/unifying the *to*-P or VP with *believed* adds the variable _C to *its* Case-list. If the projection of *believed* is governed by *have*, Case assignment to the DP in the Specifier of the *to*-P/$VP_{[+part]}$ follows by unification, giving us

(46) a. They had believed John to have left.

b. They had believed John beaten.

(with John taking the *internal* argument of *beaten* in the latter case) as desired. Note that we do not get the ungrammatical

(47) * They had believed [beaten John]

as only *had* has the property of Case-marking the internal argument of its complement, as noted above.[83] Hence *this* Case assignment cannot be applied recursively. Note again that if the Specifier position is blocked, as in (46b), then as in (43) the external θ-role is inaccessible, indicating that the unification for θ-linking is with the Specifier position. Implicit in this discussion, as in the case of Spec(COMP) discussed in §3.3.1 and Spec($V_{[+part]}$) in (43) above, is that the specifier position functions as an escape-hatch, and seems to have structural status independently of a particular Case or θ-role assignment. That is, in the normal auxiliary cases as well as here, we need to assume that the Specifier position plays a crucial role in the linking unifying of the θ-positions.

There is one more case we need to consider, namely

(48) a. * John had been beaten the dog.

b. * John had been the dog beaten.

c. * John had the dog been beaten.

[83]Cf. example (45) above. While some speakers find (46b) more felicitous with *believe* than others, the examples with the internal argument realized *in situ* are completely unacceptible.

i.e., why the case assignment mechanism cannot be iterrated via the *been* to assign Case to *the dog*, in (a) and (b) or directly in (c). We can probably rule out the first case due to the exceptional assignment properties of *have* discussed above as suggested for (47). For (b) and (c), the only θ-role available for *John* is the "benefactive" one, as noted above. R. Huybregts (*pers.comm.*) suggests that what may be going on in (48c) is that in the benefactive θ-role (as well as the "causative" θ-role: *John had the garbage taken out*) the complement must be a "true" adjectival complement: cf.

(49) a. He still had the theorem unproved by 5:00.

b. ? They had all the bunkers indestructible before the air-raid that afternoon.

where *unproved* can only be an adjective. Hence, while the participle of ordinary verbs "counts" as a true adjective, that of *be* doesn't:

(50) a. A man unknown to the police ...

b. A man beaten by the police ...

c. * A man been seen by everyone ...

How this works out in terms of the feature specification is not entirely clear, but it seems promising. This leaves us with the case of (48b) where we suggest that the copula always requires a complement which can be predicated of its Spec-position, either as an identity or linked to the unsaturated argument position of a predicate; since the external θ-role in (b) is now unavailable, the latter is impossible and the former produces nonsense, hence the Spec(*be*) gets no interpretation at all and is out by some variant of the Principle of Full Interpretation (cf. Chomsky 1986a).

If we can overcome the problems noted with the peculiarities of the QC of *be* and the ability of *have* to address the internal Case position, we then have a unified account of the A-chain phenomena. This reinforces the conclusion drawn earlier: the external argument of the past-participle, if not available for θ-raising by having the internal argument discharged by exceptional Case-marking from above, is truly unavailable, as suggested in the previous section.

Noting this, let us return to a problematical case, namely that of *believe* in English. In the two preceding sections, we have claimed that all of the A-chain cases can be reduced to a mechanism which one needs in any case for assigning θ-roles to subjects of auxiliary verbs.[84] But then structure (51) is problematic:

(51) [John$_i$ was [e_i'' believed [e_i' to have left]]]

[84]Cf. discussion of a similar suggestion in Williams (1987); his proposal is subject to the same problem discussed in this subsection, as far as I can see.

(extra e_i's omitted in the subordinate clause). The difficulty is that, in the case of passive, we have just suggested that the argument "available" for transmission is the "internal" one of the passivized verb, i.e., the "first" undischarged θ-role. In fact, believe has such a θ-role, and *it* passivizes normally in

(52) a. [The story]$_i$ was [believed θ_i by everone].

b. [That Jack left]$_i$ was [believed θ_i by no one].

c. It was [believed θ_i [that Jack left]$_i$].

Presumably we can maintain the usual line on examples like these, where the passive in (52a) is obligatory because of non-assignment of Case, and in (52b) it is optional (cf. 52c) since there is no Case requirement for C-projections (if anything, Case-resistance). However in (51), the internal θ-role is assigned to the complement; it cannot passivize itself with a phonetically present NP subject:

(53) * [John to have left] was believed

presumably for the same reasons (non-assignment of Case to its specifier) that small clauses and the dative cannot.[85] The difficulty is to suggest the mechanism by which the argument (θ-role) of the specifier of the *to*-projection takes precedence as the "available argument" of *believed* over *its* external argument, which is presumably "available", the internal argument having been "popped" by being assigned to the complement XP. Note that it is not the same as the other cases, as they are *inherently* copula-like; what we would need to insure is that passing the complement's available θ-role is *in fact* the default option. We can see that this indeed seems to be the default from similar constructions used as $\overline{\overline{\text{V}}}_{[+part]}$ adjuncts as in

(54) [$_{\text{DetP}_i}$ the$_i$ man [e_i believed e_i to have left]]

where movement is implausible.[86] Such a stipulation is highly unsatisfactory, and we leave the discovery of a better solution to further research.[87]

---

[85] Assuming that the structure of *John gave Mary a book* is

John gave [$_{\text{PP}}$ Mary [[$_{\text{P}}$ e] a book]]

as required by binary branching. Cf. Holmberg (1986) as well as Barss & Lasnik (1986) for empirical evidence for this structure. A potential problem is that some German speakers accept preposed ACI structures like *[Den Fritz ein Lied singen] hast du doch nie gehört!*

[86] Cf. discussion in Williams (1987).

[87] One might countenance a solution along traditional lines: suppose the external argument *is* assigned to *John*. But then the structure of (51) would be something like

* [John$_{ext}$ was [θ_{ext} believed [PRO$_{arb}$ to have left]]]

and this structure is ruled out by the PRO in a governed position. This is perhaps not so bad, as the deviance of the goverened PRO can be checked locally, in the sense of (34).

3.2.3 Raising adjectives

There is one additional wrinkle: the so-called raising verbs, like *seem*, have only an internal θ-role, which is assigned to their complement; this can be seen by the fact that the complement clause cannot appear in subject position (cf. Olsen 1981), and from the fact that raising is possible, i.e. the NP moves from a θ-position to a Case-marked but θ-less position:

(55) a. It seems [that John will leave].

b. * [That John will leave] seems.

c. John$_i$ seems [e_i to have left]

However, in the case of adjectives, there does seem to be a θ-role assigned to the subject position:

(56) [That John will leave] is likely.

In fact, even a normal NP can occupy the subject position:

(57) [John's success]$_{\theta_k}$ is certain.

If this is an external θ-role, as it superficially seems, then two quesions arise: firstly, how is "raising" possible (under the traditional analysis) or θ-passing, as discussed in the previous sections, since the subject would seem to be a θ-position? Presumably the answer to this is that the θ-role is no longer assigned to the subject position, because it has been absorbed by the complement clause. But then we need to ask how a superficially external θ-role, the same one as in *His success is certain*, can be assigned to a Complement position, as the clause clearly is internal to the VP (or rather AP):

(58) Certain to win, he isn't!

Suppose we assume that θ_k in (57) is in fact the internal θ-role which is assigned to the complement, and that it *is* the same one as in

(59) Fred$_{\theta_j}$ is certain [that John will win]$_{\theta_k}$.

The cases where this θ-role appears in the subject position, as in (57), are then just like the passive and auxiliary verb cases (especially *believe*) discussed earlier: if there is no complement, then the "first" available θ-role is the internal one as before, and *it* is the one which will appear in the subject position; the external one, i.e., θ_j in (59), is unavailable, and in this case cannot be recovered by a by-phrase, since it is evidently not agentive. In (59), however, the internal one has been discharged, so the external one is available to be passed up, just as in cases where the internal θ-role is taken by an NP Case-marked with the dummy preposition *of*:

(60) John is proud of his mother.

The advantage of this analysis is that we can now see why the raising *verbs* cannot take sentential subjects: there is no way for the θ-role to be passed on to the subject position, whereas in the adjectival raising cases, the auxiliary can do so. That is, *seem* assigns *its* internal θ-role to the sentential complement, and its subject (Spec) can either be a dummy *it* or a subject with the θ-role of its complement, as in the cases of the auxiliary verbs discussed earlier, but there is no *syntactic* mechanism to allow its internal θ-role to be realized externally. (Cf. discussion below) In the adjectival cases, however, this is precisely what the copula does, namely passing up a θ-role of its complement.

Furthermore, we now have a simple explanation for the difference between two other well known classes of adjectives[88]:

(61) a. [That John will leave] is likely

b. [That John will leave] is probable

c. John$_i$ is likely [t_i to leave].

d. * John$_i$ is probable [t_i to leave].

If we assume that *likely* has an internal θ-role, like *seem*, and *probably* a truly external one, then the paradigm in (61) follows immediately as the subject position is already assigned a θ-role directly in the *probable* case, but not in the case of likely.

An apparent problem is that it seems impossible to prevent

(62) * [His mother]$_i$ is proud (e_i)

meaning the same thing as (60), i.e., being its "passive" version. Whatever prevents passing this θ-role is evidently idiosyncratic, as *certain* also allows an *of*-complement:

(63) John is certain of Fred's success.

Let us look at the paradigms more carefully: in the case of *verbs* we have, in addition to transitive/intransitive pairs like *eat*, transitive/ergative pairs like *grow*:

(64) a. θ_{ext} eat θ_{int} b. θ_{ext} grow θ_{int}
c. θ_{ext} eat d. grow θ_{int}

[88]Cf. discussion in Chomsky (1986b) where he refers to it as "a rather marginal lexical property"...

where in (d) there is presumably no Case assigned to the internal θ-role, and hence no external θ-role, causing the internal argument to be realized in the external position.[89] If we look at the full paradigm of *proud* and *certain* we see that these two cases are parallel, with *proud* like *eat* on the one hand:

(65) a. John is proud [that he won] / [of his mother].

b. John is proud.

and with *certain* like *grow* on the other:

(66) a. Jack$_{\theta_{ext}}$ is certain [that Fred left]/of [Fred's success]$_{\theta_{int}}$

b. It is certain [that Fred left]$_{\theta_{int}}$/ * of Fred's success.

c. [That Fred left]/[His success]$_{\theta_{int}}$ is certain.

That is,

(67) θ_{ext} proud θ_{int} θ_{ext} certain θ_{int}
θ_{ext} proud   certain θ_{int}

What is different, and interesting, in the case of the Adjectives, is that we find some additional evidence as to *what* is specified in the lexicon: that Burzio's generalization does in fact seem to be at work. If we assume *of* to be a Case marker and allow the NP to realize the internal argument, we see that by (66b) that the [P NP] realization of the internal argument is impossible just when there is no external argument – in this case, however, the internal argument *can* be realized as a clause, which does not require case, and furthermore can also appear, optionally, in the Specifier position mitigated by the copula as in (66c).

Hence we can reduce the differences in the various classes to the same mechanism which we need to specify the ergative verb pairs in the lexicon, namely the presence or absence of Case/*of*, strengthening Burzio's generalization. In fact this makes it possible to express the intransitive/ergative distinction elegantly and succinctly: in the former case the internal θ*-role* is not specified, in the latter case, the internal *Case*.[90]

---

[89] We will not go into the controvery about whether the actual "raising" takes place in the syntax or lexicon; cf. Napoli (1988) and references therein: it would seem that the elements are *marked* in lexicon but θ-passed in syntax.

[90] Returning briefly to the case of *seem*, we note that since the removal of Case (or the equivalent feature for sentential complements) in the ergative construction is a lexical process, it need not apply across the board. Why the past-participle of *seem* (*It had seemed true at the time*) cannot be used in a *syntactic* passive (**That Fred left was seemed*) is apparently related to its status as a modal (under the analysis here) – note that in languages where other modals, unlike English *do* have participle forms, they nevertheless cannot passivize: **Die schwierigsten Sonanten van Beethoven spielen wurde von/durch Fritz gekonnt.* This underscores the crucial role of the auxiliaries in θ-role passing.

3.3 The status of Adjunct phrases

In this section we would like to ask whether adjunct-phrases undergo "movement" (or, *mutatis mutandis* are linked to an empty category) in the sense usually understood in Generative Grammar. By adjunct-phrase we mean non-arguments (modifying expressions), not argument phrases which arguably have been Chomsky-adjoined to another maximal category.[91]

How are adjuncts (in this sense) licensed? A minimum assumption is that modifier adjuncts are basically unsaturated predicates which have to be licenced by having their missing argument linked to an appropriate element. Recall from the previous section the analysis of auxiliary verbs, in which the unsaturated θ-role of the preposition or adjective[92] passed on the the specifier position of the *auxiliary* (or copula); cf. example (31), repeated here:

(31) $[_{\overline{\overline{V}}[+fin]}$ John$_i$ is $[_{PP}\ \theta_i$ [in the kitchen]]]

If the constituent is not governed by such a head (e.g., copula) and the specifier is not discharged by being assigned Case, as in a small clause construction, then it is available for linking (in the default case) as a modifier of the head. Hence in the PP [θ_i *in the kitchen*], the argument position θ_i which was linked to the subject in *John is in the kitchen* will be linked to the referent of the NP (i.e., DetP) in *the man in the kitchen*:

(68) $[_{DP_i}$ The$_i$ man [θ_i in the kitchen]]

and similarly in *a patient sick with the flu*, *a boy proud of his mother*, *the protesters beaten by the police*. Note that the θ-position of the adjunct need not be phonetically empty, as in the case of relative clauses, where it may be filled by an overt wh-pronoun. They may also under certain circumstances be linked to either the complement or specifier (cf. *Jack ate the meat quickly/raw/naked*).[93]

The exact details of this linking process are still unclear; cf. for example Travis (1987) for a discussion of the placement of adverbial expressions. For our purposes, it is sufficient to note that some sort of linking like this is the descriptive minimum for interpretation and hence, by the "Principle of Full Interpretation" (Chomsky 1986a), for the licensing of *in situ* adjuncts.

[91]Such as *meinen Sohn* to *S* in 'Gestern hat $[_S$ [meinen Sohn]$_i$ $[_S$ ein Hund e_i gebissen]]'; cf. example (27) on page 272. Cf. discussion in Saito (1985) and Thiersch (1985), among others.

[92]Its "specifier position"; cf. more detailed discussion in §3.2 (A-chains).

[93]We would like to suggest that (in the *default* case) they are linked to the referent of the head of their projection, as there seems to exist a clear preference for linking directly to the "host-projection" if this is an option at all.

3.3.1 Adjuncts in the *Vorfeld*

While one might want to suggest that the scope, or domain, for this interpretive linking is the "host" projection, and that cases of $\overline{\overline{V}}$ (i.e., $\overline{\overline{INFL}}$ or S) interpretation are generated by extraposition similarly to complements, as in the complement of the subject in *The trial began yesterday in Southern Yemen of the five terrorists who . . .*, there seems to be reason to believe that the adjunct cases are not, in fact, "movement" but rather interpretation within a local domain, e.g. $\overline{COMP}$. Let us look more closely at the question as to whether Adjuncts in the Vorfeld, i.e. Spec(COMP), such as *gestern* in

(69) Gestern ist er in die Oper gegangen.
yesterday is he in the opera gone
'He went to the opera yesterday.'

are "moved" there, i.e., receive their interpretation by being bound to an independently licensed empty category, or whether they are interpreted *in situ* in this position as well.[94] If Adjuncts in the Vorfeld *do* bind a position in the Mittelfeld, then their presence in the Vorfeld is presumably licensed in a similar manner to Arguments, by being properly bound to a licenced base position, which has a certain conceptual elegance to recommend it[95].

However, in addition to the parsing consideration of retrospective structure building noted in footnote 94, there is also a certain redundancy; if we already have the interpretive mechanism *and* the domain of interpretation can be $\overline{\overline{C}}$, the adjunct will be independently licenced, and it is not obvious that it needs to be bound to a empty category. What are the consequences if we assume that, in the normal case, adjuncts in the Vorfeld are licensed by interpretation? First

[94] This issue was brought up, in part, by work on the parser, as *arguments*, being independently licensed by a head, can simply be unified, whereas *adjuncts* involve building-up of an extra layer of phrase-structure, and displaced adjuncts involve *retrospective* structure-building in a partially completed structure. (This is independent of the so-called "attachment problem", much discussed in the parsing literature, and about which we have nothing more to say. Cf. Marcus, et al. (1983) for a promising suggestion to reduce the structure-building problem to the interpretation/attachment one.)

There might be a possible argument for retrospective structure building (interpretation via an empty category) if we were to capture scope differeces of the sort

i. The *tall* student with red hair ...

ii. The tall student with *red* hair ...

as differences in bracketing: [AP [N PP]] vs. [[AP N] PP]. The same readings seem to to be available in *We saw the tall student yesterday with read hair.* The question is whether the difference between (a) and (b) ought to be captured by differences in phrase structure at (S-structure); there are similar differences in focus where no difference in constituent structure is plausible at S-structure, e.g. in the German Mittelfeld. Cf. Höhle (1982).

[95] Thanks to Teun Hoekstra for getting the ball rolling by challenging this during a lecture.

of all, it has often been noted in the linguistics literature that adjuncts behave rather differently with respect, for example, to the Empty Category Principle. That is, they are subject to more stringent locality conditions[96], as in the canonical example

(70) a. ? What did John wonder how Fred fixed?

b. * How did John wonder what Fred fixed?

where *how* is interpreted in the subordinate clause.

One might well ask, *why* it should be the difference in government that causes the contrast; since government is presumably necessary to license an *argument* position on the basis of (obligatory) Case and θ-assignment, and adjuncts are rather licensed by interpretation, we might suspect that the difference results from the difference in licensing. That is, *arguments* in the Vorfeld are licensed by being bound in an A-bar chain to an independently licensed position, whereas *adjuncts* are interpreted in the domain $\overline{\overline{C}}$.

We can gain some insight into (70) by looking at the Spec(COMP) in German; first, containing an independently licensed element is not the only way in which Spec(COMP) (the Vorfeld) is licensed *as a position* — there seems to be some justification for the Vorfeld itself to be independently licensed,[97] at least in main clauses: First of all, we note that it is not a Case position itself, and the *es* in the following arguably has no θ-role, since it is obligatory in the main clause Vorfeld, but ungrammatical in the subordinate clause, where, being in the Mittelfeld, it would presumably be in a true argument position:

(71) a. Es wurde getanzt. (*cf.* *..., daß es getanzt wurde)
it was danced
'There was dancing.'

b. Es dünkt mich, ... (*cf.* *..., daß es mich dünkt, ...)
it thinks me
'I think that ... ' (*cf. archaic* 'Me thinks')

c. Es kamen gestern zwei Männer.
(*cf.* *Gestern kamen es zwei Männer.)
it came yesterday two men
'There came two men yesterday.'

Secondly, arguments in the Mittlefeld normally may not be omitted:

---

[96]Cf. discussion in Lasnik and Saito (1984) and references therein, and subsequent discussion in Chomsky (1986b), as well as the following discussion.

[97]Indeed, we ought to suspect this in a number of cases; otherwise one could create enormous structures by vacuously Chomsky-adjoining. Discussion of a suggested solution would take us beyond the scope of this article.

(72) * Gestern habe ich $e_{[acc.obj.]}$ nicht gesehen.
yesterday have I *e.c.* not seen
*'*I didn't see – yesterday'*

The one exception is when the Vorfeld is empty:

(73) Habe ich überhaupt nicht gesehen!
have I at all not seen
'I didn't see (it) at all!'

Sentences like (73) presumably have the analysis

(74) [OP_i habe ich e_i überhaupt nicht gesehen][98]

where OP_i is an empty operator binding the trace in argument position. That is, in order to count as a declarative clause, the Vorfeld, Spec(COMP), *must* be filled, even if only with a dummy phonetic item as in (71) or with an empty operator, as in (73). Hence we need to assume some sort of pseudo-argument status for the Specifier of COMP.[99]

If the specifier of COMP is a "potentially" available position, by virtue of its *structural* status, then we have an explanation for the grammatical example (75a), related to (70), repeated as (b-c) below:

(75) a. How_i did Frank think [e_i that Sam fixed the car]?

b. ? What did John wonder how Fred fixed? [= 70a]

c. * How did John wonder what Fred fixed? [= 70b]

The adjunct may (exceptionally) be interpreted within the lower $\overline{\overline{C}}$ by virture of being bound to the *independently licensed* Specifier of COMP.[100]

[98]See Huang (1984) and Ross(1982) for a more detailed discussion of this construction.

[99]Intuitively, we would like to distinguish between a true argument position which is assigned a θ-role directly, and the Spec-position of some constituent $\overline{\overline{X}}$, which is interpreted as fulfilling *some* θ-role, either directly (from the $\overline{X}$) or indirectly (from the complement of the X^0). In this respect Spec(COMP) is behaves similarly to Spec(INFL), i.e. Spec([+V,+Tense]):

i. Fred kicked the bucket.

ii. Tomorrow is a good time to leave.

iii. Sam seems tired.

[100] Unless, of course, one would try to develop an analysis by which the Adjunct *how* would link to the index of the lower $\overline{\overline{C}}$, which would then somehow be related to the V[+tense] ~ INFL projection, but this seems unlikely in view of examples like

The contrast in (70) follows immediately: as just noted above, the Specifier of the C-projection seems to be implicitly available on independent grounds, perhaps licensed by its status as a "pseudo-argument" position of the Head.[101] Hence in (75a) the adjunct (i.e., the empty category) may be interpreted in the second clause. If we view A-bar binding of arguments, however, as a search (either through a list or sections of a tree), then there is a possibility of recovering the displaced *argument* — i.e., unifying it with an already existing (i.e., licensed) empty category in (75b), even when Spec(COMP) is occupied; but the displaced *adjunct* in (75c) is impossible to interpret — Spec(COMP) is filled, and otherwise its domain of interpretation is its own $\overline{\overline{C}}$.[102] Hence we do not lose an explanation for the standard "ECP" case; it follows from already needed licensing conditions.

Note that this will also provide some basis for the contrast in judgements between subject and adjunct violations: while there is an assymetry between subject and object violation (the standard ECP effect contrast):

(76) a. ? What did Fred wonder who fixed ?

b. *? Who did Fred wonder what fixed?

the corresponding adjunct extraction violation (75c) is not just unacceptable, like (76a,b), but is *uninterpretable*; the reading is simply not available.

Note also that assuming that the specifier position of adjuncts is used to link for modification will also account for the island properties of adjunct phrases, the specifier "escape-hatch" is not available — arguments can be extracted with difficulty, with the usual subjacency violations, but *adjuncts* cannot be extracted at all. Recall footnote 100.

3.3.2 The "by-phrase" revisited.

We are now in a position to suggest a solution for the dangling problem of the *by*-phrase in passive, noted in § 3.2.1, namely, if we assume that the external θ-role is unavailable outside of the local domain (bottom-most V-projection), (i.e., taking the stack-model proposed in § 3.2.2 literally), we should expect the external θ-role to be *truly* unavailable in passives and in particular unable to be realized by the by-phrase.

i. * How is it time [e_k for John to fix the car]?

in which the Spec of the adjunct phrase, e_k is already occupied by being linked as a modifier (cf. discussion below), and *how* cannot modify the adjunct internal V-projection. We will not pursue this here.

[101] As it was in our proto-type parser.

[102] Actually the matter is a bit more complicated than this in the case of coordiate structures; cf. discussion in Thiersch (1988).

There is considerable discussion of this problem in the literature,[103] but we would like to ask, does the account sketched above suggest a particular solution as being the correct one? What could it mean in terms of this acccount for the agent θ-role to be "picked-up"? If transitive prepositions are, as suggested, two-place relations, then *the boy was beaten by the police* has the following structure

(77) [the boy]$_{int}$ was [beaten: $((\theta_{ext})\,\theta_{int})$] [$_{PP}$ θ_k by the police]

To what is the the external argument θ_k of the PP linked? According to the interpretation just sketched for adjuncts, it ought to be linked to the referent of the participle *beaten.* If it is the preposition *by* which assigns its complement the agent θ-role, which just coincidentally for some verbs happens also to be the external θ-role, cf.

(78) a. the window broken by John

b. * the arm broken by John [* *in the intended sense*]

then we can claim that in fact the external θ-role is *always* completely unavailable in these cases; i.e., it is by virtue of θ_k being linked to the referent of *beaten* and hence modifying it that the two cases happen to have the same meaning, just as in *The burgler stabbed her with a knife* the burgler presumably has the knife without assuming that we have a *syntactic* link between the two as in [$_{\text{DetP}_i}$ *the$_i$ burgler* [θ_i *with a knife*]].

Thus, if the assignment really does work like a stack, as suggested in § 3.2.2, we arrive at a uniform system for interpreting both specifiers and adjuncts relying on only the most minimal assumptions[104], and we are able to retain a plausible analysis for the canonical difference in the behavior of adjunct versus arguments with respect to extraction, linking it to the difference in licensing.[105] This means that we can restrict our attention to cases of A-bar movement.

4 Conclusion: Constraining "move α"

Let us take stock: Under a derivational interpretation, the inherent complexity of a principles and parameters based theory employing distinct levels of

[103]Cf. Höhle (1978), esp. chap.7 and further discussion in Zubizaretta (1986).

[104]Eliminating such mysterious concepts as "indirect θ-marking" of adjuncts (Cf. Koopman 1984).

[105]Additional evidence for licensing adjuncts in the Vorfeld by interpretive linking within $\overline{\overline{C}}$, rather than syntactic binding to a position, can be deduced from some exotic German data, the Subjektlücke (SL) construction, described in Höhle (1983). It would take us too far afield to discuss this here; cf. Thiersch (1988).

represention almost inevitably leads to computational intractability. Under a non-derivational interpretation, however, the structure corresponding to all the levels can be constructed simultaneously in an incremental fashion. The success of principles-based parsing then largely depends on the procedural as well a theoretical locality of the application of the modules. We have been pursuing two lines of argumentation: first, that one of the problems of "traditional" rule based parsers is solved by the uniform constituent hypothesis – one is not building structure by matching *arbitrary* phrase structures, for example, given by (CF) rules like $A \rightarrow BCD\ldots$, but rather that one is in fact making decisions involving two elements, a head(-projection) and satellite on the basis of straightforward and local criteria. An approach to A-chain relationships has been suggested which not only does not rely on a separately generated D-structure for licensing,[106] but is even more strictly local than the interpretation usually required for A-chains, namely the structure (34) in § 3.2, in which (aside from adjuncts of course) the discharging of the θ-role in the higher projection is mitigated by the head V_k, i.e., is *required* by the upper head. Hence in the structure noted earlier (§2, (24)) repeated here,

(24) a. Who do you believe [*e* to be funny] *referential expression*

b. Jack is believed [*e* to be funny] *anaphor*

c. Jack tries [*e* to be funny] *PRO ("pronominal anaphor")*

we know the nature of the empty category, in the best case, immediately upon seeing the governing verb *believe*, *believed*, or *try*, and in the worst case, as soon as we see the auxiliary *have* or *be*, and hence at that point we know whether or not we need to worry about binding the argument position.[107] Adjuncts (in the modifier sense), we have suggested, do not add to the proliferation of ambiguous *structure*, as they are never moved, so there is no question of placing and relocating empty categories.[108]

This only partially solves the serious problem, noted above in §2, of how to constrain the multitude of possible structures early on in the parse; the primary source of this was the enormous number of possible combinations of various adjunctions through application of "move α". That is, even if we limit "true" movement (A-bar chains) to movement from properly licensed Specifier and

[106]Which (cf. §2 (19) and footnote 28) is, strictly speaking, unnecessary once one adopts trace-theory of movement.

[107]In a left-right parse of course we have this information before we encounter the gap, but then the analagous problem arises in head-final languages.

[108]The so-called attachment problem of course remains, as noted above, but this, while a *parsing* problem, is not a *syntactic* one; that is, the solution must to some extent rely on semantics and discourse interpretation.

Complement positions,[109] we are overwhelmed with multiple structures. The villain is, of course, scrambling: if we view scrambling (and heavy NP-shift, extraposition, and a multitude of other constructions) as binding an empty category,[110] then we are still back at Square One if we allow "move α" to apply freely because of the multiplicity of possibilities. Unfortunately, sketching a proposal to restrict this would take us beyond the scope of this short article, and we leave this to forthcoming publications.

References

Abney, S. (1985) "Functor Theory and Licensing Conditions: Toward elimination of the base," unpubl. ms., MIT, Cambridge, Mass.

Aho, A. V. and J. D. Ullman (1972) *The Theory of Parsing, Translating and Compiling,* Prentice Hall, Eaglewood Cliffs, N.J.

Barss, A. and H. Lasnik (1986) "A Note on Anaphora and the Double Object Construction," *Linguistic Inquiry* 17.2, p.347–54.

Bennis, H. and T. Hoekstra (1985) "Parasitic Gaps in Dutch," NELS 15, Brown University, *Proceedings,* GLSA, U. Mass./Amherst.

Burzio, L. (1981) *Intransitive Verbs and Italian Auxiliaries,* Ph.D. Diss. MIT, Cambridge, Mass.

Burzio, L. (1986) *Italian Syntax,* Reidel, Dordrecht.

Cann, R. (1986) "Heads without Bars: a Theory of Phrase Structure," unpubl. ms, U. of Edinburgh.

Chomsky, N. (1970) "Remarks on Nominalization," in R. Jacobs and P.S. Rosenbaum (eds.) *Readings in English Transformational Grammar,* Ginn & Co., Waltham, Mass.

Chomsky, N. (1975) *Reflections on Language,* Pantheon, N.Y.

Chomsky, N. (1981) *Lectures on Government and Binding,* Foris, Dordrecht.

Chomsky, N. (1982) *Some Concepts and Consequences of the Theory of Government and Binding,* MIT Press, Cambridge, Mass.

Chomsky, N. (1986a) *Knowledge of Language,* Praeger, N.Y.

Chomsky, N. (1986b) *Barriers,* MIT Press, Cambridge, Mass.

[109]I.e., not "positions" which are not realized by virture of failing to have been assigned some feature such as Case or verbal inflection, such as the internal argument of the verbal particple in passive.

[110]and it's difficult to know how else to view most of these constructions in spite of protestations to the contrary in the literature ...

Chomsky, N. (1989) "Some Notes on Economy of Derivation and Representation," *MIT Working Papers in Linguistics 10*, Dept. of Linguistics and Philosophy, MIT, Cambridge, Mass.

Cichocki, W. (1983) "Multiple WH-Questions in Polish: a Two Comp Analysis," *Toronto Working Papers in Linguistics*, 4, p.53–71.

Comorovski, I. (1986) "Multiple WH-movement in Romanian," *Linguistic Inquiry* 17.1, p.171–77.

Corver, N. (1990) *The Syntax of Left Branch Extractions*, Diss., Kath. Universiteit Brabant, Tilburg.

Czepluch, H. (1988) "Kasusmorphologie und Kasusrelationen: Überlegungen zur Kasustheorie am Beispiel des Deutschen," *Linguistische Berichte* 116, p.275–310.

Evers, Arnold (1975) *The Transformational Cycle in Dutch and German*, Ph.D. Diss., U. Utrecht.

Felix, S. (1983) "Parasitic Gaps in German," U. Passau, *Working Papers.*

Fukui, N. and M. Spaes (1986) "Specifiers and Projections," unpubl. ms., MIT, Cambridge, Mass.

Gazdar, G., G. Pullum, and I. Sag (1982) "Auxiliaries and Related Phenomena in a Restrictive Theory of Grammar," *Language* 58.3, p.591–638.

Haegeman, Liliane and H. van Riemsdijk (1986) "Verb Projection Raising, Scope, and the Typology of Rules Affecting Verbs," *Linguistic Inquiry* 17.3, p.417–66.

Höhle, T. N. (1978) *Lexikalische Syntax*, Niemeyer, Tübingen.

Höhle, T. N. (1982) "Explikation für 'normale Betonung' und 'normale Wortstellung'," in Abraham, W. (1982) *Satzglieder im Deutschen*, Narr, Tübingen.

Höhle, T. N. (1983) "Subjektlücken in Koordinationen," unpubl. ms., U. Köln.

Holmberg, A. (1986) *Word Order and Syntactic Features*, Ph.D. Diss. U. Stockholm.

Huang, C.-T. J. (1984) "On the Distribution and Reference of Empty Pronouns," *Linguistic Inquiry*, 15.4, p.531–74.

Huybregts, R. and H. van Riemsdijk (1985) "Parasitic Gaps and ATB," NELS 15, Brown University, *Proceedings*, GSLA, U. Mass./Amherst.

Johnson, M. (1987) "Parsing as Deduction: the Use of Knowledge of Language," *Journal of Psycholinguistic Research*, 18.1.

Karttunen, Lauri (1986) "D-PATR. A Development Environment for Unification-Based Grammars," SRI/CSLI, Stanford, Calif.

Kayne, R. (1984) *Connectedness and Binary Branching,* Foris, Dordrecht.

Koster, J. (1978) *Locality Principles in Syntax,* Foris, Dordrecht.

Koster, J. (1987) *Domains and Dynasties,* Foris, Dordrecht.

Kolb, H.-P. (1989) "Op principes gebaseerde ontleding," in A. Neijt & D. Bakker (eds.) *Computerlinguistiek: een overzicht in artikelen,* Foris, Dordrecht.

Koopman, H. and D. Sportiche (1988) "Subjects," unpubl. ms. UCLA, Los Angeles, Calif.

Lasnik, H. and M. Saito (1984) "On the Nature of Proper Government," *Linguistic Inquiry* 15.2, p.235–89.

Lenerz, J. (1977) *Zur Abfolge nominaler Satzglieder im Deutschen,* Narr, Tübingen.

Marcus, M. (1978) *A Theory of Syntactic Recognition for Natural Language,* Ph.D. Diss. MIT, Cambridge, Mass.

Marcus, M., D. Hindle, and M. Fleck (1983) "Talking about Talking about Trees," *Proceedings of the 21st Meeting of the Association for Computational Linguistics.*

Moortgat, Michael (1987) "Parsing Lambek Categorial Grammars," INL Working Papers 87–05.

Muysken, P. (1982) "Parameterizing the Notion 'Head'," *Journal of Linguistic Research,* no.2.

Napoli, D. (1983) "Review of Burzio: *Italian Syntax,*" *Language* 64.1, p.130–42.

Olsen, S. (1981) *Problems of* seem/scheinen *Constructions and their Implications for the Theory of Predicate Sentential Complementation,* Niemeyer, Tübigen.

Pesetsky, D. (1982) *Paths and Categories,* Ph.D. Diss. MIT, Cambridge, Mass.

Pollock, J.-Y. (1989) "Verb Movement, Universal Grammar, and the Structure of IP," *Linguistic Inquiry* 20.3, p. 365–424.

Riemsdijk, H. van (1987) "Movement and Regeneration," unpubl. ms., Tilburg U.

Ristad, E. (1988) *Computational structure of human language,* Ph.D. Diss., published as MIT Artificial Intelligence Laboratory, technical report 1260, MIT Dept. of Electrical Engineering and Computer Science, Cambridge, Mass.

Ross., J. R. (1982) "Pronoun Deleting Processes in German," paper presented at the LSA Annual Meeting, San Diego, Calif.

Saito, M. (1985) *Some Assymetries in Japanese and their Theoretical Implications,* Ph.D. Diss. MIT, Cambridge, Mass.

Sportiche, D. (1988) "Conditions on Silent Categories," unpubl. ms., UCLA, Los Angeles, Calif.

Steedman, M. (1987) "Combinators and Grammars," in. R. T. Oehrle, E. Bach and D. Wheeler *Categorial Grammars and Natural Language Structures,* Reidel, Dordrecht.

Stowell, T. (1981) *Origins of Phrase Structure,* Ph.D. Diss. MIT, Cambridge, Mass.

Steen, G. Van der (1987) *A Program Generator for Recognition, Parsing and Transduction with Syntactic Patterns,* Proefschrift (Doctoral Diss.) U. Utrecht.

Thiersch, C. (1985) "Some Notes on Scrambling in the German Mittelfeld, VP and X-bar Theory," unpubl. ms., U. Conn & U. Köln

Thiersch, C. (1988) "A note on the Status of Adjuncts," unpubl. ms., U. Tilburg.

Thiersch, C. (1989; *forthcoming*) "Het (hulp-)werkwoord Systeem," in *Syllabus: Grammatische Analyse,* Chap. 11, U. Tilburg; English version in preparation, probably to appear in Proceedings of 1990 Geneva Workshop on G/B Parsing.

Toman, J. (1982) "Aspects of Multiple Wh-Movement in Polish and Czech," in R. May and J. Koster, eds. *Levels of Syntactic Representation,* Foris, Dordrecht.

Tomita, M. (1986) *Efficient Parsing For Natural Language. A Fast Algorithm for Practical Systems,* Kluwer, Dordrecht.

Travis, L. (1984) *Parameters and Effects of Word Order Variation,* Ph.D. Diss. MIT, Cambridge, Mass.

Travis, L. (1988) "The Syntax of Adverbs," in *McGill Working Papers in Linguistics: Proceedings of the IVth Workshop on Comparative Germanic Syntax,* McGill University, Montréal.

Verngaud, J.-R. (1985) *Dépendances et niveaux de représentation en syntaxe,* Benjamins, Amsterdam.

Williams, E. (1981) "Argument Structure and Morphology," *The Linguistic Review* 1.1, p.81–114.

Williams, E. (1986) "A Reassignment of the Functions of LF," *Linguistic Inquiry* 17.2, p.265–99.

Williams, E. (1987) "NP Trace in Theta Theory," *Linguistics and Philosophy* 10.4, p. 433–47.

Zubizarreta, M.-L. (1986) *Levels of Representation in the Lexicon and in the Syntax,* Foris, Dordrecht.

Notes on Contributors

Gisbert Fanselow
Universität Passau
Institut für allgemeine und angewandte Sprachwissenschaft
Innstr. 40
D-8390 Passau
Germany

Hubert Haider
Universität Stuttgart
Institut für Germanistik Linguistik
Keplerstr. 17
D-7000 Stuttgart 1
Germany

Tilman Höhle
Universität Tübingen
Germanistisches Seminar
Wilhelmstr. 52
D-7400 Tübingen
Germany

Katalin É. Kiss
Hungarian Academy of Science
Research Institute for Linguistics
Szentháromság utca 2.
H-1014 Budapest I
Hungary

Hans-Peter Kolb & Craig Thiersch
Katholieke Universiteit Brabant
Department of Linguistics
Postbus 90153
NL-5000 Le Tilburg
The Netherlands

Klaus Netter
Deutsches Forschungszentrum für Künstliche Intelligenz
Stuhlsatzenhausweg 3
D-6600 Saarbrücken 11
Germany

Ian Roberts
Université de Genève
Départment de Linguistique Générale
CH-1208 Genève
Switzerland

Wolfgang Sternefeld
Universität Konstanz
Fachgruppe Sprachwissenschaft
D-7750 Konstanz
Germany

Knut Tarald Taraldsen
University of Tromsø
Department of Linguistics
Rundvannet 130
Postbox 1090
N-9001 Tromsø
Norway

Index of Names

Abney, 271, 273, 274, 276, 298
Abraham, 247
Adams, 100, 133
Aho, 260, 298
Andrews, 236, 247
Aoun, 157, 171, 194, 217, 220, 227, 228, 247

Baker, 11, 14, 22–24, 34, 35, 50, 71, 81, 82, 84, 91–94, 96, 99, 106, 118, 119, 123, 133
Bakker, 300
Baltin, 77, 133
Barss, 26, 49, 50, 133, 287, 298
Basri, 160, 194
Battistella, 185, 195
Bech, 108, 134
Belletti, 27–29, 33, 34, 40, 50, 59, 68, 130, 134, 223, 238, 247
Benincà, 68, 69
Bennis, 80, 134, 273, 298
Besten, 107, 110, 124, 134
Booij, 147, 194
Bouchard, 217, 247
Bresnan, 247
Browning, 50
Burzio, 29, 32, 37, 40, 50, 253, 276, 279, 282, 290, 298, 300

Campos, 244, 247
Cann, R. 271, 298
Chomsky, N. 1, 2, 4–9, 11, 14, 15, 17, 20, 25, 28, 33, 37, 43, 47, 48, 50, 53–56, 59–62, 68, 71–73, 75, 79, 80, 82, 86, 89, 90, 93, 96, 100–107, 111, 118, 121, 122, 131, 134, 150, 188, 189, 194, 199, 201, 203, 208, 213, 214, 217–221, 225–230, 232, 234, 237, 238, 242, 244, 247, 248, 251, 254, 261, 266, 270–273, 286, 289, 291, 293, 298, 299
Christensen, 62, 63, 65, 66, 68
Cichocki, 276, 299
Cinque, 32, 50, 211, 214
Comorovski, 277, 299
Cooper, 108, 117, 123, 134
Corver, 274, 299
Czepluch, H. 273, 299

Dahl, 68, 69
de Meij, 211, 212, 215, 247
di Sciullo, 83, 137
Dowty, 148, 194
Durie, 100, 135

Edmondson, 107, 134
Emonds, 83, 90, 135
Engdahl, E. 47, 50, 173, 183, 185, 189, 194
Entjes, 141, 194
Epstein, 20, 24, 25, 50, 91, 135
Everaert, M. 222, 235, 245, 248
Evers, A. 108, 110, 118, 135, 256, 299

Fanselow, G. 9, 13, 217, 221, 223–225, 227, 231, 233, 234, 236, 243, 244, 246, 248
Faraci, 50
Felix, S. 80, 135, 273, 299
Finer, 160, 194, 197
Fleck, 300
Fodor, Janet, 158, 194
Fodor, Jerry, 132, 135, 195
Fukui, 152, 194, 271, 273, 274, 276, 299

Gabbay, D. 158, 195

Gazdar, G. 271, 274, 299
Geilfuß, 117, 135
Goodall, 147, 194
Grewendorf, G. 108, 135, 137, 229, 248
Groos, 204, 214
Guéron, 174, 185, 194

Haegeman, L. 11, 15, 86, 87, 107, 109, 110, 116–120, 135, 256, 299
Haider, H. 227, 248
Haik, 14, 15, 49, 50, 211, 214
Higginbotham, 23, 50
Hindle, 300
Hoekstra, T. 45, 51, 80, 134, 273, 292, 298
Holmberg, A. 68, 69, 276, 287, 299
Hornstein, 129, 135, 221, 226, 233, 234, 248
Höhle, T.N.12, 139, 141, 146, 147, 152, 154, 157, 167, 194, 195, 281, 292, 296, 299
Houtman, 148, 195
Huang, 8, 15, 221, 248, 294, 299
Huybregts, 116, 134, 135, 273, 286, 299

Jackendoff, R. 33, 51
Jacobs, J. 158, 160, 195
Jacobson, 185, 195
Jaeggli, U. 56, 69, 100, 135
Johnson, 22–24, 34, 35, 50, 263, 299
Jones, C., 51

Karttunen, L. 259, 300
Kasher, 158, 195
Kathol, A. 157, 195
Kayne, R. 20, 51, 62–65, 69, 128, 135, 204, 214, 217, 224, 233, 246, 249, 271, 300
Kim, 89, 135
Kiss, K.É. 9, 13, 164, 195, 199, 200, 203, 204, 208, 214, 221, 249
Kitagawa, 152, 185, 195
Klima, 19, 22, 23, 25, 51, 158, 195
Kohrt, 146, 195
Kolb, 12, 13, 251, 269, 300
Koopmann, 27, 45, 51, 278, 296, 300
Koster, J. 2, 4, 15, 104, 108, 110, 111, 113–116, 135, 139, 195, 199, 211, 214, 217, 232, 243, 244, 246, 247, 249, 266, 300, 301
Kuno, S. 79, 136

Ladusaw, 1–3, 15
Lakoff, G. 51, 125, 132, 136
Langendoen, 185, 195
Larson, 89, 135, 228, 249
Lasnik, H. 18, 19, 22, 48, 49, 51, 91, 96, 114, 136, 187, 195, 224, 244, 248, 249, 287, 293, 298, 300
Lebeaux, 26, 51
Lees, 19, 22, 23, 25, 51
Lenerz, 117, 136, 300
Lerner, 120, 136
Levin, B., 32, 35, 39, 51
Lie, 148, 196
Lötscher, 107, 117, 120, 136
Longobardi, 171, 196

Maling, J. 245, 249
Manzini, 222, 235, 249
Marácz, 14, 15, 211, 212, 215
Marantz, 40, 51
Marcus, M. 259, 261, 292, 300
May, 7, 8, 15, 18, 25, 45, 51, 89, 120, 136, 208, 215, 221, 224, 226, 249
Montalbetti, 244, 249
Moortgat, M. 260, 300
Müller, 93, 100, 117, 136

Muysken, P. 247, 249, 271, 300

Nanni, 106, 136
Napoli, 282, 290, 300
Neijt, 140, 146–148, 196, 300
Neubauer, 185, 195

Oirsouw, 147, 196
Olsen, S. 288, 300

Pafel, 158, 161, 163, 164, 196
Partee, 147, 148, 179, 183, 196, 197
Perlmutter, 29, 35, 51
Pesetsky, D. 83, 86, 89, 136, 217, 246, 249, 271, 300
Philippaki-Warburton, 244, 249
Platzack, 100, 136
Pollock, 66, 69, 219, 225, 237, 249, 270, 276, 300
Postal, 17, 19, 22, 23, 25, 29, 31, 34, 35, 51
Pullum, 271, 274, 299

Rappaport, M. 32, 35, 39, 51
Reed, 185, 196
Reinhart, T. 17, 51, 207, 215
Reis, M. 229, 249
Reyle, U. 248, 249
Riemsdijk, H. van 2, 4, 5, 11, 15, 86, 87, 107–114, 116–120, 129, 134–136, 184, 196, 204, 211, 212, 214, 215, 247, 249, 256, 273, 299, 300
Rigau, 244, 249
Ristad, 263, 300
Rizzi, L. 10, 11, 15, 19–24, 28, 29, 33, 34, 40, 41, 45, 48–50, 52, 54, 59–61, 68, 69, 88–91, 96, 100, 128, 130, 134, 137, 217, 220, 223, 226, 227, 238, 243, 247, 249, 250
Roberts, I. 10, 11, 17, 22–24, 32–35, 40, 45, 50, 52, 174, 196, 220, 227, 246, 250
Rohrbacher, 100, 136
Rohrer, C. 248, 249
Rooth, M. 148, 179, 183, 196
Ross, 125, 132, 136, 294, 300
Rouveret, 185, 196
Rudin, 221, 250

Sag, I. 158, 194, 271, 274, 299
Saito, 96, 114, 136, 171, 172, 197, 224, 249, 272, 291, 293, 300, 301
Schachter, 147, 197
Shopen, 152, 197
Spaes, 271, 273, 274, 276, 299
Sportiche, 27, 45, 51, 96, 137, 278, 300, 301
Sprouse, 55, 69
Stechow, A. von 87, 108, 114, 115, 117, 122, 129, 132, 137
Steedman, M. 260, 301
Steen, van der, 259, 301
Sternefeld, W. 11, 71, 75, 87, 108, 114, 115, 117, 118, 120–122, 129, 132, 136, 137, 248
Stockwell, 147, 197
Stowell, T. 49, 51, 236, 238, 250, 271, 301
Szabolcsi, A. 128, 137

Taraldsen, K.T. 6, 11, 53, 62, 63, 65, 66, 68
Terazu, 147, 197
Thiersch, C. 12, 13, 170, 197, 251, 270, 271, 273, 276, 277, 281, 291, 295, 296, 301
Toman, J. 146, 194, 197, 276, 301
Tomita, 259, 301
Travis, L. 255, 291, 301

Ullman, 260, 298
Uriagereka, 187, 195

Vergnaud, 185, 196, 284, 301

Vikner, S. 55, 69

Wasow, T. 35, 52, 184, 197
Webelhuth, G. 124, 134
Weinberg, A. 233, 234, 248
Weisler, 185, 197
Wesche, B. 148, 197
Wexler, 222, 235, 249
Williams, 2, 4, 5, 15, 83, 129, 136, 137, 152, 174, 184, 185, 196, 197, 211, 215, 274, 286, 287, 301

Zubizarreta, 301

Index of Subjects

1-Advancement Exclusiveness Law, 35, 40

adjunct, 13, 47, 94, 96, 122, 187, 202, 205, 218, 223–227, 230, 233, 265, 270–277, 282, 287, 291–293, 295–297
Adjunct Condition, 202, 205
adjunction, 25, 61, 77, 99, 100, 108–113, 117, 118, 121, 122, 148, 208, 219, 224, 231, 233, 254, 273
anaphor, 9, 18, 25, 27, 44, 49, 75, 77, 80, 81, 85, 90, 91, 176, 185, 220–222, 226–229, 235, 238, 240–245, 269, 279
  lexical anaphor, 185, 186, 220, 222, 223, 239, 240, 243–245
  long distance anaphor, 222, 235
  null anaphor, 146
anaphoricity, 81
argument, 7, 14, 19, 21, 22, 25, 28, 29, 32, 33, 35, 37, 39, 45, 46, 55, 56, 58–60, 64, 66, 72, 73, 76–80, 83, 84, 88, 101, 105, 115, 116, 130, 152, 200, 224, 225, 231, 252, 253, 255, 257, 264, 266, 267, 273, 274, 276–279, 281, 282, 287, 292, 293, 295, 296
  direct argument, 37, 39, 40
  empty argument, 200, 210, 211
  external argument, 32, 39, 229, 253, 274, 278, 283, 286, 287, 290, 296
  internal argument, 39, 274, 281, 283, 285–287, 290, 298
  logical-subject argument, 22, 34, 35
  potential argument, 79, 80
argument position, 53, 76, 85, 88, 115, 200, 265, 274, 275, 277, 286, 291, 293, 294, 297
argument structure, 19, 30, 40, 49, 282
AUX, 276
auxiliary, 55, 63, 65, 279, 281–286, 288, 289, 291, 297

Backward Conjunction Reduction, 146
Backward Gapping, 146
barrier, 33, 60–62, 91, 92, 94, 95, 107, 111, 112, 118, 119, 121, 203, 206, 213, 217, 220–228, 232–234, 241
binary branching, 265, 273, 287
binding, 4, 5, 12, 17, 21, 23, 75, 78, 80, 102, 104, 122, 168, 170, 173, 175, 178, 180, 184, 187, 189–191, 193, 223, 241, 243, 244, 257, 296
  A-binding, 25, 72, 73, 168, 170, 172–175, 180, 182, 190, 277–279
  Ā-binding, 12, 27, 73, 183, 184, 187, 190, 191, 193
  anaphoric binding, 217, 223, 227–230, 235, 238, 239
  f-binding, 12, 189–193
  local binding, 21, 24, 25, 49, 72, 73, 75, 88
  long distance binding, 235–237
  operator binding, 294
  s-binding, 12, 189–193
binding domain, 18, 19, 223
binding theory, 17, 18, 89, 174, 176, 199, 220, 221, 223, 242, 243,

246, 260, 264, 268, 269, 278
bottom up, 267, 268
bridge verb, 212, 213
Burzio's generalization, 32, 37, 40, 57, 253, 290

Case, 13, 19, 22, 32, 37, 39, 40, 57, 58, 65, 78, 92, 93, 101, 103, 106, 113, 119, 130, 131, 202–204, 206, 230, 233, 234, 236, 237, 242, 245, 253–255, 257, 268, 274, 279, 281–284, 286, 287, 290, 291, 293, 298
  long distance Case agreement, 236, 237
  non-Case position, 19
Case absorption, 119
Case-assign, 29, 40, 57, 65, 101, 119, 131, 204, 231, 233, 234, 236, 253, 255, 264, 278, 279, 283–286, 290
Case conflict, 236, 237
Case feature, 231, 232, 234–237, 243, 247
Case Filter, 37, 101, 217, 218, 231, 232, 234, 241, 245, 246, 283, 284
Case list, 283–285
Case-mark, 40, 42, 53, 56–58, 65, 103, 104, 152, 234, 242, 243, 245, 268, 273, 276, 285, 286, 288, 290
Case position, 19, 78, 286, 293
Case requirement, 283–285, 287
Case resistance, 283, 287
Case theory, 19, 115, 230, 245, 258, 264, 266, 268
Case transmission, 231, 233, 234
Catalan, 244
CHAIN, 104
chain, 4, 5, 11, 14, 19–25, 28, 32, 35, 45–47, 49, 57, 71–76, 79–81, 83, 84, 87, 88, 91, 92, 94, 95, 98, 100, 102–105, 150–152, 199, 205, 207, 211, 234, 268, 278, 280
  Ā-chain, 14, 25, 72, 73, 76–78, 199, 205–207, 273, 277, 297
  A-chain, 19, 25, 54, 57–60, 62, 65, 66, 68, 72, 73, 76, 77, 102, 220, 267, 270, 276–278, 280–282, 286, 291, 297
  derivational chain, 11, 73, 74, 81, 105
  history chain, 102
  representational chain, 74
  θ-chain, 19, 21, 33
  wh-chain, 4
chain formation, 4, 10, 13, 20, 24, 27–31, 35, 36, 38, 41, 42, 46, 48, 49, 71, 72, 74–77, 81, 83, 85, 86, 88–91, 94, 95, 100, 102, 105, 227, 246, 264, 266, 268
  free chain formation, 11, 72–76, 78, 81, 83, 85, 86, 88, 89, 91, 92, 98, 100, 107
  Chain Formation Algorithm, 10, 11, 20, 23, 41, 45, 96
Chinese, 8, 221, 255, 274
Chomsky-Adjunction, 265, 270, 272
clitic, 10, 19, 20, 22, 24, 59, 63, 65, 89, 90, 276
clitic climbing, 284
clitic doubling, 22, 276
cliticization, 76, 77, 89, 90
competence, 251, 261
Complex NP Constraint, 13, 43
control, 43, 44, 113, 114, 116, 118, 119, 123, 132, 236, 237, 243, 246, 257, 258, 264, 266, 280
Coordinate Structure Constraint, 141, 145, 151, 157
coordination, 12, 86, 139–142, 144,

147, 153, 154, 156, 176, 184, 193, 194, 277
asymmetric coordination, 85, 141, 152
Shared Constituent Coordination, 146
split coordination, 141
symmetric coordination, 140, 141
coreference, 75, 169, 170, 174
crossover, 10
strong crossover, 4, 17–25, 31–33, 38, 40–46, 48, 49, 168, 184, 185, 227
weak crossover, 26, 49, 184, 189–191

Danish, 55, 63
declarative (clause), 153, 157, 294
declarative (vs. procedural), 253, 261, 265, 267
disjoint reference, 170
distinctness, 92–94
domain extension, 232, 233, 246
Dutch, 80, 86, 108, 113, 141, 252, 255, 256

ECM (Exceptional Case Marking), 114, 227, 229, 235, 245, 268, 285
ECP, 27, 48, 53, 54, 58–62, 64, 66, 67, 71, 92, 93, 95, 98, 111, 114, 115, 217–224, 230–232, 235, 239, 242, 244, 246, 257, 258, 264, 266, 270, 279, 280, 295
empty category, 23, 67, 72, 79, 80, 103, 116, 150, 185, 189, 205, 206, 231, 232, 235, 239, 241, 274, 276, 278, 280, 291, 292, 295, 297, 298
English, 24, 34, 40, 101, 103, 116, 122, 146, 152, 156, 170, 172, 184–187, 189–191, 204, 221, 233–236, 239–241, 244, 245, 256, 260, 270, 276, 280, 281, 284, 286, 290
Experiencer, 29, 31–33, 35–37, 39, 40, 91
expletive, 44, 54–56, 58–60, 62, 64, 66, 67, 74, 78, 86, 103, 227, 228
expletive replacement, 58–60, 64, 66–68
expletive subject, 54, 55, 57, 60
expletive/argument linking, 11, 54, 56–60, 64, 66–68
extraposition, 74, 122, 124, 202, 270, 292, 298

feature assignment, 238, 247
feature-based minimality, 217, 218, 230, 232, 235, 246
filter, 12, 258, 264, 265, 272
Doubly Filled COMP Filter, 245
focus, 7, 8, 13, 77, 117, 120, 162, 166, 174, 185, 200–202, 207–209, 292
Forward Conjunction Reduction, 147
French, 9, 204, 220, 225, 233, 276
functional structure, 271

gapping, 143–147, 153
German, 11, 12, 74, 86, 90, 92, 101, 103, 107, 108, 113, 116–119, 121–123, 139, 141, 142, 146, 147, 153, 155–158, 160, 164, 171, 172, 176, 185, 186, 189, 191, 211, 212, 218, 221, 222, 225, 227, 228, 230, 232, 233, 236, 238–241, 256, 265, 273, 276, 280, 292, 293, 296
Gothic, 236

government, 13, 25, 39, 60, 73, 116, 118, 124, 204, 217, 220, 225, 226, 231, 232, 255, 257, 279, 293
  antecedent government, 27, 42, 65, 73, 79, 81, 94, 124, 131, 172, 187, 218–220, 222–224, 226–228, 231–233
  Case government, 124, 231
  lexical government, 218, 226
  proper government, 96, 213, 218, 219, 224
  θ-government, 218
  φ-government, 236
government domain, 204, 206
grammar, 2, 3, 6, 10, 67, 68, 101, 104, 120, 125, 126, 128–130, 132, 133, 224, 242, 247, 251, 252, 258, 261, 265, 270
  generative grammar, 2, 67, 128, 261, 291
  transformational grammar, 1, 252, 254, 258, 259
  Universal Grammar, 9, 10, 71, 74, 104, 111, 116, 118, 125, 128, 131, 133, 217, 220, 226–228, 235, 243, 246, 251, 255, 257, 259–262, 270
grammatical function, 76, 83–88, 103, 114, 115
Greek, 204, 236, 244

head, 4, 11, 19, 24, 25, 47, 48, 57, 60, 62, 65, 66, 80, 84, 85, 92–94, 98, 103, 104, 111, 118, 121, 122, 124, 199, 206, 211, 228, 229, 253, 254, 270, 272–274, 276–278, 283, 291, 292, 295, 297
Hungarian, 13, 164, 199–204, 206–208, 210, 211, 214, 221

Icelandic, 218, 227, 235–237, 245, 276
incorporation, 11, 71, 96, 100, 106, 107, 110, 111, 117, 120–124
intonation, 158, 159, 163, 164, 166, 173, 174, 177, 204
  declarative intonation, 158, 162, 163
  I-Topic-Intonation, 158, 159, 164, 165, 174
Italian, 10, 19, 20, 33, 55, 59–62, 89–91, 122, 171, 172, 187, 190, 218, 220, 221, 223, 238, 241–243, 246

Japanese, 172, 185, 221, 235

L-mark, 30, 33, 60, 61, 121, 122, 203, 206, 217–226, 233, 246
language acquisition, 9
language acquisition device, 261
Latin, 246
Left Deletion, 146
Left Dislocation, 14, 164, 199, 204–207, 209–211
level, 1, 2, 4, 6, 7, 9–12, 18, 20, 32, 49, 67, 72, 74, 81, 96, 99–101, 104, 107, 114–116, 121, 125, 127–132, 139, 142, 173, 178, 182, 193, 217, 218, 221, 232, 234, 239, 247, 251, 256–258, 263–267, 270, 272, 296, 297
lexicon, 6, 7, 12, 251, 254, 256–260, 262–264, 279, 282, 290
license, 60, 103, 143–146, 187, 188, 190, 222, 224, 238, 243, 244, 269, 270, 273–277, 291–295, 297
licensing, 64, 270, 271, 273, 275, 277, 291, 293, 295, 297
local domain, 13, 217, 227, 231, 235, 246, 267, 282, 292

locality, 13, 14, 81, 95, 207, 267–270, 278, 279, 297
locality condition, 13, 27, 44, 217, 293
locality restriction, 8, 11, 239, 246

modifier, 34, 100, 272, 273, 275, 277, 282, 291, 295, 297
modularity, 257
movement, 1, 4, 5, 7–11, 13, 14, 18, 19, 28, 30, 33, 35, 40, 43, 44, 47, 49, 55, 67, 71, 73, 75, 77, 78, 81, 84, 86, 88–96, 99, 102, 105, 107, 108, 110, 112, 114, 119–122, 129, 131, 147, 166, 199, 201, 202, 204–207, 211, 212, 214, 221, 224, 232, 252, 257, 258, 260, 265, 276, 277, 279, 287, 291, 292, 296, 297
  acyclic movement, 93, 95
  A-movement, 53
  Ā-movement, 219
  anaphor movement, 48, 221, 235
  clitic movement, 9, 11, 88, 122, 157, 171
  each-movement, 27, 30
  head movement, 74, 91–93, 95, 119, 121, 122, 124, 270, 276
  LF-movement, 7, 8, 11, 30, 54, 61, 96, 212, 213, 221–224, 227, 230, 231, 234, 238, 239, 241
  NP-movement, 7, 10, 11, 17–20, 22, 28, 36, 38, 41, 42, 44, 45, 48, 53–56, 59, 64, 67, 68, 76, 88, 95, 96, 107, 152, 170, 220, 226, 230, 234, 236, 248
  Operator movement, 9, 13, 14, 105, 121, 131, 199–204, 206–211
    long Operator-movement, 13, 106
  psych-movement, 11, 20, 28
  quantifier movement, 270
  S-structure movement, 8, 230, 231
  tough-movement, 105–107, 118
  wh-movement, 4, 5, 7, 8, 13, 17, 18, 20, 42, 43, 60, 61, 66, 129, 172, 187, 190, 211, 212, 232, 236
movement chain, 204

Norwegian, 63–66

Operator, 14, 43–49, 65, 78, 79, 105, 107, 121, 130, 199–201, 203, 207, 209–213, 224, 225, 227, 273, 274, 276, 277, 279, 294

parameter, 7, 12, 131, 225, 251, 255, 256, 259–262, 270, 271, 277
parasitic gap, 12, 47, 48, 53, 78, 79, 100, 172, 184, 187–191, 193, 224, 229, 234, 273
parsing, 251, 256, 258, 260–264, 267–269, 271, 292, 297
  incremental parsing, 12, 265
passive
  adjectival passive, 34–36, 39
  long distance passive, 116, 129
performance, 259, 261, 262
φ-feature, 231–233, 235–243, 245
Polish, 276
predicate, 28, 270, 274, 275, 277, 286, 291
preposition stranding, 233
principle
  Bijection Principle, 27, 45, 46, 48, 49
  Case Resistance Principle, 236, 238
  Full Specification Principle, 241–243, 245, 247

Projection Principle, 7, 19, 21, 22, 24, 53, 67, 82, 83, 87, 88, 96, 99, 104
Extended Projection Principle, 87, 88, 105, 107
Proper Inclusion Principle, 244, 245
PRO, 7, 43, 44, 56, 86–88, 103–105, 115, 116, 118, 119, 123, 129, 150, 152, 217, 218, 236, 237, 242–247, 269, 279–281, 287
pro, 7, 55, 60, 92, 103, 217, 218, 227, 242–244
pro-drop, 7, 100, 246
PRO-theorem, 242–244, 262
problem solving, 267
procedural, 258, 259, 265, 267, 297
projection, 271, 272
maximal projection, 12, 33, 62, 65, 66, 86–88, 91–93, 108, 109, 111, 113–115, 121, 123, 146, 152, 157, 167, 168, 170, 174, 203, 205, 208, 218, 223, 224, 229, 232, 237, 241, 245, 255, 272, 274–277, 279–282, 284, 285, 287, 291, 292, 294, 295, 297
pronoun, 4, 17–19, 26, 27, 46, 53, 65, 77, 157, 170, 176, 182, 184, 186, 188–190, 201, 202, 204, 208, 242, 244
psych-adjective, 31, 33, 34, 36
psych-nominal, 36
psych-passive, 33
psych-predicate, 28, 29, 33, 38, 40, 41, 48
psych-stem, 38, 40
psych-verb, 28–36

quantifier, 17, 18, 26–28, 30, 45, 46, 116, 119, 130, 158, 174, 178, 179, 196, 223, 224, 226, 227

raising, 11, 20, 28, 32, 41–44, 48, 74, 80, 87, 88, 92, 96, 107, 108, 114–116, 120, 121, 129, 132, 151, 170, 171, 214, 260, 279, 280, 286, 288–290
LF-raising, 30, 159, 222
NP-raising, 84, 113
quantifier raising, 13, 18, 26, 27, 120, 200, 221, 223, 226, 229, 232, 236, 258, 264, 270
verb raising, 107, 108
verb projection raising, 108–110, 112, 113, 117, 118, 120–123
reanalysis, 11, 71, 87, 88, 105, 107, 109–115, 117, 119, 129, 132, 234
reciprocal, 20, 25–28, 30, 37, 41, 42, 44
relativized minimality, 13, 226, 230, 231, 233, 235, 246
Right Node Raising, 146
Right Periphery Ellipsis, 142–149
Romanian, 276, 277

scope, 12–14, 26, 112, 116, 119, 120, 128, 139, 158–163, 165–168, 173–175, 177–180, 182, 185, 192, 196, 207–209, 211–214, 223, 224, 226, 227, 266, 270, 292
scope domain, 160
scope reversal, 159, 164
scrambling, 76, 77, 80, 88, 111, 113, 117, 124, 172, 230, 270, 272, 273, 298
SEEM, 101–104
serial verb construction, 81–84
Spanish, 244, 246
specifier, 27, 49, 60, 61, 65, 89, 105, 106, 200, 201, 207, 210, 223, 225, 228, 229, 254, 271, 273–

275, 277, 278, 280–285, 287, 290, 291, 294–297
structure building, 12, 67, 265, 267, 292
subcategorization, 7, 279, 283
subjacency, 13, 33, 53, 67, 71, 73, 79–81, 131, 199, 201–206, 246, 258, 264, 295
subjunctive, 235, 237, 238, 245
Swedish, 63, 65, 66, 92

Theme, 29, 30, 32, 37, 39, 40
θ-assignment, 82, 83, 100
θ-criterion, 19, 21, 35, 46, 47, 57, 58, 62, 72, 75–80, 82–85, 87, 88, 90, 101–103, 115, 116, 220, 227, 228
θ-role, 21, 22, 29, 32, 37, 39, 40, 46, 57, 58, 76, 82–85, 88, 90, 101, 105, 116, 202, 219
θ-role assignment, 7, 33, 57, 58
topic, 200, 202, 203, 257
topicalization, 76, 88, 111, 113, 124, 172, 205
trace, 4, 7, 11, 12, 18, 19, 31, 42, 44, 46, 49, 58–67, 75–78, 80, 83, 86, 87, 92–99, 102, 103, 105, 106, 108, 111, 114, 119, 122, 124, 141, 146, 152, 154, 155, 157–161, 163, 165–173, 175, 179, 180, 183, 185–189, 191–193, 197, 200, 211, 213, 218, 220–222, 226, 227, 231, 232, 234, 236, 245, 279, 294
  NP-trace, 18, 19, 42, 43, 131, 218–220, 222, 234, 243, 245
  trace-of, 75
  trace theory, 120
  wh-trace, 17, 18, 44, 46, 53, 172, 187, 218, 219, 227, 234, 243, 245

Uniform Constituent Hypothesis, 13, 270, 297

variable, 17, 18, 27, 45–49, 77–80, 120, 130, 131, 173, 178, 227, 283, 284

X̄-theory, 6, 7, 86, 99, 100, 109, 111, 246

Züritüütsch, 107, 108, 113, 117, 118, 123

Studies in Natural Language and Linguistic Theory

Publications

1. L. Burzio: *Italian Syntax.* A Government-binding Approach. 1986.
   ISBN Hb 90-277-2014-2; Pb 90-277-2015-0
2. W.D. Davies: *Choctaw Verb Agreement and Universal Grammar.* 1986.
   ISBN Hb 90-277-2065-7; Pb 90-277-2142-4
3. K. É. Kiss: *Configurationality in Hungarian.* 1987.
   ISBN Hb 90-277-1907-1; Pb 90-277-2456-3
4. D. Pulleyblank: *Tone in Lexical Phonology.* 1986.
   ISBN Hb 90-277-2123-8; Pb 90-277-2124-6
5. L. Hellan and K. K. Christensen: *Topics in Scandinavian Syntax.* 1986.
   ISBN Hb 90-277-2166-1; Pb 90-277-2167-X
6. K. P. Mohanan: *The Theory of Lexical Phonology.* 1986.
   ISBN Hb 90-277-2226-9; Pb 90-277-2227-7
7. J. L. Aissen: *Tzotzil Clause Structure.* 1987.
   ISBN Hb 90-277-2365-6; Pb 90-277-2441-5
8. T. Gunji: *Japanese Phrase Structure Grammar.* A Unification-based Approach. 1987. ISBN 1-55608-020-4
9. W. U. Wurzel: *Inflectional Morphology and Naturalness.* 1989
   ISBN Hb 1-55608-025-5; Pb 1-55608-026-3
10. C. Neidle: *The Role of Case in Russian Syntax.* 1988 ISBN 1-55608-042-5
11. C. Lefebvre and P. Muysken: *Mixed Categories.* Nominalizations in Quechua. 1988. ISBN Hb 1-55608-050-6; Pb 1-55608-051-4
12. K. Michelson: *A Comparative Study of Lake-Iroquoian Accent.* 1988
    ISBN 1-55608-054-9
13. K. Zagona: *Verb Phrase Syntax.* A Parametric Study of English and Spanish. 1988 ISBN Hb 1-55608-064-6; Pb 1-55608-065-4
14. R. Hendrick: *Anaphora in Celtic and Universal Grammar.* 1988
    ISBN 1-55608-066-2
15. O. Jaeggli and K.J. Safir (eds.): *The Null Subject Parameter.* 1989
    ISBN Hb 1-55608-086-7; Pb 1-55608-087-5
16. H. Lasnik: *Essays on Anaphora.* 1989
    ISBN Hb 1-55608-090-5; Pb 1-55608-091-3
17. S. Steele: *Agreement and Anti-Agreement.* A Syntax of Luiseño. 1990
    ISBN 0-7923-0260-5
18. E. Pearce: *Parameters in Old French Syntax.* Infinitival Complements. 1990
    ISBN Hb 0-7923-0432-2; Pb 0-7923-0433-0

19. Y.A. Li: *Order and Constituency in Mandarin Chinese*. 1990 ISBN 0-7923-0500-0
20. H. Lasnik: *Essays on Restrictiveness and Learnability*. 1990 ISBN Hb 0-7923-0628-7; Pb 0-7923-0629-5
21. M.J. Speas: *Phrase Structure in Natural Language*. 1990 ISBN Hb 0-7923-0755-0; Pb 0-7923-0866-2
22. H. Haider and K. Netter (eds.): *Representation and Derivation in the Theory of Grammar*. 1991. ISBN 0-7923-1150-7

Kluwer Academic Publishers – Dordrecht / Boston / London

Printed by Printforce, the Netherlands